Make the Most of
Your Digital Photos, Video, & Music

First Edition

Ton Bunzel, Dave Johnson, and Walter Glenn

201 W. 103rd Street
Indianapolis, Indiana 46290

Make the Most of Your Digital Photos, Video, & Music

First Edition

International Standard Book Number: 0-7897-2943-1

Library of Congress Catalog Card Number: 2003090825

Printed in the United States of America

First Printing: May 2003

06   05   04   03   4   3   2

Trademarks

Warning and Disclaimer

Associate Publisher
Greg Wiegand

Acquisitions Editor
Angelina Ward

Development Editor
Kevin Howard

Managing Editor
Charlotte Clapp

Project Editor
Tricia Liebig

Production Editor
Megan Wade

Indexer
Erika Millen

Interior Designer
Anne Jones

Cover Designer
Anne Jones

Page Layout
Stacey Richwine-DeRome

Graphics
Tammy Graham

Contents at a Glance

Contents at a Glance

Contents

We Want to Hear from You!

As the reader of this book, *you* are our most important critic and commentator. We value your opinion and want to know what we're doing right, what we could do better, what areas you'd like to see us publish in, and any other words of wisdom you're willing to pass our way.

As an associate publisher for Que, I welcome your comments. You can email or write me directly to let me know what you did or didn't like about this book—as well as what we can do to make our books better.

Please note that I cannot help you with technical problems related to the *topic* of this book. We do have a User Services group, however, where I will forward specific technical questions related to the book.

When you write, please be sure to include this book's title and author as well as your name, email address, and phone number. I will carefully review your comments and share them with the author and editors who worked on the book.

Email: feedback@quepublishing.com

Mail: Greg Wiegand
           Que Publishing
           201 West 103rd Street
           Indianapolis, IN 46290 USA

For more information about this book or another Que title, visit our Web site at www.quepublishing.com. Type the ISBN (excluding hyphens) or the title of a book in the Search field to find the page you're looking for.

The Complete Visual Reference

Each chapter of this book is made up of a series of short, instructional tasks, designed to help you understand all the information that you need to get the most out of your computer hardware and software.

Click: Click the left mouse button once.

Each task includes a series of easy-to-understand steps designed to guide you through the procedure.

Double-click: Click the left mouse button twice in rapid succession.

Right-click: Click the right mouse button once.

Drag: Click and hold the left mouse button, position the mouse pointer, and release.

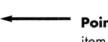

Pointer Arrow: Highlights an item on the screen you need to point to or focus on in the step or task.

Selection: Highlights the area onscreen discussed in the step or task.

Type: Click once where indicated and begin typing to enter your text or data.

Drop

Drag and Drop: Point to the starting place or object. Hold down the mouse button (right or left per instructions), move the mouse to the new location, and then release the button.

④ Export the File
Click **OK** in the Optimizing panel.

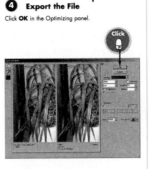

⑤ Save Your Final JPG
Click the drop-down arrow to put the image on the desktop, where you can find it (be sure to give it a name you can remember).

⑥ Attach It to Email
Open your email editor and click **Attachment** to find the file. Or, you can drag and drop it in from the desktop.

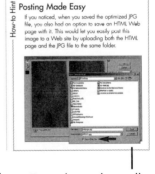

Posting Made Easy
If you noticed, when you saved the optimized JPG file, you also had an option to save an HTML Web page with it. This would let you easily post this image to a Web site by uploading both the HTML page and the JPG file to the same folder.

Each step is fully illustrated to show you how it looks onscreen.

Extra hints that tell you how to accomplish a goal are provided in most tasks.

(↵Enter) **Key icons:** Clearly indicate which key combinations to use.

Menus and items you click are shown in **bold**. Words in *italic* are defined in more detail in the glossary. Information you type is in a **special font**.

Introduction

This book is about the fun things you can do with your computer, digital photography, video, and music. Regardless of your computer experience, in no time you will be able to take quality pictures and video, edit them, and send them to your friends and family. You will also learn about digital music—how to find it, edit it, and play it. You will even be able to create your own music CDs!

To begin, you'll learn the basics of Windows XP and then learn how to install any required hardware and configure your computer for digital photography, video, and music. With pictures and step-by-step instructions, we'll make it easy for you.

With today's digital cameras, you can take high-resolution pictures and produce professional, photo-quality prints. More than that, you can see the results instantly, edit the pictures yourself to create exactly what you want, use them on the Internet, email them to friends and family, and create prints for display. Some of the topics in this section include

- Taking high-quality pictures
- Scanning existing prints
- Setting up and using your digital camera
- Keeping your photos organized
- Editing your pictures

Digital video is exciting. Imagine this: Using a camcorder, you can create a movie. Then, you can transfer the video to your PC, where—without losing one tiny scrap of resolution—you can rearrange the scenes, add music, include transitions, overlay titles, and add special effects. When you're done, you can output the completed masterpiece back to videotape, upload the movie to the Internet, or burn a copy onto CD-ROM. In this section, you learn about the following:

- Shooting video under a variety of lighting conditions

- Creating a complete movie with multiple scenes, transitions, and titles
- Adding complex, multisource audio to your movie soundtracks
- Outputting your movie to videotape
- Publishing streaming video movies to the Internet using RealPlayer
- Adding video to PowerPoint presentations

With a computer and a connection to the Internet, you have virtually unlimited access to musical entertainment. Add a CD burner and you can take that music with you! In this section you will

- Learn the various ways to listen to music on your PC
- Find and share MP3 files
- Tag and organize your MP3s
- Create and edit your MP3 files
- Create your own CD

Each topic is presented visually, step-by-step, so you can clearly see how to apply each feature to your own tasks. The illustrations show exactly what you'll see on your own computer screen, letting you easily follow along.

You can use the book as a tutorial, working through each section one task at a time, or as a reference, looking up specific features you want to learn about. There's no right or wrong way—use the method that best suits your own learning style.

Whatever your level of expertise and for whatever reason you use your computer, you will find this book a useful tool. Whether you read it cover to cover or set it aside for reference when you come across a specific task with which you need help, this book provides you with the information you need to complete the task and get on with your work. Enjoy!

Computer Basics

Task

Up and Running

This chapter discusses several things that are essential to know before you can operate your computer. Much of the information you'll learn here—such as how to turn the machine on and off and how to find your way around the keyboard—might seem obvious to those of you with even a small amount of computer experience. At the same time, these pages might reveal some new twist that you didn't know about, such as a new keyboard strategy for getting yourself out of trouble.

First, you'll learn what exactly happens when you turn on your computer—how to decode some of the sounds you'll hear and messages you'll see. Then you'll get some in-depth information about keyboards and keyboard layouts. You'll find out how to make your way around with the cursor movement keys. You'll also learn the ins and outs of some special keys, particularly the Delete and Backspace keys. In addition, you'll discover how and when to use the function keys, either by themselves or in combination with modifier keys such as Ctrl and Shift. As you'll see, you can enter numbers speedily with the numeric keypad, which can typically double as a set of extra cursor movement keys as well. Some of the most valuable keys and key combinations you'll discover are those that help you get unstuck.

You can also communicate with and control your computer via the mouse or its stand-ins: the trackball or touch pad. In this chapter, you'll learn the full variety of mousing techniques. After that, you will find out the proper way to turn off your computer. Finally, you'll learn some tips for arranging the different parts of your computer system for maximum comfort and minimum back, wrist, and eye strain.

What Happens When You Turn On Your Computer

Many personal computer systems are set up so that all the components, including the system unit and the monitor, are plugged into a single power strip. In this case, you turn on your computer (and everything else in sight) by throwing the switch on the power strip itself. If you don't have a power strip, you'll have to turn on the components one at a time. As you'll learn here, a whole sequence of events happens next.

❶ What Happens First

Your computer hardware can't do much of anything without instructions. When you turn on a computer, the first thing it does is go searching for a program that can tell it what to do next.

❷ The Boot Program

The program the CPU is looking for is a very small part of the operating system known as the boot program. This program is stored in ROM and is known as the boot program because it essentially helps the computer "pull itself up by its own bootstraps," by loading (booting) the rest of the operating system into memory. The basic input/output system (BIOS) is part of the operating system that is stored in ROM. It runs the basic startup tests for your computer.

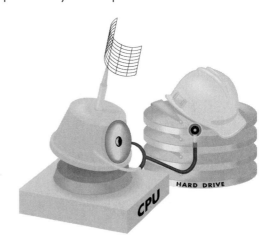

The CPU makes sure the disk drives and other components are working. The CPU takes an inventory of memory.

③ The Power On Self Test

Under the direction of this boot program, the CPU performs what is known as a power on self test (POST). During this stage, the CPU tests to see whether the various parts of the system are still alive and well. You will see a progress report during this phase. At a minimum, you will probably notice the computer counting up its memory. You might also see messages as the CPU checks out various peripherals, and little lights on your keyboard and printer might turn on and off. Finally, a beep will indicate that everything seems to be okay.

④ Searching for the Operating System

After the CPU has finished its internal inventory, it goes hunting for the rest of the operating system: the part that is stored on disk. The first place it looks is in the floppy disk drive. (If you have a PC with two floppy disk drives, it looks to the one named drive A—which is usually the leftmost or uppermost drive.) If the floppy disk drive is empty, the CPU continues its search on the hard drive.

The read/write head, under instructions from the CPU, locates the operating system on the hard disk.

⑤ If You Have a Disk in the Floppy Disk Drive

If there is a disk in the floppy disk drive, your computer checks whether it contains the operating system. If it doesn't, the computer informs you that you have an invalid system disk or a non-system disk or disk error. Just open the floppy disk-drive door or eject the disk and then press any key on your keyboard to have the CPU resume hunting for the operating system on your hard drive. (The moral of this story is that if you plan to work with a floppy disk, postpone inserting it until your system is done booting.)

⑥ When Windows Starts

As soon as the CPU locates the operating system, it loads it into memory. If you are running Windows XP, you'll see the message `Starting Windows XP` and then the Microsoft Windows XP logo. (If you are running another version of Windows, you will see that version's logo and name at this point.) If you are not part of a network, you'll probably go immediately to a screen known as the Windows desktop. (You learn all about the desktop in Chapter 2, "Using the Windows XP Desktop.")

⑦ Logging In to a Network

If you are on a network you'll need to enter your name and password before you arrive at the desktop. This process is known as *logging in*.

② Keyboards and Keyboard Layouts

Before you can use your computer effectively, you need to know your way around the keyboard. Your computer keyboard is very sensitive; you don't need to bang or lean on the keys, placing unnecessary stress on both your own wrists and the keyboard's innards; your computer recognizes and responds to the lightest key press. If you hold down a key for more than a second, your computer will respond as though you had pressed it several times in rapid succession. The effect will depend on what that key actually does in the program you are using, but it's unlikely to be the intended result. If you're not accustomed to typing at all, experiment to find the lightest touch that will work on your machine.

① The Standard Keyboard

Close to a dozen different styles of computer keyboards are available. One of the most common keyboards is shown in the figure below. Although almost all keyboards have the letter and number keys in the same places, the location of other keys can vary.

② The Feel of a Keyboard

Different brands of keyboards can also have a very different feel. On some, the keys click when you press them and on some they don't; the keys feel stiffer on some keyboards and looser on others. The nice part about this variety is that you can choose the feel and the layout you like. The unfortunate part is that if you switch computers at some point, you might need to spend some time getting used to the feel of the keyboard and searching for keys.

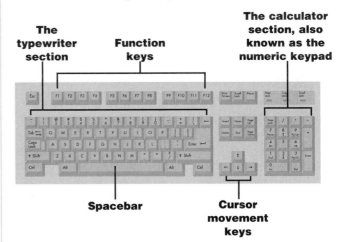

The typewriter section

Function keys

The calculator section, also known as the numeric keypad

Spacebar

Cursor movement keys

Your keyboard might have a different arrangement of keys. If you are using an older computer, or a laptop or notebook computer, you might have fewer keys altogether.

③ The Caps Lock Key

Caps Lock is what is known as a toggle key—a key you use to alternately enable and disable a particular feature. You press it once to turn the feature on and again to turn it off. Unlike the Shift Lock key on a typewriter, Caps Lock on a computer keyboard affects letters only. This means that typing a dollar sign requires holding down the Shift key while you press the 4 at the top of your keyboard, even if Caps Lock is on.

④ The Enter Key

If you first learned to type on a typewriter, you'll find that the Enter key works something like a carriage return: You press it to move to the next line when you get to the end of a paragraph. However, you don't need to press Enter at the end of each line in word processing programs; the program automatically "word wraps" text to the next line when you reach the right margin. You still need to press Enter to force the cursor to a new line before you reach the right margin, however. You also sometimes use Enter to select options from a menu (onscreen list of options) or to indicate that you are done entering instructions or data and want the program to respond. (Not sure just what the cursor is? You'll learn in a moment.)

⑤ The Tab Key

On some older PC keyboards and many laptops, the Tab key doesn't actually say Tab. It just has two arrows pointing in opposite directions, such as → ←. In some cases you get both the text and the arrows.

How-to Hint

Different Names for the Enter Key

The Enter key is labeled Return on certain older PC keyboards. In addition, some keyboards label the Enter key with the ↵ symbol. This symbol is used to indicate "Press the Enter key now" in many software manuals. Your keyboard also might have an additional Enter key, at the right of the numeric keypad, for entering numbers.

The Cursor Movement Keys

In most programs, a symbol indicates where you are on the screen at the moment—like a "you are here" indicator on a map for a park or shopping mall. When you are entering text in Windows, the "you are here" symbol is a blinking vertical line known as the insertion point. (Its DOS equivalent was the cursor.) On most keyboards, there are two groups of keys designed to move the cursor or insertion point around the screen: the arrow keys and another set of keys called Home, End, Page Up, and Page Down. You might also have a duplicate set of cursor movement keys on the numeric keypad. You can move the cursor or insertion point by using either the cursor movement keys or your mouse.

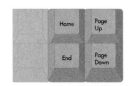

The insertion point or cursor indicates your current position on the screen.

① The Arrow Keys

The arrow keys move the cursor/insertion point one character or one unit at a time in the direction of the arrow. To move one character to the left when you are entering text in a word processing program, for example, you press the left arrow key. On most keyboards, the arrows occupy keys by themselves.

② Additional Navigation Keys

The other cursor movement keys (Home, End, Page Up, and Page Down) let you make larger jumps across the screen. On some laptop keyboards, there are no separate cursor movement keys; they are always part of the numeric keypad (the calculator section). You'll discover how to use these dual-purpose keys when you learn about the numeric keypad.

❸ The Home Key

The Home key is often used to move to the beginning of some set of data—such as the top of a document, the beginning of a line, or the upper-left corner of a spreadsheet.

❹ The End Key

The End key is often used to move to the end of some set of data—such as the bottom of a document, the end of a line, or the last number or character in a particular block of data in a spreadsheet.

❺ The Page Up Key

The Page Up key is usually used to move up one page or one screenful of data. (This key is often labeled PgUp.)

❻ The Page Down Key

The Page Down key is usually used to move down one page or one screenful of data. (This key is often labeled PgDn.)

❼ Moving the Insertion Point with the Mouse

You can also move the cursor or insertion point by using a mouse. Typically, you do this by clicking where you want the insertion point to go.

The Special Keys

The special keys include all the keys other than normal typewriter keys, cursor movement keys, the numeric keypad (the set of keys resembling a calculator), and function keys. These keys are scattered around the keyboard, and they generally perform some operation other than displaying a particular character on the screen.

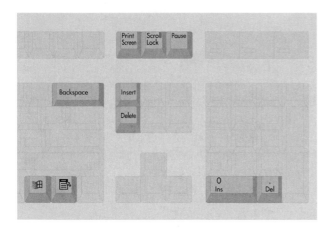

The Backspace key gobbles characters to the left of the cursor or insertion point.

The Delete key (sometimes abbreviated Del) gobbles characters to the right of the cursor or insertion point.

① The Backspace and Delete Keys

Most PC keyboards include two keys for erasing. The key labeled either Delete or Del generally deletes the character immediately to the right of the insertion point. The Backspace key deletes the character to the left of the insertion point. (On some keyboards, the key doesn't say "Backspace"; it shows a left-pointing arrow.)

② Deleting Selected Text

In most programs, you can also select a group of characters to erase using either your keyboard or the mouse. Pressing either the Backspace or the Delete key will delete any currently selected characters. (In case you don't already know, you'll learn how to select shortly, in the task "Things You Can Do with a Mouse or Trackball.")

③ The Insert Key

The Insert (or Ins) key is a toggle that determines what happens when you type new characters within existing text or numbers. If the Insert feature is on and you type new characters in the middle of a paragraph, for example, the old characters are pushed to the right to make room for the new ones. With Insert off, the new characters replace the old ones. In most programs, Insert might be set on by default, so you don't accidentally overtype what you've already entered. On some keyboards, Insert shares a key with the number 0 on the numeric keypad.

④ The Windows Logo Key

Some keyboards designed specifically to work with Windows contain two extra types of keys—Application keys and Windows Logo keys—that provide fast keyboard alternatives to many operations you'd usually perform with a mouse. For example, you can use the Windows Logo keys to open the Start menu, instead of clicking the Start button at the lower-left corner of the desktop.

⑤ The Application Key

You can use the Application key to bring up a shortcut menu relevant to what you're doing at the moment (it's the equivalent of right-clicking). If you're not sure whether your keyboard contains these keys, look a bit to the left and right of the spacebar. The Windows Logo keys contain the Windows logo (surprise). The Application key looks like a menu with an arrow pointing to it.

How-to Hint

Backspace Versus Left Arrow

Don't confuse the Backspace key and the Left Arrow key. Both of these keys contain left-pointing arrows. Although both of these keys move the insertion point to the left, the Left Arrow (like all arrow keys) doesn't change anything. In contrast, the Backspace key moves and erases at the same time. Every time you press the key, the character to the left of the insertion point is deleted and the insertion point moves left one space to take up the slack.

The Modifier and Function Keys

All PC keyboards contain three types of special keys that you use almost exclusively in combination with other keys. They don't do anything by themselves. (Many keyboards contain two keys of each type—two Shift keys, two Control keys, and so on.) This book will refer to these special keys as modifier keys. Occasionally, the modifier keys are used with a row of keys called function keys—labeled F1, F2, and so on—that you'll probably find across the top of your keyboard.

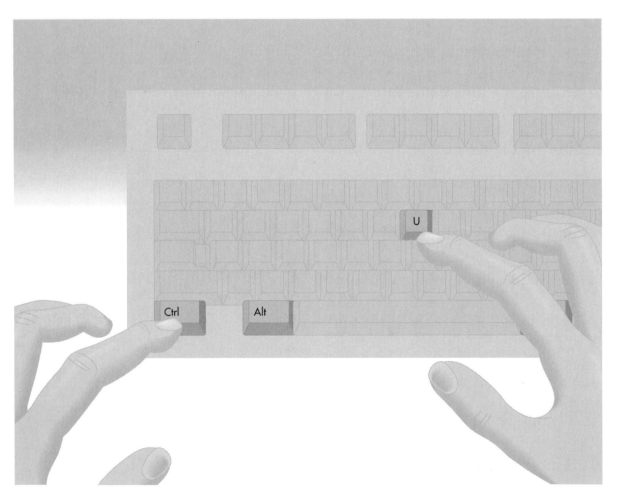

**When you use key combinations, you always press the modifier key
(in this case Ctrl) first and hold it down while you press the other key.**

❶ Modifier Keys

For those of you who've used typewriters, the Shift key on a typewriter is an example of a modifier key. Pressing the Shift key by itself does nothing. But if you hold down Shift while pressing the letter A, you get an uppercase A instead of the lowercase a you get by pressing the A key by itself.

❷ The Shift, Control, and Alt Modifier Keys

Similarly, on a PC keyboard, nothing happens when you press Shift, Control (Ctrl), or Alternate (Alt). But in many application programs, holding down a modifier key while pressing another key is a way of issuing a command. In some word processing programs, for example, holding down the Ctrl key while pressing U issues the command to underline any currently selected text (while pressing U by itself would generate a letter U and pressing Ctrl by itself would do nothing). These key combinations are often called "hot keys" or "keyboard shortcuts."

❸ Using Modifier Keys with Cursor Movement Keys

Often you can also modify the way the cursor movement keys work by using them in combination with one of the modifier keys. For example, in Microsoft Word, pressing Home moves the insertion point to the beginning of the current line, whereas pressing Ctrl+Home moves the insertion point to the beginning of the document. Shift+Home selects a block of text from the beginning of the paragraph to the insertion point.

❹ What Is a Key Combination?

A key combination is a combination of two or more keys (at least one of which is a modifier key) to perform an operation. To use a key combination, you press the modifier key first and hold it down while you press the other key. Don't try to press both keys at once; you might press the second key slightly before you press the modifier key, which has the effect of pressing that second key by itself.

❺ How Key Combinations Are Notated

When computer books or manuals refer to key combinations, they sometimes combine the names of the keys with commas, hyphens, or plus signs. In other words, if you're supposed to hold down Alt while you press the Backspace key, you might see Alt,Backspace, Alt-Backspace, or Alt+Backspace.

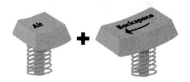

❻ Function Keys

The function keys are the keys labeled F1 through either F10 or F12 and are usually located at the top of the keyboard. In many application programs, function keys are used to issue commands. For example, F1 frequently invokes an application's Help system, which provides you with information on how to use the program. F10 sometimes activates the program's menu system. Surprisingly, in many programs many of the function keys have no function at all.

How-to Hint

Function and Modifier Keys Together

The function keys are sometimes used in combination with the modifier keys. For example, in a number of word processing programs, pressing Shift+F7 invokes the thesaurus.

The Numeric Keypad

Currently, two basic layouts exist for PC keyboards: one, often called the extended keyboard, for desktop PCs, and another for laptops. The main difference is that most desktop keyboards have both a numeric keypad and separate groups of cursor movement keys, while most laptops have a numeric keypad that doubles as a set of cursor movement keys.

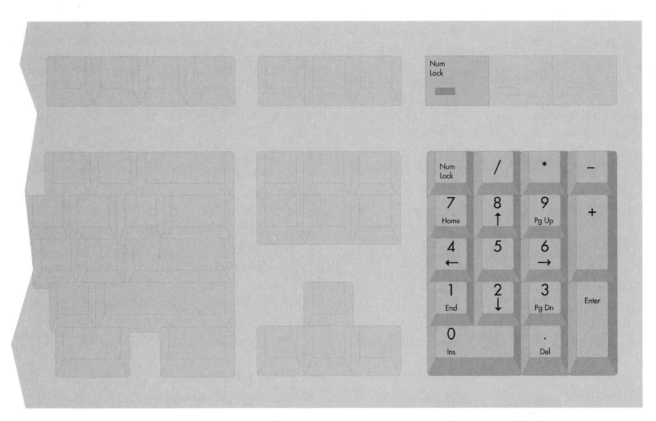

You can use the numeric keypad either for typing numbers or moving around the screen, depending on the current status of the Num Lock setting.

❶ The Two Ways to Use the Numeric Keypad

On all keyboards, you can use the numeric keypad for either of two functions: typing numbers or moving around on the screen. The status of the Num Lock (number lock) setting—which you control by pressing the Num Lock key—determines the function.

❷ The Num Lock Key

Num Lock is a toggle key: Each time you press it, the status of the Num Lock feature changes, from off to on or on to off. When Num Lock is on, the keys on the numeric keypad generate numbers. When Num Lock is off, they change to cursor movement keys. The 7 key acts like a Home key, for example, and the 8 key serves as an Up Arrow key. The function of each key is spelled out on the key itself. (The effect of the cursor movement keys was covered earlier in this chapter.)

❸ Other Keys on the Numeric Keypad

The keys other than the Num Lock key around the outside of the numeric keypad work the same regardless of the Num Lock setting. You can use them to enter mathematical symbols such as + and -. (In a number of applications, the / symbolizes division and the * symbolizes multiplication.)

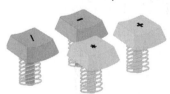

❹ The Enter, Insert, and Delete Keys on the Numeric Keypad

The Enter key on the numeric keypad works just like the Enter key in the main section of the keyboard. (If you're typing lots of numbers, you might want to use this Enter key rather than the one that's in with the typewriter keys.) The Ins and Del keys work just like the Insert and Delete keys typically found to the left of the Home and End keys.

❺ How to Tell Whether Num Lock Is On

You can usually determine whether Num Lock is on in several ways. On most keyboards, there is a little light on the key itself or a light labeled Num Lock above the key. If the light is on, the feature is on. Many application programs also display the words Num Lock or Num on the screen when Num Lock is on. If needed, you can check by pressing one of the arrow keys and see whether the cursor moves or a number is generated.

❻ Off Num Lock

Why would you want to turn off Num Lock? On many laptops, there is no separate set of arrow keys; you have to choose between using the cursor movement keys and using the numeric keypad to type numbers. If you don't need to do a lot of moving around at the moment, you might turn Num Lock on temporarily to enter a set of numbers, particularly if you're a touch-typing wiz on calculators. Otherwise, leave Num Lock off and use the number keys at the top of the keyboard to enter numbers.

How-to Hint

Entering Arithmetic Operators from the Numeric Keypad

It's often easier to type arithmetic operators (such as + and *) using keys at the side of the numeric keypad rather than keys at the top of the keyboard. If you use the keys at the top, you need to remember to hold down the Shift key; otherwise, you'll get = when you mean + or 8 when you mean *.

Options for Navigating

The Num Lock key was carried over to the newer keyboards primarily to accommodate people who were already used to navigating with keys on the numeric keypad. Some people also prefer the layout of arrow keys on the numeric keypad (with the Up Arrow key above the Left Arrow and Right Arrow keys).

What to Do When You Get Stuck

Never turn off your computer in the middle of an application if you can avoid it. (Turning off your computer is covered later in this chapter.) It can damage data and, at the least, cause you to lose any unsaved data in memory. Occasionally, however, you might just get stuck. There might be a "bug" (glitch) in the program you are using, causing an error message that won't go away; or the program might stop responding to your commands. Here are some techniques to try if you do get stuck, listed from the least drastic to the most.

❶ The Escape Key

In many application programs, the Escape (or Esc) key is a general-purpose "get me out of here" key—used to cancel or back up a step in the current operation.

❷ The Break Key

If the Escape key doesn't solve your problem, you can try the Break key. On most keyboards, either the Scroll Lock or Pause key doubles as a Break key. (You should see the word Break either on top of the key or on its front edge. If you don't find Break on either key, you can use Scroll Lock for this purpose.) By itself, Break does nothing, but holding down a Ctrl key and pressing this key will interrupt some programs or commands. This key combination is referred to as Ctrl+Break (pronounced "Control Break").

③ Rebooting Your Machine

If neither of the preceding techniques works, you can reboot your computer by holding down the Ctrl and Alt keys and then tapping the Del key. This opens a window that allows you to close specific programs or to reboot the machine by pressing Ctrl+Alt+Del a second time. Rebooting erases memory and reloads the operating system; you lose any data currently in memory. In some programs, you can damage data as well, so only use this key combination when you can't think of any other solution. Although fairly drastic, rebooting is still a bit safer than the next two options.

④ The Reset Button

Many PCs have a Reset button that lets you restart your computer without actually flicking the power switch. The main power to the computer's components is not interrupted. This saves wear and tear. (Some, but not all, Reset buttons are actually labeled Reset. If you can't find yours, check in the documentation for your computer.)

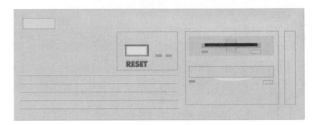

⑤ If All Else Fails

If all else fails and your computer does not have a Reset button, turn off the computer by switching off the power supply switch, wait at least 30 seconds, and then turn it on again.

How-to Hint

Closing Programs and Rebooting in Windows

If you are using Windows, pressing Ctrl+Alt+Del invokes a Close Program dialog box. From there, you can select the program you suspect is causing the problem and click the End Task button. If that doesn't work, click the Shut Down button. If you still have no luck, press Ctrl+Alt+Del again.

Using a Mouse, Trackball, or Touch Pad

Keyboards are only one of the tools available for talking to your computer. The other main tool is a mouse or trackball. A mouse is a hand-held pointing device that lets you point to, select, and manipulate objects on the screen. As you move the mouse around on your desk, a special symbol, known as the mouse pointer, moves in an analogous direction on the screen. If you move the mouse forward and backward, the mouse pointer moves up and down on the screen; if you move the mouse left and right, the mouse pointer moves left and right. Although the mouse pointer most often looks like an arrow, it can assume many other shapes, depending on which program you are running and what operation you are performing.

1 Using the Mouse

You can hold the mouse in either hand. Most people prefer to use their dominant hand—the right if right-handed or left if left-handed. (Most computer stores offer left-handed mice.) Make sure the mouse cord is pointing away from you. Then just glide the mouse lightly over the surface of your desk or mouse pad.

2 Moving the Mouse

If you reach the edge of your desk or mouse pad before you reach the desired point on the screen, just lift your mouse up and move it. The mouse pointer only moves when the mouse is flat against a hard surface; the ball underneath rolls as you move the device. If you want to move the mouse pointer to the bottom of your screen, for example, and you reach the front edge of your desk when the mouse pointer is still an inch above the desired spot, just lift the mouse, move it up a few inches, put it back down again, and continue moving it down.

3 Using a Mouse Pad

If your computer didn't come with one, you will want to purchase a mouse pad, a rectangular piece of nylon-covered rubber that you place on your desk as a platform for your mouse. A mouse often gets better traction and therefore moves more smoothly on a pad than directly on a desk, particularly one with an uneven surface.

④ Trackballs

A trackball is essentially an upside-down mouse. Instead of having a ball on the bottom, it has a ball on the top, set inside a square cradle. Rolling this ball has the same effect as moving a mouse.

⑤ Pointing Sticks

Laptop computers sometimes sport yet another type of pointing device, known as a pointing stick. This is a small cylindrical piece of plastic that looks like the eraser on the end of a pencil. It is usually positioned in the center of the keyboard. By pushing the stick in various directions, you can control the movement of the mouse pointer on your screen. (The stick itself does not actually move when pushed, but it does respond to the pressure of your finger.) Computers with pointing sticks generally have two buttons near the bottom of the keyboard that you can press to simulate left and right mouse clicks.

⑥ Touch Pads

A touch pad is a small rectangular area on some keyboards. Moving your finger across the touch pad causes the pointer to move across the screen.

⑦ The Two Mouse Buttons

Many of the operations that you perform using a mouse, trackball, or touch pad involve pushing buttons. Mice designed for PCs typically have two buttons: a left button and a right button. The buttons on a trackball are usually positioned at the far end of the device. You can press them using either your thumb or forefinger. On a touch pad, you can click by either tapping the pad with your finger or pressing the left button.

⑧ Cleaning Your Mouse

If your mouse pointer starts moving in fits and starts or moves in one direction but not another, it's probably time for a mouse cleaning. Turn the mouse upside down. Next, either slide the round lid down until it pops open or turn it counterclockwise until it reaches the open position. Drop the ball out into your palm. Clean the rollers inside the mouse using a cotton swab dipped in alcohol. Clean the ball using a soft, dry cloth. Replace the ball and the lid and you're ready to go. To reassemble a trackball after cleaning, place the ball in one hand, with your other hand, place the mouse part on top of it, and flip your hands over.

How-to Hint

How Your Mouse Will Look

When using some programs, your mouse might behave differently than it would otherwise. (The mouse pointer might look like a hand instead of an arrow.) Chapter 2 covers this mouse behavior in detail.

The IntelliMouse

Microsoft makes a mouse called the IntelliMouse that has a small wheel between the left and right mouse buttons that you can use to scroll through data or text.

Things You Can Do with a Mouse or Trackball

Moving the mouse pointer where you want it is just the first step. After you've done so, you need to use one of the available buttons, depending on which type of action you want to carry out. When you read software manuals, you are likely to encounter the following terms for the various things you can do with a mouse or trackball.

① Pointing

Point means position the mouse pointer over a particular word or object on the screen. If the mouse pointer looks like an arrow, you need to position the tip of the arrow over the desired object. Pointing is usually the precursor to actually doing anything by using one of the mouse buttons.

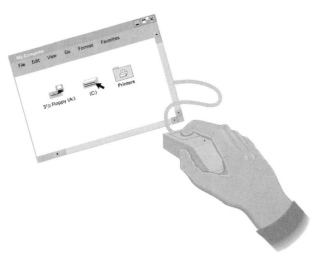

② Pressing the Mouse Button

Press means press and hold down the mouse (or trackball) button. You need to press the mouse button in preparation for dragging, which is described in a moment.

③ Clicking

Click means tap the button—pressing it in and then releasing it quickly. The term click generally means click the left mouse button. *Right-click* means tap the right mouse button. Often you click to initiate some action, such as pulling down a menu of choices. In Windows, right-clicking typically displays a shortcut menu of choices relevant to the object you clicked.

④ Double-Clicking

Double-click means click the button twice in rapid succession. Double-clicking often initiates some action right away; for example, if you have a program icon on your desktop, double-clicking that icon will launch the program.

⑤ Dragging

Drag means move the mouse or trackball while holding down the button. (*Right-drag* means move the mouse or trackball while holding down the right button.) Dragging is frequently used to move or resize items on the screen, as well as to select text or other items. When you've dragged the item to its new location, you drop it by releasing the mouse button. This procedure is called *drag-and-drop*.

Click Means the Left Mouse Button

When you see instructions to press or click the mouse button, assume that you should use the left mouse button unless explicitly told otherwise. If you are supposed to click the right mouse button, for example, the instructions will say "right-click" or "click the right mouse button" rather than just "click."

How to Click the Mouse

To click the mouse in a particular spot, move the pointer to that spot and then, without moving the mouse, just use your index finger to press the mouse button. (Some beginners try to jab the mouse key from on high, which usually jettisons the mouse pointer away from its target.) If you're double-clicking, be sure to keep the mouse in the same spot between the first and second click.

Adjusting the Double-Click Speed

If every time you try to double-click, the computer responds as if you'd only clicked once, chances are you're waiting too long between the first and second click. If you're using Windows, you can adjust the double-click speed—that is, the amount of time you're allowed to leave between clicks. To do this, open the Start menu and select Control Panel. Then double-click the mouse icon, and you'll be there.

Turning Off Your Computer

The first thing to know about turning off your computer is not to do it too often. In general, you should turn it off only when you don't plan on using it again for several hours. If you're going to lunch, leaving the computer on causes less wear and tear than turning it off and then on again. (Some people even leave their computers on night and day, presumably with the thought that this is easier on the machine in the long run, even though it might not be easier on their electricity.) However, you might want to turn off your monitor temporarily, to protect the screen and to turn off the electromagnetic radiation. The monitor also consumes the most energy.

1 Saving Your Work

When you are done using your computer for the day, save any unsaved data that you want to be able to use in future work sessions.

2 If You Close Before You Save

If you are using Windows and forget to save something, the program double-checks with you before discarding your changes.

3 Shutting Down

After confirming your choices, click the Start button in the lower-left corner of the screen to display a Start menu. Click the Turn off Computer option.

4 Turning Off Your System

When Windows displays a box with the title Turn off Computer, click the button labeled Turn off. In a moment, you'll see the message `It's now safe to turn off your computer` and you can flip the on/off switch or press the power button.

5 Automatic Shut Down

Some laptops and desktops are smart enough to turn themselves off automatically. All you do is choose the Turn off Computer option; you don't need to flip an on/off switch or press a power button.

6 When You Can Turn Your Computer Back On

If you turn your computer off and then decide to turn it on again, wait for 30 seconds first to let all the electrical charges dissipate from the machine.

How-to Hint

Shutting Down

In versions of Windows before XP, the Turn off Computer sequence was known as Shut Down. If you are using Windows 98, for example, you will see Shut Down instead of Turn off Computer. The end result is the same either way.

Safe Mode

If you turn off your computer without shutting down properly in Windows, when you turn your computer on again you might see a message indicating that the computer is starting in "safe mode." If so, let the computer finish booting, and then shut it down properly. When you see the Turn off Computer dialog box, choose Restart and then click OK. When your computer restarts, it should be in regular (rather than safe) mode.

Ergonomics: Taking Care of Your Body While You Use a Computer

You'll never learn to love (or even tolerate) a computer if it causes you discomfort or pain. If you plan to spend hours at the keyboard, it's worth taking time to make the experience as comfortable as possible. Setting up your workstation properly isn't just about feeling good (although that's a worthy goal). It's also a way of preventing painful and potentially debilitating conditions like carpal tunnel syndrome, tendonitis, repetitive motion disorder, and chronic back pain. The figure shows how to arrange your computer to cause minimum wear and tear on your body. The basic rules of thumb are as given in the following paragraphs.

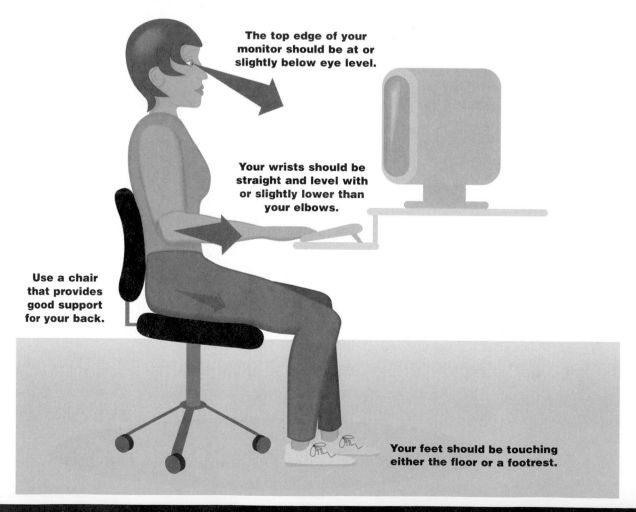

The top edge of your monitor should be at or slightly below eye level.

Your wrists should be straight and level with or slightly lower than your elbows.

Use a chair that provides good support for your back.

Your feet should be touching either the floor or a footrest.

① Your Monitor

The top edge of your monitor should be at eye level or a little below, so you're looking down just slightly. (You might need to prop up the monitor with a large book or a monitor stand.) The front edge should be 20–30 inches from your eyes.

② Desk Height and Posture

Your wrists should never be higher than your elbows. Ideally, your elbows should be bent at a 90° angle and your wrists should be straight, not flexed upward or bent downward. If you can't achieve this position using your desk, your desk is too high (or your chair seat too low). Try a typing desk or a keyboard drawer that allows the keyboard to sit lower than the desktop. Your feet should touch the floor or a footrest and the angle between your thighs and spine should be 90° or a bit more.

③ Proper Mousing

Keep your mouse close to the keyboard so you don't have to reach far to use it. This will minimize strain on your shoulders. Also, try not to sit for hours with your hand on the mouse; let go of the mouse when you're not using it. If you use the mouse even more than the keyboard, put the mouse directly in front of you and the keyboard slightly off to the side. If you do start developing strain in your mouse arm or shoulder, consider using a touch pad.

How-to Hint

Breaks Are Important

One of the best ways to baby your body while using a computer is to take frequent and regular breaks. At least once an hour, take a minute or two to stand up, stretch your arms, turn your head from side to side, roll your shoulders around, and flex and extend your wrists.

Using a Glare Screen

If you're suffering from eye strain, you might want to try a glare screen. These screens, which you can buy for about $20, are usually made of very fine wire mesh, to fit over the front of your monitor—cutting down on glare and, in many cases, sharpening the contrast between light and dark.

④ Proper Wrist Position

One of the worst things you can do to your wrists is lean the heel of your hand on the desk with your wrist flexed backward as you type. Train yourself to hold your wrists up while you're typing (like your piano teacher taught you) or rest them on a wrist rest. Some mice conform to the shape of your hand and can result in less strain. You can also alleviate wrist strain by adjusting the angle of your keyboard. You can angle most keyboards so the back is slightly higher than the front.

⑤ Ergonomic Keyboards

Part of the problem with most computer keyboards is that they force you to hold your hands at an unnatural angle to your arms; your hands are both more horizontal to the desk than they'd like to be and rotated slightly outward at the wrist. Microsoft makes an ergonomic keyboard in which the left-hand and right-hand keys are slightly separated and angled outwards. (The angle between the keys cannot be adjusted.) There are similar keyboards available from third-party vendors.

⑥ Rest Your Eyes

Many people also experience some eye strain after staring at a computer screen for a few hours. The best approach here is to rest your eyes periodically by focusing on a distant object once in awhile, and blinking often. Also make sure you have proper lighting. Avoid overhead lights; they almost always reflect off your screen. The best source of lighting is probably a desk or floor lamp or track lights that are not directly aimed at your screen. Beautiful as it is, sunlight streaming in the windows usually leads to glare as well.

⑦ Find a Good Chair

Finally, if you have back problems (or want to avoid them), a good chair is essential. Look for one that provides support for your lower back and is fully adjustable. (You should be able to change both the height of the seat and the angle of the seat and the back.)

Task

Using the Windows XP Desktop

The Windows desktop works much like its real-world counterpart; it is a place where you organize files, run programs, and coordinate your work. When you run a program or open a folder, these items open in a window on the desktop. You can keep multiple windows open at once, arrange them how you like, and switch between them easily.

In the following tasks, you will explore some of the basic features of the Windows desktop—features that you will use daily. You will learn how to log in and out of Windows, how to use a mouse, how to run a program, and how to get help when you need it. You will also learn techniques for arranging windows and switching between open programs. Finally, you will learn the proper way to shut down your computer.

How to Log On to Windows XP

Windows XP is a secure system. If more than one user account is configured on your computer, or if your computer is on a network, you must log on so that Windows knows who you are and what you are allowed to do on the computer and network. If your computer is on a network, your logon information is supplied by your network administrator. When you install Windows XP on your own computer, you supply the information during setup. Depending on how your computer is set up, you may see the new Windows XP logon screen (steps 1–3) or the traditional logon screen (steps 4–7).

1 Select the User Account

From the list of available users, click the user account with which you want to log on. If a password is not assigned to the account (that is, if the password field was left blank when Windows was installed), you will enter directly into Windows. Otherwise, you'll be asked for a password.

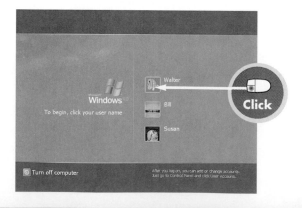

2 Enter Your Password

Type your password in the box that appears. As you type, the characters appear as dots. This prevents people looking over your shoulder from discovering your password. Note that the password is case-sensitive.

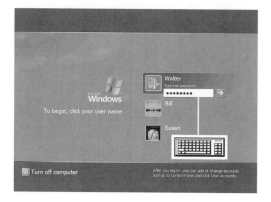

3 Log On

Click the arrow next to the password box (or press the **Enter** key on your keyboard) to submit the password and log on to Windows.

④ Press Ctrl+Alt+Del

An alternative way to log on to Windows is to use the traditional logon screen. To get to the main logon screen, you must press the **Ctrl**, **Alt**, and **Del** keys all at once. This special key combination informs Windows that you want to enter a username and password.

⑤ Enter Your Username and Password

Type your username and password into the appropriate boxes. As you type the password, the characters you enter appear on the screen only as dots. Passwords are case-sensitive. You must enter the correct combination of uppercase and lowercase characters and numbers.

⑥ Show Extra Login Options

Most of the time, a username and password are enough for you to log on to Windows XP. However, you can click the **Options** button for more choices, including choosing a different domain and logging on to just the computer instead of a network.

⑦ Shut Down

You can also shut down your computer from the logon screen. Clicking the **Shutdown** button opens a dialog box from which you can choose to shut down or restart the computer. These options are great when you need to shut down the system but don't want to wait through the logon process.

How to Use Your Mouse

Your mouse allows you to get tasks done quicker than with the keyboard. Sliding the mouse on your desk moves the pointer on the screen. The pointer usually appears as an arrow pointing up and to the left—just point it to the item you want to use. The pointer shape changes as you move over different areas of the screen—a vertical bar shows where you can enter text, for example. The shape also changes to indicate system status. An hourglass means that Windows is busy. An hourglass with an arrow means that Windows is working on something but that you can continue to do other things in the meantime.

❶ Point to an Object

An object refers to an item on your screen, usually an icon, that represents a program, file, or folder. You can point to an object by sliding the mouse so that the tip of the mouse pointer arrow is over that object.

❷ Click an Object

Clicking your left mouse button one time selects an object. When you select the object, its icon and text become highlighted with a dark blue background. Then you can perform another action on the object, such as deleting it.

❸ Double-Click an Object

Double-clicking means to move the mouse pointer over an object and click the left mouse button twice in quick succession. Double-click an object to launch it. Double-click a folder to open it; double-click a program to run it.

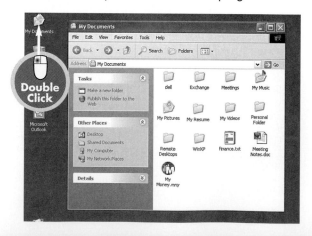

④ Right-Click an Object

When you click once on an object with the right mouse button, a shortcut menu pops up that lets you perform various actions associated with the object. The command in boldface is the action that would be performed by double-clicking the object.

The shortcut menu

⑤ Drag an Object

To drag an object, point to the item, click and hold the left mouse button, and move the mouse to reposition the item. Release the mouse button to drop the object. The drag-and-drop approach is the way to move files to new folders and to move whole windows on your desktop.

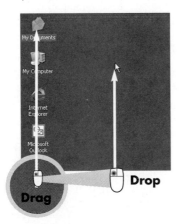

⑥ Open a Menu

Many windows, such as open folders and programs, have menus that provide access to different commands for working in the window. To open a menu, click the menu's name once.

⑦ Select a Menu Command

After a menu is open, you can click any command on the menu to have Windows perform that action.

How to Display Icons on Your Desktop

In previous versions of Windows, icons representing important parts of your system were always shown on your desktop. This may or may not be the case with Windows XP. If you buy a copy of Windows XP and install it yourself (see the Appendix), your desktop will be empty except for the Recycle Bin. If you buy your computer with Windows XP already installed, the icons may or may not be on the desktop, depending on the manufacturer of your computer. Throughout this book, many tasks assume that these icons are displayed on the desktop. If you don't see them on your desktop, you can find them on the Start menu. You can also tell Windows to show the icons on the desktop using the following steps.

1 Open the Start Menu

The Start menu lets you access all your programs and most of the Windows settings available for configuration. The first time you start a computer with Windows XP, the Start menu opens automatically. After that, you must open it yourself by clicking its button once.

2 Find the Icon You're Looking For

The icons that used to appear on the Windows desktop now appear in the upper-right part of the Start menu.

3 Click an Icon to Open Its Window

To open the window for any of the icons in the Start menu, click the icon once with the left mouse button. The Start menu closes and a window opens on your desktop.

4 Open an Icon's Shortcut Menu

Right-click any icon to open a shortcut menu with special commands for working with that icon.

5 Show the Icon on the Desktop

Click the **Show on Desktop** command in the shortcut menu to have that icon appear on the Windows desktop. (The icon will still appear on the Start menu, as well.) If you decide you don't want the icon on your desktop after all, open the **Start** menu, right-click the icon in the menu, and select **Show on Desktop** again to remove the icon from the desktop.

6 Open the Desktop Icon

After the icon is shown on your desktop, double-click it to open it.

7 Turn on Other Icons

Each of the icons shown in the upper-right portion of the Start menu can appear as icons on your desktop. Just right-click each one in turn and choose the **Show on Desktop** command from the shortcut menu.

How to Start a Program

Windows XP provides several ways to run your programs. To begin with, all your programs are conveniently located on the Start menu. This menu includes some simple programs that come with Windows (such as a calculator and a notepad) and any other programs you have installed.

1 Click the Start Button

Click the **Start** button to open the Start menu. Directly under your logon name, you'll find shortcuts to your Web browser and email program (Internet Explorer and Outlook Express, by default). Under these shortcuts, you'll find shortcuts to any programs you've run recently. On the right side of the Start menu, you'll find shortcuts to various important folders on your system and access to the help and search features.

2 Click the More Programs Button

If you don't see the program you are looking for on the Start menu, click the **All Programs** button to see a list of all the programs installed on your computer. Some might be listed in folders within the All Programs folder; just point to a subfolder to open it. Programs that have recently been installed are highlighted. When you find a program you want, click the shortcut to run it.

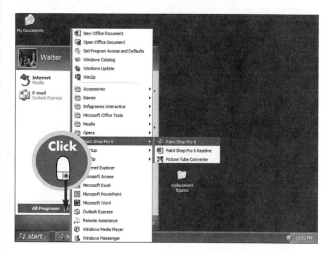

3 Click a Quick Launch Shortcut

Some programs have shortcuts on the Quick Launch toolbar, just to the right of the Start button. Click any of these shortcut buttons to launch the program. The program opens in a new window on the desktop.

4 Maximize a Program Window

Click the **Maximize** button to make the program window take up the whole screen (except for the space occupied by the taskbar).

5 Restore a Program Window

After a window is maximized, the Maximize button turns into a Restore button. Click the **Restore** button to shrink the window back to its previous size.

6 Minimize a Program Window

Click the **Minimize** button to remove the window from the desktop but leave the program running. You can tell the program is still running because its button remains in the taskbar at the bottom of the screen. Click the taskbar button to restore the window to the desktop.

7 Close a Program Window

Click the **Close** button to end the program and remove its window from the desktop. The program displays a dialog box asking you to save any unsaved work before it closes. You can also close a program by choosing the **Exit** command from the **File** menu.

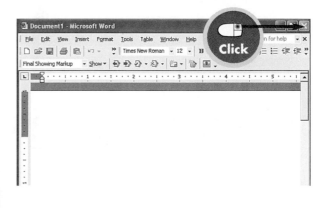

How to Arrange Windows on the Desktop

Windows offers the ability to keep many windows open at the same time. Although having multiple windows open at the same time provides the ability to easily move between tasks, using multiple windows can become confusing. Fortunately, Windows offers some clever tools for working with and arranging the windows on your desktop.

❶ Resize a Window

When you move your pointer to the outer edge or corner of a window, the pointer changes into a double-headed arrow. When the pointer changes, click and drag the edge of the window to change its size.

❷ Move a Window

You can move an entire window to a different location on the desktop by dragging its title bar. You can even move the window off the edges of your screen.

❸ Cascade Windows

You can line up Windows in a cascade by right-clicking the taskbar and choosing **Cascade Windows** from the shortcut menu.

④ Tile Windows Vertically

Another way to arrange multiple windows on your desktop is to tile them. Right-click the taskbar and choose **Tile Windows Vertically** to arrange them from left to right on your screen.

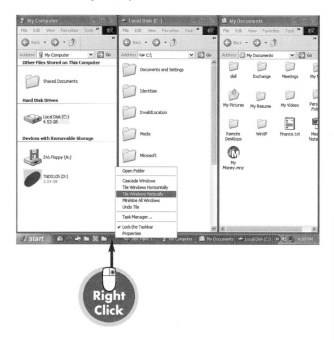

⑥ Minimize All Windows

You can minimize all open windows on your desktop at once (and thus clear them from your desktop) by right-clicking the taskbar and choosing **Minimize All Windows**. This is a great way to get to your desktop quickly.

⑤ Tile Windows Horizontally

You can also tile windows horizontally. Right-click the taskbar and choose **Tile Windows Horizontally**.

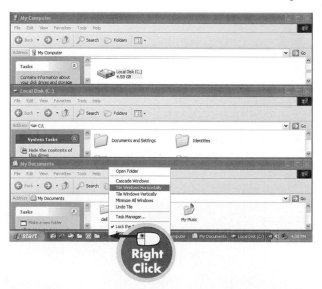

Showing the Desktop

A better way to get to your desktop quickly instead of using the Minimize All Windows command is to use the **Show Desktop** button on the **Quick Launch** toolbar. This button effectively minimizes all windows, even if some windows are showing dialog boxes (something the Minimize All Windows command can't do). Click **Show Desktop** again to reverse the action and return all the minimized windows to their previous states.

How to Switch Between Programs

When you run several programs at once, you must be able to switch between these programs easily. Windows offers three great methods for switching between open applications—two using the mouse and one using the keyboard.

❶ Click the Program's Window

The easiest way to switch to an open program is simply to click the program's window, if some portion of the window is visible. Inactive windows have a slightly dimmer title bar than the active window. Clicking anywhere on an inactive window brings it to the front and makes it active.

Click to make the inactive window active

The active window

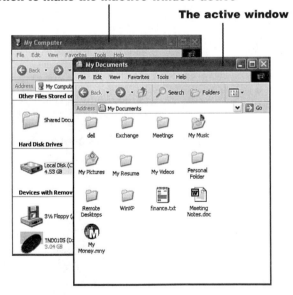

❷ Click the Taskbar Button

When you can't see the window you want, the simplest way to switch to it is to click that window's button on the taskbar. This action brings that window to the front of the desktop in whatever size and position you left it.

❸ Resize the Taskbar

When there are a lot of open windows, the buttons on the taskbar might get too small to be of much value in determining which window is which. You can hold your pointer over a button to see its full description, or you can drag the top edge of the taskbar up to make it bigger.

④ Use Grouped Taskbar Buttons

When more than one window is open for a single program, Windows XP groups those windows using a single taskbar button instead of multiple taskbar buttons. For example, you may be looking at a few different Web sites in different windows using Internet Explorer. A single taskbar button for Internet Explorer is displayed and the number of active Internet Explorer windows (five in the example shown here) is shown on the button. Click the button once to open a menu from which you can choose a specific window to activate.

⑤ Press Alt+Tab

You can also switch between open windows using your keyboard. Press and hold the **Alt** key and then press the **Tab** key once (without letting go of the Alt key). A box appears, displaying icons for each window. Press the **Tab** key to cycle through the windows. When you get to the window you want, release the Alt key to switch to it.

How-to Hint

Getting Out of Alt+Tab

If you use Alt+Tab to open the box that lets you switch between windows and then decide that you don't want to switch, just press **Esc** while you're still holding down the **Alt** key. The box disappears and puts you right back where you were.

Unlocking the Taskbar

If you find that you cannot resize the taskbar, it is probably locked. A locked taskbar cannot be resized or moved. Some people prefer to keep their taskbar locked so that no accidental changes are made to it. Others prefer to leave it unlocked so that they can easily resize it. Right-click anywhere on the taskbar and click the **Lock the Taskbar** command to deselect that command and unlock the bar.

How to Use the Notification Area

The notification area is the part of the taskbar at the far right side that holds your clock and probably several other small icons. These icons show information about programs that are running in the background on your computer. Some of the icons provide access to certain functions of the programs they represent. For example, the speaker icon lets you set your system's volume and configure audio properties.

❶ Expand the Notification Area

The notification area collapses automatically to show only the clock and any recently used icons. To view the entire notification area, click the button with the double-left arrow at the left side of the notification area. A few seconds after you move your pointer away from the area, the notification area collapses again.

❷ View the Date

Hold the mouse pointer over the clock for a moment to view a pop-up balloon with the current date.

❸ Set the Clock

Double-click the clock to open a dialog box that lets you set the current date and time, as well as configure time-zone settings.

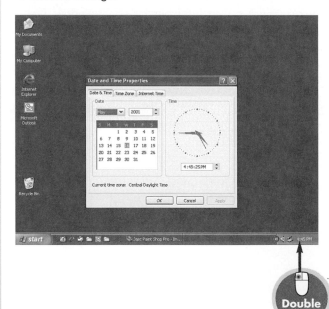

④ Set the Volume

Click the speaker icon in the notification area to open the volume control. Slide the control up or down to change the volume of your system. A beep sounds to let you know how loud the volume is set.

⑤ Use Other Notification Area Icons

Unfortunately, the notification area icons for different programs behave in different manners. Sometimes, right-clicking or left-clicking the icon once opens a dialog box for configuration of some sort (as was the case with the volume control). Sometimes, right-clicking the icon opens a shortcut menu with program options. You'll have to experiment or read the documentation for the appropriate program.

How-to Hint

Keeping the Notification Area Open

To keep the notification area open and showing all its icons all the time, right-click the taskbar and choose **Properties**. On the Taskbar tab of the dialog box that opens, disable (that is, remove the check mark next to) the **Hide Inactive Icons** option.

Turning Off Icons

You can turn off some icons in the notification area by right-clicking the icon and choosing the **Exit** command, if one exists. There also might be a command for setting options or preferences. Sometimes these settings contain an option for permanently turning off the icon. Another place you might look is in the Startup folder on your Start menu. Often, programs that are configured to start with Windows place icons on the notification area. For more about using the Startup folder, see Chapter 4, "Changing Windows XP Settings."

Updating the Clock Automatically

If you have Internet access and are not behind a firewall, Windows XP can update your clock automatically. Double-click the clock. In the dialog box that opens, select the **Internet Time** tab. Select the **Automatically Synchronize with an Internet Time Server** option and then choose an available server.

How to Browse Your Disk Drives

Your disk drives hold all the information on your computer: all the files, folders, and programs, as well as all your documents. The My Computer window gives you access to these drives, whether they are hard drives, floppy drives, CD-ROM drives, or something else. My Computer also provides a shortcut to the Windows Control Panel, which is discussed more in Chapter 4.

❶ Open My Computer

Double-click the **My Computer** icon on the desktop or Start menu to open the My Computer window.

❷ Select a Disk Drive

The My Computer window shows any drives present on your computer. Click the icon for the drive you want to investigate to select it. Your floppy drive is usually named A:, and your main hard drive is usually named C:. Information about the capacity and free space on any selected drive is shown in the Details pane to the left.

③ Open a Drive

Double-click the drive icon to open that drive.

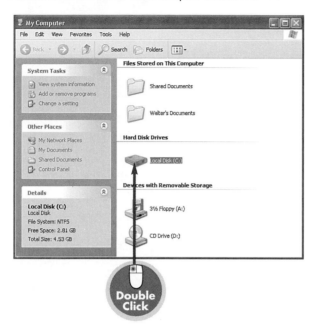

④ Open a Folder

Objects on a drive are organized into folders. *Folders* can contain both files and other folders. Double-click a folder to open it.

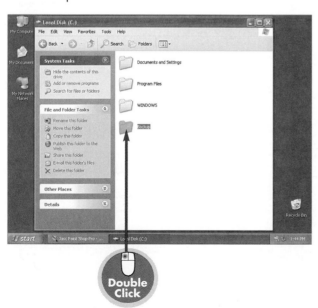

⑤ Open a File

When you select a file, a description of that file appears on the left side of the window. Double-click a file to launch the program that created the file (that is, the program *associated* with the file) and open that file within the program.

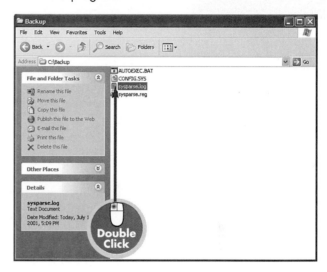

⑥ Navigate Folders

Click the **Back** button in the toolbar at the top of the folder window to go back to the folder you just came from. Click the down arrow next to the **Back** button to view a list of previous locations you can jump back to.

How to Get Help

Windows XP boasts a comprehensive Help system that lets you get details on Windows concepts and performing specific tasks. You can browse the contents of Windows Help, search for specific terms, or even ask questions in plain English.

① Open Help

To open the Windows Help system, click the **Start** button and then choose **Help and Support**. The Help and Support Center window opens.

② Enter a Search Term

If you know what topic you are looking for, type a word, phrase, or question in the **Search** box and click the **Search** button.

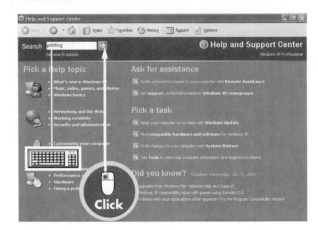

③ Select a Result

Windows shows a list of articles that match your search. Click one of the results in the left pane to view the article in the right pane. Buttons above the article let you print the article or add it to a list of favorites.

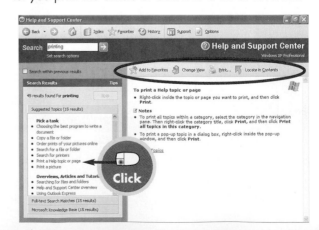

④ Pick a Help Topic

If you are not sure what the name of the topic you're looking for is, or if you just want to browse the Help system, click the link for a help topic on the main Help and Support Center page.

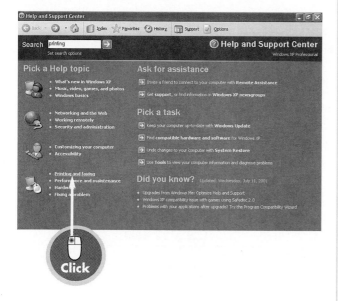

⑤ Pick a Category

In the left pane, Windows displays the categories for the topic you selected in step 4. Click a category to display a list of help articles related to that category in the right pane.

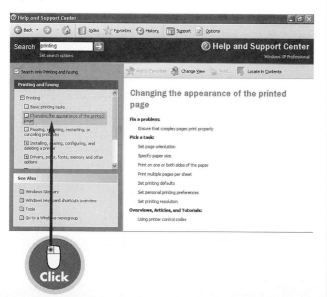

⑥ Pick an Article

Click the article in the list you want to view. Windows opens the selected article in a new window. When you're done reading the article, click the window's **Close** button to close the window and return to the Help and Support Center window.

How-to Hint

Using the F1 Key

Press the **F1** key at any time while using Windows to open a help page related to your current activity. Many programs also support the F1/Help feature.

Using the Index

Click the **Index** button on the help window's toolbar to view a searchable index of all help articles. Some people find it easier to browse the Help system this way.

How to Use the Recycle Bin

You can delete files, folders, and programs from your computer at any time. However, when you delete an item, Windows does not immediately remove it from your computer. Instead, the item is placed into the Recycle Bin. You can restore an item from the Recycle Bin later if you decide you would rather not delete it. When the Recycle Bin becomes full (depending on the amount of disk space allocated to it), Windows deletes older items permanently to make room for newer items. You can think of the Recycle Bin as sort of a buffer between your files and oblivion.

① Drag an Object to the Recycle Bin

The easiest way to delete an object is to drag it to the Recycle Bin. You can drag an item from the desktop or from any open folder. You can also delete a file by selecting it and pressing the **Delete** key on your keyboard.

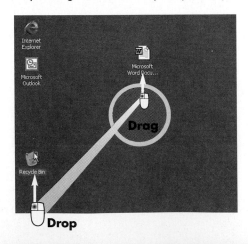

② Confirm the Deletion

When you try to delete an object, Windows asks you to confirm that you really want to delete it. Click **Yes** if you're sure; click **No** if you made a mistake and don't want to delete the object.

③ Open the Recycle Bin

Double-click the **Recycle Bin** icon on the desktop to open it. All files in the Recycle Bin are listed with their original locations and the date on which they were deleted.

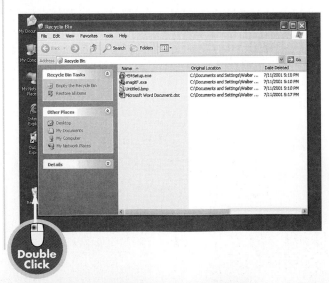

④ Restore Files

To remove a file from the Recycle Bin and restore it to its original location, select the file and click the **Restore This Item** link that appears on the left.

⑤ Delete Files

Right-click a file in the Recycle Bin list and choose **Delete** from the shortcut menu to permanently delete that file from your hard disk.

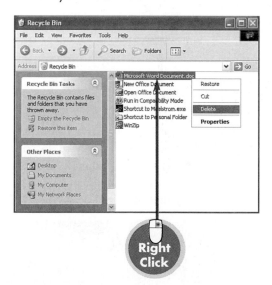

⑥ Empty the Recycle Bin

To permanently delete all the files from the Recycle Bin (which you might want to do to regain some disk space), make sure that no files are selected and click the **Empty Recycle Bin** link on the left.

How-to Hint

Another Way to Empty the Bin

You can empty the Recycle Bin without opening it by right-clicking its icon on the desktop and choosing **Empty Recycle Bin** from the shortcut menu.

Allocating Recycle Bin Space

By default, 10% of your hard drive space is reserved for use by the Recycle Bin. You can change the amount of space used by right-clicking the **Recycle Bin** and selecting the **Properties** command from the shortcut menu. On the Global tab of the Recycle Bin Properties dialog box, drag the slider to change the maximum size of the Recycle Bin.

How to Log Off Windows XP

As you learned earlier in this chapter, logging on (providing Windows with your username and maybe a password) tells Windows who is using the computer. Logging off tells Windows that you are finished with your computer session. You should log off whenever you plan to be away from the computer for a length of time (such as for lunch or at the end of the day).

1 Click Log Off

Click the **Start** button and then choose **Log Off**.

2 Switch User

If you are not finished using Windows and just want to let someone else use the computer for a short time, you can simply switch users. Click the **Switch User** button if you want to leave all your programs running and your documents open while the other person uses the computer. The logon window (shown in Task 1) opens so that the other person can log on. When that person logs off, you can switch back to your account and continue working.

3 Log Off

Logging off closes any running programs. Although Windows usually gives you the chance to save any unsaved documents before it actually logs off, you should save your files manually before you log off to make sure that your data is safe.

④ Log On Another User

As soon as you log off, Windows presents the logon screen. You can now log back on as described in Task 1.

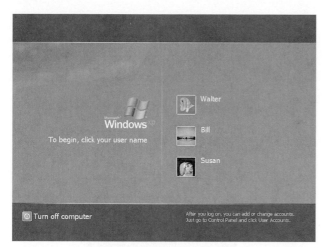

Using a Screensaver Password

Screensaver passwords let your computer automatically lock itself whenever the screen saver activates. To access the computer again, you'll have to type the password to deactivate the screen saver.

How to Turn Off Your Computer

While running, Windows keeps a lot of its information in system memory—memory that is not sustained when the computer is turned off. For this reason, you should never simply turn your computer off using the power button. You should always use the Turn Off Computer command to allow Windows to gracefully shut itself down.

❶ Click Turn Off Computer

Click the **Start** button and then choose **Turn Off Computer**. The Turn Off Computer window opens.

❷ Choose the Turn Off Option

Click the **Turn Off** button. Windows closes all open programs (giving you the opportunity to save unsaved documents) and tells you when it is safe to turn off the power. This is the option you will likely choose at the end of the day or when the computer will be unused for a lengthy period.

❸ Choose the Restart Option

Click the **Restart** button to have Windows shut itself down and then automatically restart the computer. After the computer is restarted, you can log on to Windows again. Restarting your computer is the first thing you should try if you find that Windows, another program, or a hardware component isn't working as you think it should.

④ Choose Hibernate or Standby

Some computers offer additional logoff options, including Hibernate and Standby. The Hibernate option saves all the information in your computer's memory to hard disk and then shuts the computer down. When you restart the computer, all your programs and windows are restored to the same state in which you left them. The Standby option turns off the power to most of the components of your computer, but keeps enough power going to your computer's memory that it can remember its current state. When you restore a computer from Standby (usually by pressing the power button, but different computers can vary in the method), the computer returns to the state in which you left it.

⑤ Save Any Open Files

If you attempt to shut down Windows while programs are running with unsaved documents, you are given the chance to save those documents before shut-down proceeds. Click **Yes** if you want to save the changes to the named document; click **No** if you don't want to save the changes; click **Cancel** if you want to abort the shut-down process altogether.

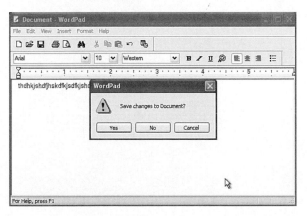

Other Active Users

Because Windows XP now allows multiple user accounts to be logged on at the same time, you may find that when you try to shut down or restart the computer, other user accounts are still logged on. Windows XP informs you that the accounts are still active and gives you a chance to cancel your request to shut down. You should log off the other accounts (or have the people to whom the accounts belong log off); if you don't, any documents open in those accounts will be lost. Windows does not give you the option of saving other people's files the way it lets you save your own when shutting down or restarting.

3

Working with Files and Folders

Everything on your computer is made up of files on your hard drive. Windows itself is just thousands of different files that interact with one another. Your programs are also collections of files that interact with one another and with Windows files. Finally, all the documents you create are themselves files.

Files are organized into folders that can hold both files and other folders. For example, suppose your C: drive contains a folder named Backup, which in turn holds a folder named July, which in turn holds a file named smith.jpg. The full description of the location of a file on a drive is called a path and includes the name of the disk drive, the names of each folder, and the name of the file—each name separated by a backslash (\). For the smith.jpg document mentioned earlier, the path would be `C:\Backup\July\smith.jpg`.

The name of a file can be 256 characters long and has a three-character extension (the three characters after the dot) that identifies the type of file it is. By default, extensions are not shown for file types that your system knows about.

How to Use Windows Explorer

Chapter 2, "Using the Windows XP Desktop," explained how to use the My Computer window to browse through the folders and files on a disk drive. In truth, you can use the My Computer window to get to any file on your computer and do anything you want with it. However, Windows offers another utility, Windows Explorer, that you might find more useful for working with the files and folders on your computer. It's really a matter of personal style.

❶ Open Explorer

You run Windows Explorer just like you do any other program. Click the **Start** button and select **All Programs**, **Accessories**, **Windows Explorer**.

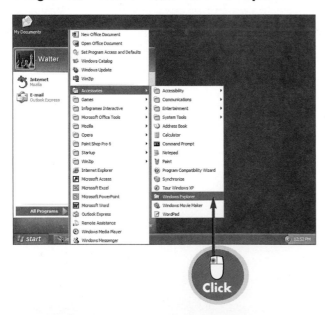

❷ Browse Folders

The left pane of the Explorer window shows a hierarchy of all the drives, folders, and desktop items on your computer. A drive or folder that contains other folders has a plus sign to the left of the icon. Click the **plus sign** to expand it and see the folders inside.

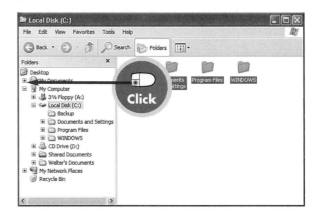

❸ Open a Folder

Click any folder in the list in the left pane; all the files and folders in that folder are shown in the right pane.

4 Open a File

The right pane works the same way as the My Computer window. You can double-click any file or folder in this pane to open it.

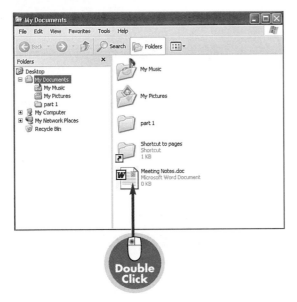

5 Move a File to Another Folder

One of the advantages of using Windows Explorer is that you can easily move a file to any other folder on your computer. Drag a file from the right pane and drop it on any folder icon in the left pane to move the file there.

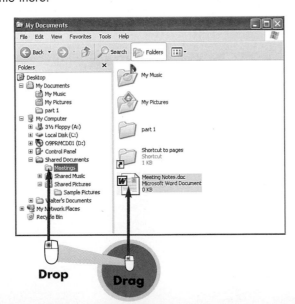

6 Copy a File to Another Drive

Copying a file to another drive is as easy as moving it. Just drag a file from the right pane to another disk drive (or a folder on another drive) to copy it there. Notice that the icon you are dragging takes on a small plus sign to let you know that the file will be copied, but not moved.

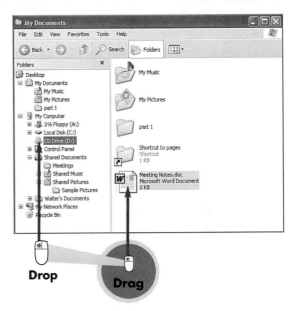

How-to Hint

Auto-Expanding

When you move a file to another folder in Windows Explorer, the folder doesn't have to be visible already. While dragging the file, hold the mouse pointer over a folder's plus sign for two seconds to automatically expand that folder.

Auto-Scrolling

While dragging a file, hold the mouse pointer at the top or bottom of the left pane for two seconds to automatically scroll up or down.

Copying or Moving to Other Locations

For more on how to move or copy files between folders and drives, see Task 11, "How to Move or Copy a File or Folder," later in this chapter.

How to Search for a File or Folder

Using Windows Explorer is great if you know where the file or folder you want is located. Sometimes, however, it's hard to remember just where you put something. Fortunately, Windows has a great search function built right in that helps you find files and folders. You can search for folders by all or part of their names, by text they might contain, or by their location. You can even search using all three of these criteria at once.

① Open the Search Window

Click the **Start** button and select **Search**. You'll also find a Search button on the toolbar of most windows that performs the same function. A search window opens.

② Select the Type of Document

The left pane holds the interface you will use for searching. Results of any search you perform are displayed in the right pane. Choose the type of document you want to search for from the list in the left pane. The pane changes to show additional search questions based on the type of file you choose.

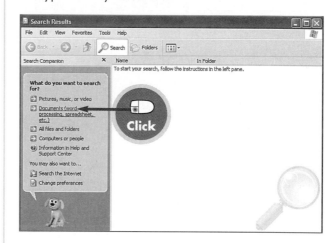

③ Type the Document Name

Type all or part of the name of the file or folder you want to search for in the text box. When you search, Windows shows all of the file and folder names that contain the text you enter.

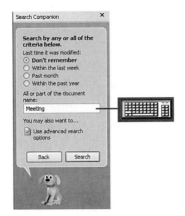

④ Select a Time Frame

If you know approximately when the document was last modified, select one of the time options. If you don't remember, just leave the **Don't Remember** option selected.

⑤ Click Search

After you have entered your search criteria, click **Search** to have Windows begin the search.

⑥ View the Results

The results of your search are displayed in the right pane. You can double-click a file to open it right from the search window.

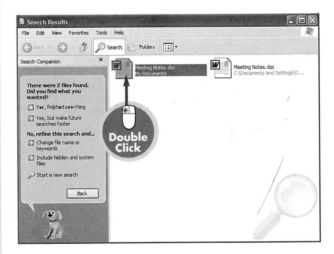

How-to Hint

Quickly Opening a File's Folder

You can quickly open the parent folder of a file you've found by right-clicking the file in the results pane and choosing **Open Containing Folder** from the shortcut menu.

How to Create a Folder

Folders help you organize your files. You create a folder using the My Computer window or Windows Explorer. You can create a folder in any existing disk drive or folder or on the Windows desktop itself.

1 Find the Place to Make the Folder

The first step in creating a folder is to decide where you want to create it. Use the My Computer window or Windows Explorer to find the place you want to be.

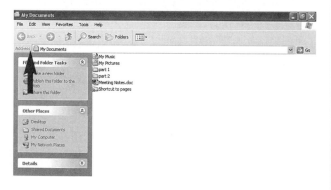

2 Create the New Folder

In the **Tasks** list, select **Make a New Folder**. Alternatively, pull down the **File** menu and select **New**, **Folder**.

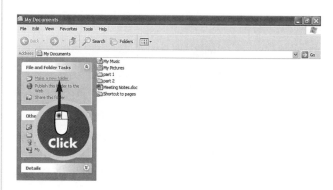

3 Rename the Folder

The new folder appears in the current location with the default name New Folder. The name is already highlighted; you can rename it by typing the name you want and pressing **Enter** or clicking somewhere outside the name field (here I've named the folder Personal Folder). You can also rename the folder later by selecting it and choosing **File**, **Rename** and then typing the new folder name. Note that renaming the folder does not affect any files contained in that folder.

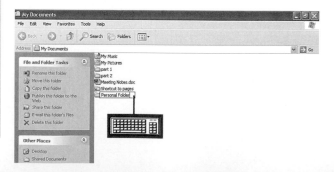

4 Create a Folder on the Desktop

To create a new folder directly on your desktop, right-click any empty area of the desktop. Point to **New** on the shortcut menu and then choose **Folder**.

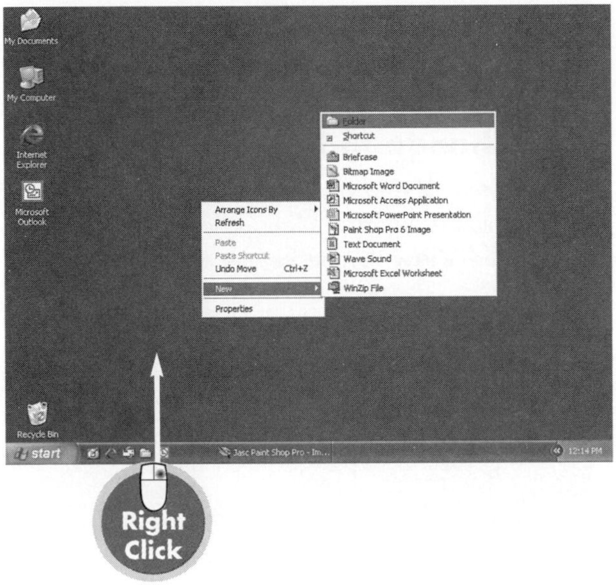

5 Name the New Folder

As you did in step 3, type a new name for the folder (its default name is New Folder) and press **Enter**.

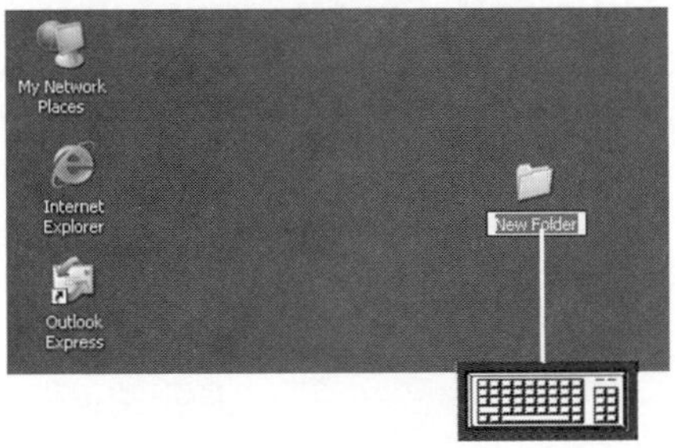

How-to Hint

Saving a Document

Some programs let you create a new folder from the same dialog box you use to save a document. There is usually a button named Create New Folder. Just click the button, name the new folder, and open it to save your document there.

Creating a Folder in the Start Menu

The Start menu is really a folder on your hard disk; you can create new folders in it to help organize your files. Right-click the **Start** button, choose **Open** from the shortcut menu, and create the folder in the window that opens using the methods described in this task. The new folder appears on your Start menu. For more on customizing your Start menu, see Chapter 4, "Changing Windows XP Settings."

How to View Items in a Folder

Normally, both the My Computer window and Windows Explorer show you the contents of a folder as large icons that represent other folders and files. This is a friendly way to view folders, but not always the most useful, especially if a folder contains large numbers of files or many files with similar names. You can also view the contents of a folder as small icons, as a list, as a list with file details, or even as thumbnails.

❶ Open a Folder

First, you need to find a folder to view. You can do this in either the My Computer window or in Windows Explorer. In this Windows Explorer example, notice that the regular large icon view looks pretty cluttered.

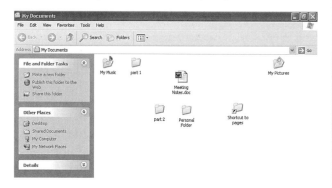

❷ Change to List View

Choose **View**, **List** to view the folder contents as a list. The contents are listed in alphabetical order. You can also use the **View** button on the toolbar to change views.

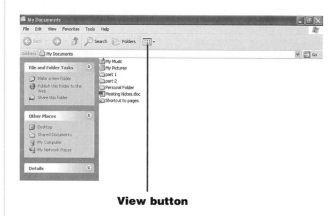

View button

❸ Change to Details View

The Detail view is perhaps the most useful way to view the contents of a folder. Choose **View**, **Details**. Contents are presented in a list with columns that include file details, such as the size and type of the file and when the file was last modified.

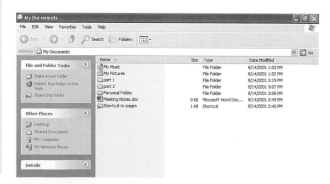

4 Change to Thumbnail View

Thumbnail view presents the contents of a folder as small thumbnails, or previews, of the actual documents. Only certain file types, such as JPEG images, support this type of viewing. Choose **View**, **Thumbnail** to display the folder contents as thumbnails. Other types of documents are displayed as larger versions of their normal icons.

5 Arrange Icons

In addition to choosing how to view the contents of a folder, you can also choose how those contents are arranged. Choose **View**, **Arrange Icons By** and then choose **Name**, **Type**, **Size**, or **Modified** (the date the files were last modified) to order the contents of the folder. You can also have the folder arrange the icons automatically.

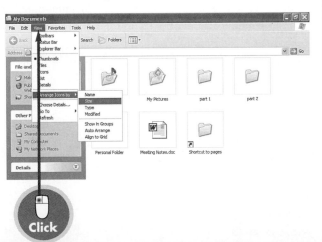

Arranging in Details View

You can easily arrange the contents of a folder in the Details view by clicking the column heading by which you want to order the contents. For example, click the **Type** column heading to group the files in the current folder by type. You can choose the columns that are shown in Details view by selecting **View**, **Choose Columns** from the menu bar. A window opens with lots of different choices for columns to display. Just select the ones you want.

Other Arrangements

Select **View**, **Arrange Icons By**, **Show in Groups** to divide a folder's window into different sections that show different types of items, such as folders, drives, and files. Within each group, icons are arranged according to your other settings on the View menu. The Auto Arrange option on the same menu automatically arranges the icons in a window by alphabetic and numerical order and groups them together at the beginning of a window. The Align to Grid option gives you the freedom to arrange your icons as you like, while making sure that they all uniformly align to an invisible grid in the window.

Cleaning Up Your Windows

Many users find that the common tasks shown on the left side of most windows take up too much space and really aren't that useful anyway. You can turn the task list off for all folders by selecting **Start**, **Control Panel**, **Folder Options**. On the General tab of the Folder Options dialog box, choose the **Use Windows Classic Folders** option. To turn the task list back on, come back to the Folder Options dialog box and choose the **Show Common Tasks in Folder** option. Unfortunately, you cannot enable the list for some folders and disable it for others.

How to Create a File

Most of the time, you will create new documents from within a particular program. For example, you usually use Microsoft Word to create a new Word document. However, Windows does offer the ability to quickly create certain types of documents without opening the associated program at all. This can be quite useful when you are creating a large number of new documents that will be edited later.

1 Locate the Parent Folder

First, you must find the folder in which you want to create the new file. You can create a file directly in any folder on your computer. Here I used Windows Explorer to navigate to the new Personal Folder folder I created in Task 3, "How to Create a Folder."

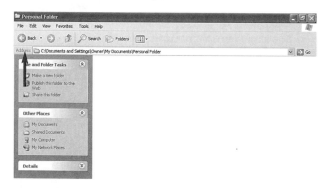

2 Create the File

Choose **File**, **New**, and then select the type of file you want to create. Note that the list of file types presented in the submenu covers basic Windows objects (such as folders, shortcuts, and text files) and objects that depend on additional software you have installed (such as Microsoft Word documents).

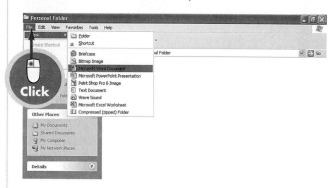

3 Locate the New Document

The new document appears in the selected folder with a generic name, such as New Microsoft Word Document. If you don't see the new file immediately, use the window's scrollbars to find it.

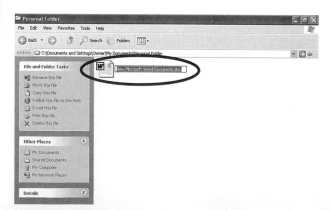

④ Rename the File

The new file appears with the name already high-lighted. Just start typing to enter a new name for the file. When you're done, press **Enter** or click somewhere outside the text box.

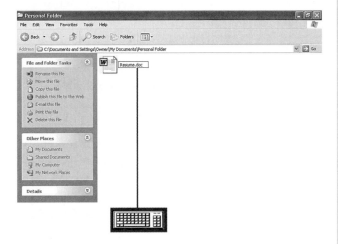

⑤ Open the File to Edit

After you have created and renamed your new file, double-click it to launch the appropriate program and open the new file with it. Now that the file is open in the appropriate application, you can work with it just as you would any other file created in that application.

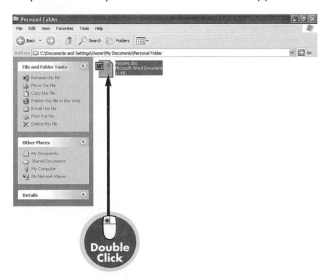

Renaming Files

Files can have names of up to 256 characters, including spaces. There are several special characters you cannot use in your file's name, including \ / : * ? " < >

Preserving the File Type

When you create a new file, Windows automatically gives it the right three-letter file extension (the three letters after the dot) to indicate the file type. If your Windows settings allow you to see the file extension (by default, they don't), be sure that you don't change the extension when you rename the file. If you do, the file won't open with the right program. Windows warns you if you try to change the file extension.

Populating a Folder Quickly

In Windows Explorer or My Computer, you can create as many new documents as you need and then go back and rename them later. To create files even more quickly, create one file, copy it by selecting it and pressing **Ctrl+C**, and then paste as many new files in the same folder as you need by pressing **Ctrl+V**. Each new file has the text Copy of and a number prepended to the filename to distinguish it from its siblings (for example, if the original file is named resume.doc, the first copy is named Copy of resume.doc; the second copy is named Copy [2] of resume.doc, and so on).

How to Open a File

There are several different ways to open a file in Windows. One way is to locate the file in the My Computer window or Windows Explorer and open it from there. You can also open a file from within the program that created it. Windows even keeps track of the files you have opened recently so that you can reopen these in one simple step using the Start menu.

1 Double-Click the File

Find the file you want to open by using the My Computer window or Windows Explorer. Double-click the file to launch the file's program and open the file with it. Here, the file Resume.doc will open in Microsoft Word.

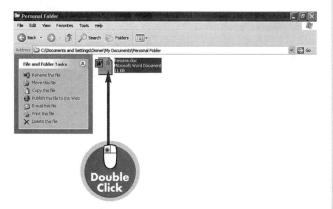

2 Open a Recently Used File

Windows keeps track of the most-recent 15 documents you have opened. To open any of these documents, click the **Start** button and point to the **My Recent Documents** option to see a list of the documents most recently opened on your computer. Select the document you want to open. If the My Recent Documents option does not show up on your Start menu, see Chapter 4 for details on how to add it.

③ Run a Program

Yet another way to open a file is from within the program that created it. The first step is to run the program. Click the **Start** button, point to **More Programs**, and find the program you want to run in the submenus that appear.

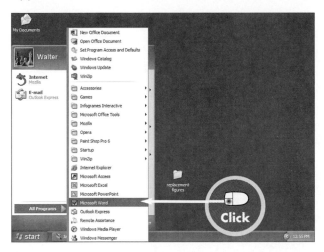

④ Choose Open from the File Menu

After the selected program opens, choose **File**, **Open** from the menu bar. The Open dialog box appears.

⑤ Find the File to Open

For most programs, the Open dialog box works a lot like the My Computer window. Navigate through the folders on your computer system to find the file you want to open, select it, and click **Open**.

How to Save a File

Saving your work is one of the most important things you'll do. After all, if you don't save your work, what's the point of doing it in the first place? Saving a file is always done while you are working on it within a program. There are two save commands in most programs. Save As lets you choose a location and name for your file. Save simply updates the file using its current location and name. The first time you save a new file, the program uses the Save As function no matter which command you choose.

1 Open the Save As Dialog Box

If you want to save a file using a particular name or to a particular location, click the **File** menu and then choose **Save As**. Note that you can use this command to save a copy of the file you are working on with a new name or to save versions of a file. The Save As dialog box opens.

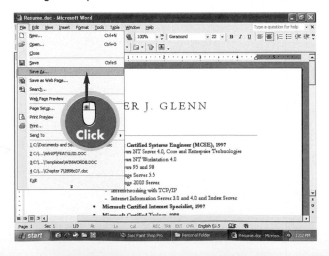

2 Choose a Location

The Save As dialog box works just like the My Computer window. Choose the disk drive to which you want to save the file using the **Save in** drop-down list. After you choose the drive, navigate to the desired folder.

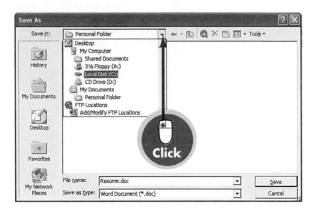

3 Choose a Favorite Place

Instead of using the drop-down list, you can choose a favorite place by clicking the icon for a folder in the bar on the left of the dialog box. You can then save your file in that folder or browse to another folder inside the folder.

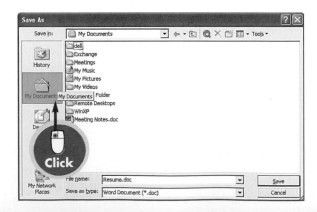

④ Create a New Folder

If you want to save the file you're working on in a new folder, navigate to the folder in which you want to store the new file, then click the **Create New Folder** button in the Save As dialog box toolbar. Type a name for the new folder and press **Enter**. Open the new folder by double-clicking it.

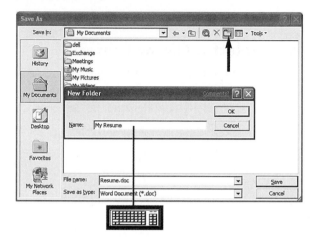

⑤ Name the File

Type the name for the document in the **File Name** box. Note that, in most applications, you do not have to include the file extension when you type the filename. The application supplies the extension for you. If you do include an extension, the application accepts it.

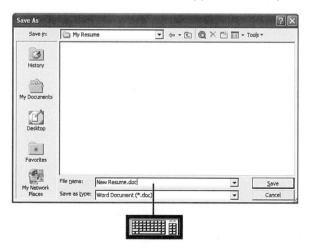

⑥ Save the File

Click **Save** to save the new file in the selected folder with the name you specified.

⑦ Save the File As You Work

Periodically as you work, save any changes to your document using the **Save** button on the program's main toolbar (or the **Save** command on the **File** menu). If you click Save and it is the first time you are saving a new document, the Save As dialog box opens and prompts you for a filename. Otherwise, the file is saved in the current location with the current filename, overwriting the last version of the file you had saved.

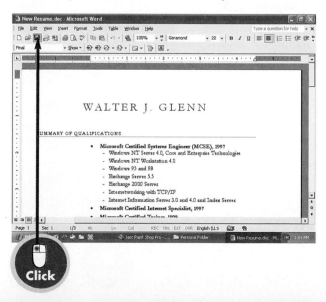

How to Create a Shortcut to a File or Folder

A shortcut is an icon that points to a file or folder somewhere on your computer. The shortcut is merely a reference to the actual object and is used to access the object without having to go to the object's location. For example, on your desktop you could place a shortcut to a frequently used document. You could then double-click the shortcut to open the file without having to go to the folder where the actual file is stored.

1 Open Windows Explorer

The first step in creating a new shortcut is to use the My Computer window or Windows Explorer to find the file or folder to which you want to make a shortcut. To open Windows Explorer, click **Start** and select **All Programs**, **Accessories**, **Windows Explorer**.

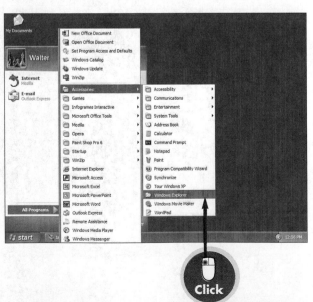

2 Select a File or Folder

In Windows Explorer, navigate to the object to which you want to make a shortcut. In this example, I want to create a shortcut to my new Personal Folder folder.

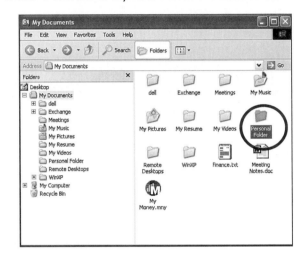

③ Drag the File to Your Desktop

Click and hold the *right* mouse button and drag the object to a blank space on the desktop. Release the right mouse button to drop the icon on the desktop.

④ Choose Create Shortcuts Here

When you release the right mouse button, a shortcut menu appears. Choose **Create Shortcuts Here**.

⑤ Rename the Shortcut

Notice that the shortcut icon has a small arrow on it, indicating that it is a shortcut. You can rename the shortcut to anything you like by right-clicking the shortcut icon and choosing **Rename** from the shortcut menu.

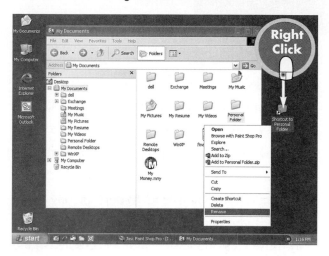

⑥ Double-Click the Shortcut

To open the original object to which you made the shortcut, double-click the shortcut icon. In this example, double-clicking the **Shortcut to Personal Folder** shortcut opens the Personal Folder folder in Windows Explorer.

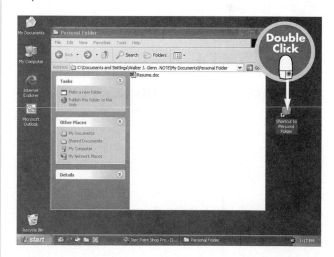

How to Rename a File or Folder

In Windows XP, you can name files or folders just about anything you want. Names are limited to 256 characters, including spaces, but there are a few special characters you are not allowed to use, including the following: \ / : * ? " < >. You can rename files and folders at any time. Note that you should be very careful to rename only those files and folders that you created in the first place. Windows and Windows programs are composed of many folders and files that have special names. Changing the names of these files can often cause a program, or even Windows itself, to malfunction.

❶ Select the File

To rename a file in the My Computer window or Windows Explorer, first select the file with a single click.

❷ Choose Rename from the File Menu

From the menu bar, choose **File**, **Rename**. A box appears around the name of the file or folder you selected in step 1 and the filename itself is highlighted.

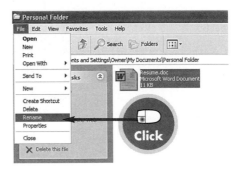

❸ Type a New Name

Type a new name for the selected file. Note that as you type, the highlighted filename is replaced by the text you type. If you want to edit (and not replace) the current filename, use the arrow keys or mouse pointer to position the insertion point, then add and delete characters from the filename as desired. When you're done with the filename, press **Enter**.

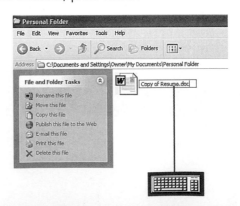

④ Click the Name Twice Slowly

A quicker way to rename a file (and one that also works on files on the desktop) is to first select the file with a single click and then click the name of the file a second later—not so fast as to suggest a double-click. You can also select the file and press the **F2** key. When the filename is highlighted, you can then type a new name.

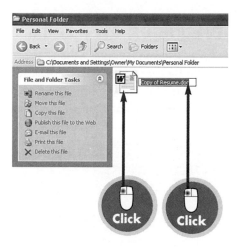

Keeping Names Simple

How-to Hint

Although you can create very long filenames in Windows, it is usually better to keep them short and simple. The reason for this is that when you view the contents of a folder, filenames are often cut off after the first 15–20 characters so that you can view more files in the folder. Keep the filenames short so that you can view the contents of a folder without having to switch to details view and adjust the default column size to see the entire filename. For more on adjusting window views, refer to Task 4, "How to View Items in a Folder."

⑤ Right-Click the File

Yet another way to rename a file is to right-click the file and choose **Rename** from the shortcut menu. You can then type a new name as explained in step 3.

How to Delete a File or Folder

When you delete a file or folder in Windows, the object is not immediately removed from your computer. It is first placed into the Recycle Bin, where it is kept temporarily before being permanently deleted. The Recycle Bin gives you the chance to recover files you might have accidentally deleted. For more information about the Recycle Bin, see Chapter 2, Task 10, "How to Use the Recycle Bin." There are a few ways to delete objects in Windows, including dragging them to the Recycle Bin or deleting them directly using the keyboard or Windows Explorer.

❶ Select a Group of Files

Place the mouse pointer in a blank spot near a group of objects you want to delete. Click and hold the left mouse button and drag the pointer toward the objects. A dotted rectangle (named the lasso) appears behind the pointer. Drag the lasso over all the objects to select them all at once.

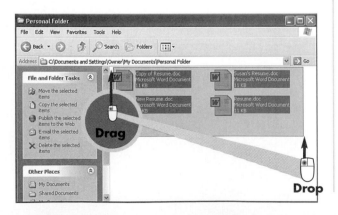

❷ Drag to the Recycle Bin

After you have selected a group of files, drag them to the Recycle Bin by clicking any single selected file and holding the mouse button while you drag the pointer over the Recycle Bin. Release the mouse button when the Recycle Bin icon becomes highlighted to drop the selected files into the Recycle Bin.

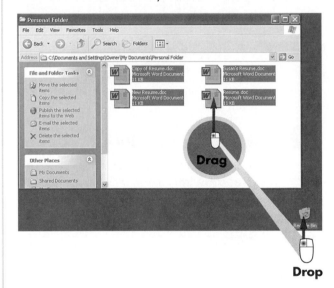

③ Select a File

It is also easy to delete files without using the Recycle Bin, which is helpful when you can't see your desktop. First, select the file you want to delete by clicking it once.

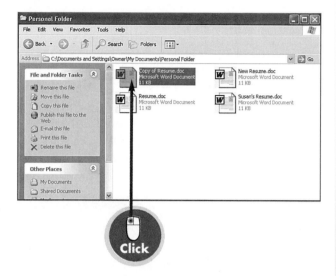

④ Use the Delete Key

Press the **Delete** key on your keyboard to send the selected file (or files) to the Recycle Bin.

⑤ Choose Delete from the File Menu

After a file is selected, you can also open the **File** menu and choose **Delete** to send the file to the Recycle Bin.

Disabling the Recycle Bin

If you would rather not use the Recycle Bin, right-click the **Recycle Bin** icon on the desktop and choose **Properties** from the shortcut menu. Select the **Do Not Move Files to the Recycle Bin** option. Be careful, though. When this option is selected, files that you delete are permanently removed from your system, giving you no chance to recover them.

Changing the Recycle Bin Settings

There are several ways you can customize the operation of your Recycle Bin. For more information on this, see Chapter 2.

How to Move or Copy a File or Folder

Most people move objects around from folder to folder by simply dragging them using the left mouse button. This usually works fine, but it might not provide the exact results you want. Depending on where you drag an object, you can move the object or you can copy it to the new location. For better results, try using the right mouse button instead of the left when you drag files to a new location.

❶ Find the Parent Folder

Use the My Computer window or Windows Explorer to find the folder that contains the object you want to move or copy.

❷ Locate an Object

Locate an object you want to move. The object can be a file or a folder. Note that if you move a folder, you move the contents (all the files and folders contained in that folder) as well. If you copy a folder, you copy the contents of the folder as well.

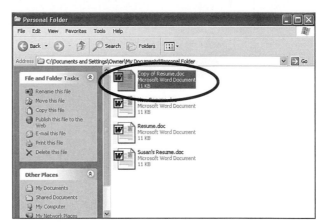

③ Drag the File to a New Location

Place the mouse pointer over the object, click and hold the right mouse button, and drag the object to the target location. In this example, I am dragging the document file to the desktop. Release the right mouse button to drop the object in its new location.

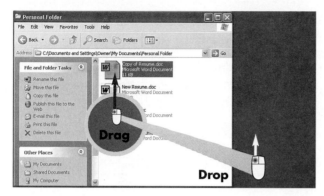

④ Choose Copy Here

When you release the right mouse button, a shortcut menu appears. Choose **Copy Here** to place an exact copy of the selected item in the new location and keep the original object in the old location.

⑤ Choose Move Here

Choose **Move Here** from the shortcut menu to move the object to the new location and remove it from the old location.

How-to Hint

Left-Dragging

When you use the left mouse button to drag a file, the icon you drag changes to reflect what action will be performed. If the icon has a small plus sign on it, the file will be copied when you release the mouse button. If the icon has a small arrow, a shortcut will be created. If the icon has nothing extra on it, the object will be moved.

Right-Dragging

A better way to move files is to drag them using the right mouse button (instead of the left). When you release a file or folder you have dragged with the right button, a menu pops up asking whether you want to copy, move, or create a shortcut.

Dragging with Keys

When you drag using the left mouse button, you can hold down the Shift and Ctrl keys to get different effects. For example, hold down the **Shift** key while dragging a file to move the file instead of copying it. Hold down the **Ctrl** key while dragging a file to copy the file instead of moving it.

How to Format a Floppy Disk

When you buy floppy disks from a store, they are usually formatted. Make sure that you buy disks formatted for your system. The package should read "IBM Formatted" if the floppy disks are to work with Windows. If you have an unformatted disk, it is easy enough to format in Windows. Formatting is also a quick way to erase all the files that you don't need anymore from a disk. Before you start the steps in this task, insert the floppy disk to be formatted in your floppy drive.

1 Open My Computer

Double-click the **My Computer** icon on your desktop to open the My Computer folder.

2 Right-Click the Floppy Drive

Right-click the drive labeled 31/2 Floppy (A:) and select the **Format** command from the shortcut menu. The Format dialog box opens.

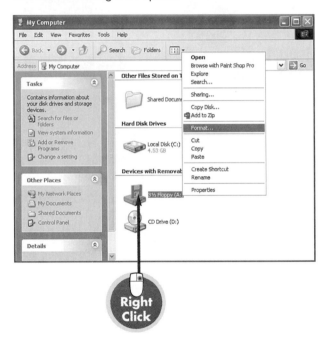

③ Choose a Capacity

Almost all computers today use 1.44MB floppy drives, which is the default choice in this dialog box. If you are formatting an older floppy (or one for an older computer), choose the 720K size from the **Capacity** drop-down list.

⑤ Perform a Quick Format

If you are formatting a disk that has been previously formatted by Windows (as you would do when erasing a disk), choose the **Quick Format** option to significantly shorten the time needed to format the disk.

④ Enter a Volume Label

Type a label into the **Volume Label** box. The volume label is the name of the floppy disk. You can leave this blank if you do not want a label (most people do leave this field blank).

⑥ Format the Disk

Click **Start** to begin formatting the disk. A progress indicator at the bottom of the dialog box shows the formatting progress. Another dialog box opens to inform you when the format is done.

How-to Hint

Be Careful When Selecting a Drive

The Format dialog box lets you select any drive on your system to format. Be sure that the correct drive is selected before formatting. Formatting a hard drive erases all its contents!

How to Send a File to the Floppy Drive

Floppy disks are often used to back up files or transfer files to another computer. In Windows, the floppy drive is always labeled A: in the My Computer window and Windows Explorer. As with most other tasks, Windows offers a couple different ways to send files to a floppy disk. Before you begin this task, make sure that a properly formatted floppy disk is in the floppy disk drive.

① Open My Documents

Double-click the **My Documents** icon on your desktop to open the My Documents folder. If you don't see the My Documents icon on your desktop, you can find it on the Start menu or add it to your desktop as explained in Chapter 2.

② Open My Computer

Double-click the **My Computer** icon on your desktop to open the My Computer window.

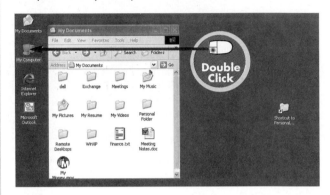

③ Tile Your Windows

Right-click the taskbar and choose **Tile Windows Vertically** so that you can see both the My Computer and the My Documents windows at the same time.

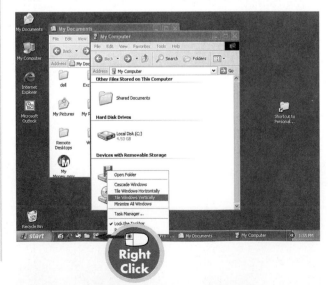

④ Drag the File to the Floppy Drive

Place the mouse pointer over the file in the My Documents window that you want to copy. Click and hold the left mouse button while dragging the file to the floppy drive icon in the My Computer window.

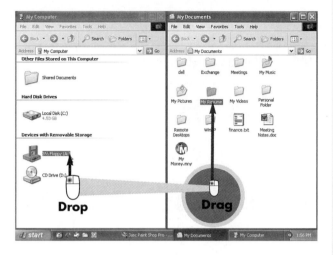

Drop **Drag**

⑤ Copy the File

Release the left mouse button to drop the file on the floppy drive icon. A dialog box appears to track the progress of the copy operation.

⑥ Select a File

Another way to send a file to the floppy drive is to choose a command rather than dragging and dropping the file. Start by selecting the file (click it once).

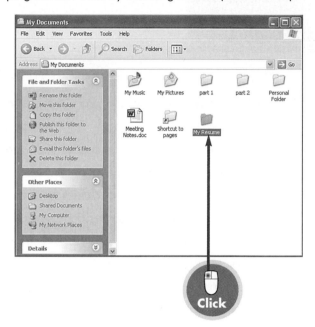

Click

⑦ Choose Send to Floppy Drive

Right-click the selected file, point to the **Send To** command on the shortcut menu, then choose the floppy drive option. Windows copies the file to the floppy disk in the drive.

How to Open a File with a Different Program

Files usually have a certain program associated with them, normally the program that created them. A text file, for example, is associated with Notepad. Windows knows what program to use to open a file because of the three-character extension following the file's name. For example, a text file might be named `Groceries.txt`. Windows knows that files with the `.txt` extension should be opened in Notepad. Sometimes, however, you might want to open a file with a different program or even change the program associated with the file altogether.

1 Right-Click the File

Right-click the file you want to open with a special program and choose **Open With** from the shortcut menu. The Open With dialog box opens.

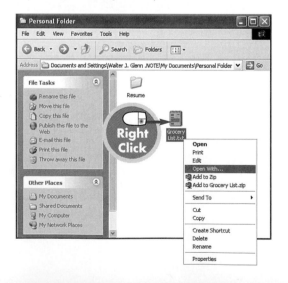

2 Choose the Program

Select the program you want to use to open the file.

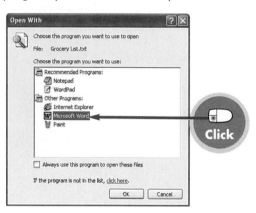

3 Find Another Program

If the program you want to use does not appear in the list, click the **Click Here** link to find the program file on your computer yourself. Most of the programs installed on your computer are located in the Program Files folder on your C: drive. If you don't find the program there, consult the documentation for the program to get more information.

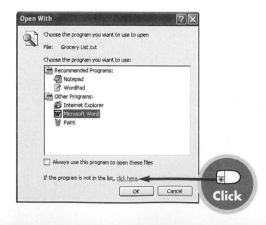

④ Make It the Default Choice

If you want to change an extension's association (that is, to make all files of that type open with the new program you've selected from now on), enable the **Always Use This Program to Open These Files** option.

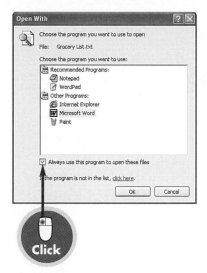

⑤ Open the File

Click **OK** to open the file in the selected program.

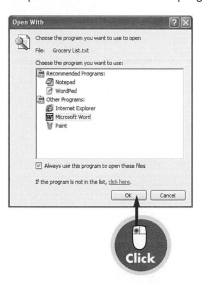

How-to Hint

Viewing File Associations

You can view a complete list of file associations in Windows. Click **Start** and choose **Control Panel**. In the Control Panel window, double-click **Folder Options**. In the dialog box that appears, click the **File Types** tab. All associations are listed here. You can create new associations and change existing ones.

Task

Changing Windows XP Settings

After you have worked with Windows XP for a while and gotten used to the way things work, you might find that there are changes you would like to make. Windows XP is wonderfully customizable and provides many options for changing its interface to suit the way you work.

Most of the changes you will make take place using the Windows Control Panel, which is a special folder that contains many small programs that adjust settings for a particular part of your system. For example, Display lets you change display settings such as background color, window colors, screen saver, and screen size. You can access the Control Panel through either the Start menu or the My Computer window, as you will see in the tasks in this chapter.

You'll also find that many of the Control Panel settings are also directly available from the shortcut menu of various desktop items. For example, right-clicking the desktop and choosing Properties from the shortcut menu that opens is exactly the same as opening the Display applet from the Control Panel. You'll see several such ways for accessing common controls in the following tasks.

How to Change the Volume

If you have speakers hooked up to your computer, you've probably noticed that some programs and certain things that Windows does (called events) make sounds. Many speakers have physical volume control knobs on them, but there is also a convenient way to change the volume from within Windows itself.

❶ Click the Volume Icon

A small volume icon that looks like a speaker appears in the system tray next to your clock to indicate that sound is configured on your computer. Click the icon once with your left mouse button to open the Volume dialog box.

❷ Change the Volume Setting

Click and drag the slider with your left mouse button to adjust the volume. Your computer beeps when you release the slider to give you an idea of the volume you've set.

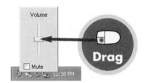

❸ Mute Your Speakers

Click the Mute option to silence your speakers. While your speakers are muted, the volume icon is overlaid with a red circle and slash. When you want the speakers to play again, open the Volume dialog box again and deselect the **Mute** option.

4 **Close the Dialog Box**

Click anywhere out on your desktop once to close the Volume dialog box.

Double-Clicking

The main volume control adjusts the volume for all the sounds on your computer, no matter where that sound comes from. Double-click the **Volume** dialog box to open a more sophisticated volume control that lets you adjust the volume for each audio device configured on your system. For example, you might want to lower the volume for CD-ROMs but leave the volume for Wave files (which are used for Windows system events) alone.

Where's My Volume Icon?

On some computers, the volume icon on the system tray may be disabled. If you don't see one, but would like to, first open the **Start** menu and click **Control Panel**. In the Control Panel window, double-click the **Sounds and Audio Devices** icon. On the Volume tab of the Sounds and Audio Devices Properties dialog box that opens, select the **Place Volume Icon in the Taskbar** option.

How to Set Up a Screen Saver

On older monitors (those more than ten years old), screen savers help prevent a phenomenon called burn-in, where items on your display can actually be permanently burned in to your monitor if left for a long time. Newer monitors don't really have a problem with this, but screen savers are still kind of fun and do help prevent passersby from seeing what's on your computer when you're away. Windows XP provides a number of built-in screen savers.

1 Open the Display Properties

Right-click any open space on your desktop and choose the **Properties** command from the shortcut menu. The Display Properties dialog box opens.

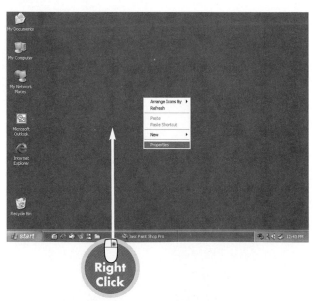

2 Switch to the Screen Saver Tab

Switch to the **Screen Saver** tab by clicking it once.

3 Choose a Screen Saver

By default, Windows comes with no screen saver active. Click the arrow next to the **Screen Saver** drop-down list to choose from the available screen savers.

4 Preview the Screen Saver

When you choose a screen saver, Windows displays a small preview of it right on the picture of a monitor in the dialog box. To see how the screen saver will look when it's actually working, click the **Preview** button. Move the mouse or press a key during the preview to get back to the dialog box.

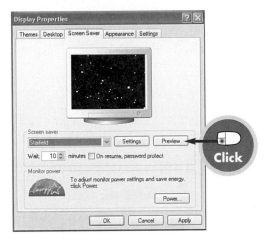

6 Adjust Wait Time

The Wait field specifies how long your computer must be idle before the screen saver kicks in. By default, this value is 15 minutes, but you can change it to whatever you want by using the scroll buttons. You can make a screen saver password protected by clicking the **Password Protect** option on the Screen Saver tab.

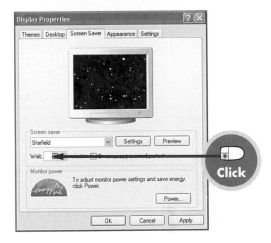

5 Adjust Settings

Each screen saver has its own specific settings so that you can change how the screen saver behaves. Settings for the Starfield screen saver, for example, let you control how many stars are displayed and how fast they move. Click the **Settings** button to experiment with options for any screen saver.

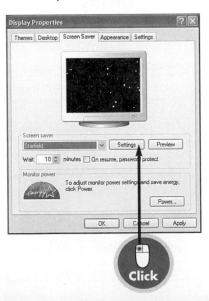

Getting Back to Work

After the screen saver kicks in, you won't be able to see the work that was on your screen because the screen saver "takes over." To get back to work, banish the screen saver simply by moving the mouse or pressing any key on the keyboard. The screen saver will come back on after the next lull in your activity.

Getting New Screen Savers

New screen savers are available for purchase at most software stores; many are available for free on the Internet. When you download a screen saver, it usually appears as a file with the extension .scr. Just copy the file to the System32 folder inside your Windows folder to have it show up on the list in step 3.

How to Change Your Desktop Theme

A desktop theme determines the overall look and feel of your desktop. A theme includes a background picture, a set of desktop icons, a color scheme for window elements, a predetermined set of sounds for Windows events, and a set of display fonts. All these aspects of the theme are customizable.

1 Open Display Properties

Right-click any open space on your desktop and choose the **Properties** command from the shortcut menu. The Display Properties dialog box opens.

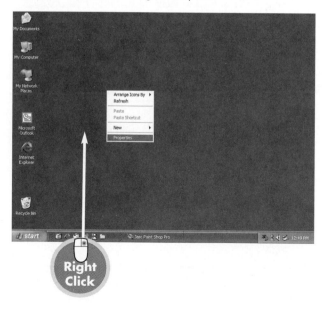

Right Click

2 View the Current Theme

On the Themes tab of the dialog box, the name of the current theme is displayed along with a sample of what the theme looks like on your desktop.

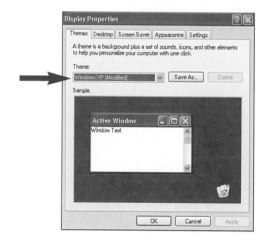

3 Select a Theme

Click the arrow next to the **Theme** drop-down list and choose a different theme.

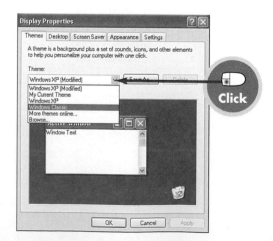

Click

4 Sample the New Theme

A sample of the selected theme is displayed in the Sample window so that you can see what the theme will look like before actually applying it to your desktop.

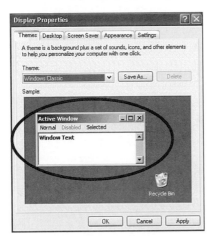

5 Set the New Theme

To apply the new theme to your desktop and close the Display Properties window, click **OK**. To apply the theme and keep the dialog box open, click **Apply**.

How-to Hint

Finding More Themes

Use the **More Themes Online** selection from the **Theme** drop-down list to go to the Windows Media Web site. There, you'll find a number of desktop themes you can download. After you download them, they will appear in your Theme list.

Browsing for Themes

If you downloaded a theme from a Web site other than the Windows Media site, it may be saved somewhere on your hard disk and not show up in your Theme list. Select the **Browse** option from the **Theme** drop-down list to open a standard dialog box that lets you find the theme on your hard disk. Theme files have a .theme extension.

How to Change Your Wallpaper

Wallpaper is a pattern or picture that is displayed on your desktop just to make things a bit more fun. By default, Windows uses no wallpaper; you see only the standard blue desktop color. Windows XP includes a number of interesting wallpapers you can use to spruce up your display.

1 Open Display Properties

Right-click any open space on your desktop and choose the **Properties** command from the shortcut menu. The Display Properties dialog box opens.

2 Switch to the Desktop Tab

Click the **Desktop** tab once to bring that page to the front.

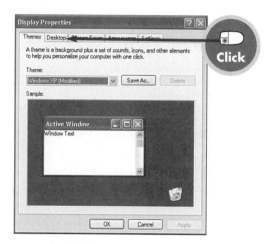

3 Choose a Wallpaper

Choose any wallpaper from the **Background** list by clicking it once. Whatever wallpaper you choose is displayed in the picture of a monitor in the dialog box.

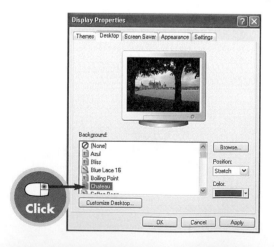

4 Use Your Own Picture

If you have a picture file on your computer that you want to use as wallpaper, click the **Browse** button to open a dialog box that lets you locate the file. Background pictures can have the following extensions: .bmp, .gif, .jpg, .dib, and .htm.

5 Adjust the Picture Display

You can display background pictures in one of three ways. You can center a picture on the screen, stretch a picture so that it fills the screen, or tile a small picture so that it appears multiple times to fill the screen. Click the **Position** drop-down list to experiment with these options.

6 Set a Color

If you would rather not use a picture, but are tired of staring at a blue desktop, try setting a different color. Click the down arrow next to the current color to open a palette for choosing a new color.

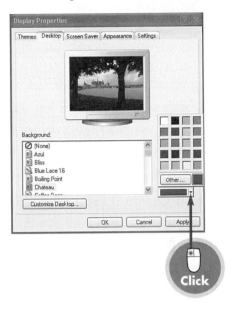

7 Apply the Settings

Click the **Apply** button to apply any new wallpaper to your desktop and keep the Display Properties dialog box open so that you can more easily experiment with backgrounds. After you find a background you like, click the **OK** button to get back to work.

How to Change Desktop Appearance

Changing your desktop appearance can really affect how you work. Windows lets you change the colors used on your desktop background, parts of windows, and even menus. For example, if you find yourself squinting at the text on the monitor, you can adjust the point size of the display font. If you don't like blue title bars on dialog boxes, you can change the color of that element, too.

1 Open Display Properties

Right-click any open space on your desktop and choose the **Properties** command from the shortcut menu. The Display Properties dialog box opens.

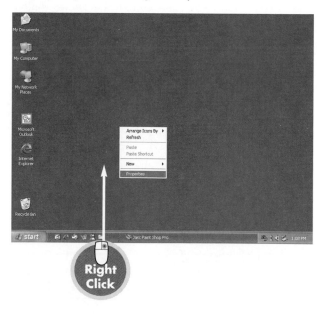

2 Switch to the Appearance Tab

Switch to the **Appearance** tab by clicking it once.

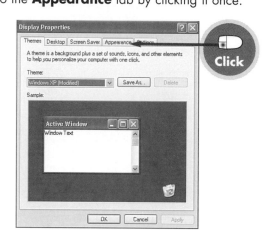

3 Choose a Style

The Windows XP style uses the new rounded windows and stylized buttons. Windows Classic uses windows and buttons that look like previous versions of Windows. In Windows Classic style, the Advanced button (not available in the Windows XP style) lets you set colors for the different window elements.

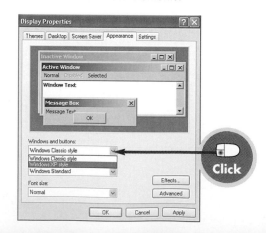

④ Choose a New Color Scheme

If you're using the Windows XP style, you have only a few choices for the color scheme, including blue (the default), olive, and silver. If you're using the Windows Classic style, you can choose from many predefined color schemes. Choose a scheme using the **Color Scheme** drop-down list. The sample window in the dialog box changes to show you what a color scheme will look like.

⑤ Adjust Font Size

Some of the color schemes allow for more than one font size to be used when displaying menus, window text, and dialog boxes. Use the **Font Size** drop-down list to choose a **Normal**, **Large**, or **Extra Large** display font.

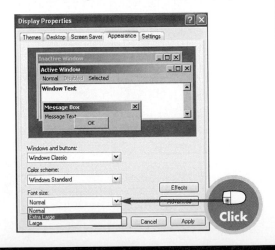

⑥ Open the Effects Dialog Box

Click the **Effects** button to open a separate dialog box for adjusting special desktop settings.

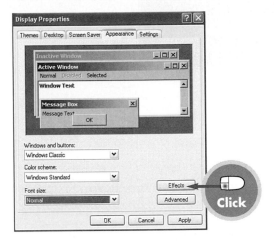

⑦ Adjust Effects

Many of the effects you can choose in this dialog box affect the speed with which windows are displayed on your computer. Using transition effects for menus, showing window contents while dragging the windows, and showing shadows under menus all make displaying windows on the desktop take just a little longer. Consider turning them off if you have a slower computer. Click **OK** twice to close both dialog boxes and apply the settings.

How to Change Display Settings

Display settings control various aspects of your video adapter and monitor. You can change the display settings to control the screen resolution (how many pixels are shown on your screen) and the color quality (how many colors are available for the display to use). Using a higher resolution lets you fit more on your desktop. Using better color quality makes things look better. However, both options depend on the quality of your video card and monitor, and using higher settings can slow down your system a bit.

❶ Open Display Properties

Right-click any open space on your desktop and choose the **Properties** command from the shortcut menu. The Display Properties dialog box opens.

❷ Switch to the Settings Tab

Switch to the **Settings** tab by clicking it once.

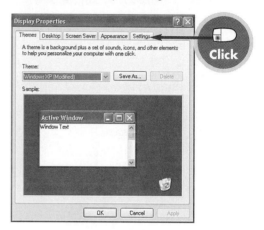

❸ Choose a New Color Depth

Color depth refers to the number of colors your screen can display. Click the **Color Quality** drop-down list to choose a new color setting. And although using the highest available color quality is usually the better choice, it can slow down your system just a bit. You'll have to play with the settings to find what you like best.

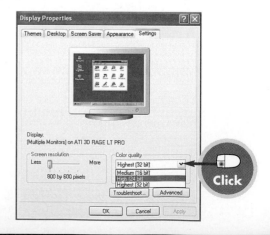

④ Choose a New Screen Resolution

Screen resolution refers to the size of items displayed on your screen. Increasing the area means that you can see more items on your screen at once, but also means that those items will appear smaller. Adjust the screen area by dragging the **Screen Resolution** slider.

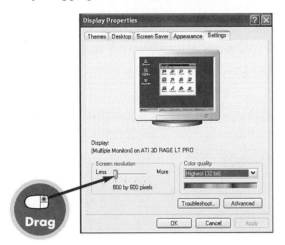

⑤ Start the Display Troubleshooter

If you are having display problems, click the **Troubleshoot** button to open the Windows Help system and go directly to the display troubleshooter.

⑥ Open Advanced Properties

Click the **Advanced** button to open a separate dialog box with controls for changing the video adapter and monitor drivers your computer is using, along with other advanced display settings.

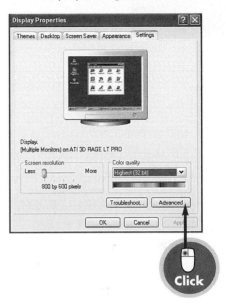

Using Advanced Settings

Be careful when changing the advanced display settings. Although these setting can be useful, they can also cause problems. Incorrectly changing the drivers for your adapter or monitor can cause your display to stop working. Changing the refresh rate on your monitor can result in a more stable image, but changing it to a rate your monitor doesn't support can damage the monitor. In general, you should probably leave these settings alone if your display is working fine.

How to Change Mouse Settings

Because the mouse will likely be your main tool for getting around in Windows, it should come as no surprise that Windows allows you to change the way your mouse works. Among other things, you can change the clicking speed that makes for a successful double-click and the speed at which the pointer moves across the screen.

1 Open the Control Panel

Click **Start** and then select **Control Panel** to open the Control Panel window.

2 Open the Mouse Icon

Double-click the **Mouse** icon to open the Mouse Properties dialog box.

3 Change Button Configuration

Choose the **Switch Primary and Secondary Buttons** option to swap the functions of the left and right buttons. This option is useful if you use your mouse with your left hand.

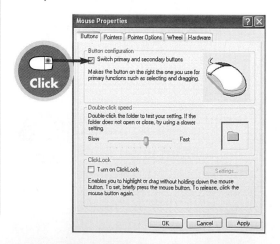

4 Adjust Double-Click Speed

The Double-click Speed option refers to how close together two clicks of the mouse button must be for Windows to consider them a double-click rather than two single clicks. Drag the slider with your left mouse button to adjust the speed and then test it by double-clicking the folder icon in the test area.

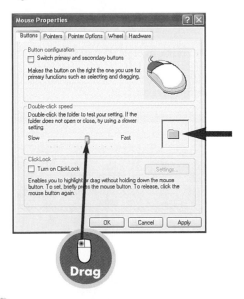

5 Adjust the Pointer Speed

Click the **Pointer Options** tab to switch to that page. Here you can set several options relating to how the mouse pointer moves. Drag the **Motion** slider to set how fast the pointer moves across the screen when you move the mouse. Click the **Apply** button to experiment with any settings you make while keeping the Mouse Properties dialog box open.

6 Enable Acceleration

Acceleration refers to whether the movement of your pointer accelerates if you begin moving your mouse more quickly. Without this option, the pointer keeps moving at a single speed no matter how quickly you move your mouse. Usually, you want this option enabled so that the speed you move the mouse on the table top is mimicked in the speed at which the mouse pointer moves onscreen. However, you sometimes may find that the mouse pointer moves too quickly or acts erratically with this option enabled.

7 Snap to Default

Normally, when a new dialog box opens, the mouse pointer stays right where it is; you must move it to the buttons on the dialog box to do anything. With the **Snap to** option enabled, the mouse pointer automatically jumps to whatever the default button is.

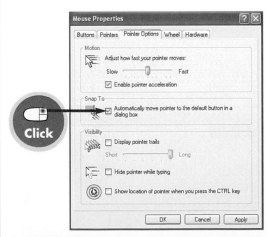

How to Change Keyboard Settings

Windows allows you to change a number of settings related to how your keyboard works. You can change the delay that occurs between when you press a key and when the key starts to repeat from holding it down. You can also change the rate at which the key repeats. Finally, you can change the blink rate for your cursor (the little vertical line that blinks where you are about to type something).

① Open the Control Panel

Click **Start** and then choose **Control Panel** to open the Control Panel window.

② Open the Keyboard Icon

Double-click the **Keyboard** icon to open the Keyboard Properties dialog box.

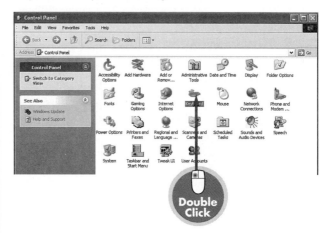

③ Change the Repeat Delay

The Repeat Delay option specifies the delay that occurs between when you press a key and when the key starts to repeat from holding it down. Drag the slider to change the rate.

4. Change the Repeat Rate

When you hold a key down longer than the repeat delay you specified in the previous step, the key begins to repeat. Drag the **Repeat Rate** slider to change the repeat rate.

5. Test Your Settings

Click in the test box and then press and hold any key to test your repeat delay and repeat rate settings.

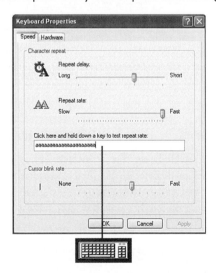

6. Change the Cursor Blink Rate

Whenever you click in a text box to type a value or to type a document, a little vertical line called a cursor blinks to let you know where the characters you type will appear. The cursor is sometimes also called the insertion point. Drag the **Cursor Blink Rate** slider to change the rate at which the cursor blinks. A sample cursor to the left of the slider blinks according to your settings.

How to Customize the Taskbar

The taskbar is one of the more important tools you use when working in Windows XP. There are several ways you can customize its use, as you will see in the following steps.

① Open Taskbar Properties

Right-click anywhere on the taskbar and click **Properties**. The Taskbar and Start Menu Properties dialog box opens.

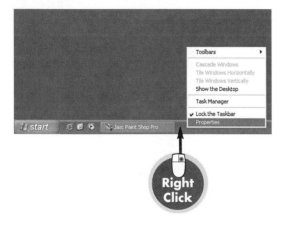

② Lock the Taskbar

By default, you can drag the taskbar to other edges of the screen, resize the taskbar, and adjust the size of the system tray and Quick Launch portions of the taskbar. Enable the **Lock the Taskbar** option to prevent this from happening.

③ Make the Taskbar Autohide

Enable the **Auto-hide the Taskbar** option to have the taskbar automatically scroll off the edge of the screen when it's not in use. Move your pointer to the edge of the screen to make the taskbar scroll back into view. This option cannot be used when the taskbar is locked.

④ Keep the Taskbar on Top

By default, the taskbar is always on the top of your display. Thus, when you move a window into the same space occupied by the taskbar, the taskbar still appears in front of the window. Disable the **Keep the Taskbar on Top of Other Windows** option so that other items can appear in front of the taskbar.

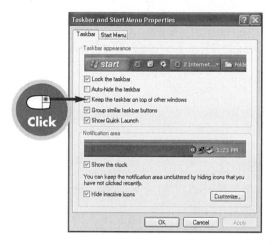

⑤ Group Similar Buttons

When you start a program (such as Internet Explorer) more than once, a separate button appears on the taskbar for each instance of the program. When you enable the Group Similar Taskbar Buttons option, only one button appears for each program and a number to the side indicates how many documents for that program are open.

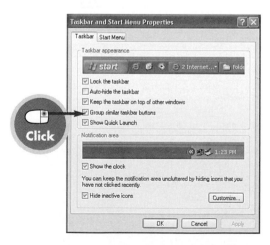

⑥ Show the Clock

The Show the Clock option causes Windows to display the clock in the system tray at the far right of your taskbar. Disable this option to hide the clock. Double-click the clock to open a dialog box that lets you set the time and date.

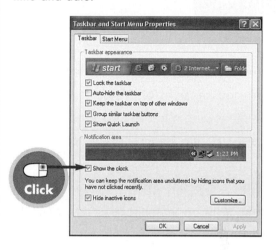

⑦ Hide Inactive Icons

By default, the system tray is collapsed so that only the most frequently used icons are shown. If you don't like this space-saving feature, turn it off by disabling the **Hide Inactive Icons** check box.

How to Change Folder Options

Windows XP handles folders in much the same way as previous versions of Windows. You have the option of viewing a folder as a Web page, in which a pane on the left side of the folder view gives you information about any selected item. You also have the option of having Windows open a new window for each folder you want to open. The following steps explain how to access these options using the Control Panel. You can also access the Folder Options dialog box from the View menu at the top of any open folder.

❶ Open the Control Panel

Click the **Start** button and then choose **Control Panel**. The Control Panel window opens.

❷ Open the Folder Options Icon

Double-click the **Folder Options** icon to open the Folder Options dialog box.

❸ Use Web View

Web View is an option that shows Web content in folders. Normally, this just means that a pane at the left of a folder window shows information about selected items in that folder. Some folders, however, might have more specialized content. Enable the **Use Windows Classic Folders** option to disable this feature.

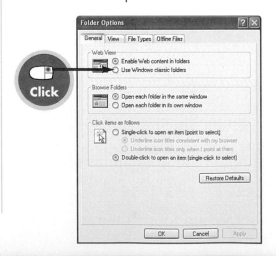

④ Change Folder Browsing

Normally when you open a folder, that folder opens in whatever window you are using at the time. If you would rather Windows open a whole new window for each folder you open, select the **Open Each Folder in Its Own Window** option here.

⑤ Change Click Settings

By default, you single-click items to select them and double-click items to open them. If you prefer, enable the **Single-click to Open an Item (Point to Select)** option so that you only have to single-click items to open them, much like you do in Internet Explorer. With this option enabled, holding the mouse pointer over an item for a second selects the item.

⑥ Restore Defaults

If you find that you don't like the folder settings you have already made, click the **Restore Defaults** button to change the settings back to their original configuration.

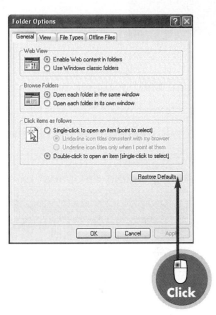

How-to Hint

Advanced Options

The View tab of the Folder Options dialog box features a long list of specific settings relating to how folders work, such as whether hidden system files should be displayed, whether file extensions should be displayed or hidden, and whether Windows should remember the view for each folder you open. After you are familiar with using Windows, you may want to check the options on this list and see whether any appeal to you.

How to Change Power Options

You might find it useful to adjust the way Windows handles your power settings. To save energy, Windows can automatically turn off parts of your computer, such as the hard drive and monitor, after a certain amount of time. The next time you try to access these devices, the power is immediately restored and you can proceed with your tasks without delay.

❶ Open Control Panel

Click **Start** and then choose **Control Panel**. The Control Panel window opens.

❷ Open the Power Options Icon

Double-click the **Power Options** icon to open the Power Options Properties dialog box.

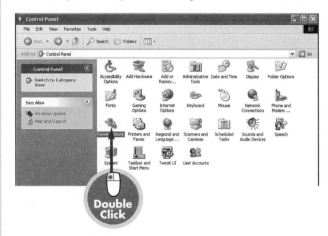

❸ Choose a Power Scheme

The easiest way to configure power settings is to choose a custom scheme designed to fit the way you use your computer. Click the **Power Schemes** drop-down list to choose from a number of schemes.

④ Turn Off Monitor

If you want to customize power settings beyond just choosing a scheme, you can choose how long the computer should be idle before certain devices are turned off. Click the **Turn Off Monitor** drop-down menu to specify how long the computer should be idle before your monitor is turned off. Note that you can specify a different delay time if your computer is running on batteries.

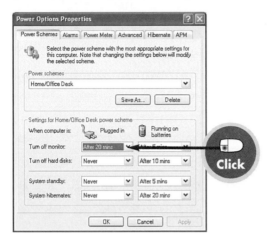

⑤ Turn Off Hard Disks

Click the **Turn Off Hard Disks** drop-down menu to specify how long the computer should be idle before your hard drive is turned off. Note that you can specify a different delay time if your computer is running on batteries.

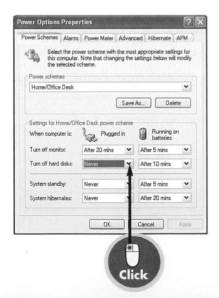

⑥ Send System to Standby

Some computers have the capability to go into standby, where only a trickle of power is used to keep track of what's in your computer's memory. When you come back from standby, everything should be as you left it. Use the drop-down menu to specify how long the computer should be idle before it goes into standby. Note that you can specify a different delay time if your computer is running on batteries.

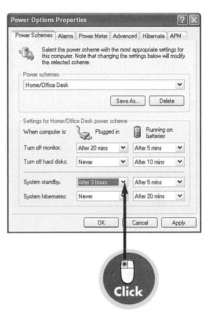

How-to Hint

Where Are All Those Options?

Depending on the type of computer and type of hardware installed, the Power Options Properties dialog box you see may be different than the one shown in this task. Notebook computers, for example, have settings both for when the computer is plugged in and when it is running on batteries. Notebooks also boast several more tabs on the dialog box to configure such things as advanced standby and hibernation modes. The best place to find out information about these advanced options is in the documentation for the computer itself.

How to Change System Sounds

If you have speakers on your computer, you might have noticed that certain things you do in Windows (such as emptying the Recycle Bin, starting Windows, and logging off) make certain sounds. These things are called events. Windows events also include things you don't do yourself, such as when an error dialog box is displayed or when e-mail is received. You can easily change the sounds associated with Windows events by using the following steps.

① Open the Control Panel

Click **Start** and then choose **Control Panel**. The Control Panel window opens.

② Open the Sounds and Audio Devices Icon

Double-click the **Sounds and Audio Devices** icon to open the Sounds and Audio Devices Properties dialog box.

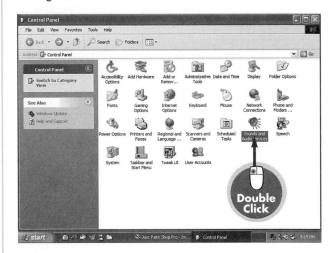

③ Switch to the Sounds Tab

Click the **Sounds** tab to bring it to the front.

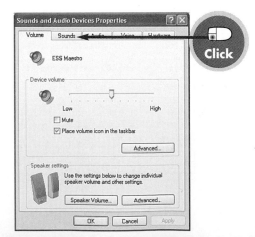

4 Choose an Event

From the **Program Events** list, select any system event, such as **Default Beep**.

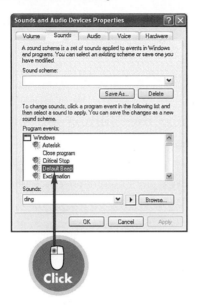

5 Choose a Sound File

Click the arrow next to the **Sounds** drop-down list to select a sound to associate with the selected event. You can also use your own sound file (any .wav file) by clicking the **Browse** button.

6 Play the Sound

Click the **Play** button to hear the selected sound.

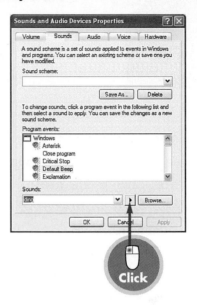

7 Choose a Sound Scheme

Windows comes with a couple of different sound schemes, which are sets of sounds similar in effect that are applied to all the major system events at once. Use the **Sound Scheme** drop-down list to choose a scheme.

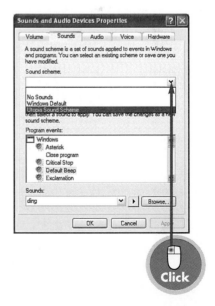

How to Add an Item to the Start Menu

The Start menu is loaded with shortcuts to various programs and folders on your computer. Whenever you install a new program, that program usually adds a shortcut of its own to the Start menu automatically. You can also add items of your own. You can add shortcuts to programs, documents, or even folders.

❶ Find the Item You Want to Add

Use the My Computer or My Documents window to find the item you want to add to the Start menu. This item can be a document, a program, or even a folder.

❷ Drag the Item over the Start Menu

Using the left mouse button, click and drag the item over the **Start** button, but *do not* release the mouse button yet.

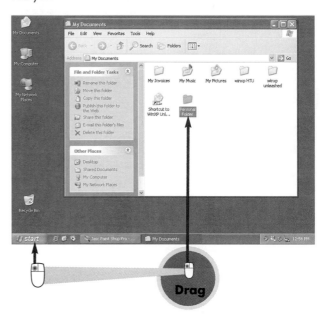

③ Place the Item in the More Programs Folder

After holding the item over the **Start** button for about two seconds, the Start menu opens. Continue dragging the item over the **All Programs** folder and then onto the **All Programs** menu that appears. When you find where you want to place the item (a horizontal line appears to guide placement), let go of the mouse button. After you have placed the shortcut, just click it to launch the original program.

④ Rename the Shortcut

Right-click the new shortcut and choose **Rename** from the shortcut menu to give the shortcut a new name. This name appears in a pop-up window when you hold your pointer over the shortcut for a second.

⑤ Delete the Shortcut

Right-click the shortcut in the **Start** menu and choose **Delete** from the shortcut menu to remove the shortcut from the Start menu.

How to Add an Item to the Quick Launch Bar

The Quick Launch bar is handy feature located in the task bar next to the Start button. You can use it to open certain programs with a single click. Only three shortcuts appear by default on the Quick Launch bar: one to launch Internet Explorer, one to launch Outlook Express, and one to show your desktop when there are windows in the way. Fortunately, it's pretty easy to add new shortcuts for programs, documents, and folders. In fact, many programs (such as Microsoft Outlook) add their own shortcuts during installation.

❶ Find the Item You Want to Add

Use the My Computer or My Documents window to find the item to which you want to make a Quick Launch shortcut.

❷ Drag the Item to the Quick Launch Bar

Click the item with your left mouse button and, while holding the button down, drag the item into a blank space on the Quick Launch bar. You can even drag the item between two existing shortcuts to put it exactly where you want.

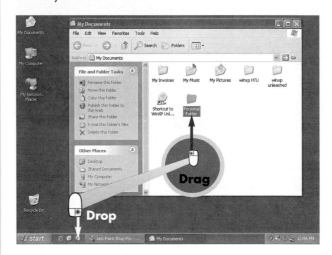

❸ Rename the Shortcut

Right-click the new shortcut and choose **Rename** from the shortcut menu to give the shortcut a new name. This name appears in a pop-up window when you hold the mouse pointer over the shortcut icon for a second.

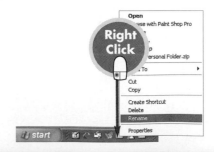

④ Delete the Shortcut

Right-click the shortcut and choose **Delete** from the shortcut menu to remove the shortcut from the Quick Launch bar and place it in the Recycle Bin. Hold the **Shift** key down when selecting **Delete** to permanently delete the shortcut without sending it to the Recycle Bin.

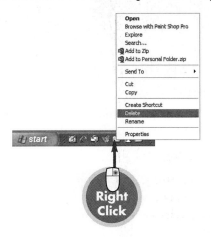

How-to Hint

Rearranging Shortcuts

You can rearrange existing shortcuts in the Quick Launch bar by simply dragging them to new locations on the Quick Launch bar.

Moving the Quick Launch Bar

You can move the Quick Launch bar separately from the taskbar by clicking at the leftmost edge of the Quick Launch bar (marked by two rows of small, dimpled dots) and dragging it. You can move the bar to one of the other edges of your display or into the center of the window.

Don't See a Quick Launch Bar?

On some computers, the Quick Launch bar may be disabled. If you don't see the Quick Launch bar and want to add it, right-click anywhere on your taskbar and choose **Properties**. On the Taskbar tab of the Taskbar and Start Menu Properties dialog box that opens, choose the **Show Quick Launch** option.

How to Start a Program When Windows Starts

Windows maintains a special folder named Startup that lets you specify programs, folders, and even documents that open every time Windows starts. You can see the Startup folder and what's in it by selecting **Start**, **All Programs**, **Startup**. The following steps show you how to add shortcuts to that folder.

① Find the Item You Want to Add

Use the My Computer or My Documents window to find the item you want to add to the Startup folder menu. This item can be a document, program, or even a folder.

② Drag the Item over the Start Menu

Using the left mouse button, click and drag the item over the **Start** button, but *do not* release the mouse button yet.

③ Drag the Item over the All Programs Folder

Continue dragging the item and hold it over the **All Programs** option on the Start menu. Do not release the mouse button yet.

④ Place the Item in the Startup Folder

When the All Programs folder opens, drag the item to the **Startup** folder and drop it there.

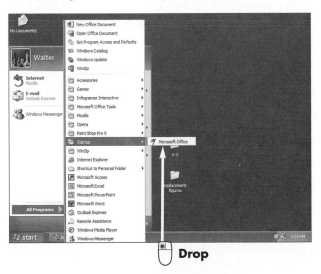

Drop

How to Set Accessibility Options

Windows includes a number of accessibility options intended for people with disabilities (some people without disabilities find these settings useful, as well). These options include a small window that magnifies whatever part of the screen your mouse pointer is on and the ability to make Windows flash the display instead of making sounds. All these options are available through the Windows Control Panel.

① Open the Control Panel

Click the **Start** button and then choose **Control Panel**. The Control Panel window opens.

② Open Accessibility Options

Double-click the **Accessibility Options** icon. The Accessibility Options dialog box opens.

③ Set Keyboard Options

Switch to the **Keyboard** tab to set various accessibility options for working with the keyboard. The StickyKeys option lets you press one key at a time (Ctrl and then Shift, for example) instead of having to press them simultaneously. The FilterKeys option tells Windows to ignore brief or quickly repeated keystrokes that may be caused by unsteady hands on the keyboard. The ToggleKeys option plays sounds to indicate when the Caps Lock, Num Lock, and Scroll Lock keys are turned on or off.

④ Set Sound Options

Switch to the **Sound** tab to set options for using sound in addition to the visual feedback your computer gives you in certain circumstances. The SoundSentry option generates visual warnings (such as flashes) when your system would otherwise just play a sound. The ShowSounds option generates captions for the speech and sounds made by certain programs.

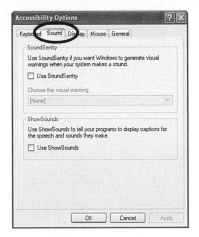

⑤ Set Display Options

Switch to the Display tab to find settings that make it easier to read the screen. The High Contrast option causes Windows to display the desktop using colors and fonts that are easier to read. The Cursor Options adjust the size and blink rate of the cursor that appears where text is about to be typed.

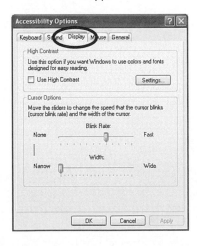

⑥ Set Mouse Options

Switch to the **Mouse** tab to enable MouseKeys, a feature that lets you use your keyboard's number pad to control the mouse pointer. Click the **Settings** button to open a dialog box that lets you control the pointer speed and turn on and off the MouseKeys feature using the **Num Lock** key on your keyboard.

⑦ Set General Options

Switch to the **General** tab to set options that pertain to all accessibility features, such as when they are used and whether they are automatically turned off after a period of time. When you have specified all the options you want, click **OK** to apply the settings and close the dialog box.

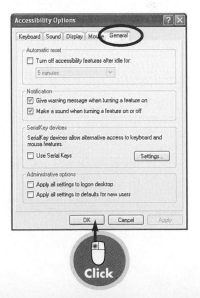

Click

Task

5

Using the System Tools

Computers are pretty complicated. A lot of things can happen during the course of normal use that can slow a computer down or keep certain things from working as they should. If you are connected to a network, the chances are that you have a network administrator to rely on for fixing problems when they occur. If you don't have an administrator, you'll have to take things into your own hands. There are a few things you can do to help make sure that your computer is performing well and your work is not lost if something does go wrong. Windows XP provides a number of important system tools to help you protect your files and maintain your computer.

How to Free Up Space on Your Hard Disk

Even with the size of today's large hard drives, you might still find conservation of disk space an issue. During normal operation, Windows and the programs you run on it create temporary and backup files. Unfortunately, these programs (Windows included) are sometimes not very good at cleaning up after themselves. Windows includes a tool named Disk Cleanup that you can use to search for and delete unnecessary files.

❶ Run Disk Cleanup

Click the **Start** button and choose **All Programs**, **Accessories**, **System Tools**, **Disk Cleanup**.

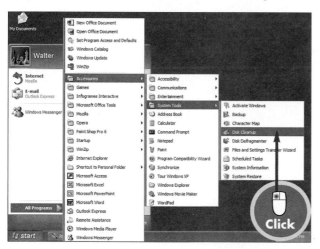

❷ Select the Drive to Clean Up

Use the drop-down list to select the hard drive on which you want to free up space. Click the **OK** button after you have chosen your drive. Disk Cleanup scans the specified drive for files. This process might take a few minutes.

❸ Select the Items to Remove

After Disk Cleanup has finished scanning your drive, it presents a list of categories for files it has found. Next to each category, Windows shows how much drive space all the files in that category take up. You can mark categories for deletion by clicking the check boxes next to them.

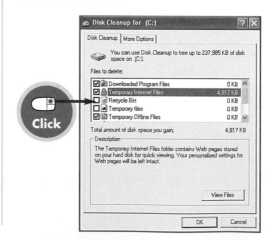

4 View Files

Categories that are already checked, such as Downloaded Program Files, are always safe to delete. Other categories might contain important files, and it is up to you to decide whether they should be deleted. Select a category by clicking its name once and click the **View Files** button to see what's contained in that category.

5 Click OK

When you have selected all the categories for files you want to delete, click the **OK** button to proceed. Windows asks whether you are sure you want to delete the files. If you are, click the **Yes** button.

How-to Hint

Taking Out the Trash

One way to keep space free on your hard drive is to regularly empty your Recycle Bin. Right-click the bin and choose **Empty Recycle Bin** from the shortcut menu to delete all the files it holds. You can also double-click the **Recycle Bin** to display a list of the files it contains and then delete individual files.

Deleting Only Certain Files

When you click the View Files button (as described in step 4), a standard window opens showing the files in that location. If you want to delete only some of the files, select them in this window and delete them by pressing the Delete key. Make sure that you deselect the folder when you return to the Disk Cleanup Wizard or you'll end up deleting all the files anyway. Also, when you delete selected files using the View Files method, the files are moved to the Recycle Bin. You must empty the Recycle Bin to finish freeing the disk space. When you remove files using the Disk Cleanup Wizard, the files are permanently deleted.

How to Defragment Your Hard Disk

When you delete a file on your computer, Windows doesn't really remove it. It just marks that space as available for new information to be written. When a new file is written to disk, part of the file might be written to one available section of disk space, part might be written to another, and part to yet another space. This process fitting files in pieces on the disk is called fragmentation. It is a normal process, and Windows keeps track of files just fine. The problem is that when a drive has a lot of fragmentation, it can take Windows longer to find the information it is looking for. You can speed up drive access significantly by periodically defragmenting your drive.

❶ Run Disk Defragmenter

Click the **Start** button and choose **All Programs**, **Accessories**, **System Tools**, **Disk Defragmenter**.

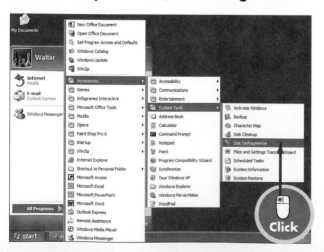

❷ Choose a Drive

The window at the top of the screen lists all the hard drives on your computer. Select the drive you want to defragment by clicking it once.

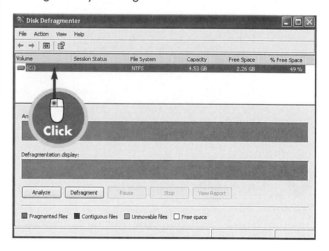

③ Analyze the Drive

Click the **Analyze** button to have Disk Defragmenter analyze the selected drive for the amount of fragmentation on it. This process might take a few minutes, and the process is depicted graphically for you while you wait.

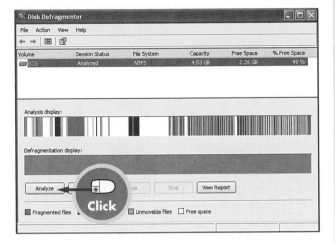

⑤ Defragment the Drive

Should the analysis and report prove that your drive needs to be defragmented, you can start the procedure by clicking the **Defragment** button. This process can take a while—even an hour or so—depending on the size of your hard drive and how fragmented it is.

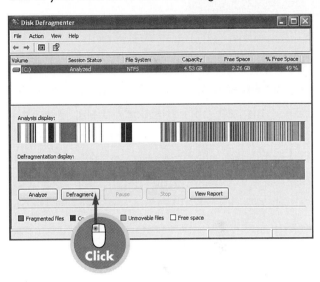

④ View the Report

When the analysis is done, a dialog box appears that lets you view a report or go ahead with defragmentation. You can also perform these actions from the main program window itself. Click the **View Report** button to view a detailed report of the fragmented files that the analysis has discovered.

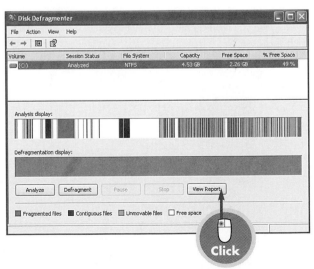

How-to Hint

Some Helpful Tips

Make sure that you close all programs before beginning the defragmentation process. Also make sure that all documents are finished printing, scanning, downloading, and so on. In other words, your computer should not be busy doing anything else. During the defragmentation process, you will not be able to run any other programs. Unless you enjoy watching the defragmentation process, take a coffee break.

How to Schedule a Task to Occur Automatically

Windows XP includes a task scheduler that lets you schedule certain programs to run automatically. This can be particularly useful with programs such as Disk Cleanup and Disk Defragmenter, although you can schedule virtually any program. You might, for example, schedule Disk Cleanup to run automatically every Friday night after work and Disk Defragmenter to run once a month or so, saving you the time of running these programs when you have better things to do.

① Start Scheduled Tasks

Click the **Start** button and choose **All Programs**, **Accessories**, **System Tools**, **Scheduled Tasks**.

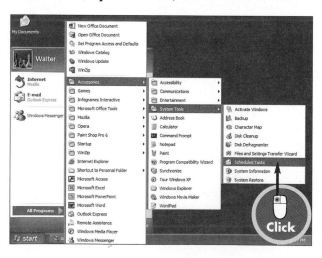

② Add a Scheduled Task

Double-click the **Add Scheduled Task** icon to start the Scheduled Task Wizard. The first page of the wizard is just a welcome page. Click the **Next** button to go on.

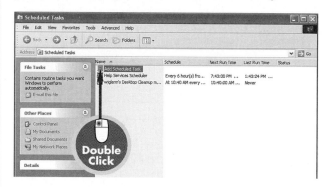

③ Choose a Program to Run

Select the program you want to schedule from the list by clicking it once. If you don't see the program on the list, you can try to locate it by clicking the **Browse** button. After you've selected the program, click the **Next** button to go on.

④ Choose When to Run the Program

If you want to change the default name of the task, type a new name in the text box. Choose when you want to perform the task by enabling that option. When you're done, click the **Next** button to go on.

⑤ Choose a Time and Day

If you chose to run the program daily, weekly, or monthly, you must also specify the time of day to run the program. Type in a time or use the scroll buttons. You must also select the day or days you want the program to run by clicking the appropriate check boxes. Click the **Next** button to go on.

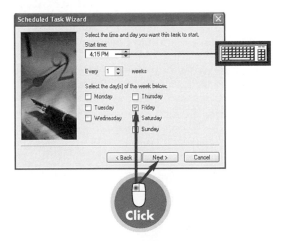

⑥ Enter a Username and Password

To run a program in Windows, Task Scheduler must have your username and password. Type this information into the boxes on this page, and then click the **Next** button to go on.

⑦ Finish

Click the **Finish** button to schedule your new task. When the specified day and time roll around, the selected program starts and runs with the default settings. If you want the selected program to start using any other settings, you'll have to consult the Help file for the program to see whether it supports changing settings in a scheduled task.

How to Use the Windows Troubleshooters

If your computer is on a corporate office network, you are probably fortunate enough to have a network administrator to call when your computer has problems. In a home office situation where you are the network administrator, or for a standalone installation, you will be relieved to know that Windows includes a few useful troubleshooters that can help you diagnose and repair problems.

① Start Help

Click the **Start** button and then choose **Help and Support**.

② Open the Fixing a Problem Category

Click the **Fixing a Problem** subject once to expand it.

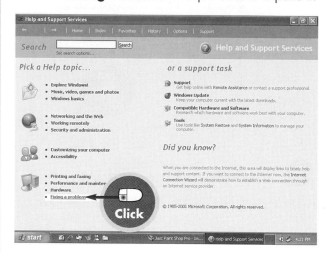

③ Choose a Type of Problem

From the list on the left side of the window, choose the type of problem you are having by clicking it once.

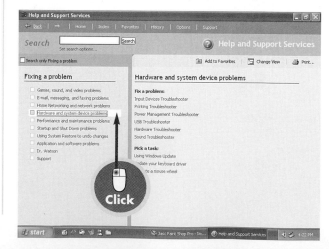

4 Choose a Troubleshooter

From the window on the right, locate the troubleshooter you want to run. After you find the troubleshooter you want, **Printing** for example, click it once to start it.

5 Work Through the Steps

Troubleshooters work just like wizards. Each page asks a question. Choose the answer by clicking it once, and then click the **Next** button to go on. Some pages offer steps for you to try to fix your problem. If the steps work, you're done. If the steps don't work, the troubleshooter continues. If the troubleshooter can't fix your problem, it recommends where you should go (Web sites and Microsoft technical support) for more information.

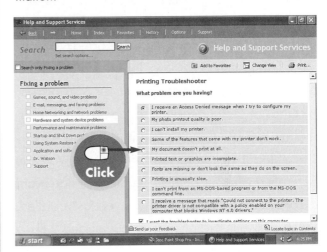

How to Get System Information

Often, fixing a problem requires that you find more information about your computer or your installation of Windows than is normally necessary. Fortunately, Windows includes a useful tool named System Information that lets you browse all kinds of useful information. Some of this information can be useful to you in determining why something is not working. For example, you can determine whether an existing piece of hardware is conflicting with the new piece you just installed. Much of the information is technical and will be useful when you're speaking with a technical support person.

1 Start System Information

Click the **Start** button and choose **More Programs**, **Accessories**, **System Tools**, **System Information**.

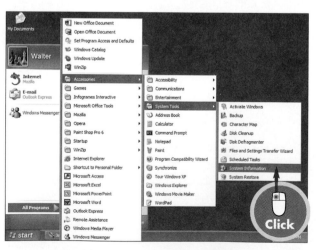

2 View System Summary

The right side of the Help and Support Services window that opens contains a brief summary of your system, including the exact version of Windows installed and a snapshot of your basic hardware.

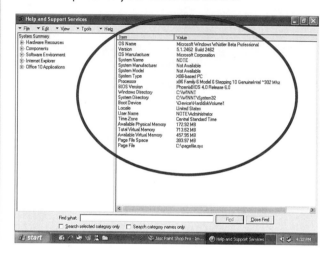

③ View Hardware Resources

Expand the **Hardware Resources** item in the left side of the window by clicking the plus sign next to it. Inside, you'll find various types of resources you can check on. Click any of these resources, such as **IRQs**, to view details on that resource.

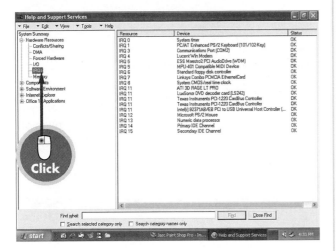

④ View Components

Expand the **Components** item to view details about many of the hardware components on your system. Click any subcategory, such as **CD-ROM**, to view details about that particular component.

⑤ Access Tools

Many useful tools are available on the Tools menu in the Help and Support Services window. Some of the tools are not available anywhere else in Windows. A good example is the DirectX Diagnostic Tool, which can help you diagnose video problems related to the Windows DirectX drivers.

How-to Hint

Printing and Exporting System Information

The File menu of the Help and Support Services window offers the ability to print and export your system information. When exporting, a text file is created. The entire set of system information (not just the page you're looking at) is printed or exported.

How to Use System Restore

Windows XP automatically creates system restore points at regular intervals. These restore points are basically backups of vital system settings and information. If you make a major change to your system, such as installing a new application or hardware driver, and then discover that the change has caused unwanted side effects, you can return to a previous restore point. The System Restore tool is used both to restore the computer to a previous point and to manually create a restore point.

❶ Start System Restore

Click the **Start** button and choose **All Programs**, **Accessories**, **System Tools**, **System Restore**.

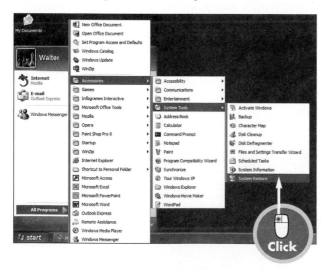

❷ Create a Restore Point

Although Windows creates restore points automatically, you can manually set a restore point before you make some change to your system that you think might adversely affect system performance. In the System Restore window that opens, select the **Create a Restore Point** option and then click **Next**.

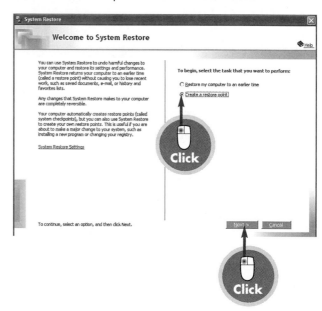

③ Name the Restore Point

Type a name for the restore point that describes it well enough to help you remember it. For example, you might name the restore point after the date, an action you just performed (or are about to perform), or after the fact that you have installed Windows and have everything working the way you want.

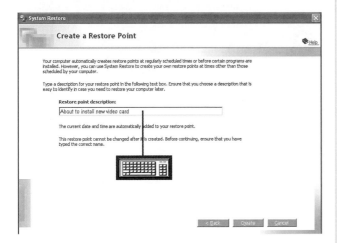

④ Create the Restore Point

When you have named the new restore point, click **Create**.

⑤ Close System Restore

When Windows has successfully created the restore point, it displays a message to that effect. To return to the Welcome to System Restore screen shown in step 2, click **Home**. Otherwise, click **Close**.

Restoring a Restore Point

How-to Hint

Returning your computer to a restore point is just as easy as setting one. On the initial page of the System Restore Wizard, select the **Restore My Computer to an Earlier Time** option. The wizard will guide you through choosing the restore point to which you want to return your system. The necessary files will be restored, your computer will be restarted, and you'll be back in business in no time. If you use System Restore to return your computer settings to a point before a software installation that went bad, note that System Restore just returns your Windows settings to the restore point—it does not remove the software from your computer.

How to Compress Files and Folders

Windows XP includes a built-in compression tool. You can compress files and folders to help save hard disk space. While compressed, the items are still accessible. In fact, you probably won't notice any difference between files you've compressed and those you haven't. On large files, however, you may notice that access is a bit slower than normal because of the compression. But if disk space is an issue, you may decide that it's better to have the large file and wait through the file-access hesitation.

❶ Open an Item's Properties

In the My Documents or My Computer window, right-click the file or folder you want to compress and choose the **Properties** command from the shortcut menu.

❷ Open Advanced Options

On the General tab of the Properties dialog box, click the **Advanced** button to open the Advanced Attributes dialog box.

❸ Compress the Item

Select the **Compress Contents to Save Disk Space** option. Note that there is also an option here that lets you encrypt the item. You cannot use both compression and encryption at the same time.

④ Close the Dialog Boxes

Click the **OK** button to close the Advanced Attributes dialog box. Click the **OK** button on the General tab of the folder's Properties dialog box to close it.

⑤ Compress Files and Subfolders

A dialog box appears that lets you choose whether to compress only the selected folder or also to compress the files and subfolders within that folder. Choose the option you want and click the **OK** button. The file or folder is compressed.

Decompressing a Folder

To decompress a folder, simply follow the preceding steps and disable the **Compress Contents to Save Disk Space** option on the Advanced Attributes dialog box in step 3.

Visual Indicator

When you compress a file or folder, by default Windows gives no visual indicator that compression is present. To see whether an item is compressed, you must open its Properties dialog box and see whether the Compress Contents to Save Disk Space option is enabled. However, you can tell Windows to display compressed files in a different color: Open the Control Panel and double-click **Folder Options**. On the View tab of the dialog box that opens, enable the **Display Compressed Files and Folder in Alternate Color** option.

Sending Compressed Files

If you send a compressed file as an email attachment or transfer a compressed file or folder to another computer using a network or a removable disk, the compression is removed on the copy that is sent. For example, if you email a compressed file to a friend, the file remains compressed on your drive but the attachment is not compressed when your friend receives it.

Having Fun with Windows XP

You can't work all the time, and when you want to have some fun with your computer, Windows XP is ready for you with several built-in "fun" programs.

Windows Media Player can play audio CDs, MP3 music files, and movies in a variety of formats. You can use Windows Media Player to search for music on the Internet and even record your own CDs.

With Windows Movie Maker, you can take still pictures, movie files, home movies, and even music and put them all together to create your own movie. You can edit and play that movie at any time and even send it to friends.

Windows also includes a number of great games, from the classic Solitaire and Hearts to fast-action Pinball. With the variety of Internet games that are available at sites all over the world, you'll never be without a gaming partner again.

How to Play Music and Movies

Unless you have set up a different player program as your default player, Windows plays music and video files using the Windows Media Player. When you insert an audio CD, video CD, or DVD into your disc drive or double-click a music or movie file stored on your computer, Windows Media Player opens automatically and begins playing. To start this task, use Windows Explorer or the My Documents window to browse to a music file (a file with the extension .mp3, .wav, and so on) or a video file (a file with the extension .mpg, .avi, .asf, and so on); double-click it to launch the Windows Media Player.

❶ Pause

You can pause the playback of the audio or video file by clicking the **Pause** button once. While playback is paused, the Pause button changes to a Play button; click the **Play** button to start playback where you left off.

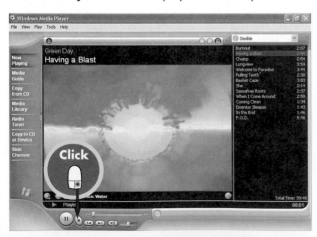

❷ Stop

You can stop playback by clicking the **Stop** button. When playback is stopped, the Pause button turns into a Play button.

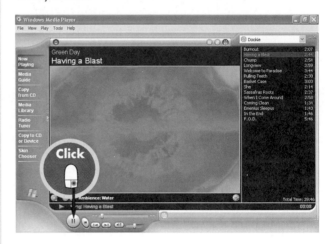

❸ Play

When no music or movie is being played or when the movie or audio file is paused, a Play button appears. Click it once to start playback.

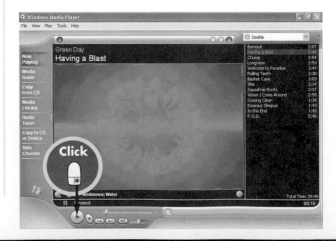

4 Change Volume

Change the volume for the music or video being played by dragging the **Volume** slider to the right (for louder) or to the left (for softer).

5 Go Backward and Forward

During playback, you can skip to the previous or next tracks by clicking the single arrows with lines next to them. During playback of some sorts of media (such as movies), you might also see rewind and fast-forward buttons which are small left- and right-facing double arrows.

Rewind —
Back One —
Track
— Forward One Track
— Fast Forward

6 Pick a Track

If you are playing a CD or DVD with multiple tracks, each track is shown in the playlist on the right side of the player screen. Click any track to begin playing it.

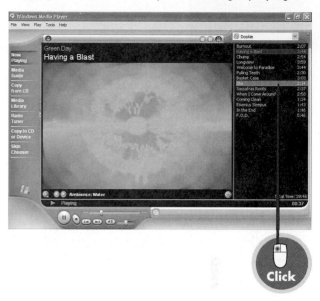

7 Select a Visualization

Visualizations are graphics that move along with the music file as it plays. Windows Media Player includes a number of interesting visualizations. Click the left and right arrows under the visualization window to browse through the available visualizations one at a time; alternatively, click the button with an asterisk to choose a particular visualization from a drop-down list.

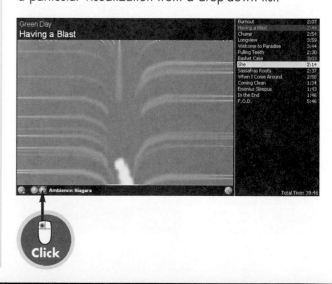

Windows Media Player makes copying tracks from audio CDs easy. You can record songs from an existing audio CD to a file on your hard disk or to another CD if you have a recordable CD drive. You can also convert songs to the popular MP3 format. You can even listen to songs as they're being copied. Copying music for anything other than strictly personal use is a violation of copyright laws. If you want to copy a song to a CD that you can play in your car, you're probably okay. If you want to use a song in a presentation at the office, you're on shaky legal ground.

❶ Start Windows Media Player

Select **Start**, **All Programs**, **Accessories**, **Entertainment**, and then click **Windows Media Player**.

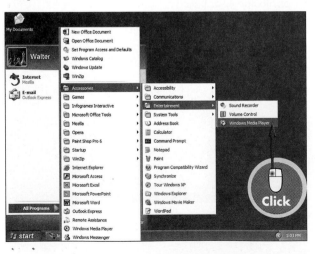

❷ Switch to Copy from CD

Click the **Copy from CD** button. If your CD is not in the computer's CD-ROM drive, insert it now. If the music begins playing, click the **Stop** button to stop playback.

❸ Find Album Information

If Windows Media Player does not display the album and track information for your CD, click the **Get Names** button. A wizard opens, asks a few questions, and helps you search the Internet for album information.

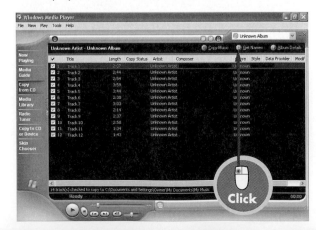

④ Select Tracks to Copy

By default, all the tracks on the CD are selected to be copied. Deselect a track by clearing the check from the box next to the track (click the box once). Only tracks with check marks will be copied.

⑤ Open the Options Dialog Box

By default, tracks are copied to the My Music folder inside your My Documents folder. You can change this location and specify some additional settings from the Options dialog box. Open it by choosing **Tools**, **Options**.

⑥ Set Options

On the Copy Music tab, you can change where the tracks are copied, the file format (such as MP3 and several others) in which the tracks are copied, whether content copy protection is enabled (which basically means that the recording you make can't be further copied and shared), and the quality of the recording (higher quality takes up more disk space). When you've made your selections, click **OK**.

⑦ Copy the Music

Click the **Copy Music** button to begin copying the selected tracks to the location specified in the Options dialog box, with the selected options.

How to Find Music Online

Windows Media Player provides two ways to find music on the Internet. The Media Guide feature lets you browse for downloadable music and video files. The Radio Tuner lets you tune in to streaming Internet audio in dozens of different formats.

1 Start Windows Media Player

Select **Start**, **All Programs**, **Accessories**, **Entertainment**, and then click **Windows Media Player**.

2 Switch to Media Guide

Click the **Media Guide** button to open an Internet connection and jump to the WindowsMedia.com Web site.

3 Browse the Web Site

Use the WindowsMedia.com Web site to browse for all kinds of files you can play in Windows Media Player.

❹ Switch to Radio Tuner

If you want to listen to a radio station across town or across the globe, switch to the Radio Tuner feature. Many radio stations around the world (but not all) broadcast over the Internet. Click the **Radio Tuner** button.

❺ Start a Preset List

Just as you can with the radio in your car, Windows Media Player lets you create preset lists of stations. Unlike your car radio (which has a limited number of preset buttons), you can create any number of lists and fill each list with as many stations as you want. A list named My Stations is created for you. Switch to it by clicking its link.

❻ Find a Station

To find stations to add to your list, use the list of categories on the right side of the window to browse for stations. You can also search for stations by keyword or click the **Find More Stations** link to browse a complete list of radio stations available on the Web.

❼ Listen

After you have displayed a list of stations, select a station and then click the **Play** link to begin listening. Click the **Add to My Stations** link to add the selected station to your list.

How to Make Movies

Windows XP includes a program named Windows Movie Maker that lets you import pictures and movies, edit them, and put them together as a movie. Movie Maker is complex enough that an entire book could be written about it, but this task should give you an idea of what it can do.

1 Start Movie Maker

Select **Start**, **All Programs**, **Accessories**, **Windows Movie Maker** to launch the program.

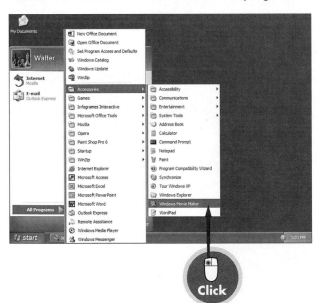

2 Import Files

To import picture or movie files already on your computer into Movie Maker, select **File**, **Import** from the menu bar.

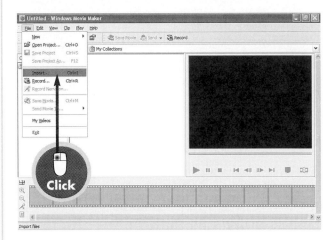

3 Record Video

To record video from a VCR or camcorder, select the **Record** command from the File menu. To use this feature, you must have a video card that supports recording from an external device, and the device must be hooked up correctly to this video card.

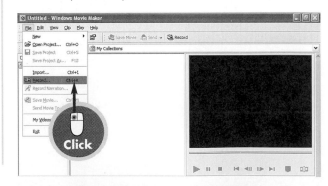

4 View a Collection

When you import pictures or record video into Movie Maker, the files are displayed as part of a collection. By default, the media files are placed into a collection named My Collection. When you select a collection from the Collections list on the left side of the screen, the files in that collection are displayed as thumbnails on the right side of the screen.

5 Create a New Collection

To organize the files you access in Movie Maker, you can create new collections. Right-click anywhere in the **Collections** list and choose **New Collection** from the shortcut menu.

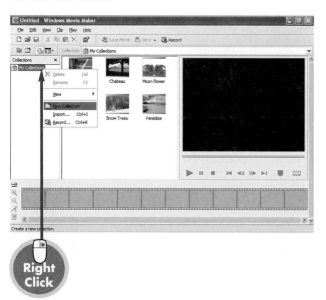

6 Name the New Collection

As soon as you create a new collection, you are given the chance to rename it. Type a name for the new collection.

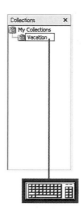

7 Move Files to the New Collection

To move files between collections, select the thumbnails of the files you want to move (the same way you do in Windows), drag them to the new collection in the Collections list, and drop the files.

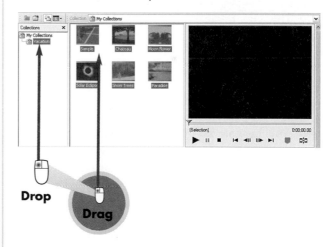

⑧ Move Pictures to the Storyboard

The storyboard is the filmstrip at the bottom of the Movie Maker window. It represents the movie you are currently creating. Each frame of the filmstrip is a picture in the movie. Drag each picture individually to a frame on the storyboard. This task shows the steps to make a slideshow movie out of still pictures.

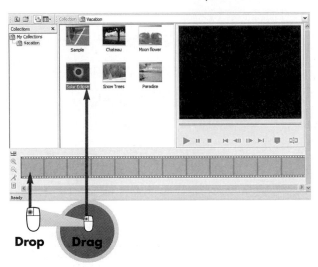

Drop   **Drag**

⑨ Show the Timeline

After you have moved all the pictures to the storyboard, you can display the timeline for the movie. The timeline helps you adjust the length of each frame (just slide the divider between frames to adjust the size) and position an audio soundtrack should you decide to include one.

⑩ Select All Clips on Storyboard

After you have adjusted the lengths of your frames and are ready to make your movie, select all the clips on the storyboard (hold down the **Ctrl** key and click each of the clips in turn).

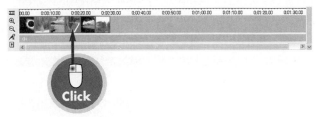

⑪ Combine the Clips

Combining the clips tells Movie Maker that you want each picture to play in succession when you play the movie. With all clips selected, choose **Clip**, **Combine** from the menu bar.

⑫ Play the Movie

To see what your movie looks like at any time, click the **Play** button. All the frames shown in the storyboard play in sequence. You can assess the flow of the scenes and adjust the duration of the frames in the storyboard.

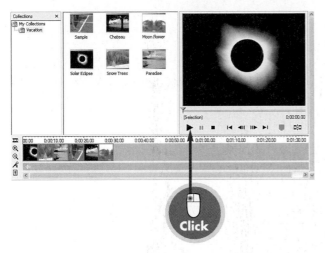

⑬ Save the Movie

When you are satisfied with your movie, choose **File**, **Save Movie** from the menu bar. This command opens the Save Movie dialog box.

⑭ Click OK

Use the Save Movie dialog box to adjust the quality of the saved movie. Higher-quality movies take up more disk space. When you have made your selection from the Setting drop-down list and provided any labeling information, click **OK** to save the movie. Movie Maker converts all the clips and individual pictures files in the storyboard into a single movie file. After the movie is saved, you are given the chance to watch it in Windows Media Player.

How-to Hint

Recording Audio

You can record your own narration or even include a music soundtrack for your movie. To record narration, just click the button that looks like a microphone to open the Record Narration Track dialog box. Click the **Record** button and speak into your computer's microphone to narrate your movie. To add music, click the **Change** button on the Record Narration Track and choose a source for the audio. You can record audio from a music CD or another audio device (such as digital tape) that you have hooked up to your computer's sound card.

How to Work with Pictures

Most Windows applications store picture files in a folder named My Pictures, which you'll find inside the My Documents folder. This folder was created to include tools that are specific to working with picture files.

1 Open My Documents

Double-click the **My Documents** icon on your desktop to open the My Documents window. If you don't see the My Documents icon on your desktop, you can find it on your Start menu.

2 Open My Pictures

Double-click the **My Pictures** icon to open the My Pictures folder.

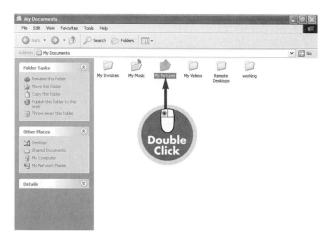

3 Select a Picture

Select any picture in the My Pictures folder by clicking it once.

④ Print Pictures

To print the selected picture or pictures, click the **Print Pictures** link in the Picture Tasks list on the left side of the window.

⑤ View As Slideshow

If no pictures are selected or if multiple pictures are selected, click the **View As a Slide Show** link in the Picture Tasks list. Windows shows the selected pictures one by one in full-screen mode. You are given controls to advance, rewind, and stop the slide show.

⑥ View As Filmstrip

Select the **Filmstrip** command from the View menu.

⑦ Work with the Picture

In filmstrip view, the selected picture is shown enlarged. Use the tools under the enlarged picture to zoom in and out on, resize, and rotate the picture. These adjustments affect only the display of the picture and not the picture file itself. In filmstrip view, you can use the **Next** and **Previous** buttons to move through the slides one at a time.

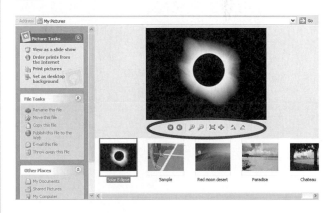

How to Play Games

Windows XP includes a number of games that you can play when you get tired of working. Some games you can play by yourself (such as the classic Solitaire); other games require you to sign on to the Internet to find other online gamers you can challenge to rounds of checkers, spades, and backgammon.

1 Start Solitaire

Select **Start**, **All Programs**, **Games**, **Solitaire**. The game opens in a new window.

2 Move Cards

To move a card, click it with the left mouse button and drag it to its new location on the seven row stacks. Double-click a card to move it directly to one of the four suit stacks in the top-right corner of the board.

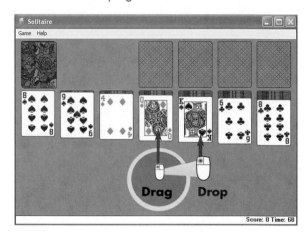

3 Get Help

To learn about the rules of the game and how to play the game, choose **Help**, **Contents** from the menu bar.

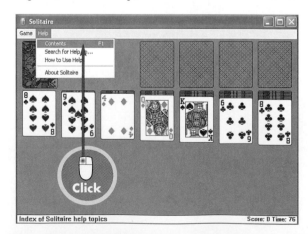

④ Start an Internet Game

Several Internet games are included with Windows. Start one the same way you would a game that can be played from your computer's hard disk: Click **Start** and choose **All Programs**, **Games**; then choose the name of the Internet game you want to play.

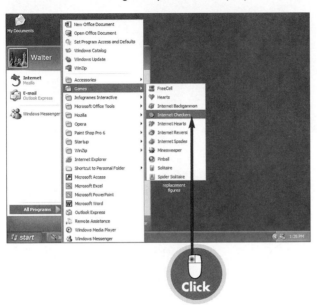

⑤ Enter Zone.com

To play on the Internet, you must connect to Microsoft's Zone.com Web site by clicking **Play**. You do not have to register or give any personal information. An opponent of your skill level will be selected for you, and the game will begin immediately. Set your skill level using the **File** menu of any open game.

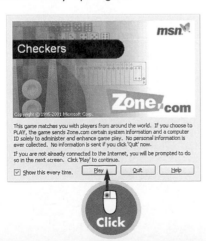

⑥ Play

Play the game the way you would play a normal "non-computer" game. In checkers, for example, just drag a checker where you want it to go.

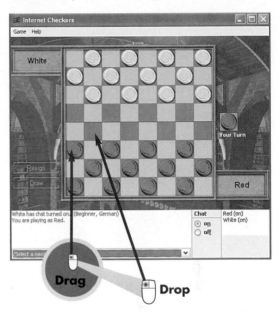

⑦ Send a Message

During play, you can send any of a number of preset messages to your opponent. Select one from the drop-down list at the bottom of the screen. Unfortunately, you cannot type your own messages.

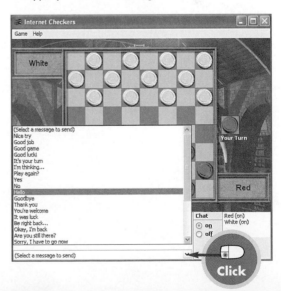

Prepare Your Computer

II

Task

7

Performing Computer Maintenance

When it comes to taking care of your computer, the old adage, "An ounce of prevention is worth a pound of cure," couldn't be more true. The best way to help ensure that you won't need to needlessly repair your PC is to perform basic computer maintenance—doing things such as scanning your hard disk for errors, using antivirus software, and cleaning out the inside of your PC.

In this chapter, we look at the basic computer maintenance you should perform regularly—everything from backing up your hard disk, to defragmenting your hard disk, to making sure you always have the latest drivers for your hardware, to blowing dust out of the inside of your computer. If you follow this advice every several weeks, your computer will be more likely to keep running at tip-top shape.

And we also look at basic troubleshooting tips, should something go wrong with your PC. Before calling in a technician, or deciding to replace a computer part, there are a variety of steps you can take that can save you time and money. Doing basic things such as checking whether your add-in boards are properly secured, whether the cables are all tight, and even whether everything is plugged in means less hours of computing frustration—and less money spent on needless repairs.

Software Maintenance You Should Perform

The best way to ensure that nothing goes wrong with your computer is to perform computer maintenance on your software and hard disk regularly. Take the following steps, and you'll help ensure that you fix problems with your computer—before they happen.

1 Create a Windows Startup Disk

A Windows Startup disk lets you start your computer from its floppy drive, if something goes wrong with your computer or hard disk and it won't start. To create a Windows Startup disk, select **Settings** from the Start menu, and then select **Control Panel**. After Control Panel opens, double-click **Add/Remove Programs**. From the window that appears, click the **Startup Disk** tab and follow the instructions for creating a Startup disk. Use a blank floppy disk or one with data you don't mind losing.

Click

2 Scan Your Hard Disk

As you use your computer, you can get disk "errors," which can result in the loss of data, programs not running, and even worse. To be sure that you've cleaned up any disk errors, run the ScanDisk program in Windows. To use it, click the **Start** menu and select **Programs**, **Accessories**. From the Accessories menu, select **System Tools**, **ScanDisk**.

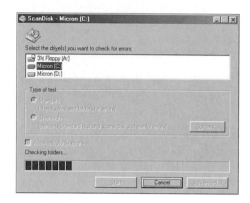

3 Defragment Your Hard Drive

As you use your hard disk, the files on it become fragmented and spread out over your entire hard disk. So, your hard disk has to work harder. Most versions of Windows have defragmentation software. To use it, click the **Start** menu and select **Programs**, **Accessories**. From the Accessories menu, select **System Tools**, **Disk Defragmenter**.

④ Run Antivirus Software

You can get a computer virus from anywhere. To ensure that your computer doesn't get infected, buy and run antivirus software, such as Norton's AntiVirus. Most antivirus software has an "auto-protect" feature in which the antivirus runs all the time. To be safe, use the auto-protect feature.

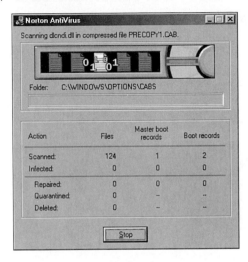

⑤ Back Up Your Hard Disk

To ensure that you don't lose any vital information, back up your hard disk to a removable drive, your company's network, or even the Internet. Windows includes backup software. To use it, click the **Start** menu and select **Programs**, **Accessories**. From the Accessories menu, select **System Tools**, **Backup**. You also can buy special backup software.

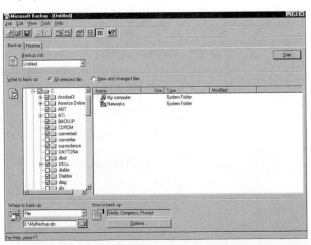

⑥ Check the Web Sites

Drivers are required for hardware such as printers, modems, graphics cards, and other devices to work with Windows. Sometimes the drivers have small bugs in them or become outdated. To ensure that you don't run into hardware problems, you should regularly check manufacturers' Web sites to see whether they have new versions of drivers that you can download and install. Video and sound drivers are often updated every three to six months.

Physical Maintenance of Your PC

Physical problems with your PC are a frequent cause of computer problems—and there's a lot you can do to ensure those problems never occur. Dirt and dust can damage your components by acting as a blanket and trapping heat, which can overheat the components. Additionally, dirt and dust can cause electrical shorts inside the components of your computer. Canned air, which you can buy in many computer stores, is invaluable in cleaning out dust.

Other physical things can go wrong as well. Connectors and boards can come loose, and grime can disturb the contacts between devices.

① Swab Any Heavy Dust Areas

Debris and grime, in addition to dust, might have accumulated on the motherboard and any expansion boards. To loosen and clean it, use foam rubber swabs. Don't use any kind of cleaning solution, unless the solution has been specifically designed for electronic components. Be careful not to use brushes, cotton swabs, or pieces of cloth because they can leave a residue and produce static charges.

② Blow Out Accumulated Dust

Using the nozzle of the canned air, blow out any dust that might have accumulated on the motherboard and the sides of the expansion cards. Be sure to blow the dust out from a variety of angles to ensure you clean out the hidden areas. Also remove backplates from where you screw in add-in cards so you can blow dust out of them.

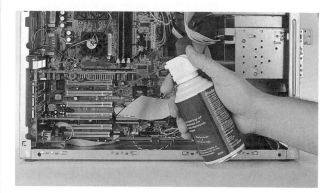

③ Spray the Power Supply

Dust and grime accumulating in your power supply can freeze it. So clear it by spraying air through all the supply's vent openings. Be careful not to open the power supply because it retains a powerful electric charge even when turned off. Also spray inside your floppy drives, and spray their cable connections as well.

4 Clean the Keyboard

A great deal of dust, hair, grime, grit, and paper accumulate inside your keyboard by falling through the cracks. Spray between the cracks of the keyboard and hold it upside down to enable the particles to fall out. A swab will also enable you to clean between the keys.

5 Clean the Mouse

Clean the mouse by taking off the twist-lock on the bottom, taking out the ball, and cleaning the ball as well as the hole into which the ball is normally seated. This will prevent grime and dust from causing erratic mouse movements.

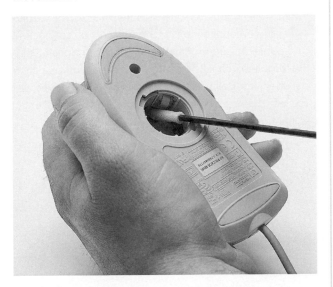

6 Clean Connectors

If connectors and contacts get grimy, your computer might not work properly. Using a foam rubber swab and special electronics cleaning solution, clean all the connections and contacts.

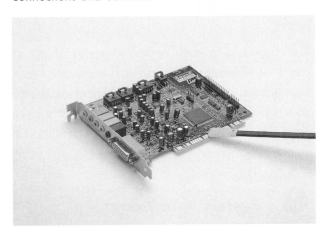

Watch Out!

- Only use special electronics cleaning fluid, which you can buy at computer stores and electronics outlets. Any other kind of fluid or liquid can seriously harm your computer.

- Don't smoke or allow anyone to smoke near your computer. The smoke contains chemicals that can damage your computer and corrode its parts.

What to Check for When You Run into Problems

Computers are such complex pieces of equipment that literally thousands of unique problems can occur—and it often can be almost impossible to track down the source of the problem. Here, however, are things you should do when you run into a problem on your PC.

1 Restart Your Computer

Problems might occur for unexplained reasons and then never happen again. Often the simplest way to fix them is to restart your computer. Shut the computer down by clicking the **Start** menu and selecting **Shut Down**. If that doesn't work, try pressing **Ctrl+Alt+Delete** twice. If neither of those works, try pressing the **Reset** switch on your computer. If that doesn't work, or if your computer doesn't have a reset switch, press the **Power** button to turn it off, and then press it again to turn it back on.

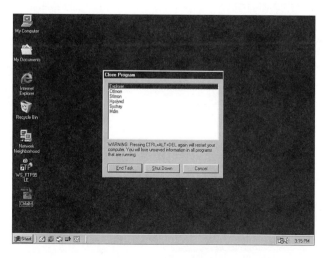

2 Ensure Things Are Plugged In

You'd be surprised how frequently the cause of a computing problem is simply that not all the hardware has been plugged in and turned on. As technical support personnel will tell you, many printer "problems" are caused by the printer not being plugged in.

3 Check Your Cables

Often, the cause of the problem is loose cables, switches, or connections. Check external connections and cables to see that they're tight. If that doesn't solve the problem, check the internal connections, such as between controller cards and cables, or drives and cables, to ensure they're tight. Pay particular attention to the connections of your power supply cable.

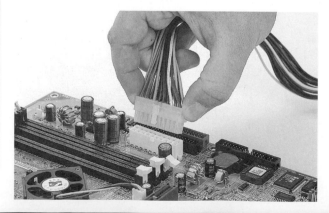

④ Use the Device Manager

The Windows Device Manager checks your hardware to see whether everything is working properly, so it's a good place to troubleshoot problems. To get to it, right-click **My Computer** and select **Properties**. Then, click the **Device Manager** tab. If Windows detects problems with a device, you'll see an exclamation mark.

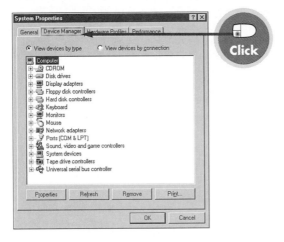

⑤ Look for Signs of Overheating

Turn off your PC and let it cool down for an hour. Then, turn it back on again. If the problem goes away but then returns after your PC has been on for a while, the problem might be caused by overheating. If your micro-processor chip has a cooling fan, make sure it's connected and working. Check any other fans inside your case as well, including any on chips. Use canned air to blow away dust—dust can lead to overheating. You will need to replace any fans that aren't working properly.

⑥ Reseat Add-In Boards and Chips

The problem could be caused by an add-in card that was loose. You won't be able to tell that they're loose by looking at them, so you'll have to reseat each of them. Make sure each is firmly seated into the slot on the motherboard. Also check the chips on your mother-board, such as the CPU, to see whether they've come loose. Reseat each of them to ensure that they're firmly in position. And make sure your RAM is connected tightly as well.

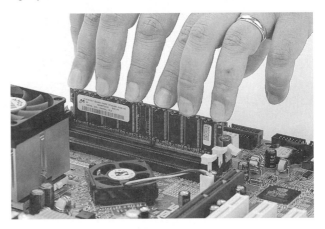

How-to Hint

• If you have a PC with many drives, add-in cards, and other devices, your power supply might not provide enough electricity to power them. Consider buying a new power supply that has a higher rating than your current one. Make sure you buy it from a well-known manufacturer.

Watch Out!

• Make sure that your home's or office's power outlets are grounded properly. Improperly grounded outlets can cause problems, as can unreliable PC power supplies.

The Tools You Need

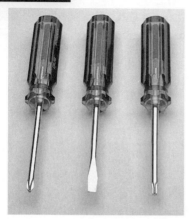

Screwdriver

You'll need some type of screwdriver to open the cases of most PCs and to add or remove expansion cards inside the PC. Get both a Phillips screwdriver and a medium-sized flathead screwdriver (left). Some computers also use special star-headed screws called Torx screws, so if your computer uses these special screws, you'll need a Torx screwdriver (right). Screwdrivers that are 3/8" are best.

Nutdriver

Many screws used in a PC also have hexagonal heads, so a hexagonal-head nutdriver will work on them; in fact, they often work better because they surround the head of the screw, making it less likely that a slip will strip the screw head. A 1/4" nutdriver is your best bet because it's a standard size for computer equipment, and is can be used when adding some heatsinks.

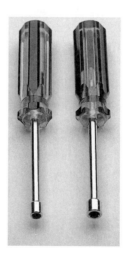

Small flathead screwdriver

You'll need a small, flathead screwdriver about 1/8" across. You'll mainly use it to tighten cables attached to serial, parallel, and other ports. It is also helpful for setting various switches.

Grounding wrist strap

Static electricity you pick up can seriously damage some components of your computer. To ensure you don't zap an electronic part, wear this. Wrap it tightly around your wrist, and then attach the other end to a grounded piece of metal, such as a metal table leg, or clipped to the metal case of the PC. You can also use an antistatic mat.

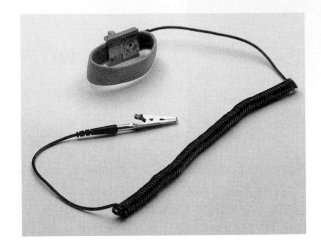

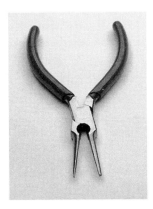

Needle-nose pliers

A good, all-around tool for holding screws, getting objects that are too heavy for the pickup tool, or a hundred other things.

Chip puller

Good for extracting chips that otherwise would be difficult to remove. You won't need this tool for newer memory or processors.

Tweezers

These are good for holding small objects and changing settings on an expansion board. Get the cross-locked kind, pictured here.

How to Prepare for Your Upgrade

Anytime you upgrade your computer, you need to take certain basic steps to ensure that you can recover your system information if things go bad and to ensure that your PC can handle your upgrade. Shown here are the steps you should take particularly when installing critical components such as new drives, cards, or a new motherboard in your computer.

① Back Up Using Windows

You should always have a copy of your hard disk, so that you can restore everything if something goes wrong. You might want to back up only your data (the data files you want to keep, such as word processing documents), or you might want to copy the operating system and your programs. Back up your hard drive to a CD-R or CD-RW, tape drive, Zip drive, or similar removable media. Backup software is built into Windows. To use it, click the **Start** menu and select **Programs**, **Accessories**. From the Accessories menu, select **System Tools**, **Backup**.

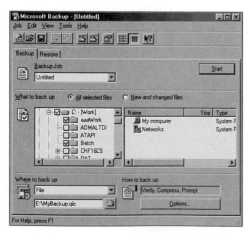

② Back Up Your Hard Drive

You can buy special software that offers more options than the software built into Windows to back up your hard disk. NTI Backup Now Deluxe is specially designed for backing up to CD-R and CD-RW drives, while Backup Plus can back up to any device.

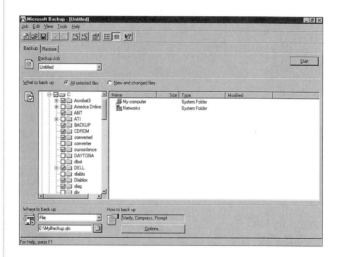

③ Put Backup in a Safe Place

Make sure that your backup is secure and in a safe place where it won't be damaged. That way, you can be sure you can restore your hard disk. Consider buying a small fireproof safe and putting CD backups in the safe.

4 Create a Bootable Floppy

Make a bootable floppy disk so that you can start (also known as *boot*) your computer even if something goes wrong with your hard disk during an upgrade. To do that, put a disk in your floppy drive. Open the Control Panel by double-clicking **My Computer** and double-clicking **Control Panel**. Next, double-click **Add/Remove Programs** and click the **Startup Disk** tab. From the tab, click **Create Disk** and follow the instructions.

5 Check Your BIOS Settings

In many types of upgrades, particularly when you're upgrading a drive, you need to know your BIOS settings. And it's generally a good idea to have these handy, in case something goes wrong with the installation and you must reinstall an old hard drive. Go to the CMOS screen and write down all the information it contains about your hard drive.

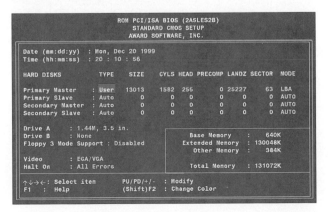

How-to Hint

- Remember to record your BIOS information before taking out your old hard drive or installing a new one.

- Always make a boot disk before installing a new hard drive or adding a second one.

How to Open the Case

To expand or upgrade almost anything, you have to get inside the case of your PC. Although there are variations in how you do this, you'll be able to safely open the case of just about every computer by following these steps.

① Turn Off Your PC

Before doing anything, you have to turn off your PC. If you try to upgrade or repair the computer while it's on, you can do damage to the computer as well as to yourself. Be sure to turn off anything attached to your computer, such as a printer or monitor.

② Unplug the Power Cord

If you open the case of your PC while it's plugged in, you could hurt yourself or your computer, so unplug it first. The power cord usually plugs into the back of your PC. Unplug it from there, not from the wall or the power strip. If you unplug it from the wall or power strip, you could accidentally unplug the wrong device and end up opening your PC with the power cord still attached. You might find your monitor plugged into your power supply, so remove that as well.

③ Get Rid of Static Electricity

You often build up a static charge simply by walking on carpets and upholstery, especially during the winter months when the air is dry. You can destroy some PC components if you accidentally discharge static electricity onto them. Because of that, always get rid of any static charge you might carry before opening the case. One way is to use a grounding wrist strap. You can also touch a grounded object, such as the power supply of your PC.

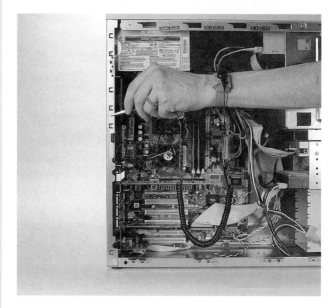

④ Find the Screws on the Case

If you have a desktop model, usually three to five screws hold it in place. A minitower usually has two or more screws, and a full tower might have as many as eight or ten. In some instances, instead of screws, there are thumbscrews you can unscrew by hand. Many cases now have snap-on front covers that, when removed, reveal the screws that hold on the cases. Some cases forgo these kinds of screws altogether and instead use one or more thumbscrews to hold them in place.

⑤ Remove the Screws

You might need a Phillips screwdriver, flathead screwdriver, or Torx screwdriver, depending on the type of screw. Better yet would be to use a hexagonal nutdriver if your screws have hexagonal heads, because that way you'll be less likely to strip the screws. Be sure to place the screws in a safe place, such as a paper cup. You also might want to tape them to the case until you need them again.

⑥ Remove the Case

You usually remove the case by sliding the cover toward the front or rear of the computer and then lifting it off its rails. After you've removed the case, you should ground yourself again before reaching inside to do whatever work you're planning, if you are not using a wrist strap.

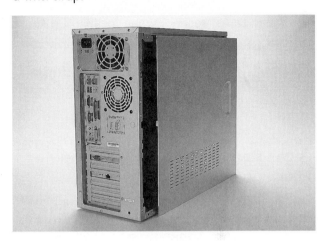

Watch Out!
- Remember to turn off any devices attached to your PC, as well as the PC itself, before opening the case.
- Be sure that you're grounded so that you don't damage any delicate internal components.

How-to Hint
- When you remove the screws, put them nearby in a safe place, or tape them to the case after it's opened—you'll need them when you reattach the case.

How to Remove an Existing Card

In many cases, such as when installing a sound card or graphics card, you might have to remove an existing card from your system before installing a new one. Follow these steps to remove a card from your system.

❶ Remove the Drivers and Software

Before installing a new sound card, uninstall drivers and other software for your existing card. To do this, right-click the **My Computer** icon in Windows and select **Properties** and the **Device Manager** tab. Click on the hardware you're planning to remove and select your sound card. Click **Remove** and follow the instructions. To remove any special software that works specifically with the card, double-click **Add/Remove Programs** from the Control Panel, select the program you want to remove, and click **Add/Remove, Yes**.

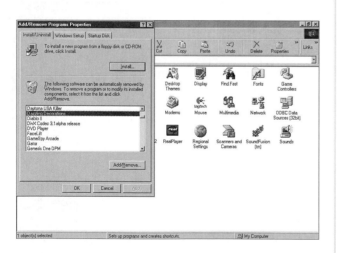

❷ Turn Off and Remove Case

Follow the steps outlined earlier in this chapter in Task 5, "How to Open the Case," to turn off your computer and remove its case.

❸ Detach Devices and Cables

If you look on the back of your card (the side that faces the outside of your computer) you will most likely see one or more connectors and plugs. A variety of devices might be connected to the card. Unplug the devices. Cables and devices might be attached internally to your card as well. Disconnect them.

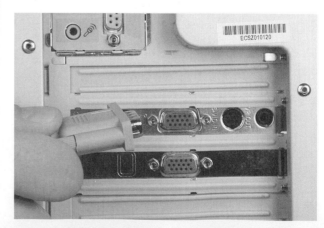

4. Remove Backplate and Card

The card is secured to your system by a screw connecting it to the backplate. Remove that screw, probably with a Phillips screwdriver. Then lift the card free from the system. Hold the card by its top edge with two hands and lift straight up. If the card doesn't move, pull up one edge slightly first and then lift the other.

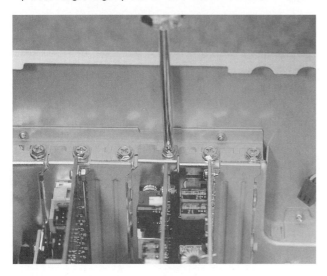

5. Attach Case and Turn On PC

Put the case back on, and once it's secure, turn on your computer. If you're going to be installing a new card in place of your old one, don't do this step yet. Instead, install your new card first.

6. Double-Check Software

You want to be absolutely sure that all the old software and drivers for the old card are gone from your system. Run the **Add/Remove Wizard** from the Control Panel. In most cases, the wizard won't find any software associated with the old card, but if it does, tell it to remove the software.

How-to Hint

- When you remove the screw for the slot, put it nearby in a safe place—you'll need it when you install your new card.

How to Install a Basic Card

You could need to install a new card on your system for many reasons: You might be adding a sound card or graphics card, or you might need to add a card to attach a device to it, such as a removable drive or SCSI device. Before you install a card, turn off your PC and remove its case, following the instructions earlier in this chapter in Task 5, "How to Open the Case." Then follow these steps.

1 Find and Verify a Free Slot

After you remove your computer's case, look on the motherboard and locate an empty slot. Ensure that the free slot matches the type of card you're installing. For example, if installing a graphics card, you might require a free AGP slot, while many other types of cards require a free PCI slot. Check your computer's or motherboard's documentation for information. When checking the documentation, ensure the free slot is not an Audio Modem Riser (AMR) or Communications and Networking Riser (CNR) slot, since these can't be used by general-purpose cards.

2 Remove the Slot's Backplate

To install the card, you have to remove the small metal flap protecting the slot, called a *backplate*. The flap is held in place by a small screw. Remove the screw (usually a Phillips screw), and then remove the flap. Put the screw in a safe place. (You'll need it to secure the card you're inserting.) In some instances, you must punch out a blank instead of unscrewing the backplate.

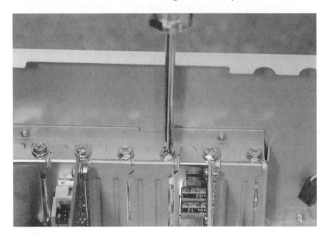

3 Set Jumpers

In some instances, before you install the card, you must set its jumpers. Check the card documentation to see whether you need to set jumpers.

④ Install the Card

Align the card in the free slot, making sure the connectors on the card line up properly with the slot into which you're inserting the card. Then, using two hands, apply gentle, even pressure to push the card down into the slot. After the card is in place, press down firmly to ensure that it's all the way into the slot.

⑤ Screw the Card into Place

To ensure that the card doesn't come loose, you need to screw it into the backplate. Using a Phillips screwdriver, screw in the sound card, but be careful not to overtighten it so that you don't strip the screw.

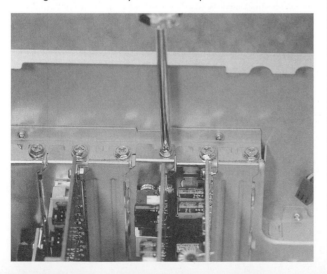

⑥ Attach Devices and Cables and Restart

Some cards have devices and cables attached to them internally and externally. Attach them, then put the case back on, plug in your PC, and restart the computer. A wizard for installing hardware might appear. If so, follow the instructions. In many cases, you'll now have to install drivers for your new card to work. To learn how to install drivers, see Task 10, "How to Install Hardware Drivers," later in this chapter.

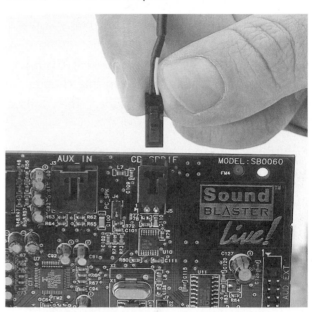

Watch Out!

- Be sure that the card is seated firmly—if it isn't, the card won't work.
- Don't press too hard when inserting the card or you could damage the card or motherboard.

How to Remove an Old Drive

When installing certain kinds of drives such as a floppy drive, you first should remove your old drive. You take the same basic steps for removing most drives, so follow these steps when you need to remove an old drive. Before you remove a drive, turn off your PC and remove its case, following the instructions earlier in this chapter in Task 5, "How to Open the Case." Then follow these steps.

❶ Locate the Drive You Want to Remove

Your PC will have several drives in it, so after you open the case, be sure to find the drive you want to remove—you don't want to accidentally remove the wrong drive.

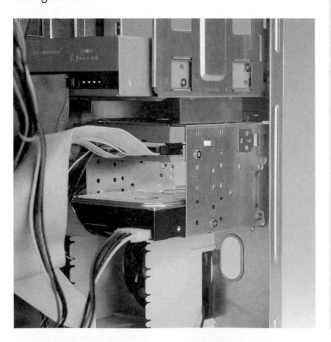

❷ Remove the Ribbon Cable

A flat ribbon cable runs from the motherboard or a controller card to a drive. Data runs back and forth along this cable. A plug connects the cable to the drive. Remove the cable from the drive by pulling it straight off. It should come off easily.

❸ Remove the Power Cables

Power cables run from the power supply to the drive, supplying it with power. These cables are attached to the drive by connectors. Pull the connectors off the drive. It might take more force to pull these off than it did to take off the ribbon connectors.

④ Take Off Mounting Screws

Some drives are held onto the computer by small rails that slide into your computer, along with the floppy drive. If your drive uses rails, look for the mounting screws and remove them. If it doesn't use rails, the mounting screws will be along the sides. Unscrew the mounting screws and keep them in a safe place.

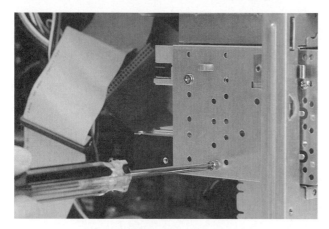

⑤ Slide the Drive Out

Now that all the cables are off and the mounting screws are taken out, the drive can easily be taken out of the computer. Simply slide it out of the computer. It should come out easily.

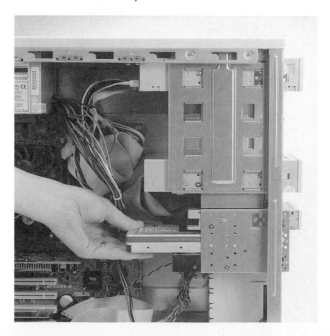

Watch Out!

- Be careful not to strip the heads off the drive's mounting screws.

How-to Hint

- When you take off the case, put the screws in a safe place because you'll need them to put the case back on.
- It will require more force to remove the power cable than it will to take off the ribbon cable.

How to Install a Basic Drive

Many of the devices you'll install in your PC are drives of some sort: floppy drives, hard drives, CD drives, and DVD drives. The instructions for how to install each varies, so turn to the specific chapter on how to install that particular drive. Here are instructions for installing a basic drive. Before you remove a drive, turn off your PC and remove its case, following the instructions earlier in this chapter in Task 5, "How to Open the Case." Then follow these steps.

1 Find a Free Bay

If you're going to install a drive of any type, you need a free drive bay. After you remove your computer's case, look inside to see which drive bay you have free. Drives come in 3 1/2" and 5 1/4" sizes, so be sure your bay accommodates the drive you buy. You can fit a 3 1/2" hard drive into a 5 1/4" bay by getting a special adapter kit, but a 5 1/4" hard drive won't fit into a 3 1/2" bay. Additionally, some hard drives are mounted inside bays via mounting rails or adapter kits. Look at how your current hard drive is mounted to see whether you need a kit or rails.

2 Remove the Faceplate for the Drive

A faceplate will cover the front or back of your computer, in front of the empty bay. Remove the faceplate. It might be a blank that you need to punch out, or it might need to be unscrewed.

3 Attach Mounting Rails or Spacers

Many drives need to be mounted using special rails or spacers. Follow the instructions for installing them.

④ Set Jumpers

In some instances, before installing the drive, you must set its jumpers. Check the drive documentation to see whether to set jumpers.

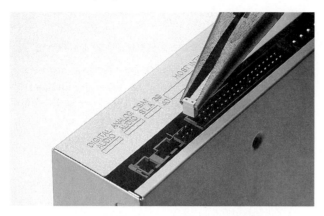

⑤ Slide in and Secure the Drive

Slide the drive into the drive bay, and screw it into the drive bay or railings. Connect all the screws so that the drive is held firmly in place, but don't overtighten or strip the screws.

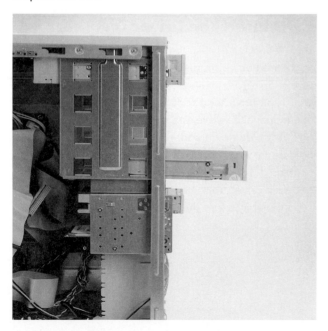

⑥ Attach the Cables and Restart

Depending on the type of drive you're installing, you must attach a cable or variety of cables, such as controller cables or power cables. Turn to the relevant chapter about the kind of drive you're installing for more information about which cables to attach.

Watch Out!
- Ensure that all the cable connectors are tight before putting the case back on your PC.

How to Install Hardware Drivers

Whenever you install a new piece of hardware, you also have to install drivers. *Drivers* are software that mediate between your hardware and your operating system—they're what enable your hardware to work with the software in your computer.

You install drivers after you install the hardware. With Windows, installing drivers is relatively easy. Be aware that Windows will automatically install its own drivers for your hardware if you don't provide them on disc or downloaded from the Internet.

❶ Turn Your Computer Back On

Turn on the computer if you've had to turn it off during installation of the hardware. That way, the operating system should recognize that you've installed new hardware, if what you've added supports plug-and-play. If you didn't have to turn off the computer, or if the operating system didn't recognize that you added new hardware, tell the operating system to find your new hardware. Click the **Start** menu and select **Control Panel** from the **Settings** menu. Then, double-click the **Add New Hardware** icon and follow the onscreen instructions.

❷ Identify the New Hardware

Your computer will now search for the new hardware you've installed. This could take several minutes. At some point it might ask whether it should search for the hardware itself or whether you want to specify the hardware you've added. Tell it to find it itself.

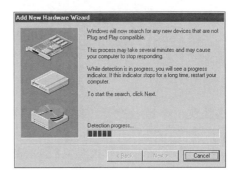

❸ Insert the Driver Disc

After several minutes, the computer will identify the hardware you've installed. It will ask you whether you have a disc from the manufacturer that contains the driver. If you have that disc, insert it into your drive and then indicate the drive and subdirectory where it should look. If you've downloaded the driver from the Internet, indicate in which drive and subdirectory the driver is located. If you don't have the disc or haven't downloaded a driver from the Internet, insert your Windows CD and tell it to find the driver on that disc.

④ Finish Installing the Driver

The operating system will find the driver and start to install it. Follow the directions onscreen to finish the installation. At each step, you'll click the **Next** button, until at the end, when you'll click **Finish**. At this point, your new hardware should be ready to use.

⑤ Confirm the Driver Works

To confirm that the hardware has been installed properly, go back to the **Control Panel** and double-click **System**. Then, click the **Device Manager** tab. Click the small cross next to the type of device you've installed, such as a modem. If the driver has been installed properly, you'll see its name there—if it hasn't, you'll see an error message of some sort. Try installing the driver again by turning off your computer and then turning it back on.

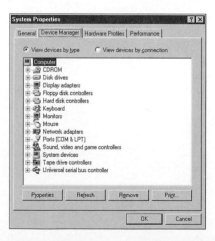

⑥ Check the Web for Newer Drivers

After you've installed a piece of hardware, you should go to the hardware manufacturer's Web site, download any newer versions of the driver, and then install them.

Watch Out!

- If you don't have a driver for the specific device you're installing, use a generic one from the Windows CD.
- Remove the previous drivers before installing new ones—if you don't, the new hardware might not work.

How-to Hint

- Check the manufacturer's Web site frequently—as often as once a month—to check for new drivers. However, be aware that newer drivers aren't always better. If your current driver works without problems, and new drivers don't offer extra features, there's no need to get the newest drivers.

Task

8

Installing USB and FireWire Devices

Perhaps the best news in the last several years for those who want to expand and upgrade their computers is the advent of the Universal Serial Bus (USB) and FireWire, sometimes known by its formal name IEEE-1394, or simply 1394. They provide the easiest way yet to attach devices such as scanners, joysticks, keyboards, mouse devices, modems, removable drives, CD and DVD drives, MP3 players, digital cameras, digital camcorders, and more to your computer.

Another plus of USB is that you can daisy-chain up to 127 devices to your computer using its USB. Sometimes, devices let you plug other USB devices into them. For example, if you install a scanner, it might have a second USB port, into which you can plug another USB device. You won't have to plug that device into your computer's USB port; instead, plug it into the extra port on another USB device. However, not all USB devices have these extra ports, and a solution is to buy a USB hub, a device that plugs into your computer's USB port, and into which you can plug several USB devices. It is by using many hubs that you can connect up to 127 devices to your USB port. FireWire devices can also be connected in a daisy-chain or by using a FireWire hub or hubs.

If you bought a computer in the past several years, odds are that it comes with one or more USB ports. FireWire ports are rarer, but do come on some PCs.

Note the two speeds of USB: the older USB 1.1, which allows devices to communicate with your PC at 12Mbps, and the newer USB 2.0 standard, which allows devices to communicate at 40 times that speed, or 480Mbps. Many computers use the 1.1 standard, because the USB 2.0 standard only came into use in 2002. FireWire allows for communications at 400Mbps, although a faster FireWire standard that would communicate at 1,600Mbps has been proposed.

In this chapter, you'll see how to install USB and FireWire devices. You'll learn how to install a USB hub to make it easy to daisy-chain many USB devices. FireWire devices and hubs install much like their USB cousins, so follow the same directions for both.

How the Universal Serial Bus Works

Daisy-chained devices

The USB enables up to 127 devices to be attached in a daisy chain to your computer via the USB port. A USB controller in your PC is the brains of USB. If you don't have a USB port and controller, you can add them by installing a USB card on your PC, but only if you have Windows 98 or above.

USB ports

Computers have one or more USB ports. Whether you have one or more ports, however, up to 127 devices can be daisy-chained via USB to a computer. Plugs from USB devices attach to USB ports. In this way, you can connect USB devices to your computer without opening the case. USB ports are marked with the special symbol in this illustration.

USB hubs

You can connect up to 127 devices to your USB port by using USB hubs. A hub attaches to a USB port or to another USB hub. These hubs have USB ports on them, enabling numerous USB devices to be plugged into them.

Power

D+

D-

Ground

USB cables

Inside USB cables are four wires. Two provide electricity to the USB devices attached to your computer: One provides the electricity, while the other is a ground. (Some USB devices, such as scanners, require more electricity than the USB cables can provide and still need to be plugged into a power outlet.) The other two wires, D+ and D-, transmit data and commands.

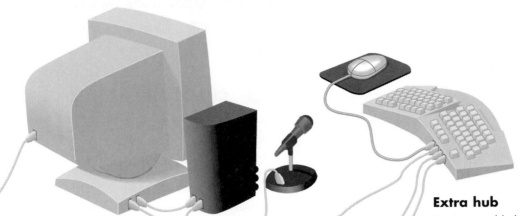

USB device as a hub

Some USB devices include extra USB ports so that they can function like a hub. For example, a monitor could have USB speakers, a microphone, and a keyboard plugged into it.

Extra hub

Devices and hubs can be daisy-chained, enabling devices to be attached to one another. As pictured here, a keyboard that has been plugged into a monitor can in turn have a mouse, a digitizing pen, and other devices plugged into it.

Automatic configuration

After you install a new USB device, the USB controller communicates with the device, in essence asking it to identify itself. This helps the controller decide whether the device is a high-speed device such as a monitor, scanner, or printer, that can communicate at 6Mbps–12Mbps, or a slower device, such as a keyboard or mouse, that transfers data at 15Mbps. In the newer USB 2.0 standard, devices can communicate at 480Mbps. (By way of comparison, a serial port communicates at 100Kbps, whereas a parallel port communicates at about 1.5Mbps.) The USB controller also assigns the device an identification number.

Data transfer priorities

The USB controller assigns three different levels of priority to devices attached to it, in this order:

Highest priority

This is assigned to an *isochronous* or real-time device such as a video camera or a sound device. In these devices, the data is not allowed to be interrupted.

Medium priority

This is assigned to devices such as keyboards, mice, and joysticks, which don't always need to use USB to communicate with the computer because they're not in constant use. However, when they are in use, the data must be transferred immediately.

Lowest priority

This is assigned to devices such as printers, scanners, and digital cameras, in which a great deal of data must be sent at once, but in which slight delays in transfer won't be a problem.

How to Install Universal Serial Bus and FireWire Devices

Because you don't need to remove the case of your PC to install USB or FireWire devices, they are among the easiest devices to install. Almost all USB and FireWire devices are *hot swappable*, meaning you can connect and disconnect them while your machine is running; digital cameras and joysticks are good examples of this. Here's how to install a USB or FireWire device. For more information on how to install specific devices, refer to the chapters that cover them more directly.

❶ Make Sure You Have a Port

You can install a USB or FireWire device only if you have a USB or FireWire port on your PC. Look for one or two rectangular ports on the front, side, or rear of your PC. USB ports have the USB symbol next to them, whereas FireWire ports will generally have 1394 printed next to them.

❷ Check Device Manager

Most versions of Windows support USB and FireWire, although Windows 95 support is erratic. To ensure that your computer properly supports USB or FireWire, check the Device Manager and look for the USB setting or the IEEE-1394 setting. To do that, right-click the **My Compute**r icon and select **Properties**. Then, click the **Device Manager** tab and scroll down. You should see a USB controller entry or an IEEE-1394 entry. It shouldn't be expanded to show any exclamation points next to any of the entries within it.

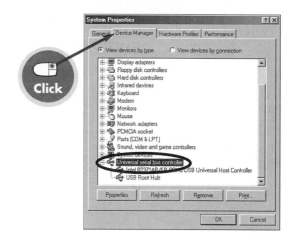

❸ Install Device Software

Some devices, such as scanners, require special software to work. If your device requires special software, install it now.

④ Turn On the Device

First, connect the device's power cable. Some devices need to be plugged into a wall outlet. If the device needs to be plugged in, plug it in and turn it on.

⑤ Connect the Cable

The device comes with a USB or FireWire cable. USB cables have a rectangular connector, called *Series A*, and a square connector, called *Series B*. Plug the square, Series A end into the device and the rectangular, Series B end into the computer. The USB cable connects only one way, so don't force it. If you don't have a free USB port on your PC, you can buy a USB hub to give you extra USB ports to plug devices into. FireWire cables have four-pin (for self-powered devices) or small six-pin connectors.

⑥ Restart Your Computer

With some devices, you'll have to restart your computer. When you do, Windows recognizes that you've added new hardware and an Add New Hardware Wizard launches. Follow the directions for installing your new hardware. If you have a disk from the manufacturer, insert it when asked to, so Windows will use the manufacturer's drivers. You can install most USB and FireWire devices while the computer is still running. In that case, wait a few seconds after you install it, and the Add New Hardware Wizard will appear. (Note that many USB and FireWire devices don't require restarting your computer when you install them.)

Watch Out!

- Check the Device Manager to ensure that your system properly recognizes your USB or FireWire port.
- Check your CMOS to ensure that USB is enabled in it.
- Be sure that all the USB or FireWire connectors are tight.
- Use the manufacturer's disk when the Add New Hardware Wizard asks if you have a disk from the manufacturer.

How to Install a Universal Serial Bus or FireWire Hub

In theory, USB and FireWire allow you to daisy-chain up to 127 devices from a single USB. But most PCs come with only one or two USB or FireWire ports, and most devices don't have any extra ports into which you can attach other devices. So in practice, it appears that you can attach only one or two USB or FireWire devices to your PC at one time. The way around the problem is to buy a USB or FireWire hub. These inexpensive devices plug into your USB or FireWire port and give you four or more ports into which you can plug other devices. And you can daisy-chain hubs by plugging them into one another, so they're an easy way to connect as many devices as you need. This section shows how to install a USB hub, but a FireWire hub installs in the same way.

❶ Attach the AC Adapter

Most hubs come with an AC adapter so they can receive electricity from a power outlet. Although a hub can get its electricity from your computer, some devices are power-hungry, so you should use the AC adapter, especially when first installing the hub. Plug the AC adapter into the hub, and then plug the adapter into a power outlet.

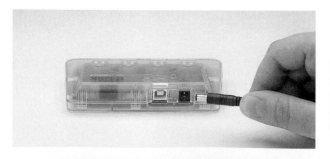

❷ Connect the Cable to Your PC

The USB hub comes with a cable that has a rectangular plug and a square plug. (The rectangular plug is called the *USB-A connector*, whereas the square plug is called the *USB-B connector*.) Plug the rectangular end (the USB-A connector) into the matching USB port on your computer. The USB cable connects only one way, so don't force it.

❸ Connect the USB Cable to the Hub

Connect the square plug on the USB cable to the matching port on your USB hub. (This port will be the USB-B connector type.) Usually, the port on the hub will be set away from the other USB ports, all of which are the rectangular, USB-A connector type. Sometimes this port will be called the *root port*. The USB cable connects only one way, so don't force it.

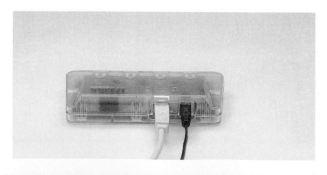

④ Connect the USB Devices to the Hub

Following the instructions in the previous task, connect USB devices to your hub the same way you would connect them to your PC. Remember that the rectangular plug connects to the USB hub, and the square plug connects to the USB device.

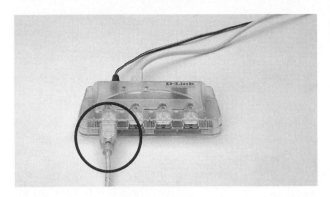

⑤ Try the Devices

Try using each of the devices to verify that they work. If one or more doesn't work, check that the connectors are seated firmly in their ports.

⑥ Test the Devices Without AC Power

If you want to run the hub without AC power, unplug the AC adapter and test each device in turn. If they all work properly, you can run the hub without the external AC power. However, if you have problems running any of them, you need to use the AC power. Also, some hubs require AC power, so check the documentation before trying to run the hub without external power.

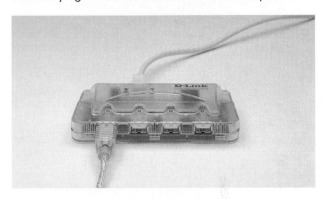

Watch Out!

- Some USB devices, such as some USB CD-RW drives, require connection directly to the computer, not to a hub. Read the devices' documentation to see if they can be connected to a hub.
- Double-check that you connect your PC to the hub via the hub's root port; otherwise, the hub won't work.

How-to Hint

- Some motherboards have a connector that will let you add a backplate that contains USB ports. If you want more USB ports on your computer, you can do that instead of adding a hub, although it will take much more work.
- Some portable devices, such as MP3 players and digital cameras, have a smaller-than-normal USB B connector (called a *mini-B connector*). If a cable that fits it didn't come with the device, you can buy one at a computer store.

Task

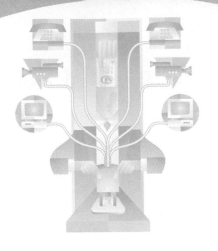

9

Installing a Digital Camera

Digital cameras are quickly replacing the more traditional kind. They enable you to preview pictures before taking them, and after you take the photos, no film is required—all you need is your computer. And if you take a photo you don't like, you don't waste any film—just delete it from your camera and try again.

Your pictures are stored on a memory card of some type in the camera. You can buy more than one card so that you can take more pictures and also a card reader that connects to your PC. If you do that, you'll never have to connect the camera to your computer—you'll only need to put the card into the reader; then you'll be able to transfer pictures to your computer that way.

Upgrade Advisor

All digital cameras are not created alike, and it's very important before buying one that you carefully check its specifications. Unlike hard disks and CD drives, they're not commodity items, so you'll need to do a bit of homework before buying.

The first thing to consider is the resolution of your camera. Camera resolutions are measured in pixels. In general, the more pixels, the better the resolution. And the more pixels, the more expensive the camera and the larger the print you'll be able to make on your printer at a reasonable image quality.

Resolution is measured in megapixels, or one million pixels. There's no reason to buy a camera under 1-megapixel—the quality of images taken with cameras with lower resolutions simply isn't acceptable. If you can afford it, consider cameras with resolutions of 2- or 3-megapixels and above.

Also consider whether you want zoom, and if so, how much zoom you want. But be sure you read the fine print and understand what type of zoom the camera has. You want a true, optical zoom—in other words, the camera lens itself can zoom in. In some instances, a camera does digital zoom, merely by using software, and in that case, you're not getting a true zoom. All you're doing is taking the same picture at the same resolution, so the quality isn't there.

Buy a camera with a USB or FireWire connection. These are faster and easier to install and use than those that connect via a serial cable.

How a Digital Camera Works

5 Image manipulation

The data from the pixels on the CCD passes through a series of camera components that turn the individual pixels into a single image. The image is also compressed so it takes up less memory in the camera.

6 Flash memory

After the image is compressed, it's stored on memory inside the camera. Usually, this memory is a kind called *flash memory*. Even when no batteries are in the camera, or the camera is powered off, flash memory holds the images safely.

1 Shutter and lens

When you hold down the shutter button to take a picture, a metering cell takes a light reading and determines how much light is required for the exposure. It then instructs the shutter to stay open for a specific amount of time. The lens focuses the image, as it does in a traditional camera.

7 **PC transfer**

To manipulate and print the pictures, you must transfer them to a computer. The digital camera attaches to the computer via a cable of some sort, often a USB or serial connection. Even after you transfer the pictures to your computer, they stay on the digital camera until you delete them either using the PC software or using the camera itself. Some printers let you attach camera memory cards to them and print from the cards. In those instances, you don't need to first transfer the pictures to your PC.

4 **Digital conversion**

After the exposure, each pixel's charge is converted into a digital number, corresponding to the amount of light that fell on that particular pixel.

View screen

Digital cameras generally include a view screen that lets you preview your pictures before you take them, and they also let you view the pictures stored on your camera.

2 **Image sensor**

Instead of hitting film, as in a traditional camera, the light hits an image sensor, called a charged-coupling device (CCD). The image sensor is a silicon chip about the size of a fingernail and contains a grid made up of millions of photo-sensitive pixels.

3 **Pixels**

Each site on the CCD captures a single pixel—either red, blue, or green. Where that color light falls on the pixel, it records the color; if the color doesn't fall on the pixel, it remains dark. Each pixel can record only a single, specific color. So, if red light falls on a blue-recording pixel, for example, that pixel doesn't record any data. Each pixel retains a charge that corresponds to the brightness of the light falling on it. So, when a great deal of light falls on a pixel, it has a high charge, and if little light falls on it, it has a low charge.

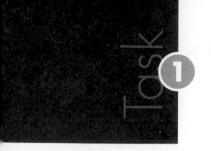
How to Install a Digital Camera

Two major things must be done to install a digital camera. First, you must prepare the camera so it can be used on its own. Second, you must connect the camera to your PC and install software so the camera can transfer pictures to your PC. To prepare the camera, you must install batteries and a storage card, which holds the camera's pictures. Then, you connect the camera to your PC with a cable and install the camera software.

① Install the Batteries

Open the battery compartment and insert the batteries, taking care to line up the positive and negative terminals properly.

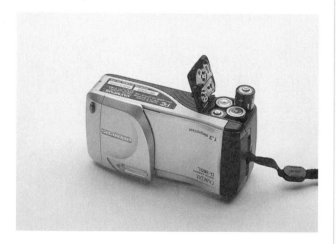

② Insert the Memory Card

Most digital cameras require you to install a small memory card called flash memory or a smart card. This memory card is what holds your pictures. You can even buy additional memory cards and swap them to store more images. Next, insert the memory card into the camera. Some cameras also require that you format the memory card after you've installed it. Follow the camera's directions for how to format the card—each camera does it differently.

③ Turn On the Power

For many digital cameras, to turn on the power, all you need to do is slide open the lens protector on the front of the camera. If your memory card needs to be formatted, you'll usually get an error message telling you a problem exists with the card, so now is the time to format.

④ Connect the Camera

Some cameras connect via a USB cable, whereas others connect via a serial port. Either way, the cables will connect only one way, so don't force them. If you don't have a free USB port on your PC, you can buy a USB hub to give you four USB ports into which you can plug devices. If you don't have a USB port, you can install one in your computer. (To learn how to install USB hubs and ports, refer to Chapter 8, "Installing USB and FireWire Devices.")

⑤ Run the Software

If you're connecting via a USB cable, your computer will recognize that you're adding a digital camera. The Add New Hardware Wizard will appear, or an installation routine will automatically start. Follow the onscreen directions for completing the installation. For serial connections, your computer might not recognize the camera, so you must install the software that came with your camera. Even if you install via USB, however, be sure you install the software for your camera after you follow the installation instructions. In either case, you might have to go through two installation routines: one to install drivers for the camera and one to install software to work with the camera.

⑥ Take Pictures and Transfer Them

After you've installed the camera, unplug it and take pictures, following the camera's instructions. Then, use the camera software you installed to view the pictures on your camera and transfer them to your PC.

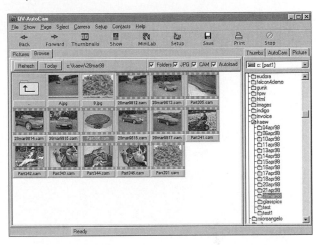

Watch Out!

- Be sure you install the correct type of memory card into your camera. There is more than one standard for memory, so match the proper card to your camera's specifications.

- Keep memory cards away from extreme heat and magnets—both can destroy data.

- Use only the type of batteries specified by the camera manufacturer. Some cameras can be damaged by overheating if you use manganese batteries.

Task

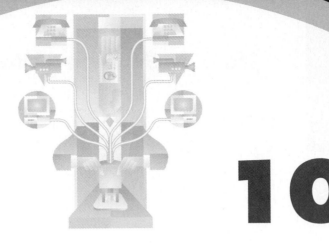

10

Installing a Scanner

Scanners enable you to take images and text from pictures, photographs, paper printouts, books, or other sources and transfer them to your computer. To get the text and images into your computer, you first place the image source, such as paper, on a flatbed scanner, which then scans the image or text from the paper into your PC. This chapter shows you how to install a flatbed scanner; you can install other types of scanners, including handheld and page-fed scanners, the same way as you install flatbed scanners.

In general, scanners attach to a PC via the parallel port, a USB port, a FireWire connection, or a SCSI connection. The SCSI connection transfers text and images to your PC from the scanner at the highest rate of speed, although it is also the most difficult to install. The easiest scanner to install is via the USB port, which transfers data faster than a parallel port scanner.

Upgrade Advisor

A flatbed is the most common type of scanner—with it you lay a photo or sheet of paper on the scanner's surface and scan a single page at a time. If you're using the scanner for text-scanning instead, get a sheetfed scanner or a flatbed scanner with an automatic document feeder. This will let you place many pages at a time into the scanner, and it will scan one page after another automatically.

For scanning in pictures, of primary importance is the quality of the scan. Generally, the more money you pay, the better the quality of the scanned image. The way to compare scanners' quality is by comparing their resolutions and bit depths. Resolution is measured in dots per inch (dpi); all other things being equal, the higher the dpi, the better the image quality. Be careful when comparing dpi between scanners that you compare what's called the *optical* dpi. The optical dpi tells you the actual resolution of what the scanner can see. You might instead be given an interpolated resolution. An *interpolated* resolution is the result of a scanner using software to increase the dpi. But interpolated resolution is not as high quality as optical resolution.

Most scanners you buy will have at least a 600 dpi rating, and it's best not to buy a scanner rated at less than that. For many purposes a 600 dpi rating is adequate. But if you're planning to scan photographs or slides and want very high-quality output, choose a 1200 dpi scanner or better.

The bit depth of a scanner tells you the number of gradients of color the scanner can recognize. A 24-bit depth scanner is more than adequate for most purposes, although if you are scanning photographs or slides and want very high-quality output, you'd be better off with a 36-bit scanner.

How a Scanner Works

Image

The process begins by placing an image face down on a glass window in the scanner. Beneath the glass window is a light source and a scanning mechanism—the scan head.

PC connection

The pixels are sent to the PC via one of a variety of physical connections. Some scanners are connected via the parallel port, others via a USB port, and still others via a SCSI connection. No matter which connection is used, the data is stored on the PC in a digital format. Parallel port scanners have the slowest transfer rates. USB transfer rates are higher than the parallel port but slower than SCSI.

Scan head

As light bounces off the page from the light source, the scan head moves by means of a small motor beneath the glass. As the scan head moves, it captures the light that bounces off the page. The head can read very small portions of the page—less than 1/90,000 of a square inch. If a scanner head goes bad, you must either have it repaired or buy a new scanner. Scanners are generally inexpensive devices, so unless you have an expensive scanner, it's often a good idea to simply buy a new one.

Analog-to-digital converter

A device called an *analog-to-digital converter (ADC)* reads this constantly changing stream of electrical voltage. It converts this analog stream into a series of thousands of digital pixels. Depending on the resolution of the scanner, it creates from 300 to 1,200 pixels per inch. In a color scanner, light is first directed through red, green, or blue filters before hitting the image being scanned. The quality of the ADC is one element in determining the ultimate quality of the scan.

How to Install a Scanner

Scanners attach to your PC in a variety of ways, including via the parallel port, the USB port, and a SCSI connection. Although the actual attachment can vary, the basics of how you install a scanner remain the same. So follow these steps for installing a scanner. For more details on how to install a USB device, refer to Chapter 8, "Installing USB and FireWire Devices." If you want to install a USB scanner but don't have a USB port on your PC, you can add one in. Refer to Chapter 8 to see how.

① Place the Scanner on a Flat Surface

Before doing anything, turn off your PC. Next, put the scanner on a level, flat nearby surface, and make sure it's close enough to your PC so that its cable can reach your computer. If the surface is not level, the quality of the scan can be affected.

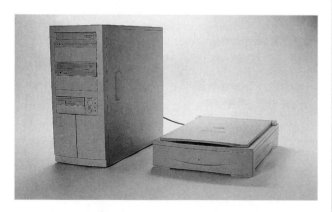

② Plug In the Cable

What you do now depends on how you'll connect the scanner to your PC. If you have a parallel port scanner, unplug the printer's parallel cable from your PC and plug the scanner's parallel cable into your computer, into the port where the printer's cable was attached. If you want to use your printer as well as your scanner, connect the printer to your scanner with cable, and then connect your scanner to your computer. For USB and SCSI scanners, attach them as you would any USB or SCSI device

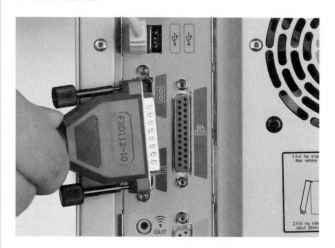

③ Turn On the Scanner

Plug the scanner's power cord into an outlet. When you plug it in, the scanner might turn on by itself. Some scanners need you to turn them on; others don't need to be turned on. If yours has an on/off switch, turn the switch on after you plug in the cord.

4 Turn On Your PC

When you turn on your computer, Windows will know new hardware has been added. If, when you turn on your PC, it doesn't automatically recognize that new hardware has been added, you can tell your computer that new hardware is present. To add the new hardware, first go to the Windows Control Panel by clicking the **Start** button and then selecting **Settings**, **Control Panel**. Double-click **Add New Hardware**. A wizard launches that will guide you through the installation process.

5 Insert the Driver Disk

At some point, the wizard will ask whether you have a disk for your new scanner. If you have one, insert it at the correct time; then select the device's INF file from the disk.

6 Calibrate the Scanner

Most scanners come with extra software you can use for scanning and using scanned images. Check the documentation to see whether yours does. If it does, install the software. For best scanning results, calibrate your scanner before you begin to use it. Check your scanner's documentation for details on how to do that.

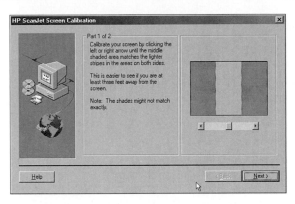

Watch Out!

- Before adding a parallel port scanner to a machine with an existing printer, you should go to the printer vendor's site and update to the latest drivers.

- Check the scanner's documentation to see whether the scanner requires an Enhanced (EPP, SPP, ECP) Parallel Port. If so, you might need to change this option under your CMOS.

- If this is the first USB device you install, be sure your USB ports are enabled in your CMOS.

- If you installed a SCSI controller with your scanner, when you turn on your computer, Windows will first have to install the SCSI controller before installing the scanner.

- If the SCSCI connection doesn't match your existing SCSI connector, buy a SCSI converter that will let you attach it.

Task

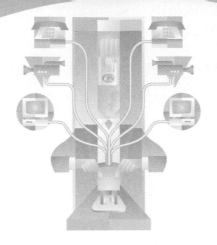

11

Installing a Portable MP3 Player

MP3 players are small, portable devices that can play music recorded in a variety of digital formats, notably in the MP3 format. Although the devices are typically called MP3 players, they often can play music recorded in other formats, such as the Windows Media format (WMA).

You get music to place in an MP3 player in several ways. Digital music can be downloaded from the Internet, or you can insert an audio CD into your computer and convert that music into the MP3 format (or another music format). Converting music to MP3 format from a CD is called *ripping* music from a CD. Many portable MP3 players come with software that will rip music in this way. Ripping software is also widely available on the Internet. Once the music is on your PC, you transfer it to an MP3 player via a USB cable and software that comes with the MP3 player.

The music is commonly stored in flash memory on the MP3 player, although other types of storage are available as well. MP3 players usually come with at least 64MB, and sometimes more memory, and can be expanded by adding flash memory cards to a special slot in the MP3 player. And some MP3 players now come with hard disks of several gigabytes so that hundreds of songs can be stored on them.

Upgrade Advisor

One of the most important features of an MP3 player is rarely, if ever, advertised, yet it's the entire point of the device: The quality of the sound. It's not true that all MP3 players sound alike; some feature a better sound than others. So when buying an MP3 player, test the sounds of several before buying.

Sometimes, the difference in the quality of the sound is because of the headphones. Better headphones can add to the cost of an MP3 player, and considering that most manufacturers try to advertise a lower price, you'll find that sometimes they skimp on the quality of the headphones.

Another excellent upgrade to your MP3 player is an addition that lets you play it through your car's stereo system. Typically, one end of these is shaped like an audio cassette and slips into your car's cassette system, and the other end fits into the headphone jack. For those who travel often by car and always want their customized music, it's a great, inexpensive upgrade.

How an MP3 Player Works

CD ripping

Music has to be in a digital music format such as MP3 for it to be transferred to a portable MP3 player and played. One way of getting music into MP3 format is to *rip* it from a CD—use software to convert it to an MP3 format. This kind of software generally comes with the MP3 player, or can be downloaded from the Internet.

Playlists

To transfer music from your PC to the MP3 player, you use software that comes with the MP3 player to create playlists. A playlist is a group of MP3 files, put in the order in which you want to listen to them.

Downloading music

Another way to transfer music to an MP3 player is by downloading MP3 files from the Internet. File-sharing software such as Kazaa can be used to locate and download MP3 files.

USB cable

To transfer files from a PC to an MP3 player, MP3 players use a USB connection. A USB cable connects the USB port on the PC to the USB port on the MP3 player. MP3 files are sent over the cable from the PC to the MP3 player, using software that comes with the MP3 player or software downloaded from the Internet.

Music processing

Inside the MP3 player, a variety of processors, controllers, and other devices converts the digital data in the MP3 file into analog data—music the human ear can understand.

Flash memory

MP3 files are stored in flash memory chips in the MP3 player. Anything stored in flash memory chips stays stored on them, even when the MP3 player is off—similar to a computer's hard drive. Many MP3 players have an empty slot into which a flash memory card can be installed, as a way to increase the amount of music that can be stored and played from the MP3 player.

How to Install an MP3 Player

Installing an MP3 player is easy. Whereas older players sometimes require you to connect them to your computer via a serial port to copy MP3 files to them, the newer ones all connect via a USB port. To install the player, you install software, connect the USB cables, and then install drivers. After the player is installed, you transfer files to the player via the USB port and delete files from the player that way, as well.

❶ Install the Software

You transfer files to your MP3 player and delete files from the player by using software you install on your PC. Before connecting the MP3 player, install the software that came with the MP3 player. You also can use jukebox software to do this, such as Real JukeBox or MusicMatch JukeBox. Both are available for free from download sites on the Internet.

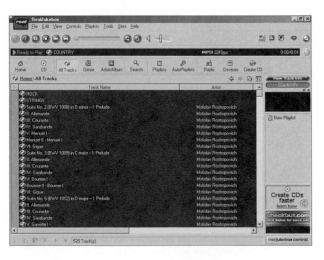

❷ Turn On the MP3 Player

Look for the switch—sometimes it's a very small one. And remember to first install a battery. MP3 players typically run on batteries—usually AA batteries. They often need only one.

❸ Connect the MP3 USB Cable

The MP3 player comes with a USB cable that may look different than most common USB cables. It's called a mini-B. One end is small and designed to fit into a special port on the MP3 player. Find the port and plug in the cable.

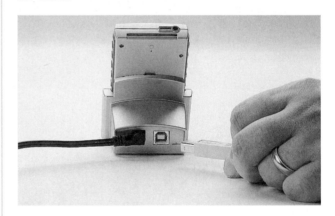

④ Connect the USB Cable to the PC

The other end of the USB cable is rectangular and designed to plug into a PC. The USB cable connects only one way, so don't force it. If you don't have a free USB port on your PC, you can buy a USB hub that will give you four USB ports into which you can plug devices. If you don't have a USB port, you can install one in your computer. (To learn how to install USB hubs and ports, refer to Chapter 8, "Installing USB and FireWire Devices.")

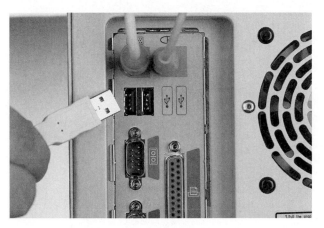

⑤ Follow Any Installation Instructions

When you plug in the USB cables, your computer will recognize that you're adding an MP3 player. The Add New Hardware Wizard will appear, or an installation routine will automatically start. Follow the onscreen directions for completing the installation.

⑥ Run the Jukebox Software

Now that your MP3 player is installed, you should transfer MP3 files to it so you can listen to them. To transfer the MP3 files, when your MP3 player is connected to your PC, run the software that came with the player—or use other software you can download from the Internet—and transfer music files to the MP3 player. JukeBox software also can be used to convert music from audio CDs into MP3 files.

Watch Out!
- Some tof the MP3 files you can get from the Internet might violate copyright laws because the recording artists haven't agreed to have those files posted online.

How-to Hint
- If you notice that MP3 files "skip" or are in some other way distorted, it might be that the CDs from which you're recording have small scratches or dirt on their undersides. Wipe the bottom sides of CDs with a soft cloth before converting them—that might solve the problem.

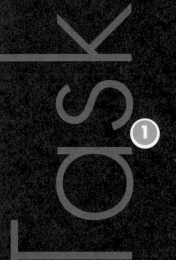

Task

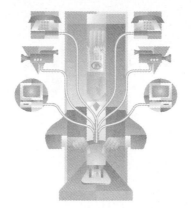

12

Installing a Video Capture Card

Your computer is a key ingredient in your digital video-editing suite. It must be fast enough, with just the right hardware to process video without dropping frames or garbling audio. A few years ago, that was a tall order, but today almost any modern PC is ready to rock.

The video capture card—called IEEE1394 or FireWire—connects the PC to your digital camcorder and lets you copy the video from the tape to your hard drive. After the video is on the computer, you can edit your movie and then send it back to tape (through the FireWire card, of course) so that you can give copies of your masterpiece to friends, family, co-workers, and so on.

How to Install a Video Capture Card

If you were lucky enough to buy a video-ready multimedia PC, your computer might already be poised to begin importing video clips from a camcorder. If not, you'll have to install a video capture card. I recommend that you get a FireWire card (also called an IEEE1394 card) to go with a DV camcorder. An analog video capture card will work too, but at a lower overall video resolution. Regardless of the kind of card you choose, it takes only a screwdriver and a few minutes to install it.

Close up the PC—you're ready to edit video!

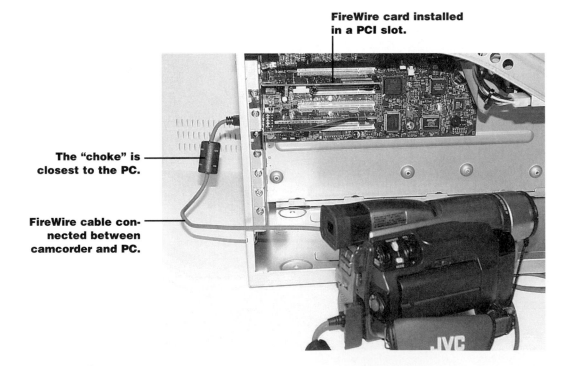

FireWire card installed in a PCI slot.

The "choke" is closest to the PC.

FireWire cable connected between camcorder and PC.

① Open Your PC

Start by opening your PC, usually by removing several screws from the back. Remember to ground yourself (touch some other grounded metal object) before you touch anything inside the computer.

② Slip the Card in Place

Find an empty PCI slot in the computer and unscrew the plate from the back of the computer (retain the screw). Take the card out of its anti-static bag and press it into the empty slot. It might help to rock the card back and forth to get it in place. Be firm, but don't press so hard that the card bends and cracks. Use the plate screw to screw the card in place.

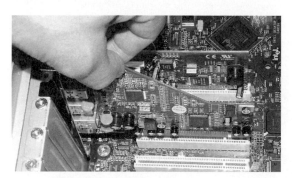

③ Attach the Cables

If you're installing a FireWire card, all you have to do is attach a single FireWire cable to the card (the other end plugs into your DV camcorder). If you've installed a traditional analog capture card, you'll have to plug in a video cable and audio cables as well.

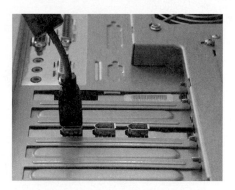

④ Install the Software

Follow the directions that came with the card to install the software. There will be a driver that tells your PC about the card, as well as video editing software. You can use that editing software or another package, such as VideoWave or Premiere, as long as the card and the software are compatible. After the driver is installed, you'll see the capture card in your PC's System Properties dialog box.

How-to Hint

Choosing a Video Card

A video capture card is essential to the video editing process because the card is what lets you import video from your camcorder to the PC. Most capture devices are internal models that slip into a PCI slot, but there are also USB models around that are completely external—a real convenience. Remember, though, that video capture hardware is finicky. Make sure that your capture card is certified to work with the software you plan to use (such as VideoWave or Premiere) before you buy and install it. Adobe, for instance, lists compatible FireWire cards at **www.adobe.com/premiere**.

Task

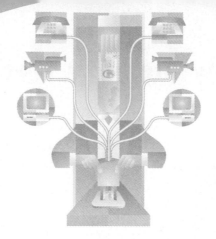

13

Adding Memory to Your PC

One of the easiest and cheapest ways to make your computer run faster is to upgrade it by adding more memory, called random access memory (RAM). If your PC seems sluggish, especially when you run several applications at once, you might be in need of a memory upgrade. When your computer doesn't have enough memory, it can't hold all your programs and data in RAM, so it has to take some of those programs and data and put them temporarily on your hard disk. Your hard disk is much slower than RAM, causing your computer to work sluggishly. If your computer is constantly reading from your hard disk, you might be in line for a RAM upgrade. RAM doesn't cost very much these days and is getting less expensive all the time. It's one of the least expensive and most effective ways to upgrade your PC.

Upgrade Advisor

How much memory do you need to buy for your PC? The short answer is as much as you can afford. However, there are certain basic RAM requirements to keep in mind when upgrading your system. In general, newer versions of Windows need more RAM than older versions. So if you have Windows 95, for example, you can get by with 16MB of RAM, but with Windows 98, you'd be better off with at least 64MB. If you run many programs simultaneously or use RAM-hungry applications such as graphics and multimedia programs, you might need even more. So to be as safe as possible, buy more RAM than you think you need. Given the low prices of RAM, it'll still be a bargain, even if you buy more than you really need.

How Memory Works

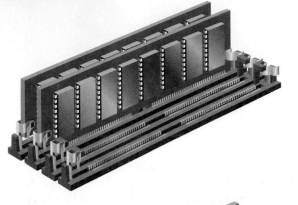

RAM (random access memory)

Memory is put on your computer using RAM chips placed into special slots or sockets. When your computer is turned off, RAM is empty—unlike a hard disk, it can't store data unless the RAM is powered by electricity. Generally, the more RAM you have, the faster your computer runs because RAM is much faster than a hard disk. If you don't have enough RAM, your computer has to read data from your hard disk frequently, slowing things down. But if you have enough RAM, the data you need is often stored in RAM, which can be accessed much faster than a hard disk can, so your computer is speeded up.

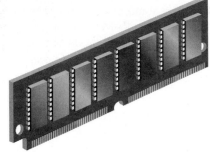

Single inline memory modules

SIMMs (Single inline memory modules) plug into long, matching sockets on your motherboard. They're an older form of memory and work only with older computers. Typically, a motherboard has several banks of SIMM sockets into which you plug SIMMs. SIMMs come in 30-pin and 72-pin formats. Generally, 30-pin SIMMs are outdated because they have little memory capacity, often 256K, 1MB, 2MB, and 4MB. 72-pin SIMMs have more capacity and come in 1MB, 2MB, 4MB, 8MB, 16MB, and 32MB.

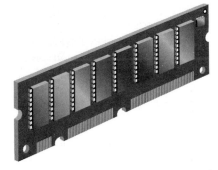

DIMMs

DIMMs (dual inline memory modules) look much like SIMMs, but they come in 168-pin and 184-pin formats. They are a faster and higher-performance memory than SIMMs. They have much higher capacities than do SIMMs.

RIMMs

Rambus inline memory modules (RIMMs) look like DIMMs and SIMMs but are even larger and come in a 184-pin format. They are a higher-speed memory than SIMMs and DIMMs.

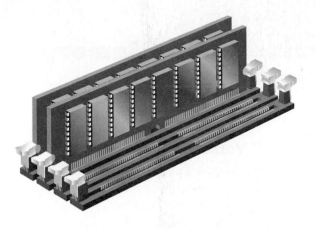

Socket

RAM modules connect to the motherboard via a socket. The socket will be different according to the type of RAM the motherboard requires. The most common type of socket is a DIMM socket, which has a locking tab at either end to secure the module into the socket.

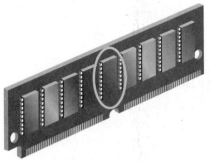

ECC Versus Non-ECC

A SIMM or DIMM may use techniques called parity or error-correcting code (ECC) to make sure that there are no memory errors. In the vast majority of instances, your memory will not use parity or ECC—those techniques are usually reserved for expensive, high-end computers called *servers*. However, to make sure, check your PC or motherboard's manual to see which kind of memory your PC requires.

Speed

The faster the memory, the faster data can be shuttled between RAM and the CPU, and the faster a computer operates. Memory comes rated at different speeds, and the faster the memory, the more it costs. Memory speed is often measured in nanoseconds, and the lower the nanosecond rating, the faster the memory. For example, a 2.5-nanosecond chip is faster than an 8-nanosecond chip. Be sure that the memory you buy is as fast as the memory you're replacing.

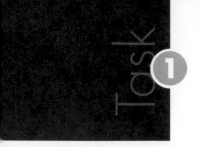
How to Determine What Memory You Need

The most difficult parts of upgrading your computer's memory are figuring out the specific kind of memory you need and knowing how much memory you can add in what configuration. The best way to answer these questions will be in your owner's manual. Here's what you need to know.

1 Determine How Much Memory You Have

You can see how much memory you have in several ways. When you first start your computer, you see information flash by on the bootup screen, including how much memory you have. In Windows, however, there's an even easier way. Right-click the **My Computer** icon and select **Properties**. The screen shows how much memory you have. In some cases, however, this screen might not accurately report your memory, so it's safer to look at the information in the bootup screen.

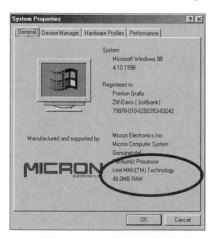

2 ECC Versus Non-ECC

Some computers require parity memory or ECC memory. Check your system's documentation or motherboard manual (or head to the manufacturer's Web site or call technical support) to see whether yours requires parity memory, nonparity memory, ECC memory, or non-ECC memory.

3 Determine the Connector Type

Check your system documentation to see how your memory connects to the motherboard. Alternatively, open the computer case and look. Look inside at the memory chips and see what kind of memory is in the bank. SIMMs have either 30 or 72 pins. DIMMs are larger and usually have 168 pins. RIMMs are also larger and have 184 pins, as do DDR DIMMs. If you're adding memory to a notebook computer, you might have SO-DIMMs, which have 72 pins or 144 pins, or SO-RIMMs, which have 160 pins. To be absolutely sure about what kind of memory you need, check your computer or motherboard documentation.

SIMM   DIMM   RIMM

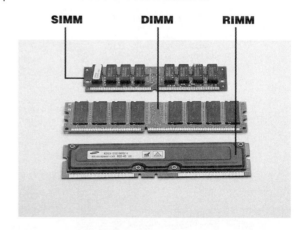

④ Determine the Memory Type

Several different standards for memory exist. Newer systems can have Rambus Dynamic RAM (RDRAM) or Double Data RAM (DDR), while older systems might use Extended Data Out RAM (EDO RAM) or Synchronous Data RAM (SDRAM). Check your computer or motherboard documentation to see what kind you need.

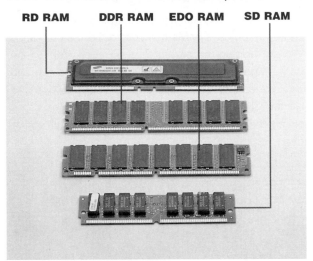

RD RAM   DDR RAM   EDO RAM   SD RAM

⑤ Determine the Memory Speed

Get memory at least as fast as the memory in your PC. Check your system documentation or call technical support to find out how fast the memory in your PC is.

⑥ Determine the Configuration

Your computer has a set of memory slots, and the motherboard can handle a maximum amount of memory. To find out the maximum amount, check the manual or the manufacturer's Web site, or call technical support. Some computers can handle memory modules only in certain configurations, so you might have to throw away your existing memory and buy all new memory. Also, some memory requires that you add memory modules in pairs rather than singly. Check your computer or motherboard documentation for details.

⑦ Determine If You Need Proprietary Memory

Although many computers accept memory chips from a variety of manufacturers, some computers accept memory only from the manufacturer of the computer. If that's the case, you have to buy the memory from the manufacturer. Proprietary memory typically costs more than other types of memory.

Watch Out!

- You can use memory with parity chips on a computer that doesn't require parity chips. Memory without parity chips, however, won't work on a computer that requires them.
- Combining different types of memory modules on the same motherboard will not work, so make sure to buy all of the same type.

How to Add or Replace Memory

After you've figured out the type of memory and the configuration of RAM chips you need to put in your computer, the hardest work is done. But you still have to open the case, take out the old memory, and put in the new. Here's how to do the final steps in a memory upgrade. Before you begin, turn off your PC and open the case as outlined in Task 5, "How to Open the Case," in Chapter 7, "Performing Computer Maintenance." You won't need any special tools to add or replace memory. It should take you under an hour to do the job.

❶ Locate the Memory Sockets

Memory sockets are long sockets with some or all the sockets occupied by memory modules.

❷ Remove Existing SIMMs

To upgrade SIMM memory, you might have to remove existing modules. SIMMs hold on to the memory slots by metal holders or plastic tabs on each side of the SIMM. A good way to remove the SIMM is to use two small flathead screwdrivers to press the tabs outward until the SIMM is released. If instead metal tabs are holding the SIMM, you can still use the small screwdrivers, although it is often easier to use your thumbnails.

❸ Install the SIMM Modules

Locate the notch on the SIMM; it enables memory to be installed in only one way. Match up the notch to the module. You usually tilt the SIMM at a 45° angle, push gently until it goes into the slot, and then tilt it upward to an upright position. Often you hear a small click as it fits into place. For other SIMMs, press them straight in first, and then down at an angle. The bottom of the SIMM should completely fit into the slot and should be perfectly level before pulling or pushing the SIMM upward from the 45° angle.

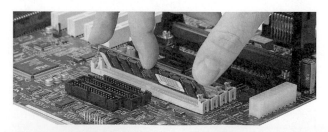

4 Remove the DIMMs or RIMMs

To upgrade DIMM memory or RIMM memory, you might have to remove existing modules. DIMMs generally are easier to remove than SIMMs. DIMMs have tabs on each side, often made of plastic. Push down on these tabs at the same time, and the tabs push the DIMM out of its socket. RIMM modules are removed similarly, except in some instances, in which a RIMM module might have a terminator that attaches to the motherboard to fill empty RIMM slots. If it does, remove the terminator (also known as a continuity module).

5 Install the DIMMs and RIMMs

DIMMs have two notches on the bottom that match the DIMM socket. Align the slots properly with the socket. Press down evenly across the top of the DIMM until the tabs on each side of the DIMM slip up into place. DIMM memory is removed similarly, except that in some instances with RIMMs you will have to attach a terminator to the motherboard. Check your documentation.

6 Turn On the Computer

Your computer might automatically boot into the CMOS screen, and the BIOS will automatically recognize the new memory. You have to exit the CMOS screen for the settings to take effect, and your computer might then reboot. If, when you first turn on your PC, you get an error message, bring up the CMOS screen, and the BIOS will automatically recognize the new memory. Exit the screen and save the CMOS settings for them to take effect.

Task

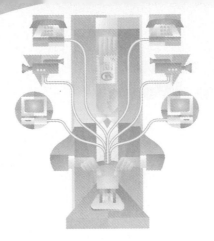

14

Adding or Replacing a Hard Drive

To a certain extent, your hard drive *is* your computer. It's where you store all your data, all your files, and all your programs.

You might need to add or replace a hard drive for many reasons. You might be running out of hard drive space, or the hard drive might be continually reporting errors, which might mean it's time for a replacement. Or you might simply want a new hard drive that's faster and holds more data than your current one. You have the option of either replacing your existing hard drive or adding a second one. The main hard disk on your system, from which your system boots, is called the *master*. A second hard drive is called a *slave*.

A hard drive can connect to the rest of your computer in several ways, notably via an ATA connection (also known as an IDE or IDE/EIDE connection) or a SCSI connection. The most common kind of connection is via ATA, and that's what this chapter covers.

Upgrade Advisor

When getting a new hard drive, a simple rule to follow is that bigger and faster is better. It's not uncommon for hard disks today to be 40GB, 60GB, 80GB, and up. Buy as large as you can afford because another rule about hard disk storage is that you fill up hard disks faster than you think you will. If you use graphics or video or store MP3s on your hard disk, you'll find that space goes very quickly, and you should consider getting an 80GB drive or more. If you use primarily word processing and similar files, you can get by with a 40GB or 60GB drive.

When measuring speed, manufacturers might tout two specs: average seek time and transfer rate. The average seek time measures the average time it takes to move the heads on a hard disk cylinder from one spot to another. It's measured in milliseconds (ms), and the smaller the number, the better. A very fast hard drive will have an average seek time of 4ms–5ms. Transfer rate measures how much data can be transferred from a hard disk in a second. The problem with this measurement is that for a single hard drive, depending on what you are measuring, there can be many different transfer rates. For a single drive, for example, these can range from 30MB per second to 100MB per second.

How a Hard Drive Works

Ribbon cable

The controller sends and receives information to and from the hard drive via a 40-pin, 40-wire ribbon cable, or a 40-pin, 80-wire cable. (In an 80-wire cable, 40 of the wires are ground wires.) A connector at each end of the cable plugs into the hard drive and into the controller. Some ribbons are marked with a different color to indicate the first pin. Knowing this makes connecting them easier. The connectors are also keyed so that improper connections can't be made.

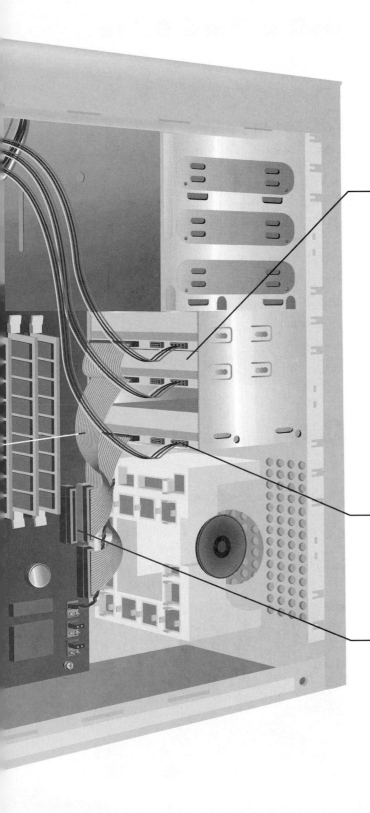

Hard drive

The hard drive, inside its sealed metal housing, fits into a drive bay on a computer. Magnetized platters in the hard drive store the data and spin at high speeds—up to 15,000 revolutions per minute. As a general rule, the faster the rotation speeds, the faster the hard disk. Read/write heads move across the spinning platter to retrieve and store information. The space between the read/write heads and the spinning platters is minute so that data can be read accurately—typically less than the width of a human hair, at 2/100,000 of an inch. Several standards exist for ATA drives, including ATA/33, ATA/66, and ATA/100. The higher the number, the faster the hard disk, so an ATA/100 hard disk is faster than an ATA/33 hard disk.

Power connection

The hard drive gets its power from the power supply. It connects to the power supply by a cable and a universal connector that plugs into the hard drive.

Controller

A controller sends instructions back and forth between your PC and the hard drive, sending information to be stored or asking for information to be retrieved. Sometimes the controller is on a separate board, although usually it is on the motherboard itself. Several kinds of controllers exist, most notably ATA (also known as IDE) and SCSI. A hard drive with a SCSI controller is usually faster than one with an ATA controller, although SCSI controllers and hard drives are more difficult to install.

How to Install a Hard Drive

In most cases, when you put a new hard drive in your PC, you're going to keep your existing hard drive. If you're replacing a hard drive, first remove your hard drive. Turn to Task 8, "How to Remove an Old Drive," in Chapter 7, "Performing Computer Maintenance," and follow the instructions on how to remove an existing drive. Because you'll be copying data from your old hard drive to your new one, turn to Task 4, "How to Prepare for Your Upgrade" (also in Chapter 7) to learn how to back up a hard drive. To begin, you will need to turn off your PC and remove the case. See Task 5, "How to Open the Case," in Chapter 7 and follow the instructions for removing the case.

1 Find a Free Bay

To install a hard drive, you need a free drive bay. After you remove your computer's case, take a look inside and see which drive bay you have free. Drives come in 3 1/2'' and 5 1/4'' sizes, so be sure your bay accommodates the drive you buy. Most often, you'll have a 3 1/2'' drive. You can fit a 3 1/2'' hard drive into a 5 1/4'' bay by getting a special adapter kit, but a 5 1/4'' hard drive won't fit into a 3 1/2'' bay.

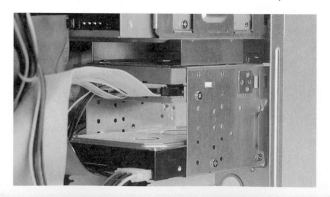

2 Set Jumpers

In some instances, before you install the drive you will have to set its jumpers. You can make your new hard drive either a master or slave. Check the drive documentation to see whether you need to set jumpers, and if so, how to set them.

3 Slide In and Secure the Drive

Slide the drive into the drive bay, and screw it into the drive bay or railings. Secure all the screws so that the drive is held firmly in place, but don't overtighten or strip the screws. Some hard drives are mounted inside bays via mounting rails or adapter kits. Install the mounting rails or adapter kit before sliding in the drive. Also, make sure a free data cable and power cable to which you'll attach the drive are present.

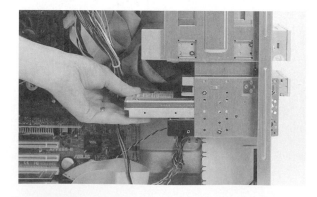

④ Connect the Data Cable

The data cable, a wide ribbon cable, runs from your motherboard to your hard drive. If there is no free connector on the cable, you have to buy a new one. In either event, connect the ribbon cable connector to the slot on the hard drive. The ribbon cable has a stripe on one side of it, indicating that that side of the cable plugs into pin 1 on the hard drive connector—the pin closest to the power supply connector.

⑤ Connect the Power Supply

Your hard drive needs power to work, so you must connect it to your power supply. The power supply cable has a connector on the end of it, which is usually four sockets encased in a small sheath of white plastic. Plug that into the connector on your hard drive. Then, close the case and restart your PC.

⑥ Set CMOS and Format the Disk

Before you can use your hard drive, you have to tell your computer about it by using the CMOS setup screen to change the BIOS settings. You must also format the hard drive so your computer can use it. For information about changing BIOS settings and formatting your hard drive, turn to the section "How to Format and Partition a Hard Drive" later in this chapter.

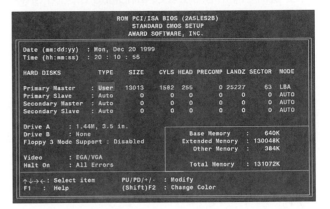

Watch Out!

- You won't be able to use your new hard drive until you change the CMOS settings, partition it, and format it, as seen in the next spread.
- If you're installing a second hard drive and both are attached to the same interface, double-check that you've set the jumper settings on the drives properly so that one is the master and the other is the slave.

How-to Hint

- Be sure to have a spare connector on your ribbon cable to attach to the new hard drive.
- If you have more than four devices attached to your controller, you might need to get a new one.
- Make sure to use rails or an adapter kit if your new hard drive doesn't fit in your drive bay.

How to Format and Partition a Hard Drive

Physically installing your hard drive is only the first part of the process of installing a hard drive. After you've made the proper physical connections, you have to tell your computer to recognize the hard drive, partition it (divide it into pieces), and finally format it so that it can be used.

If your computer or new hard disk comes with special software, use it and skip this section. Check the documentation closely for details.

❶ Run CMOS Setup

Press whatever key you need to for entering CMOS information. Often, your new hard drive will be automatically recognized and you won't have to do anything more to the BIOS. If it is not recognized, you have to select the hard drive in the CMOS setup screen and then enter information about the hard drive's cylinder, heads, and sectors.

```
                    ROM PCI/ISA BIOS (2A5LES2B)
                        STANDARD CMOS SETUP
                        AWARD SOFTWARE, INC.

 Date (mm:dd:yy)  : Mon, Dec 20 1999
 Time (hh:mm:ss)  : 20 : 10 : 56

 HARD DISKS          TYPE   SIZE   CYLS HEAD PRECOMP LANDZ SECTOR  MODE

 Primary Master   : User   13013  1582  255       0 25227     63  LBA
 Primary Slave    : Auto       0     0    0       0     0      0  AUTO
 Secondary Master : Auto       0     0    0       0     0      0  AUTO
 Secondary Slave  : Auto       0     0    0       0     0      0  AUTO

 Drive A   : 1.44M, 3.5 in.
 Drive B   : None
 Floppy 3 Mode Support : Disabled        Base Memory     :    640K
                                         Extended Memory : 130048K
 Video     : EGA/VGA                     Other Memory    :    384K
 Halt On   : All Errors                  Total Memory    : 131072K

 ↑↓→←: Select item         PU/PD/+/-  : Modify
 F1  : Help                (Shift)F2  : Change Color
```

❷ Boot from a Boot Disk

When you exit the CMOS setup screen, the computer should restart if you're replacing your hard drive. Put in a boot disk (it can be a floppy or a CD) that you've prepared before it restarts. If you are using Windows 95, you see a prompt that looks like this: `A:\>`. If you're using a later version of Windows, you get a startup menu asking you if you want to start the computer with or without CD-ROM support. Select **CD-ROM Support**. In Windows 98, a RAM drive will be created. Write down the letter of the RAM drive; you'll need it later.

❸ Partition Your Hard Drive

You can have a single partition, or you can divide your disk into separate drives. To partition your hard drive, type `FDISK` at the DOS prompt and follow the instructions. If you're replacing your old hard drive with a new one, be sure to select **Create DOS Partition** and then **Create Primary DOS Partition**. If you're adding a second hard drive instead of replacing your old one, you see the option **Change Current Fixed Disk Drive**. Select that, and then choose to create a Logical DOS partition to make your new drive D: (or E:, if you already have a D: drive). If you're partitioning your C: drive into several partitions, you *must* set the primary partition to **Active**.

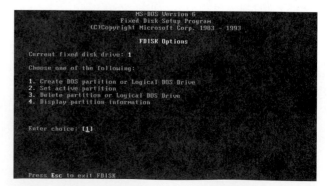

④ Format Your Hard Drive

If you're replacing an old hard drive with a new one, you need to restart your computer, so leave in your boot floppy. After it reboots, type `Format C: /S` at the DOS prompt to format your new hard drive and put the DOS operating system onto it. With Windows 98, the operating system files copy to your new hard drive from the RAM drive that Windows 98 previously created. Assuming that the RAM drive was letter *D*, type the following to format your hard drive and put basic operating system files onto it: `D:\Format C: /S`. If you're not replacing your old hard drive from the DOS prompt, type `Format D:` (or whatever letter your new drive will be). If you've created separate partitions instead of just one, format each of them in turn.

⑤ Reinstall Your Operating System

If you're replacing an old hard drive with a new one, you have to reinstall your operating system. To do that, use your Windows disks or CD to reinstall Windows onto your new hard drive. If you're not replacing your old hard drive and are only adding a second one, you won't need to put the operating system on it.

⑥ Copy Backed-Up Data and Files

After you've confirmed that the hard drive is working properly, copy all the data and files you've previously backed up to your new hard drive. Make sure you've first backed up your hard disk. For information about how to back up your hard disk, turn to Task 4 in Chapter 7.

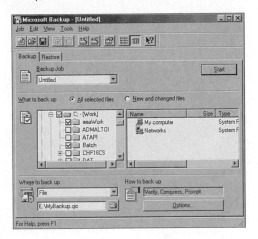

Watch Out!

- If you're replacing your old hard drive, when you format your new hard drive, be sure to use the `/S` parameter, which will add system files to the new hard drive so that it's bootable.

15

Installing New Software and Hardware

If your computer is connected to your company's network, a network administrator is probably responsible for adding and removing hardware and software on your computer and for keeping Windows up-to-date. If so, you should take advantage of her expertise. However, with Windows XP, adding components to your system has never been easier. If you are administering your own computer or network, this part shows how to install your own hardware and software and how to update Windows XP. This part also covers the installation of Windows XP Service Pack 1 and shows the major changes this service pack makes to your system.

How to Add a Program to Your Computer

Programs are the reason you use your computer. Almost all new programs today come on CD-ROM. When you insert the CD-ROM into your drive, Windows should automatically run the setup program for you. If this is the case, you won't need to follow the procedure in this task. If the setup process does not start automatically, or if your program is on floppy disk, the following steps show you how to start the installation yourself. If you download a program from the Internet, the setup process is much the same. You'll just have to tell Windows where the files are located. If the program is compressed (such as in a ZIP file), you'll have to expand it before installing.

① Open the Control Panel

Click the **Start** button and choose **Control Panel**. The Control Panel window opens.

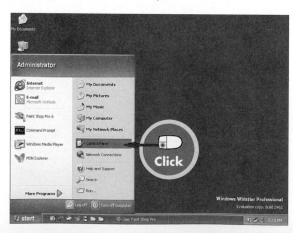

② Open Add/Remove Programs

Double-click the **Add or Remove Programs** icon to open it.

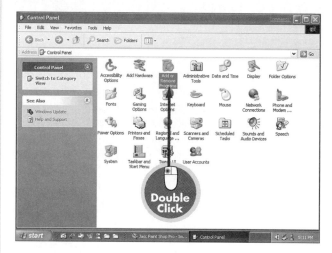

③ Add New Programs

Click the **Add New Programs** button to install a new program.

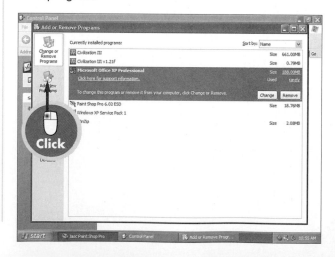

Choose CD or Floppy

If programs are available for installation on your network, they are shown in the window. Click the **CD or Floppy** button to install a program from disk. Click **Next** to skip the initial welcome page of the wizard that appears.

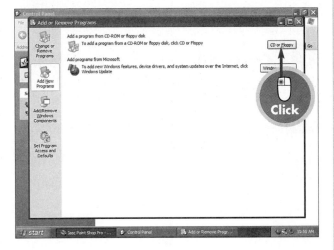

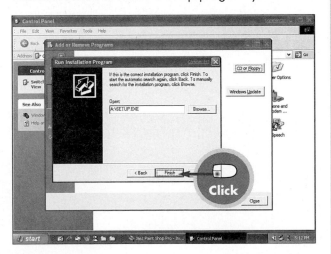 **Finish**

Windows searches both your floppy and CD-ROM drives for a setup program. If it finds one, the path to the program is displayed for your approval. If you think Windows found the right one, click the **Finish** button to launch the setup program. You can also click the **Browse** button to locate a setup program yourself.

Installing from the My Computer Window

You can also run a setup program manually without using the Add/Remove Programs applet. Just open the My Computer window and locate the setup program yourself on the floppy or CD-ROM drive. It is almost always a program named `setup.exe`. If it is not named `setup.exe`, it will be another program with the `.exe` extension. If you can't figure out which program is used to start the installation, check whether the folder has a text file that explains the installation process (this file is often named `readme.txt` or `setup.txt`). When you determine the setup program, double-click it to start.

The Program Files Folder

Your `c:` drive has a folder on it named Program Files. Most new programs that you install create a folder for themselves inside this folder that is used to store the program's files.

Restarting

Different programs have different installation routines. Some require that you restart your computer after the program has been installed. This is one reason why it is best to save any work and exit any running programs before you install new software.

How to Change or Remove a Program

Some programs, such as Microsoft Office, let you customize the installation of the program to include only the components that you want in the installation. You can then add new components later if you want. The Add/Remove Programs applet lets you change the installation of a program, and it lets you remove the installation altogether (a process sometimes called uninstalling a program).

1 Open the Control Panel

Select the **Start** button and then choose **Control Panel**. The Control Panel window opens.

2 Open Add/Remove Programs

Double-click the **Add or Remove Programs** icon to open it.

③ Select a Program

Choose a program from the list of currently installed programs by clicking it once. Notice that Windows lets you know how much disk space each program takes up and how often you use the program.

④ Click Change/Remove

Programs that do not let you change the installation show only a **Change/Remove** button. Programs that do let you change the installation show both a Change button and a Remove button. Click whatever button provides the action you want.

⑤ Follow the Program's Instructions

Every program has a slightly different routine for changing or removing the installation. Follow the onscreen instructions for the program you are using.

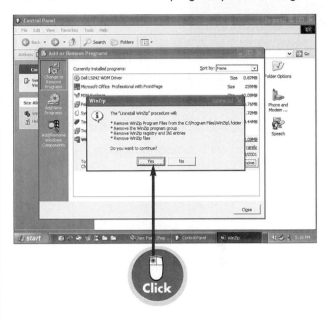

How-to Hint

Be Careful

Some programs automatically go forward with a removal without giving you a chance to confirm as soon as you click the Change/Remove or Remove button. Be sure you want to remove a program before clicking either of these buttons.

How to Add Windows Components from the CD

Windows XP comes with literally hundreds of components—and not all of them are installed during a normal installation of the operating system. You can add components from the Windows XP CD-ROM at any time after installation.

1 Open the Control Panel

Click the **Start** button and then choose **Control Panel**. The Control Panel window opens.

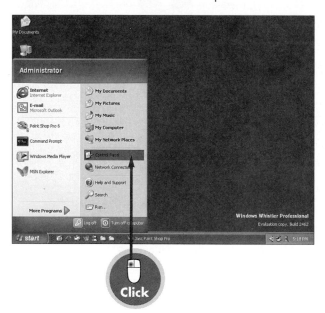

2 Open Add/Remove Programs

Double-click the **Add or Remove Programs** icon to open it.

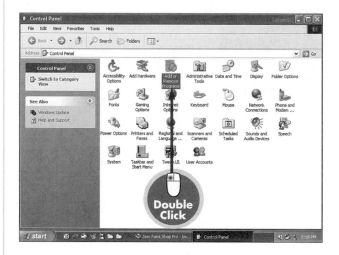

3 Choose Add/Remove Windows Components

Click the **Add/Remove Windows Components** button to display a list of the components you can install from the original Windows installation CD-ROM.

④ Select a Component

Select a component from the list of available components by enabling the check box next to it. Some components have subcomponents that you can choose from. If so, the Details button becomes active, and you can click it to see a list of subcomponents to choose from.

⑤ Next

After you have selected all the components you want to install, click the **Next** button. Windows builds a list of files that must be installed and copies them to your drive. Windows might prompt you to insert your Windows CD-ROM during this process.

⑥ Finish

After Windows has installed the components, it lets you know that the process has been completed successfully. Click the **Finish** button to finish. Depending on the components you added, Windows might need to restart your computer.

How-to Hint

Installing Windows

Many components are installed when you initially set up Windows. When you finish installing Windows, you should always check the installed components using the procedure described in this task to see what goodies you might be missing.

How to Add Windows Components from the Internet

Microsoft maintains a Web site named Windows Update that contains the newest versions of Windows components that you can download and add to your system. These components are updated versions of the components that come with Windows as well as new components and updates that Microsoft makes available. If, for some reason, the shortcut to the Windows update site does not work, you can also get there using the address `http://windowsupdate.microsoft.com/`.

1 Start Windows Update

Click the **Start** button, point to **More Programs**, and select **Windows Update**. This command launches the Windows Update Web site in Internet Explorer.

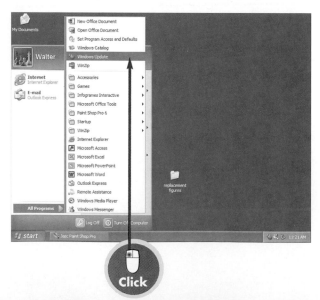

2 Scan for Updates

Click the **Scan for Updates** link. The Windows Update site seaches for components that you can download.

Automatic Updating

Windows can automatically download and install updates when it detects that they are available—provided that you have Internet access. Turn on this feature by opening the **System Control Panel** applet (open the **Control Panel** window and double-click the **System** icon) and switching to the **Automatic Updates** tab. You can have Windows download updates and install them automatically, notify you when updates are available so that you can choose the update time, or disable the service. When automatic updating is active, an icon appears in the system tray to let you know the status.

③ Review and Install Updates

Critical updates (bug fixes and security patches) are automatically selected for download. If that's all you want, click the **Review and Install Critical Updates** link. Additional non-critical updates are available in the Windows Update section on the left. Click the **Review and Install Critical Updates** link when you are ready to continue.

④ Choose Components to Update

Scroll down the Update Basket window to review the list of updates selected for download. Click the **Remove** button next to any update to remove it from the download list.

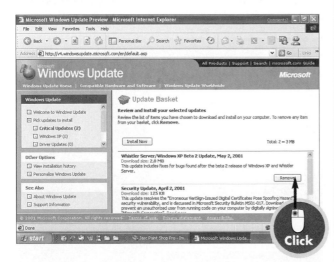

⑤ Install the Updates

When you are satisfied with the list of updates, click the **Install Now** button to download *and* install the components.

⑥ Accept the Licensing Agreement

Before you can download the updates, you must accept the Microsoft licensing agreement. Click **Accept** to continue. The files are then downloaded and installed to your computer. Windows will let you know when the process is finished and whether you have to restart your computer.

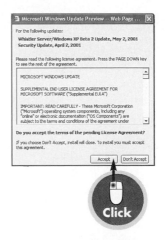

How to Find Out About Your Installed Hardware

Windows uses a tool named the Device Manager to help you find out about the hardware on your system. You can see what is installed, what resources are used, and what devices might be having or causing problems.

1 Open System Properties

Right-click the **My Computer** icon on your desktop and choose the **Properties** command from the shortcut menu. The Systems Properties dialog box opens.

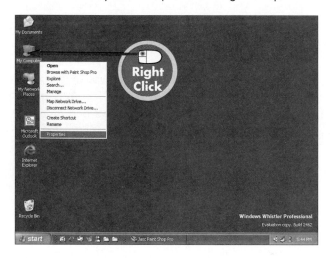

2 Switch to Hardware Tab

Switch to the **Hardware** tab by clicking it once.

3 Open the Device Manager

Click the **Device Manager** button to open the Device Manager window.

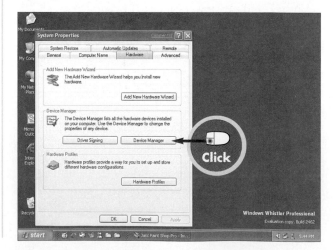

4 Expand a Category

The Device Manager window lists hardware categories for the hardware installed on your computer. Click the plus sign next to a category to expand that category and show the actual devices attached to your computer.

5 Identify Problem Hardware

Devices having problems are identified with a little yellow exclamation point. Another type of symbol you might see is a red X, which indicates a device that is turned off.

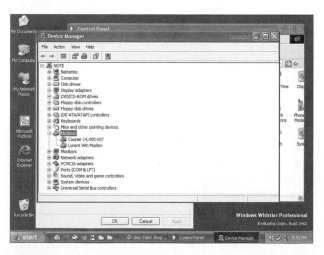

6 Open Hardware Properties

You can open a detailed Properties dialog box for any device by double-clicking the device's icon. The dialog box tells you whether the device is working properly and lets you disable the device. Other tabs let you reinstall software drivers for the device and view the resources it uses.

How-to Hint

Reinstalling a Device

If you see a device that isn't working, try running the Add Hardware applet (you'll find it in the Control Panel window). Windows scans your system for devices and presents a list of what it finds. The malfunctioning device should show up in the list, and you can try to reinstall it.

How to Tell Whether a Windows Service Pack Is Installed

Microsoft occasionally releases collections of updates to Windows in the form of a service pack. Service packs are numbered because more than one is normally released over the years that an operating system is in production. At the time of this writing, Windows XP Service Pack 1 is the only one that has been released for Windows XP. This task shows how to tell whether a service pack has already been applied to Windows or whether you will need to install one yourself.

① Open the Start Menu

Click **Start** to open the Start menu.

② Right-Click the My Computer Icon

Right-click the **My Computer** icon on your Start menu. If a My Computer icon is on your desktop, you can right-click that one instead.

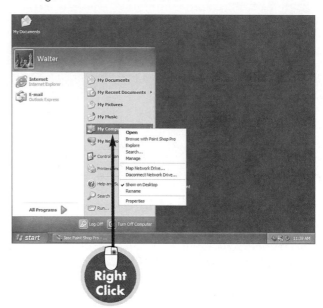

③ Open the Properties Dialog Box

Choose the **Properties** command on the My Computer icon's shortcut menu to open the System Properties dialog box.

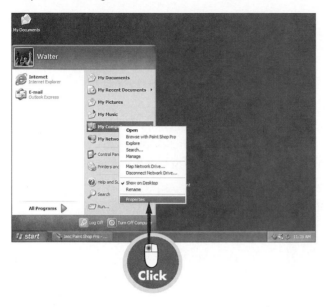

Click

④ Determine Your Version of Windows

The General tab of the System Properties dialog box displays information about Windows and about the basic hardware on your computer. Look in the System section to find out if a service pack has been installed on your computer. If a service pack has not been installed, you will not see this line at all.

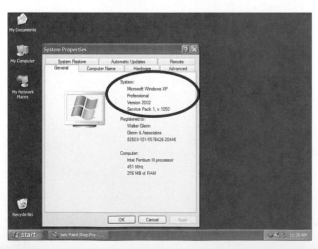

How-to Hint

Service Packs Are Cumulative

When more service packs are released in the future, you can add them to your computer with no problem. Service packs are cumulative, in that each new service pack issued contains all the features included in previous service packs. So, if you have a computer with no service pack installed, you should only apply the latest service pack available.

How to Install Windows XP Service Pack 1

You can obtain a service pack in a few ways. If you are part of a corporate network, your administrator might make the service pack available for you on the network (and in fact, will probably install it for you). If you are installing it yourself, you will either download Service Pack 1 (SP1) from the Windows Update site or install it from a CD-ROM. Use the steps in Task 4 of this part to find and start the download of SP1 from the Internet, or insert your CD and run the program **XPSP1.EXE** on the CD. Whichever method you choose, the steps for the installation are the same.

❶ Read the Welcome Page

The welcome page of the Windows XP Service Pack 1 Setup Wizard has some good advice. Before installing, you should update your system repair disk and back up your computer. If you have done this, click **Next** to continue installation.

❷ Accept the Licensing Agreement

Read the licensing agreement for Service Pack 1. Select the **I Agree** option and click **Next** to continue installation. If you select the I Do Not Agree option, the setup program ends.

③ Choose Whether to Archive Old Files

If you want to uninstall Service Pack 1 at a later date, you must archive the current Windows files in a backup location on your computer. Archiving files takes a large amount of disk space but ensures that you can return your computer to its previous state if Service Pack 1 causes you any problems. Make your choice and click **Next**.

④ Finish the Installation

At this point, Windows begins to copy files. When it is done, you are shown the final page of the Setup Wizard. Click **Finish** to complete the installation and restart your computer. You can select the Do Not Restart Now option to finish the wizard without restarting, but you must restart your computer before the Service Pack 1 installation is complete.

How to Set Program Access and Defaults

Service Pack 1 includes security updates and support for new hardware devices, such as the tablet PC. The other big addition is a simple interface for letting Windows know whether you want to use built-in Microsoft programs (such as Internet Explorer and Outlook Express) or other programs installed on your computer. This is done using a feature named Set Program Access and Defaults, which is part of the Add/Remove Programs Control Panel utility.

1 Open the Set Program Access and Defaults Tool

Click **Start**, point to **All Programs**, and select **Set Program Access and Defaults**. You can also get to this tool by opening the Add/Remove Programs utility from the Control Panel window.

2 Use the Microsoft Windows Option

You have three choices for setting program defaults. The first is the Microsoft Windows option. When this option is set, Windows uses the built-in Microsoft programs for familiar functions: Internet Explorer for Web pages, Outlook Express for email, Windows Media Player for sounds and video, and Windows Messaging for instant messaging. There is also a setting for controlling what application loads Java applets on the Internet, but Microsoft does not provide a program for that. Click the **Microsoft Windows** option to use this setting.

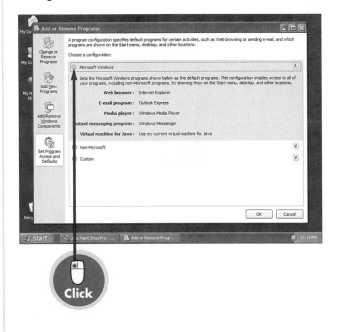

③ Use the Non-Microsoft Option

Another choice you have is the Non-Microsoft option. This option uses whatever programs are currently set as your default programs for the listed functions. Whenever you install a new program (such as Netscape Navigator for browsing the Web), that program makes itself the default. Click the **Non-Microsoft** option to retain the default programs the way you have them set and to hide the icons for the Microsoft applications from your desktop and Start menu.

④ Use the Custom Option

Click the **Custom** option to exert a little more control over your default program settings. A section for each type of program (Web browser, email, and so on) lets you select whether to use the current default program or the Microsoft program, and whether the Microsoft program should be displayed on your desktop and Start menu.

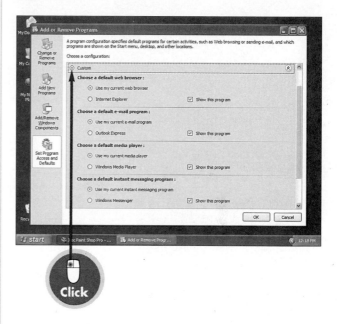

Why Is This Feature Here?

The Set Program Access and Defaults feature was really added to satisfy requirements set by the Department of Justice. It provides computer manufacturers a way to install programs that they choose to bundle with their computers and to hide the Microsoft equivalents from the casual Windows user. Interestingly, the program also provides an easy way for users who don't like the alternate programs that might come with a new computer to switch back to the Microsoft alternatives.

Digital Photography

Task

Taking the Best Picture

16

Generally, you'll be pleased with a photograph if it captures the moment or memory you intended. Nonetheless, you want to learn the best techniques for making those captured moments as visually faithful to the original, so that your memory will truly be jarred into recollection. In addition, you might want to convey a message to the viewer beyond a memory—it can be for a presentation, an educational event, or some other personal or professional purpose.

How to Cover the Basics

In every process that can be handled as a hobby or profession, such as photography, small details separate highly skilled practitioners from amateurs. Here are some starting points to consider.

❶ Take Your Camera Along

This might seem like a crazy thing to point out, but if the shot of a lifetime comes along, and you didn't have room in your pocket or briefcase, you're plain out of luck.

❷ Don't Run Out of Memory

With pocket flash memory cards decreasing in price, be sure you have enough real estate in your digital camera to accommodate your intended project. One way to save memory is to preview shots on your LCD screen before keeping them.

❸ Check Your Battery

Using the liquid crystal display (LCD) is a big part of battery wear. Keep an extra set of batteries handy, or take along that clunky recharger.

4 Use a Tripod

If you don't have the steadiest hands in the world, or your camera is heavy, this is almost a must. But for serious shots, invest in a tripod for still shots.

5 Pay Attention to the Shot

Be sure there are no extra arms or legs dangling into the picture or other extraneous objects floating around (although you'll soon learn how to crop them out digitally).

6 Learn About Image Types

Although most cameras use a compressed format (JPG), some cameras allow you to shoot in an uncompressed mode that you can download and compress later if desired. This format can be TIF or RAW.

Learning to Handle the Lag Time

Remember that with a digital camera a delay occurs between the time you press the shutter release and the moment the picture is actually taken. Make any portrait subjects aware of this, and in the case of outdoor shots where you have no control, try to anticipate a second or two into the future of any movement you want to capture.

How to Compose a Good Picture

If you're out with friends or shooting your family, the subject is the most important part of the story anyway, so too much forethought is probably an inhibition to fun photos. But experimentation in general will make you a better photographer. With this in mind, here are some pointers on what to shoot.

1 Opt for Simplicity

A single shot of a compelling subject, captured at the optimal moment with its reflection, is a great example of a simple yet effective photo.

2 Try an Off-Center Approach

The "rule of thirds" suggests that locating a subject off-center can also be effective.

3 Include the Foreground

Especially with the ability to crop digitally later, giving a subject a visual context (the shot on the left) generally improves a photograph.

4 Frame Your Subject Naturally

This takes creativity but makes for interesting shots—but watch your lighting.

5 Look for Lines and Patterns

Nature has a way of manifesting in parallel shapes and patterns—if you are observant enough like this photographer, you can create a fine composition.

6 Create a Sense of Scale (with the Horizon)

This photographer broke a rule of never putting the horizon at the center of a photo to dramatize the size of the bridge.

There's No Film to Waste

How-to Hint

You don't have to be stingy with your trigger finger on a digital camera. You can always purge photos using the LCD panel and make room for more shots, and you only need to download, and eventually print, the very best or your very favorites.

How to Control Lighting

Lighting is a tricky issue and less important for point-and-shoot cameras than for SLRs. Learning how to work with lighting effectively, however, can greatly enhance your digital photos. Let's quickly take a look at white balance, flash, ambient lighting, and exposure as important matters to consider.

1 White Balance

Some of Canon's high-end cameras have an automatic white balance setting, manual setting, and five presets (sunlight, cloudy, incandescent, fluorescent, and flash). Each of these compensates for natural conditions, although more experienced photographers use the manual controls to refine the settings. All cameras have automatic white balance adjustments, but the more you can help the camera know what it's shooting, the better the result.

2 Control Flash

Flash lets you shoot in low-light conditions, but it can introduce red eye problems in live subjects. The Flash modes available on some digital cameras are as follows: Auto(no human intervention involved), Manual (makes the flash go off even if the camera thinks there's enough light), Slow Sync (causes the camera to expose the background with no flash effect and fires the flash at the end of the exposure), Red-Eye Reduction (compensates for red-eye), and No Flash (disable this flash for sunsets, cityscapes, and low-light conditions that would be harmed by a flash).

3 Use an Extra Flash or Light Source

If you're a serious photographer or need to augment the flash unit on the camera, a slave flash or external light source can be very helpful. Make sure that it's placed outside the area of the photograph and fires in synchronicity with your camera. As you can see from this picture, two flashes can eliminate shadows.

④ Set Exposure

Even though digital cameras have built-in automatic light meters, you might want to override these settings in extreme conditions. Different cameras use different types of controls, generally marked + (plus) and – (minus), to change exposure compensation. For example, Nikon has you hold down a +/– button while turning a knob on the top of the camera to increase or decrease exposure compensation.

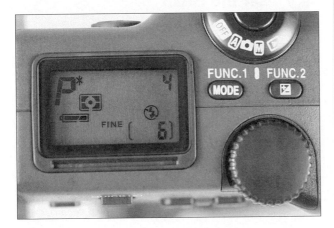

⑤ Exposure Bracketing

Even though you can take a series of test shots to choose the correct exposure, some cameras have a feature that lets you bracket different images at different exposures above and below a setting you specify. Then, you can choose the one you want either on the LCD or from a series of shots you download.

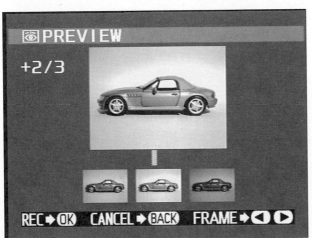

⑥ Extreme Contrast

Scenes with a large variation of lighting pose special problems for digital cameras. Zooming in and holding the AE (autoexposure lock) when you zoom out (maintaining the zoomed exposure) can help you accentuate the parts of a composition that automatic exposure would lose.

How-to Hint

Keeping the Focus and Exposure Separate

On many cameras, the AE locks both the focus and exposure. In the preceding shot, having the focus and exposure separate lets you refocus and set the exposure for the full or restricted image and then keep it for a different zoom setting.

How to Shoot Close-ups

There are close-ups and there are *close-ups*—by which we mean using the macro mode.

① Easy Close-ups

This is really just a matter of using your zoom (digital or optical) to place your subject into the optimal range of the camera.

② Close-up Mode

The close-up mode on a digital camera, however, goes beyond zoom and lets you get the closest possible shot using what is called the *macro* lens.

③ How Close Is Close Enough?

Macro capability varies among digital cameras and is a feature you should consider and have demonstrated to you. These photos were taken with the Canon D30 (with an extra adapter ring), the Sony DSC-85, and the Nikon CoolPix 995.

④ Set the Flash

This can be tricky in macro mode because the flash can be outside the range of the shot. Also, the light from the flash might be too strong at close range and cause reflection and glare.

> **How-to Hint**
>
> ## Using Accessories
>
> For small objects and macro close-ups, try the following accessories: a tabletop tripod, an off-camera flash, a paper or aluminum foil reflector, and possibly a remote control to allow you to work more closely with the subject.

How to Maintain Focus

If you use your optical viewfinder, you can think your shot is in focus even when it isn't because the lens is still out of focus. But, the image on the LCD display is almost the same as what the camera captures when you snap the picture, plus another possible 10% of the image outside the LCD composition.

1 Zoom Lens Controls

Locating the zoom control lets you move between W – wide angle and T – telephoto (tight). Some zooms are automatic, but a few (on SLR cameras) are manual, such as this Minolta Dimage.

2 Use Autofocus

In most cases, autofocus enables you to take perfectly acceptable pictures. But in some situations you want a refined setting, and some cameras use settings on the LCD panel to focus on portions of the composition. Here, the Nikon 900 uses five selectable focus points.

3 Manual Focus

The ability to set your focus manually is one reason to choose an SLR digital camera. Sometimes there are cues in the LCD panel after you switch the camera into Manual Focus mode, with a keypad containing up and down arrows to make the adjustment. Higher-end cameras let you see the actual image through the viewfinder, such as the Olympus E-10 that has manual focus control right on the lens barrel.

4 Infinity Focus

Infinity focus is used for distant objects, scenery, landscapes, and cityscapes. Locking your camera's focus into this setting for these types of shots focuses on the furthest point and is essentially a convenient way to combine the best aspects of manual and automatic focus settings.

17

Selecting a Camera

Like all technology products, prices on digital camera will typically drop just before the new greatest thing or version comes along. To maximize your use and enjoyment, make a list of the features you want and go to a store to compare the various models.

1. **Point-and Shoot-or SLR**   The automatic point-and-shoot cameras will most likely be within your price range. SLR cameras will be significantly more expensive, but they give you more versatility.

2. **How Many Megapixels**   A *megapixel* is a million pixels, which equates to 1000×1000 pixels, or roughly 20% greater screen area than the 1024×768 screen resolution you might be using on your computer. Therefore, if you're only going to be viewing the images on your computer (or putting them online), a megapixel, theoretically, is enough. But if you're looking for print-quality output from your images, then the more megapixels, the better. (It takes 2 megapixels to create a 5×7 print).

3. **What About Zoom**   Most point-and-shoot (P&S) cameras have 2X or 3X zoom capability—optical zoom. Digital zoom is touted by some manufacturers, but it is an electronic magnification that distorts the image and reduces quality.

4. **LCD and Display Features**   You should check the camera for the user-friendliness of its display features and the LCD panel itself. Some cameras have a tilt and swivel capability on the LCD panel so that you can move the body and keep the screen in the same position.

5. **Flash and Power**   Take a good look at the type of power supply and its ease of use. Does it have simple batteries, or do you need to recharge them? Is there an easy way to keep the camera charged up? Check the range of the flash and, if it's important, the presence of an extra flash connector.

6. **Connectivity and Software**   Find out how the images will be downloaded into your computer, and make sure you have a compatible connector. See whether a good utility software package is bundled with the camera and whether software with which you are already familiar will work with it. (In Windows XP, most USB cameras are recognized by the operating system.)

7. **Video Output**   You might want to display your images directly to a TV monitor, or even record them on a VCR. If this is appealing, ask about a video output feature for your digital camera.

How to Choose Accessories

Besides the camera itself, you will want some other items that will make your digital photography experience easier. To prepare for accessorizing, check what type of memory your camera uses. Then, depending on other peripherals or computers you might have, at least partially base your choice of the camera on the type of memory it uses.

For example, a relatively new standard is the Sony Memory Stick. You might not normally look for this in a camera, but if you own a Vaio laptop with a memory stick port, this would be a good feature to get.

1 Extra Memory

Memory for digital cameras comes in three basic types: CompactFlash, SmartMedia cards, and the Memory Stick from Sony. (A few cameras can save to floppy disks and CDs.) These flash standards are all different, so when you buy your camera, you're locked into the standard you have selected. If you are going to purchase these cards for mass storage, price the models that will work with your camera. Here's how they look.

2 Try a Tripod

Although a full-size tripod is great for outdoor shots, you might be able to get by with a tabletop model if you're shooting inside.

3 External Card Readers

If you're going to use multiple storage devices and not always have the camera available for downloads, you might want to get an external card reader that connects to your PC to transfer images.

④ Lenses and Filters

A wide-angle lens can expand the view of your camera, but it also requires threading on the camera lens to accept it. This is something to consider when purchasing the camera itself. Remember that longer lenses also make the camera harder to hold steady—so try a tripod. Polarizing filters can remove glare and reflection.

⑤ Batteries and Chargers

Alkaline batteries might not last very long in your camera, so you should buy extras. Rechargeable lithium-ion batteries last much longer, but they can be expensive. Chargers are available for NiMh and NiCd batteries; these are similar batteries but use different chargers, although some units can charge both. These batteries lose their charge naturally when not used, so keep them charged. They can also have different capacity ratings for batteries made by the same manufacturer, so use the right ones for your camera.

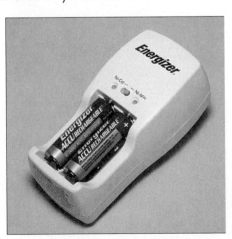

⑥ External Flash

If your camera has a hot shoe mount, it will support an external flash that is connected directly to the camera. If you don't have a hot shoe connection, you can get a slave trigger or photo sensor that will fire when it detects your main flash going off. Using an external unit like this at an angle can also help reduce red-eye problems. These pictures show the differences between a single flash and an external flash on a Fuji digital camera.

Are You on the Level?

If you're going to the trouble of using a tripod, you don't want to trust that it's not tilted. An inexpensive circular level can tip you off that you're slanted or okay.

18

Setting Up and Using a Digital Camera

Most electronic devices, such as digital cameras, are set up with defaults that are perfectly functional right out of the box. But the key to versatility and efficiency is the ability to set options. So, the reason most digital cameras have a liquid crystal display (LCD) screen is two-fold—first to frame the picture you are about to take, and second to provide a setup screen for options. In general, this means pressing a button called *menu* or *settings*, cycling through a series of choices and subchoices, and choosing or selecting the ones you want to use. You've used similar menus on digital watches, VCRs, and PDAs, now you'll do it on a camera.

You'll use a popular mid-range point-and-shoot camera: the Canon Digital Elph (PowerShot S230) with a 3.2-megapixel capability.

How to Use the Setup Screen

The first thing you need to do is get comfortable with the menu structure and how to set various options.

1 See the Controls

Let's take a look at the LCD panel of the camera. Notice the familiar buttons: Set, Menu, and Display.

2 Turn On the Camera

When the camera is turned on in camera mode (that's the default, as opposed to review), you can briefly see the settings currently in effect.

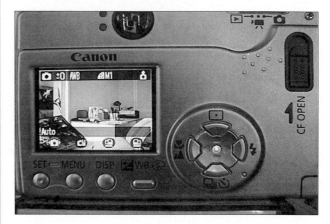

3 Ready to Shoot

In a brief moment, the settings disappear, and you're ready to fire. To see them onscreen again, press the **DISP** button.

4 Open the Menu

Press the **Menu** button to go to the first control screen.

5 Move Through the Menu

Not surprisingly, pressing down scrolls through the menu, top to bottom. The first item is resolution.

6 Move Through the Options

Pressing right or left scrolls through the options on a level. Here, it's moving through the resolution options.

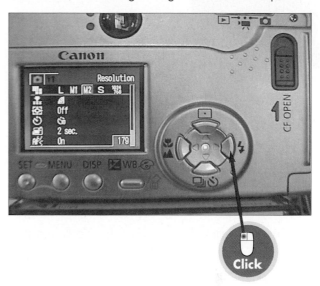

Using Menus

Not all cameras work the same way, but almost all electronic menus do. So, if you can work Windows XP, you can certainly set options on a digital camera.

Implementing a Selection

As this point, you can probably guess that to implement a selection, you press the **Set** button.

How to Choose Image Quality

You already saw a bit of the resolution settings in the previous task because they're at the top of the setup menu. You will need to experiment with various image sizes to see what you really need. Basically, choose the highest resolution for images you want to print. To save time for Web images, such as email or a Web site, use a smaller resolution. If you have time to edit the pictures, you don't need to change the resolution downward unless you have no room in memory. You can reduce the resolution in your image editing program.

❶ Open the Setup Menu

Press the **Menu** button on the back panel when the camera is on.

❷ Go to Resolution

Press the **Down** button to go to the Resolution settings. Your current resolution is shown, along with the actual screen dimensions of a computer image after it is downloaded (1600×1200).

❸ Reduce the Size

If your screen resolution is 1024×768, you might want to try the next size down. Press the **Right** button to move through the options. Notice that you now have the correct proportions for your computer screen.

④ See the Other Choices

Keep pressing **Right** or **Left** to toggle through the four main choices: from L (largest) 2048×1636 to S (smallest) 640×480.

⑤ Set a Selection

With the screen resolution at a size you want, press **Set** and move on.

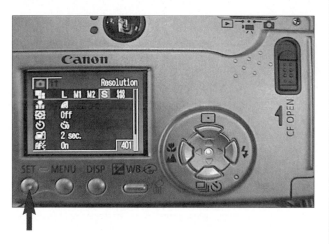

How to Set Compression

Besides resolution, the other setting that affects image quality is compression. This also affects the file size of the stored and downloaded image. However, if you have ample storage on your camera, you can use the least amount of compression to take and store your photos and use and image editor to reduce them, if necessary, later.

1 Open Menu Setup

With the camera on, return to the Setup area by pressing **Menu**.

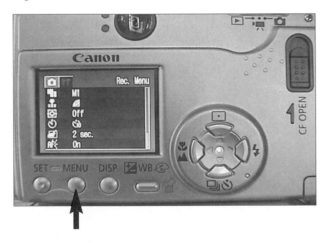

2 Check Your Main Settings

To see how much memory you have on board, press **Right** on the first Menu screen to go to the Main (or global) settings for all camera modes.

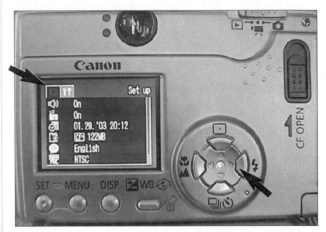

3 Check Memory

Notice that your Flash memory onboard is 122MB. That's a lot more than some cameras have as a default, so you can use the least compression.

❹ Return to Camera Settings

Press **Left** to go back to your Camera settings, then go down two levels to reach Compression.

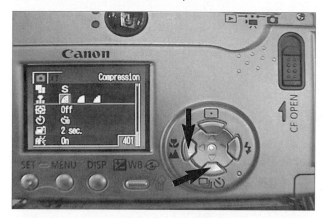

❺ Understand the Choices

The three choices for compression are represented by smoothest, smooth, and jaggy. These correspond to how a computer image looks when it is compressed for the Web: The less digital information in an image, the more jagged its edges. So, by choosing the smoothest icon, you're selecting the least compression. Press **Right** to go through the selections.

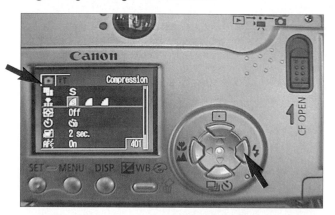

❻ Set the Compression

Don't forget to press the **Set** button to implement the compression selection (or any other setting) you make.

How to Set Other Options

We introduced the Main (or global) area in the previous task to check out Flash memory. Let's quickly take a look at some other options you can set.

① Go to Setup

Turn on the Menu and press **Right** to go to the Camera Setup area.

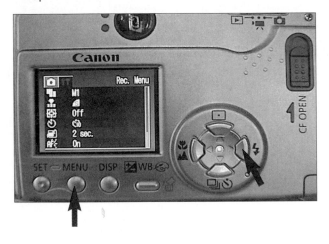

② Check Digital Zoom

Digital Zoom can create distortion. Because it is right below Compression, you can press **Down** three times to find the setting.

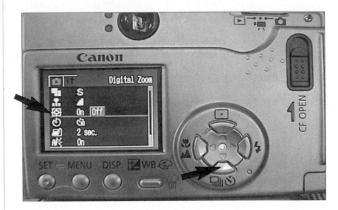

③ Autofocus Setting

If you press Down again, you'll see the self timer and review timer. Then, you'll see the AF-Beam, which lets you set Autofocus on or off.

4 Other Camera Settings

Final settings on the camera menu are AutoRotate and File Number Reset, with toggles for on and off.

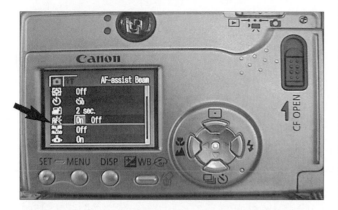

5 Review the Main Menu

Go to the top of the Menu to go Right to the Main or global menu again.

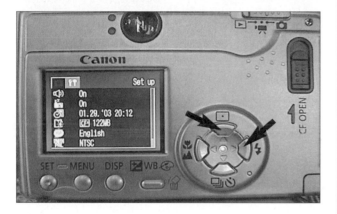

6 Other Main Options

The other options are for NTSC (American broadcast standard versus European), auto power shut down (On/Off to save batteries), the date and time (let's not mess with that), and finally something called Normal. This is the setting that enables this camera to connect, via USB, to the computer.

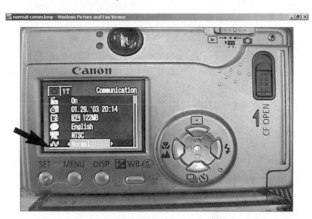

How to View and Delete Photos

So far, you've used Camera mode, where you shoot the pictures. Remember, though, that you can review a shot right after it's taken for the time period you set in the options panel, or you can go back and review all your shots later. Let's see how that's done.

❶ Change the Mode

To move from Camera mode to Review mode, move the slider at the top rear of the camera to the left.

❷ See Your Shots

Now you can use the Left and Right buttons to toggle through your shots.

③ Zoom and Tile

Different preview screens let you zoom into a photo or tile all the photos in a panel to see how they look.

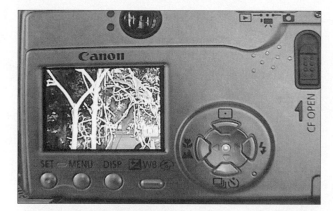

④ See the Other Sessions

You canmove to a previous session or set of shots when you see the slider at the bottom of the Review panel on the LCD.

⑤ Delete a Photo

When you locate a photo you want to delete, simply press the **Trash Can** button. (This serves the same purpose as the White Balance button in Camera mode.)

Using Review Mode

Just as you can set options in Camera mode, pressing the Menu button takes you to a separate option panel for Review mode. This lets you delete all photos (rather than formatting the flash card), clear your memory, set a slideshow review session, and make other settings with respect to seeing your photos on the camera.

Using TV or AV Mode

Moving the mode slider on the top rear of the camera in the middle takes you to TV or AV mode, in which you can use another cable supplied with the Canon Elph to view your photos on a TV or VCR without downloading them to a computer.

19

Getting Prints into Your Computer

For many people, using a digital camera is the easiest way to acquire photographic content in a computer program.

But there are other ways; many of you already have prints that have been processed from standard 35mm or other film camera. How do you acquire those for a Web site or other computer project? Let's look at two options.

How to Scan Your Prints

If you have a flatbed scanner, you can easily scan one or more photographs directly into an imaging program. A scanner (like a digital camera) is a *Twain* source, which means that any compatible Windows program should be capable of taking advantage of it. Let's use a common program, Adobe Photoshop Elements, to acquire several photos. The process is similar to other computer graphics programs.

① Select Acquire

When Elements opens, immediately select the **Acquire** option. (If you don't see this screen, select **File**, **Import** and select your scanner.)

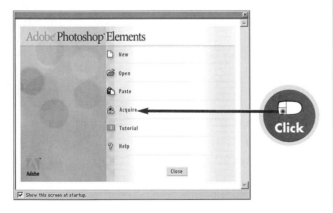

② Choose Your Source

You need to tell Elements which peripheral will be supplying your image. Select your scanner and click **OK**. [*Hint: Guess what other Twain source you'll soon be selecting? Right, the digital camera.*]

③ Ready to Scan

Generally, a Twain peripheral has a utility program that does its main work, such as scanning. As a Twain-compliant product, its utility program visits inside the application to which you want to acquire the material, in this case Elements. You should be able to acquire (or sometimes import) your peripheral assets (images) into any Windows program that supports and edits those types of files. Generally, you will use the options for the utility program to acquire your image, so select **Color Picture** and click **Scan**.

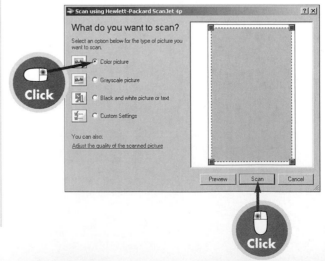

4 Quality Adjustments

You can also preview the scan first or use advanced options to set image characteristics or quality.

5 More Than One Photo?

One thing you can do with a scanner is combine more than one image at a time and then split them up. This saves time and demonstrates some of the features of the standard image editor. Notice that the preview of the image you are seeing is only 16.7% of its actual size. If you explode it to full size, it will dwarf your 800×600 display.

6 See It Full Screen

Press **Ctrl++** (Ctrl and the plus key) until the image is 100% to demonstrate its true size—only one of the three photos in the composition is visible, and only a portion at that.

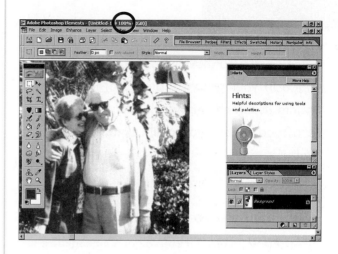

How-to Hint

Preview Size Versus Actual Size

This is an important distinction: The preview size of the image is not its actual size, which you will adjust in the next task. If you were to save this image as a JPG for the Web, not only would it be enormous in file size (bytes), but it would also require the user to slide around the entire image to view it.

How to Crop and Save the Image

Now that you have this enormous scanned image in your graphics program, let's break it up into its three components and save each one as a separate file you could email or post to a Web site.

1 Return to Normal View

Select **View**, **Fit to Screen** to get a manageable version of the image back onto the screen. (You can also press Ctrl+O.)

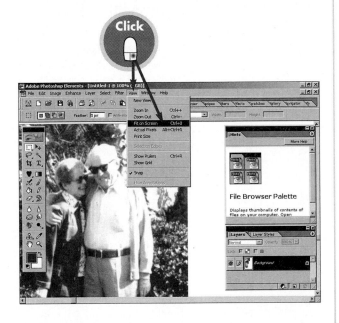

2 Select a Portion of the Image

First, click the **Window** square to show your title bar for more information. Probably the most important part of the toolbar is the Selection tool. Click the **Selection** tool, and drag a box (or marquee) around the first portion of the image you want to break out.

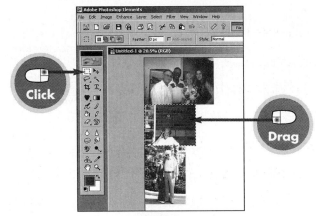

3 Crop the Image

Cropping is one of the first steps in most image processing. Remember the dangling legs in one of the photos? This is how you can get rid of them. Select **Image**, **Crop**.

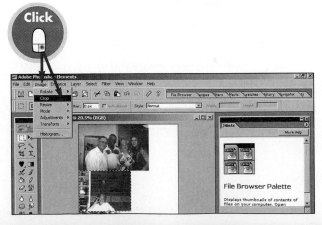

④ Save the Cropped Version

With the cropped version onscreen, select **File**, **Save As**.

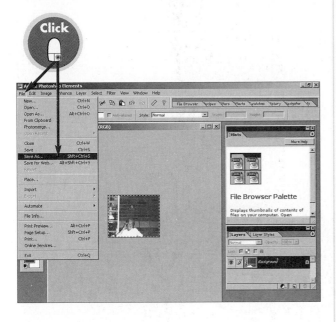

⑥ Start Over with Undo

Because you've saved the version you want, click the **Undo** icon (Step Backward) to return to the previous version with three images. Now, you can repeat the process for the other two portions.

⑤ Set a Location and File Type

The default location is My Pictures in My Documents. Use the drop-down arrow to change to a Web-friendly file type, such as JPG. Accept the default options for now. Then, give it a name and click **Save**.

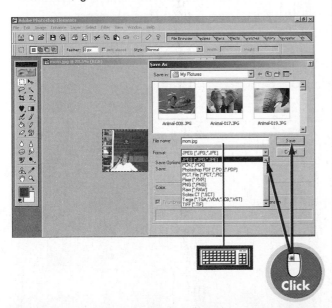

Saving the Original

Notice that the original file format symbol shown on the title bar represents Photoshop or Elements (PSD). This enables you to create multiple changes in your composition, which will be merged in any new file that you save in most other formats. You should learn to save a PSD version of your original file, along with the final versions that you can use online or in other programs.

How to Work with Photo CD

Besides scanning, you can have your photo processing lab output your images directly to a CD that is specially formatted as a Photo CD. This is fairly inexpensive, especially for a large quantity of prints, and it lets you choose from different resolutions of each image. Let's work with such a disc.

① Explore Your Photo CD

Double-click your Photo CD disc in Explorer or My Computer.

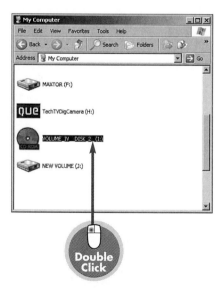

② Note the Two Resolution Choices

Your choices are high-resolution and low-resolution images.

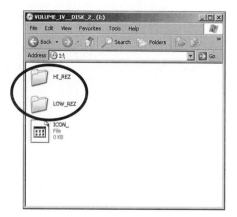

③ Explore Low Resolution

Select a folder and double-click it to see a thumbnails view.

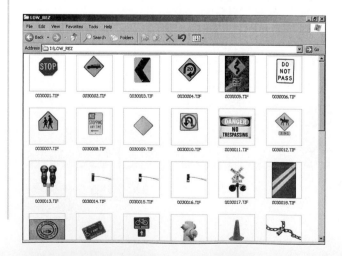

4 Access Photoshop Elements

Open Elements again from the taskbar, and drag to resize both windows so that they're side by side.

Drag

6 Save It

Don't forget to save this picture onto your hard drive into the proper folder and as the file type you want to use.

5 Acquire the Image

Having visually located an image you like from the CD, drag and drop it into Elements.

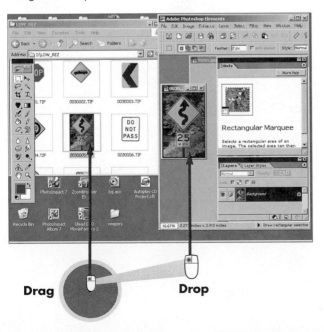

Drag   Drop

Task

Downloading and Organizing Photos

You've gone through your digital camera options, and you've seen how to acquire photos from a scanner. Now, let's work with the download program and see how you can organize what you've shot, edit the photos, print them, and possibly email and post them online.

How to Download Images

You need to connect your digital camera to the PC, and the most common connection today is the USB cable. With the Canon model, you first must install the software program and driver for the Elph. Then, when the camera is turned on (and sometimes even if it isn't), making the connection to the Windows XP computer leads to instant recognition. The message New hardware found displays on the system tray.

1 Select an AutoPlay Option

Just like any other source of content, when the camera is found, its content can be accessed from a number of possible programs. Select the **Canon Zoom Browser EX** (the default), and click **OK**.

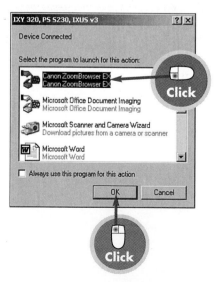

2 Use the ZoomBrowser

Starting with the utility program from the digital camera manufacturer gives you the most obvious options: Download, Print, View As Slideshow), and Connect to Internet.

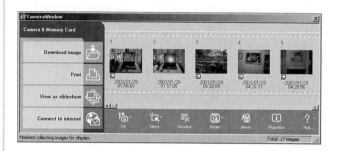

3 Select Your Images

Click an image and click **Select All** to select all the images.

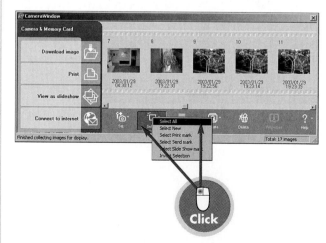

4 Save to Folder

Although you can easily add the photos to a default folder such as My Pictures, this program lets you take advantage of an instant new folder named by date. Click it, and then click **OK**.

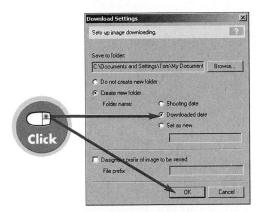

5 Watch the Transfer

There's nothing quite as exciting as watching the images zoom down to the computer from the camera, except perhaps downloading a patch for Windows XP.

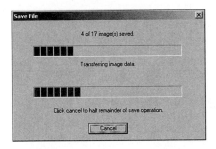

6 Expand the Folder

This folder will most likely join others in the Browser window. You can just double-click the icon to view the thumbnails of the latest shot.

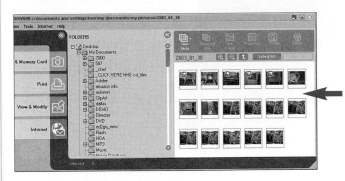

Instant Cataloging!

Let's examine this browser more carefully. In fact, it instantly catalogs every photographic image on your entire hard drive! You can drag up through your file hierarchy to locate the newly named folder (by date) in My Pictures, inside My Computer.

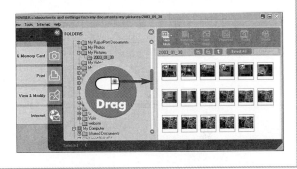

How to Organize the Images

As you shoot and download scores of images, having them in dated folders is a good start. But let's pretend that some of the images are for a special purpose. I shot scenes of my apartment—perhaps they're for insurance. Let's organize them.

1 Make a New Folder

Just as you would in My Computer, right-click the main (in this case, **My Pictures**) folder to create a new folder.

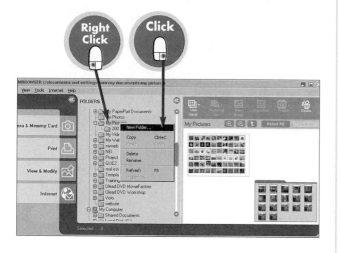

2 Give It a Name

Let's call it Insurance. Type in **Insurance**, and click **OK**.

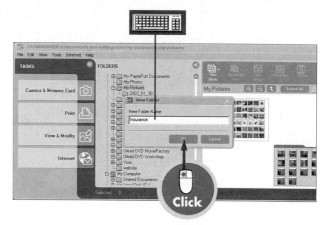

3 Select the Images

Using the Ctrl key, you can select one or more images from among the whole group by clicking them individually.

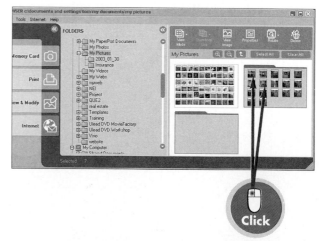

4 Move Them to the New Folder

With the images selected, drag and drop them to the newly named **Insurance** folder.

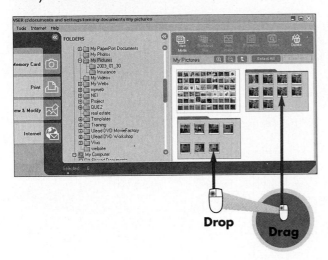

Drop

Drag

5 View the Results

Expand the new folder to see your apartment images separated from the others.

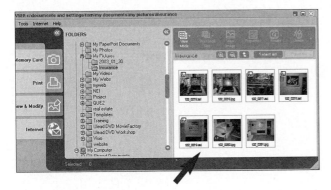

6 See It in My Computer

Select the **View** menu, and then set the Folder options in My Computer to **Thumbnail**. This lets you see a similar folder view of your images.

Click

Task

Editing Your Digital Photos

You In this hour, you'll continue to fine-tune and examine your images with your image editing software. This book uses Adobe Photoshop Elements, but the same functionality is found in most imaging software. At some point you will become familiar with the various palettes and options, but let this serve as a quick tour and introduction to the main features and concepts.

The best way to learn a program like this is to do your own project with your own images. If you get stuck, there are ToolTips over many of the icons, and a good help system is available both in the program itself and online at the Adobe Web site.

How to Open and Compare Images

Now that you know where your images are, you can easily open one or more of them in Adobe Photoshop Elements. First, let's reopen the program to get started.

1 Open Your Files

Just like any other program, Elements uses the File, Open selection command to access a default folder—in this case My Pictures.

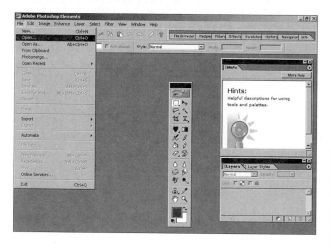

2 Open the Right Folder

You're going to review a set of similar images that remain in the dated folder you created with the Canon browser. As you click through them, you can see thumbnails and their actual file sizes.

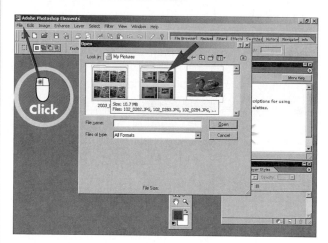

3 Examine the Images

As you click each image in turn, you can see how you used different resolution and compression settings on the camera. A broad range in file sizes is reflected in the dialog box.

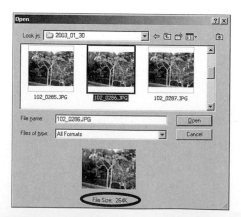

④ Open Them All

Press **Ctrl+A** to select all the images; then, click **Open**. One image appears to open in the program.

⑥ Separate the Images

Select **Window**, **Cascade** to get all the images onscreen; then, you can select them by their title bars.

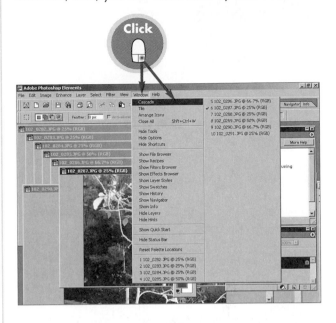

⑤ Identify the Images

Even though it looks, at first, as though only one image has opened, if you click **Window**, you can see that more than a dozen separate files are available for editing. (Hint: Your system has a lot of memory.)

— How-to Hint

Using the Smallest Preview

Examining the images with the smallest preview (25%) by selecting Image, Resize, Image Size shows that it is indeed the largest resolution you set in the camera, and it is a hefty 9MB in size.

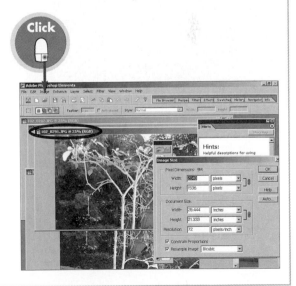

How to Adjust Brightness and Contrast

You can make a number of adjustments to any image you select by clicking its title bar.

1 Choose Enhance Image

Under the Enhance menu, select **Brightness/Contrast**, **Brightness/Contrast**.

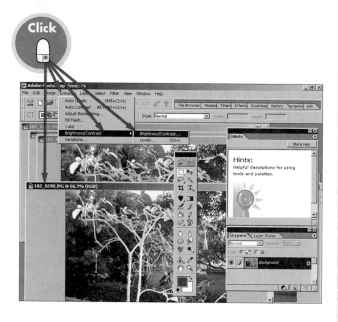

2 Set the Slider

Drag the sliders in either direction to get the effect you want, and then click **OK**.

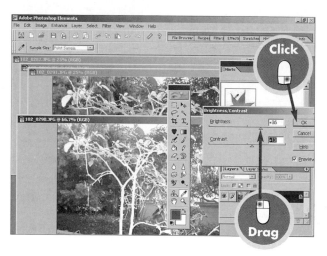

3 Save the New Image

Select **Save As** to save this version under a different name.

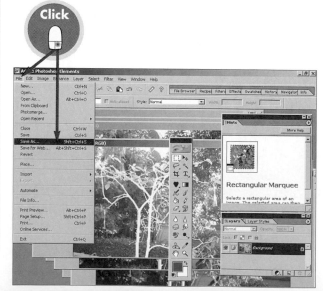

④ Give It a Name and Location

Name the image **(bright)** and give it a location to separate it from the others.

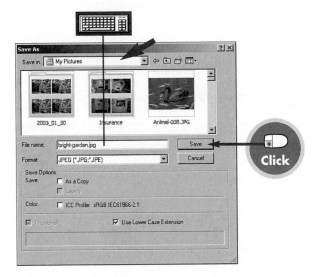

⑤ Change the File Type

Some Windows programs prefer BMP files. You can change the file type, but keeping it in the PSD format (Photoshop) will enable you to work with advanced features such as layers.

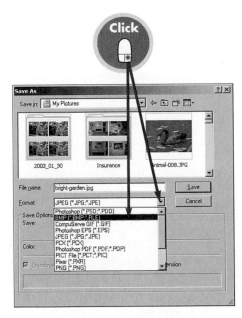

How to Adjust Color Balance and Variations

Color balance and saturation are other image attributes that you can easily change in Elements.

1 Select an Image

Select the image you want to change by clicking its title bar.

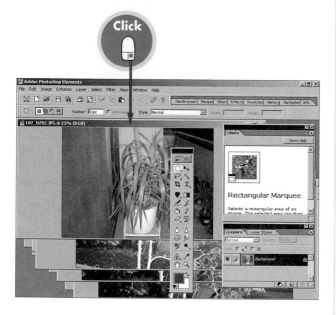

2 Open Variations

This time under the Enhance menu, select **Variations**.

3 Examine the Choices

Use this Trial and Error screen to get the effect you want, click the choices for **Red**, **Green**, and **Blue** to begin to move your image into that direction.

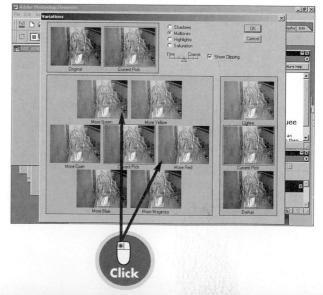

④ Other Options

You work with shadow and saturation the same way: Keep your original choices in mind at the top of the screen, and click to return to them. When you're done, click **OK**.

Click

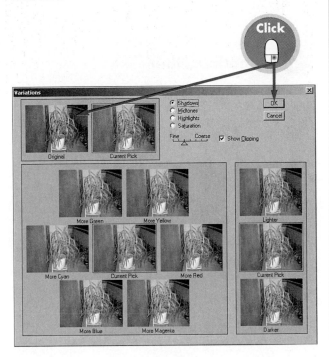

⑤ Save Your Final Version(s)

Remember that Undo takes you back to square one. You can also save incrementally to be able to return to a former version you then altered (for example, a file called `red-hues-shadows.jpg`), or you can save it as a copy.

How to Apply Special Effects

Let's try some other enhancements that will really make your photos artistic. In this task, you'll use the Filters feature, which makes having filters on our digital camera nice but almost unnecessary.

1 Sharpen the Image

Under Filters, select **Sharpen**; this won't make up for the incorrect focus, but it can enhance many images.

2 Another Filter

You can also reapply Sharpen or Sharpen More. Then, select **Pixelate-Mosaic**.

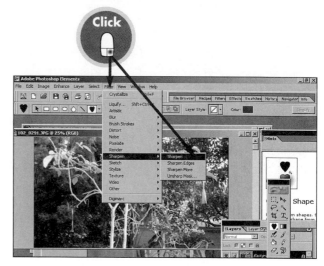

3 Select Options

You'll need to experiment with the various options, but try the default for now. Click **OK**.

4. Check the Results

You're starting to make a statement with these photos and are giving them some artistic qualities. Remember that you can use the Undo or Step Backward option.

5. Select an Area

The real power of Elements is selecting a portion of the image to which to apply any of these effects. Select the **Lasso** tool, and trace a circle around a portion of the image, closing it into a marching ants selection area.

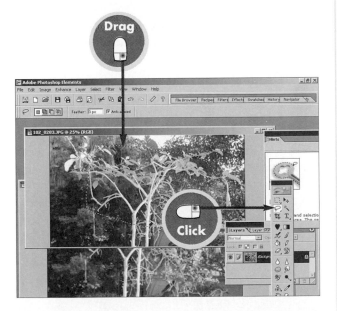

6. Apply Selectively

Now any of the enhancements you choose will be applied only to the selected area.

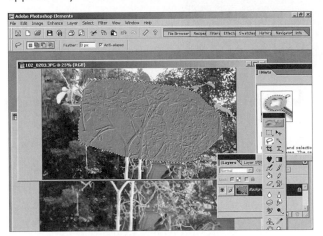

How to Create Layers

Let's take a quick look at the power of Layers, a feature that sets the great graphics programs apart. Think of using Layers as being able to separate a flat surface into a series of planes and then being able to work on each plane independently—that's what Layers lets you do. Select another image to work with by clicking its title pane.

1 Select a Part of the Image

Using the **Lasso** tool, and holding down the **Alt** key to select specific points, trace and select an object.

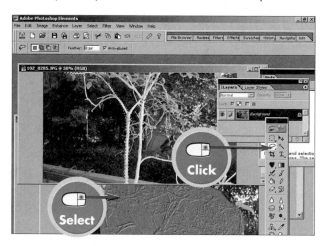

2 Cut the Image

Select **Edit**, **Cut** or press **Ctrl +X** on your keyboard to see how it will look. The tree is in memory.

3 Make a New Layer

Select **Layer New**, and give it a name (**tree**). Then, click **OK**.

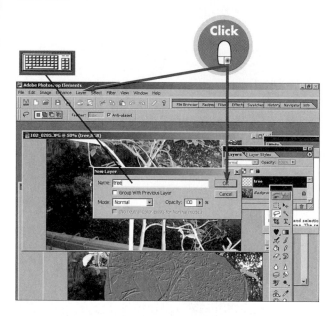

4 Locate the Layer Panel

You'll see a new layer with the name on the Layer Panel.

⑤ Paste the Image

Make sure the new layer is active by clicking it. Then, click **Edit Paste** or press **Ctrl+V** to paste the image into the new layer. It enters the image in the center.

⑥ Move It Back

Select the **Move** tool on the toolbar; then, grab the pasted tree and drag it back over the empty area.

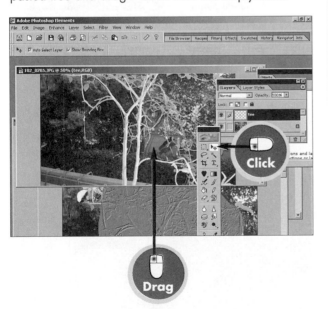

⑦ Add Another Layer

Click to add another layer, and name it `text`.

⑧ Add Text

With the layer active or selected, click the **Text** tool and add this text: `Tree`. With the text selected (drag through it), you can use the Text menu at the top of the screen to change its size and color to make it stand out.

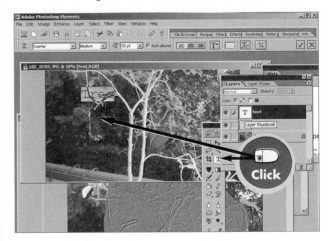

How to Use Layers

Now that you've created these three layers, let's see the results. With this simple example, you can see how you can isolate elements of a composition and apply your filters and enhancements to them first by selection and then by putting them on separate layers.

❶ See What You Have

At this point, you should have three layers—a background, a layer with the cut-and-pasted tree moved to its original position, and a layer with some text.

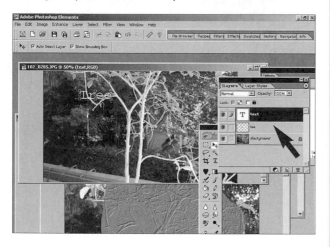

❷ Move the Text

On the image itself, use the **Move** tool and drag the text over the tree.

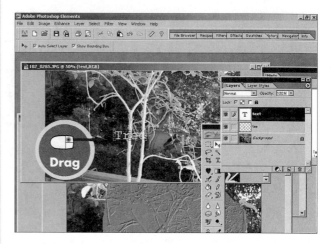

❸ Change the Order of the Layer

Now, on the Layers palette, drag and drop the tree layer between the other two layers from its position at the top.

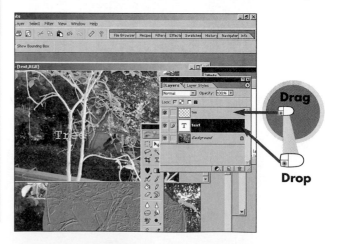

④ What Happened?

If you look carefully, you will see that the tree is now in the nearest layer and in front of the text! You moved the text behind the tree.

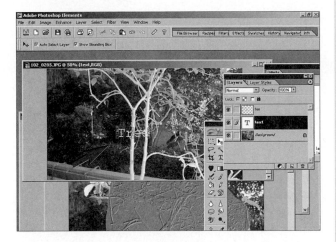

⑤ Change Opacity

Select the **Text** layer again, and change the opacity to 50% by dragging the slider.

⑥ Save the File

Now when you click Save As, the default choice for file format, and the one you should use to preserve your layers, is PSD. Notice that your layers are also being saved.

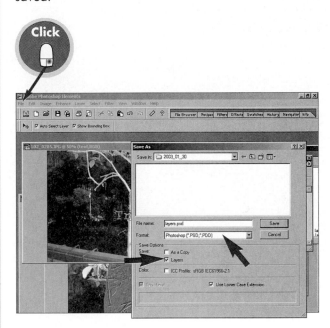

Task

22

Preparing Photos for Email and the Web

Adobe Photoshop Elements, and most imaging programs, can also help you prepare your photos for the Web. You've already learned a lot about editing and manipulating them, and if you use layers and learn Elements or another graphics software in depth, you can accomplish some amazing things. But you still need to know how to change a picture's properties to reduce its size to use in email or on the Web.

After all, if you were to email the 8MB file you downloaded at high resolution from the camera to someone, he would probably not be very happy.

How to Begin to Reduce File Sizes

As you've seen, file sizes are mainly a function of resolution (dimensions) and compression (the amount of information stored inside them). Reducing them effectively is a matter of trade-offs, such as how much reduction in quality is tolerable.

The two main file types for the Web are JPG and GIF. Although you can use GIFs for photographs, high-color images have too many colors to effectively display as GIFs (which are limited to 256 colors).

1 Choose a Large File

Open a large image file in Elements. How do you know it's large? Good question. One clue is that, when it opens, it displays at 25% (a small fraction) of its actual size.

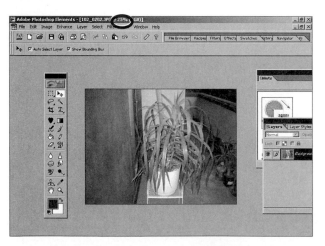

2 Open Its Image Properties

Select **Image**, **Resize**, **Image Size** to see the image properties dialog box.

3 Examine the Properties

At 1600×1200, this image is already twice as large as most people's entire Web browsers. And at 5.5MB, it's way too large to send or post online.

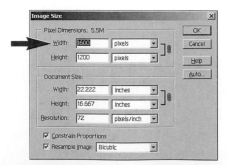

4 Play the Percentages

Let's change the way you use dimensions to percentage, for now. Click the drop-down arrow, and note that the aspect ratio of the dimension remains fixed.

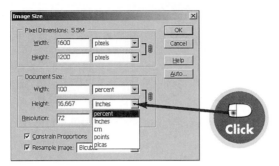

5 Make It Half Its Size

Make the image 50% of its original size; note that the resulting image will be full-screen in most Web browsers. The image is now 1.38MB, which is still big but not impossible.

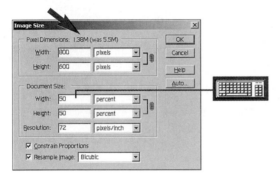

6 Change the View

Remember that it's still displayed at 25%. Press **Ctrl++** to change it to 2/3 of full-screen view. Now it looks much better.

How to Further Reduce File Sizes

Now you can continue to work with the image that began at 1600×1200 and see what else you can do to reduce its size.

1 Check the Image Mode

Under the Image menu, select **Mode**.

2 Change to Indexed Color

Click the same combination again, and select **Indexed Color**.

3 Set It to 256 Colors

Click **OK** at the default.

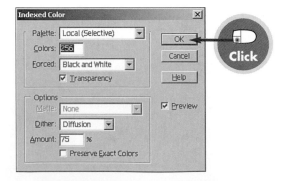

④ Check the Size

Select **Image**, **Resizing**, **Image Size**; then, check the results. The size is down to 469KB.

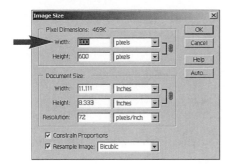

⑤ Save for Web

Select **File**, **Save for Web**.

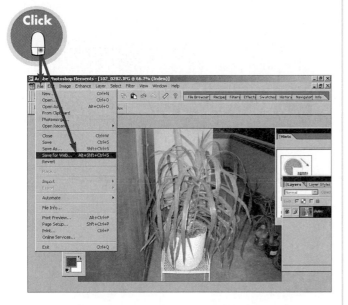

⑥ Optimize the Image

Grab the image to see some details. Select **JPG** from the drop-down menu (or try GIF). Select **JPG-Low**, and check the results. The image is now 28KB—can you tell the difference?

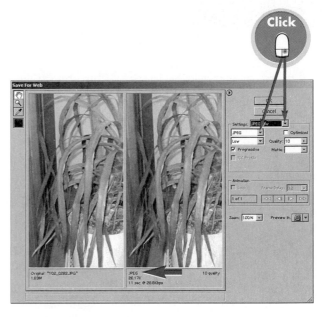

How-to Hint

Converting Color

You might have noticed that under the Image, Mode selection were selections for Black and White (and Gray Scale). That's how you can convert your pictures for these parameters without worrying about camera settings.

How to Attach It to Email

You're almost ready to send this image via email (or post it to a Web site). You've used the Optimize for Web dialog box and reduced the size to 28KB. What happens next?

① Select an Image Type

Let's see whether GIF is any better and what the results might be. The size is more than 228KB.

Click

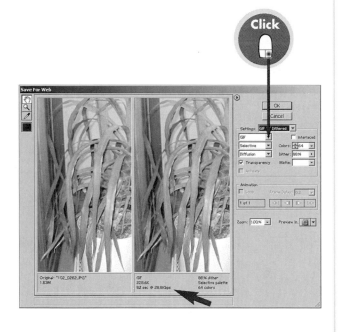

② Save the JPG

You can reoptimize by selecting **JPG-Low** and preview it in Internet Explorer.

Click

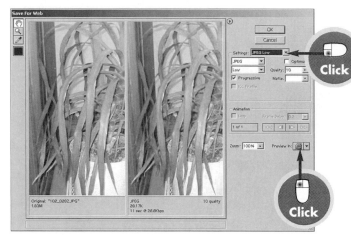

Click

③ Reduce Again

The image looks great. If you need even more reduction, though, you can reduce the dimensions again.

④ Export the File

Click **OK** in the Optimizing panel.

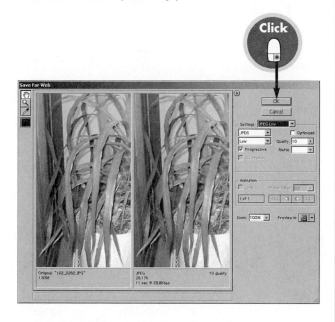

⑤ Save Your Final JPG

Click the drop-down arrow to put the image on the desktop, where you can find it (be sure to give it a name you can remember).

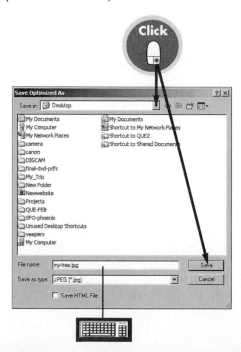

⑥ Attach It to Email

Open your email editor and click **Attachment** to find the file. Or, you can drag and drop it in from the desktop.

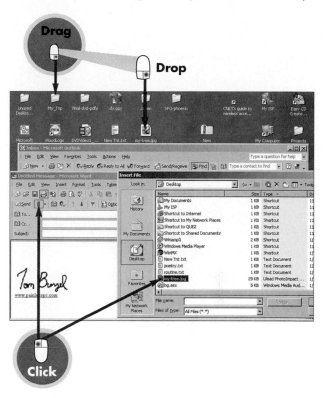

Posting Made Easy

If you noticed, when you saved the optimized JPG file, you also had an option to save an HTML Web page with it. This would let you easily post this image to a Web site by uploading both the HTML page and the JPG file to the same folder.

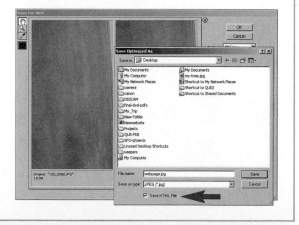

Task

23

Printing Your Finished Pictures

After you finish editing your photo, you might want to print for display or to pass around to your friends and family. You have two choices: You can print it yourself or send it to your local photo lab. Your photo lab will probably produce the best results and longevity, but so many high-quality color printers are available at inexpensive prices that it is a viable option to print them yourself. You might not even be able to notice the difference!

Color printing is a matter of learning the printer settings and doing a bit of experimentation. It helps if the camera, software, and printer are in the same family—Canon, HP, and so on—but you will still get some good results and some not so good.

Be sure you've loaded the correct type of paper specified by your printer, and for the best results, you should probably use high-gloss paper. Although you can print out of your graphics program, you can actually import your images into Microsoft Word or PowerPoint—or, for best results, use the bundled software.

How to Begin Printing Your Images

Let's use the Canon ZoomBrowser to begin printing some of your images. We'll work with the insurance photos I took of my apartment. Because I organized them into their own folder, they should be easy to find.

① Open the ZoomBrowser

Click the **Start** button; then, select **All Programs**, **Canon Utilities**, **ZoomBrowser EX**.

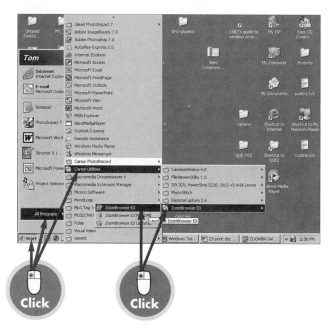

② Locate the Folder

There are my image files, right inside My Pictures in My Documents. Click to see the thumbnails.

③ Select the Images

Press the **Ctrl** key and click to select one or more images.

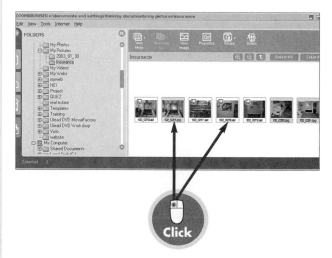

4 Begin to Print

Maximize the screen; then, click the **Print** icon.

5 Try a Layout

Select the **Layout Print** option.

6 Attach a Comment

You can automatically attach a comment, the date, and a filename. You can also print captions by clicking Select Captions for Printing. Just click **Open Layout Print**.

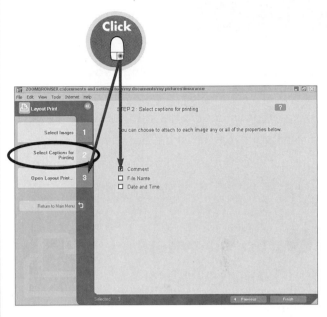

7 Begin Printing Options

Select your printer now, and then continue with a customized layout.

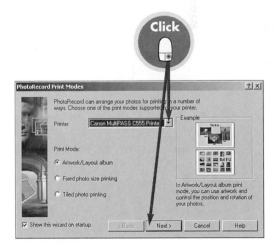

How to Continue Printing Images

By choosing layout printing, your utility has opened a subprogram that can create a layout from various templates and designs. In fact, many digital cameras and printers provide quick-and-dirty layout programs just like this to create a nice effect for printing digital files.

① Use the Wizard

Select **Layout** and click **Next** to see a preview of the page you're starting with. The default is Landscape; click **Next** to continue.

② Use Automatic Layout

Select the **Automatic Layout** option, and then click **Finish**. You can revise the page in the PhotoRecord editor.

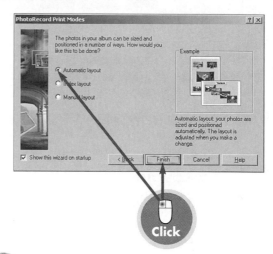

③ Select a New Layout

Click one of the circle icons to select a completely different look.

④ Resize the Images

Drag the **Photo Size** slider to expand or contract the images.

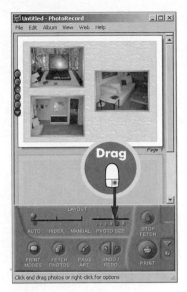

⑤ Use Some Artwork

Click **Page Art** to bring up a panel of preset backgrounds that you can attach. Click **Apply** to set the background.

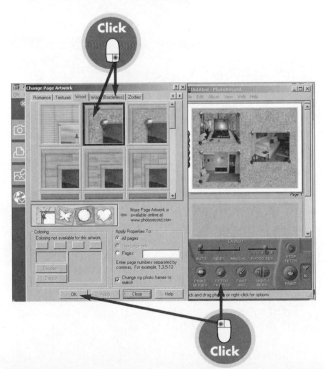

⑥ Fetch Another Photo

Select **Fetch Photo** to grab another image and put it into a second page.

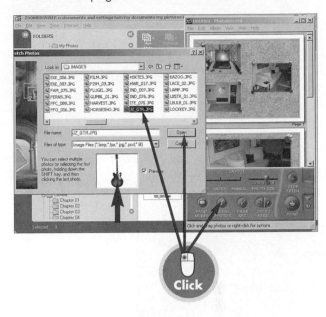

Automatic Resizing

You can drag and drop the image onto the original page, and the images will be resized automatically.

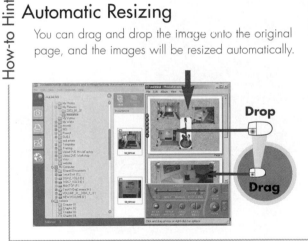

How-to Hint

IV

Digital Video

Task

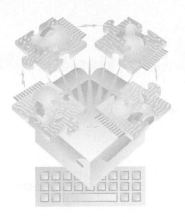

24

Getting Started with Digital Video

Welcome to the exciting world of digital video! Using your camcorder, a PC, and some editing software, you can now create movies that rival the kind of stuff you see on television. The problem is knowing exactly where to start. That's why I've tried to make it easy—in this part of the book, I've created some roadmaps for you. Start with the Video Production Roadmap. There, you'll find every major step along the path to video production laid out in snapshot form. Not only can you see the major steps along the way to making your first movie, you can also see where in the book you can turn for detailed instructions.

After that, you can check out guided tours of a typical digital camcorder along with VideoWave and Premiere. These tours show you the major interface elements of the programs so that you can dive right into the step-by-step instructions in the rest of the book.

A Video Production Roadmap

Video editing isn't as complicated as it might seem. Sure, there are a lot of things to learn—but you had to master your word processor once, too. In the next few pages, I lay out all the major ingredients in making a video. Follow along for a sneak peek at what this book has to offer.

❶ Create a Plan

Your plan—called a *storyboard* in video parlance—helps you decide what video to shoot and how to assemble all the video clips into a single video production.

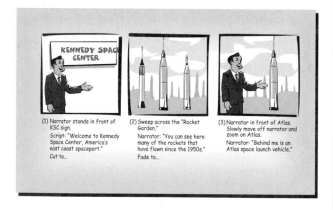

(1) Narrator stands in front of KSC sign.
Script: "Welcome to Kennedy Space Center, America's east coast spaceport."
Cut to...

(2) Sweep across the "Rocket Garden."
Narrator: "You can see here many of the rockets that have flown since the 1950s."
Fade to...

(3) Narrator in front of Atlas. Slowly move off narrator and zoom on Atlas.
Narrator: "Behind me is an Atlas space launch vehicle."

❷ Have Enough Memory

Make sure that your computer has enough memory; otherwise, your video may be jittery because the computer runs out of RAM and has to use the hard disk's slower swap file to generate video frames.

❸ How Big Is Your Hard Drive?

You'll need about 250MB of hard drive space for every minute of video you shoot. Is your hard drive big enough? If not, get a new one.

④ Install a Video Capture Card

You need a video capture card that's compatible with your editing software and with the kind of camcorder you are using.

⑤ Start Shooting

Load the film in your camcorder, perform a white balance to ensure that you've got good color balance in your video, and start shooting!

⑥ Capture Video

Then you'll have to grab the video from your camcorder and "capture" it into your PC before you can start editing the video.

⑦ Organize Your Movie

Organize all the video clips you've just captured to your hard drive by referring to your storyboard and dragging your clips to the video Storyline.

⑧ Trim Your Video

Fine-tune your clips by trimming the fat. Your clips should be sharp, focused, and to the point.

⑨ Grab Still Frames

Take snapshots of scenes in your movie or import photographs into your video to give some variety and additional interest to the final production.

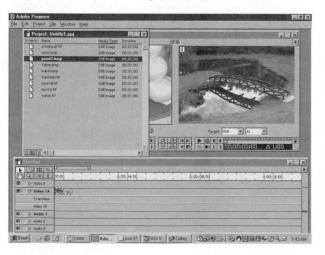

⑩ Capture CD Audio

Grab music from CDs and insert the audio tracks into your movie. Note that copyright laws prohibit you from using commercial sound tracks in anything other than a video intended for personal use.

⑪ Mix Sound

Add sound from narration, music, and other sources into your movie's soundtrack.

12 Fix Audio Glitches

Your audio and video don't always line up perfectly. Engineer the sound so that it all looks and sounds great.

13 Add Transitions

Transitions can be an elegant way to move from one scene to another. Choose from wipes, fades, and dozens of other effects, but use transitions in moderation.

14 Add Titles

Overlay titles on video or on color panels. Create titles, subtitles, and captions to help identify your video to your viewers.

15 Add Special Effects

Overlay a video clip on top of another clip for very cool results!

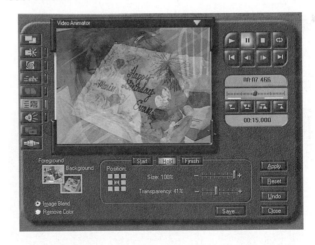

16 Create a Video Slideshow

Synchronize music and still images as a slideshow interlude in the middle of your video.

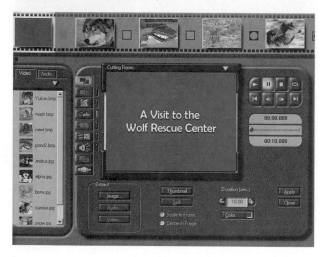

17 Roll the Credits

Add rolling credits to the end of your video production to identify all those involved in the film or just to have the final word.

18 Preview Your Production

At any point in the production, you can preview your creation on the computer screen to get a rough idea of what it will look like when done.

19 Produce the Movie

When the production is complete, generate the finished movie file.

20 Copy It to Videotape

Create a videotape from your produced movie file.

21 Put It on the Web

Take small movie files and upload them to a Web page where anyone can appreciate them.

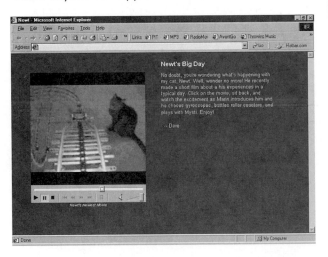

22 Burn a CD-ROM

Copy your video to CD and distribute it just as you would a digital videotape.

23 Insert Video into PowerPoint

Take your video clips and insert them into a presentation in PowerPoint.

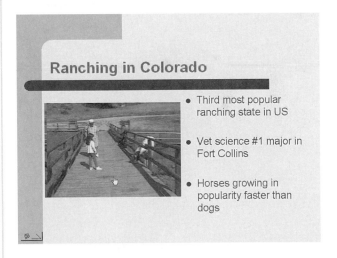

How to Get Around Your Camcorder

No two camcorders are exactly alike, but they tend to share many things in common. I've used this very popular JVC CyberCam to point out the most important features of whatever camcorder you use. Shooting clips using a digital camcorder is the same as using an analog camera; the differences generally become apparent only when you are transferring video from the camera to the PC. With a digital camcorder, you transfer video digitally with a FireWire connector; older VHS or 8mm camcorders need an analog capture card. Familiarize yourself with the features and controls of your camera so that when you're actually shooting video, you won't have to interrupt the shoot to find the zoom feature of your camera.

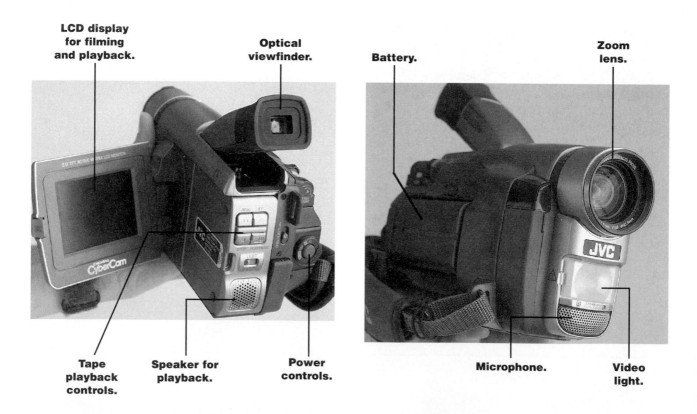

LCD display for filming and playback.

Optical viewfinder.

Battery.

Zoom lens.

Tape playback controls.

Speaker for playback.

Power controls.

Microphone.

Video light.

① Inputs

DV camcorders connect to the PC with a FireWire connector, also known as IEEE1394. If you have an analog camcorder, you'll use composite audio and video cables instead.

② Menu Controls

When your camera is in Manual mode, you can access the onscreen menus by pressing the menu dial and turning it.

③ Inside the Viewscreen

Menus are displayed on the LCD viewscreen and in the viewfinder.

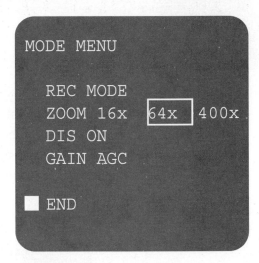

④ Tripod Connector

Most camcorders have a threaded socket in the bottom of the camera for attaching a tripod. You should use a tripod in low-light conditions or when panning an action scene to eliminate the shake that's typical when you hold the camera in your hand.

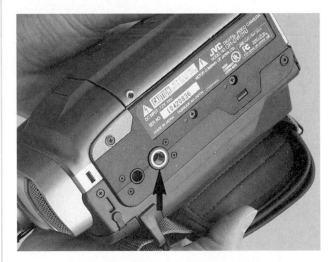

How to Get Around MGI VideoWave III

VideoWave is a great program because it has perhaps 80% of the most important features in a high-end program such as Adobe Premiere, yet it's easy to learn and almost impossible to "get lost" in. VideoWave uses a Storyline at the top of the screen for arranging your clips, a library on the left side of the screen, and a multipurpose editing room in the middle. The function of the middle of the screen changes depending on what mode you're in.

Click and drag the Storyline to see any panels that are offscreen.

Menu button.

Empty panel.

A panel in the Storyline with a video scene.

Storyline.

Transition place-holder.

Library.

Viewscreen.

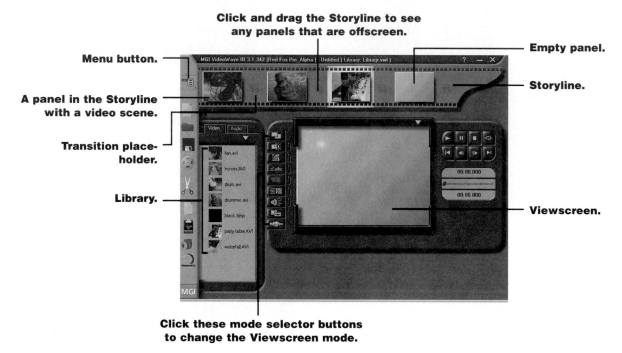

Click these mode selector buttons to change the Viewscreen mode.

File Formats

You'll see a variety of file formats when you edit video in programs such as VideoWave and Premiere, and some of them might be new to you. Here are the most common formats:

- **AVI**—The Video for Windows format is commonly used as the "delivery method" for playing video on a Windows PC. Your finished movies will often be in this format.
- **MPG**—The MPG (or MPEG) format is a great video format when you're playing back from the Web or CD-ROM because it highly compresses your movie.
- **WAV**—The WAV format is a common way of encoding and playing sound files.
- **MP3**—MP3s are a relatively new audio format, most commonly used to copy songs from audio CDs.
- **TIF**—TIF is a high-quality format for still images.
- **JPG**—The JPG (or JPEG) format is a great format for displaying still images on the Web because it compresses the file size significantly while having minimal effect on image quality.

① Access the Menus

VideoWave has several menus, but they're not in a menu bar at the top of the screen as you might expect. Instead, the main menu is found by clicking the menu button at the top left of the screen. Other menus are indicated by the arrowheads that point down at the Library and Viewscreen.

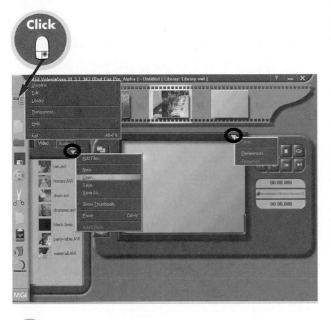

② Control Effects

Many elements in your videos can change during the course of a scene. Click the **Start** button to set the initial conditions of the scene; click the **Hold** button to set what happens in the middle of the scene; click the **Finish** button to set the conditions for the end of the scene.

③ Control Effect Timing

You can control not just the effect itself, but the timing of the Start, Hold, and Finish effects. The four buttons under the slider let you "punch-in" the point at which the effect starts and ends, as well as when and how long the hold effect occurs. To avoid an extended hold period but to move smoothly from start to finish, click the **Hold Start** and **Hold Finish** buttons at the same point in the timeline.

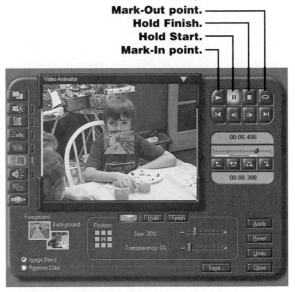

④ Use VCR Controls

If you need to play a video clip, use the VCR controls to control the video. The buttons do just what you'd expect them to do if you found them on a cassette tape player—only now, you're playing video clips.

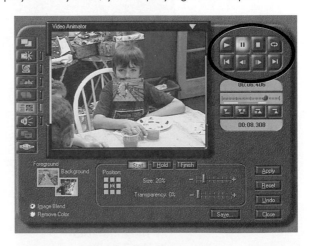

How to Get Around Adobe Premiere 5.1

Throughout this book, I've included alternative steps that involve Premiere instead of VideoWave. I did that for two reasons: First, it's an easy way to learn both programs at the same time. Second, there are effects I wanted to teach you that are simply impossible to do in VideoWave, but are easily accomplished in Premiere. So, this book is two for the price of one: When you're ready to step up to Premiere, you've already got a handy guide.

Setting Premiere's Workspace

In Task 3, I showed you how to set VideoWave to record and edit video on a specific hard disk. You should do the same in Premiere. Start the program and select **File**, **Preferences**, **Scratch Disks/Device Control**. From the dialog box that appears, select your fastest hard disk (preferably a dedicated drive) for your video work.

Premiere Steps Identified

To help you identify instructions in this book that are for Adobe Premiere, the background color for the steps changes and the icon appears next to the step heading. If you don't see these cues, the instructions are for MGI VideoWave.

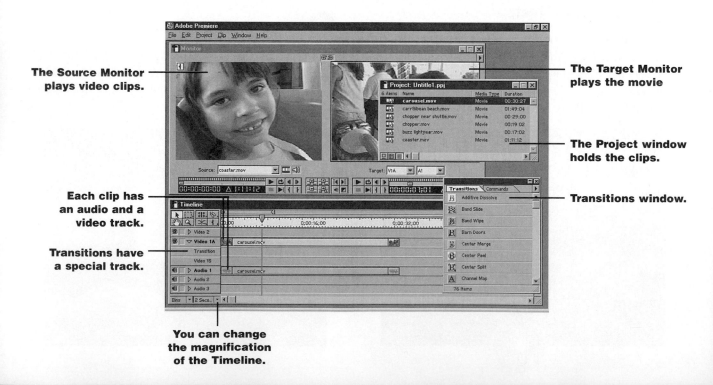

The Source Monitor plays video clips.

The Target Monitor plays the movie

The Project window holds the clips.

Each clip has an audio and a video track.

Transitions window.

Transitions have a special track.

You can change the magnification of the Timeline.

① Configure Your Project

When you first start Premiere, you should configure the program to use the right settings for the kind of movie you plan to make. Select an appropriate compressor in the series of Project Settings dialog boxes, for instance, as well as the proper frame size for your movie. (Click **Prev** and **Next** to move between the pages of this dialog box.)

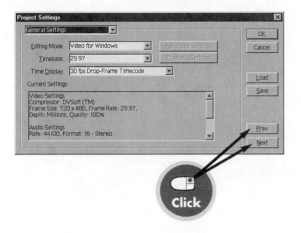

② Display Windows

You can close windows you aren't using in Premiere, but you need to know how to get them open again. Select **Window** from the menu bar; you'll find the Project, Monitor, Timeline, and Transition windows there.

③ The Timeline

Unlike VideoWave's Storyline, the Premiere Timeline lets you add clips one after another in tracks (the default track is Video 1A). To perform special effects such as superimposing video and adding transitions, you add clips on alternate tracks. There can be up to 99 video tracks and an additional 99 audio tracks available for each clip in Premiere.

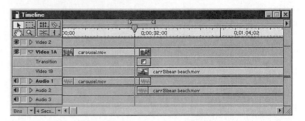

④ Trim Clips

The Source Monitor window contains controls for locating specific frames of video and marking them as the start and end of the scene. An Apply button appears over the clip. Click the **Apply** button to save the edits and update the scene in the Timeline.

Task

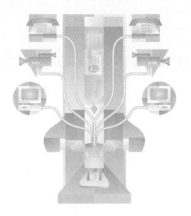

25

Working with Your Camcorder

Before you can start editing your video like a digital version of a Steven Spielberg blockbuster film, you must first create your video footage. For that, you must become familiar with your camcorder and learn how to get the most out of it.

Modern camcorders are wonders of automation; in general, all you need to do to get acceptable results is press the red Record button and start filming. But there's a lot more you can do to knock the socks off your audience. By mastering the manual controls on your camera, you can create video that is noticeably better. If you plan ahead, you can optimize your footage for the movie you plan to piece together eventually on your PC.

The tasks in this part of the book help you learn to plan the video you have to shoot to ultimately create the movie. You'll learn about some of the basic features of most of today's camcorders as well as some simple props and techniques you can use to improve the quality of the video you shoot. You don't have to be a member of an Oscar-award–winning film crew to get great results, but you should be familiar with the techniques presented in the following tasks.

How to Use a Storyboard

Most film projects benefit from a bit of planning and preparation. One of the first things you should do when you set out to make a video is to storyboard it. A *storyboard* describes the events of the film in thumbnail form. You'll find a storyboard handy for staying on track and on schedule.

How-to Hint

Revising the Storyboard

If you do a good job creating a storyboard, you'll have an easy time filming your video. Remember, however, that you might need to revise your storyboard when you get into the editing stage. Be thinking about special effects, music, and titles, which you won't add yet but will need in the editing phase.

Use this as a guide to filming and editing.

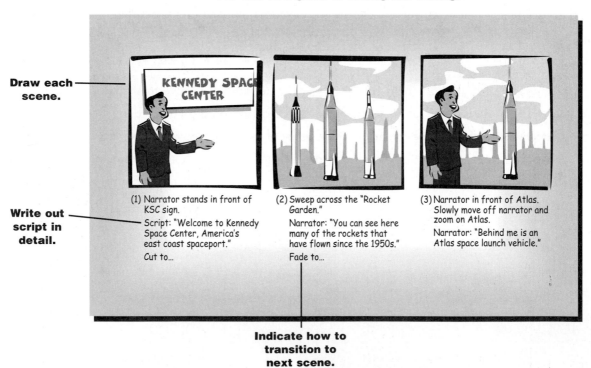

Draw each scene.

Write out script in detail.

(1) Narrator stands in front of KSC sign.
Script: "Welcome to Kennedy Space Center, America's east coast spaceport."
Cut to...

(2) Sweep across the "Rocket Garden."
Narrator: "You can see here many of the rockets that have flown since the 1950s."
Fade to...

(3) Narrator in front of Atlas. Slowly move off narrator and zoom on Atlas.
Narrator: "Behind me is an Atlas space launch vehicle."

Indicate how to transition to next scene.

① Sketch the Key Scenes

A storyboard is a cartoon you draw that describes, scene by scene or frame by frame, what happens in your movie. Draw all the events, depicting the video from key camera angles you intend to shoot. You can use a storyboard as a road map to filming the video.

② Add Narrative

Under each frame, describe what is happening, who is in the scene, and what everyone is saying. You can also describe the mood or any other key elements.

Close up of Susan.

Zoom out as Peter enters scene and they look at each other.

③ Write the Script

At this stage, it's also important to write a script that identifies what everyone is going to say. The script will help identify any weaknesses in the storyboard and also flesh out the video you are about to film.

Close up of Susan.

Zoom out as Peter enters scene and they look at each other.

Script: Susan: "Where's the money?"

Peter: "I couldn't get it away from Tony."

④ Build the Props List

The last thing you need to do is detail any costumes, props, and other essential items you must have available. Place this information under each frame of the storyboard where appropriate.

Close up of Susan.

Zoom out as Peter enters scene and they look at each other.

Script: Susan: "Where's the money?"

Peter: "I couldn't get it away from Tony."

Props: Peter has gun

How to Handle DV Tapes

Although I refer to them as DV camcorders, they're really MiniDV, a smaller version of the DV standard. That's actually great because the MiniDV tapes that these camcorders use are tiny—about the size of a pair of AA batteries. Handle them carefully, and they'll take great movies.

How-to Hint

Fixing Broken Tapes

It's possible for tapes to break, especially if they are used over and over again. Many camera and video shops will fix broken tapes for a small fee, usually under $15. If the break occurs in the middle of the tape, you'll lose a few seconds of video; if the tape breaks in the leader, it's possible that no data will be lost at all.

Tapes come in a variety of lengths.

The compact size of the cassette means that it is easy to carry.

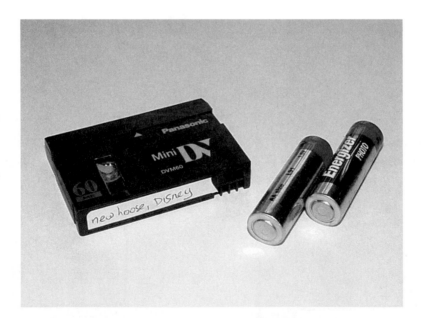

The new MiniDV cassettes are about the size of a couple of AA batteries.

① Open the Camera

DV camcorders must be turned on before you can load and eject tapes. Turn your camera on and then press and release the **Eject** button. The camera will open, exposing the loading mechanism.

② Insert the Tape

Insert the tape cassette so that its spindles face down into the camera's mechanism and the tape faces the read/write heads at the front of the camera. It's not possible to put the tape in backward or upside down, so if you encounter resistance, check the cassette's orientation.

③ Close the Camera

Now you must close the camera—*but be careful!* You can damage the camera by applying pressure to the wrong part. You should press down to lock the cassette in place, taking note of any labels on the camera to indicate where to press.

④ Tension the Tape

The first time you use a tape, it's a good idea to fast-forward to the end, and then rewind the tape back to the beginning. This action applies a uniform level of tension across all parts of the tape.

How to Zoom Effectively

The zoom feature on your camcorder is a valuable tool for composing your shots and capturing just the right elements in each scene. Specific *focal lengths* also give your movies a certain look. Telephoto shots, for instance, compress the foreground and background while keeping only the subject in sharp focus; more moderate lens magnifications are good for keeping everything in the image in focus at the same time.

Digital Zoom Warning

People often buy a particular camcorder because it offers a massive zoom—something along the lines of 200X or 300X. In reality, that number refers to a *digital zoom*, not an *optical zoom*. Optical zooms use the camera's optics to enlarge the image. But digital zooms use electronic trickery to increase the magnification, and the results are often noisy, grainy, and ugly. Avoid using the digital zoom very often—try to stick within the limits of the camera's optical zoom.

Subject is in sharp focus.

High zoom magnification blurs the background.

Zooming eliminates background clutter.

① Set a Slow Shutter Speed

You can get decent motion blur even with your camera set on full automatic, but the slower your shutter speed is set, the better your results will be. I suggest that you set your camera's shutter to manual mode and try 1/30 or 1/60 second.

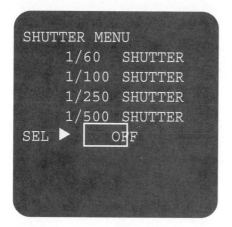

SHUTTER MENU
1/60   SHUTTER
1/100 SHUTTER
1/250 SHUTTER
1/500 SHUTTER
SEL ▶ [OFF]

② Set the Focus Manually

In certain situations, you might not be able to keep the moving subject in the middle of the frame where the auto-focus sensors are located. If that's the case, set the focus to manual and dial in the focus to where the moving subject will be when you start shooting.

Prefocus to this distance before filming or use autofocus

③ Zoom Out

Before the shot begins, make sure that you're not zoomed in too far. If you can't see enough of the background, the effect of the motion blur will be lost.

④ Pan and Film

Time to get the shot. Start recording and pan with the moving object. Ideally, it will move from left to right (or right to left) across your field of view. Just turn with the moving object to keep it in the frame throughout the shot.

Pan

How to Light the Scene

Properly exposing video is a bit different than setting the exposure on a still camera, but the principles are the same. You can keep your camera in auto mode all the time, or you can take control and get better results with manual overrides. Every camcorder is different; to learn how to access your camera's manual exposure mode, refer to the documentation that came with the camcorder.

Exposure Explained

The camera exposes the scene by balancing the *shutter speed* (the amount of time each frame of film is exposed to light) with the *aperture setting* (the size of the opening that lets light through the lens). The bigger the aperture's f/stop—expressed as f/2, f/5.6, or f/22, for instance—the smaller the aperture opening.

Lower lighting level reduces depth of focus, blurring background.

Filming in the shade reduces harsh light.

Reflector adds light to face.

① Stay in the Shade

When you shoot outdoors, direct sunlight can overwhelm your camcorder and create unflattering lighting or harsh shadows on your subject. Film in a shaded area whenever possible, and keep the sun to your left or right, never directly in front or behind you.

② Go Manual When Moving

When you move from indoors to outdoors within a scene, the sudden change in lighting conditions can radically underexpose or overexpose the subject for a few seconds while the camera adjusts. To avoid that problem, set the exposure manually and leave it there through the scene transition. The background is less important than the subject is!

③ Use a Reflector

A reflector is especially useful outdoors, where you can position someone who is holding it off to the side of your subject. This kind of light is more flattering to people than harsh, direct sunlight.

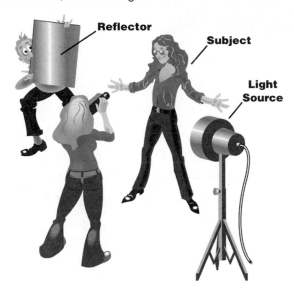

④ Use Multiple Lights

When filming indoors, you have a lot more control over the lighting. If you're in a really controlled situation, such as shooting a talking head or an interview, I recommend that you use two or three lights to illuminate your subject.

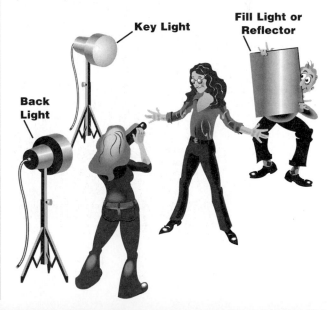

How to Control Depth of Focus

Beginning videographers rarely think about the subtleties of filmmaking, but it's the little things that can really make your projects look professional and have that extra punch. One such aspect is *depth of field*, which determines how much of the scene is in sharp focus. Creative use of depth of field can have a powerful, dramatic role in your films.

Depth of Field Explained

Depth of field—the amount of the scene that remains in focus in front and in back of the focused subject—depends on both the amount of zoom and the aperture setting of the camera. Use depth of field to isolate the subject from the foreground and background or to keep the entire scene in focus. Unlike the process with a 35 mm SLR camera, you don't have to do anything special to "check" the depth of field you are filming; what you see through the viewfinder is what you get on film.

This effect is achieved with a telephoto zoom or an open aperture.

A blurred background makes the subject stand out.

❶ Zoom In: Less Depth

An easy way to reduce depth of field to isolate your subject is to work at the telephoto end of the optical zoom on your camera. However, note that zooming into the digital zoom ratios on your camera has no effect on depth of field.

❷ Zoom Out: More Depth

You achieve the most depth of field by zooming out to the camera's most wide-angle setting. At this setting, virtually all of the scene should be in sharp focus.

❸ Open Aperture: Less Depth

If you can switch to the camcorder's manual mode, opening the aperture to admit more light also has the effect of reducing depth of field. In this example, note that although the camera lens is zoomed out to capture both children, the wide-open aperture setting narrows depth of field so that the focus is only on the child in front.

❹ Close Aperture: More Depth

In manual exposure mode, if you shut down the aperture to smaller values, you reduce the light entering the lens and simultaneously increase depth of field, making more of the scene in focus. In this example, note that the lens is zoomed out about the same as it was for the children in the preceding step, but the smaller aperture setting forces a deeper field of focus.

How to White-Balance Your Scene

Camcorders have to be tuned to the particular color of light you are filming in; otherwise, colors (such as flesh tones) look wrong. When your camcorder knows what color white is, all the other colors come out accurately as well. This adjustment is usually done automatically, but you can get better results by manually white-balancing your camcorder—especially indoors, in low-light situations, when using a camera light, or with unusually tinted overhead lights.

Why Balance Your Whites?

Different light sources (such as light provided by sunrise, midday sun, candlelight, and fluorescent bulbs) have different color temperatures, and this affects the way your camera displays color. An improperly balanced scene will appear reddish or bluish, depending on the color temperature. For the most accurate video, balance your whites often, and don't trust the automatic controls unless you have to.

Remember to reset your white balance whenever conditions change. If you use manual white balance settings from indoors when you film outdoors, you'll get very unusual results.

Have your subject or an assistant hold a paper near the subject's face, where color accuracy is most important.

Switch to automatic white balance or recalibrate when conditions change.

Use plain white paper to perform a manual white balance.

Experiment with white balance to see what kinds of locations require manual settings.

① Enter the Menu

The exact procedure for balancing whites manually depends on the kind of camera you have, but most white balancing procedures are similar. Start by opening the **White Balance** menu and selecting **Manual Mode**.

② Focus on White Paper

Have someone hold a piece of bright white paper in front of the camera. Position yourself so that the paper fills the frame and is in focus. Also, be sure that the paper is bathed in the light that you plan to shoot your subjects in so that you balance the camera properly.

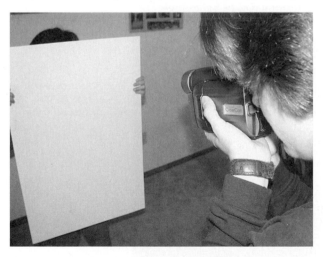

③ Set the Balance

Refer to your camera's documentation to learn how to set the white balance. (The JVC camera in this example uses the Menu dial to lock in the white balance.) Then select the appropriate control on the camera to "memorize" the color value of the paper. This sets the white balance for the current lighting conditions.

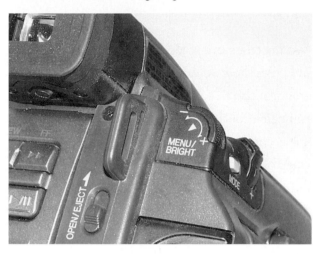

④ Exit the Menu

Finish the process by exiting the White Balance menu. The camera is now set for filming. Remember that when you're done filming this scene, you should either set the camera back to automatic white balance or recalibrate the manual white balance for the next set of lighting conditions.

How to Take Low-Light Movies

Camcorders are rated by their *lux value*, which indicates how low the light can be before the camera can't record an image. Lux values are subjective and are not standard, but typically a 2-lux camera can work in candlelight. That's not bad, but you need to know how to get the most out of low-light situations.

Low-Light Pitfalls

Although you can film in low-light situations with most camcorders, keep these tips in mind for best results:

- Auto-focus systems fail in low light. You might need to resort to manual focusing if you're filming by candlelight.

- The quality of light varies dramatically in a dark room. When you set the white balance, put the white card exactly where you plan to film.

- The quality of video recorded in low light will be dramatically lower than the quality of video recorded in daylight.

Manual white balance corrects the color of the scene (using the automatic white balance, these flames would be orange).

Use overhead lights if available.

Video is grainy in low-light situations.

Camera light fills in the subject's face.

❶ Set White Balance

Low-light situations are almost certainly outside the camera's preset white balance values. Whenever filming in these situations, the first thing you should do is set the camera's white balance. If the lighting changes during the shoot, reset the white balance as often as necessary.

❷ Use Lights

Camera lights are often harsh and unforgiving, but they are essential if you're trying to film in very low-light conditions. Your camera might have a built-in light you can turn on, or you can purchase a clip-on camera light.

❸ Avoid Digital Zoom

In low-light situations, the image will probably be grainy—this is digital noise that occurs when there isn't enough light to make a good shot. Digital zooming introduces noise of its own, so avoid that feature when you film in the dark.

Here is 64X digital zoom in ordinary lighting.

❹ Use Night Vision

In near or absolute darkness, you might be able to use another feature: infrared recording. This feature is found in Sony Handycams, where it goes by the name NightShot. NightShot works only up to about 10 feet away from the camera and creates a greenish monochrome image similar to what you would see through night-vision goggles.

How to Reduce Camera Shake

Many digital cameras come with a feature known as *digital image stabilization*. Image stabilization can be used to reduce the apparent jitter or shakiness in a scene, especially when you're using the zoom. There are other ways to stabilize your image, too.

When Not to Stabilize

Electronic stabilization tries to mimic the SteadiCam, a device used by pros to reduce vibration when filming with a moving camera. Unfortunately, digital artifacts can be obvious when using this feature. Avoid it when filming in low light, when using the digital zoom, or when shooting scenes with lots of obvious stripes (such as Venetian blinds). All these situations increase the potential for digital noise on film if your camera is set to use its electronic stabilization feature.

A tripod is the best way to reduce shake.

Mount the tripod on solid ground.

Always try to shoot in adequate light.

Securely tighten all tripod elements except the head.

Leave the tripod head loose so that you can pan around the action.

① Enable the Stabilization Mode

When you're in a situation where you want to minimize the jitters that come from camera shake, enable your camera's digital image stabilization mode. You can find it in the camera's menu; refer to the manual for details on where to find it.

② Move Slowly

Regardless of whether you're using electronic stabilization, try to move the camera slowly and steadily. Don't jerk the camera around. Note that fast zooming can induce motion sickness in your audience. Zoom slowly and keep any zooming you do to a minimum.

③ Use a Tripod

The best way to stabilize a scene is by mounting your camcorder on a tripod. Leave the swivel head loose so that you can move the camera from side to side and up and down while you film.

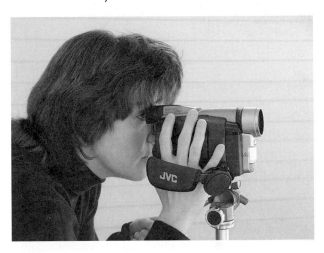

④ Get Support from a Doorway

If you can't use a tripod, try leaning your body against something solid (such as a doorway, a fence, or a post) for support. This trick really works.

How to Film with a Blue Screen

Special effects in movies are often done with a *blue screen*. By filming the action in front of a specially colored backdrop, another video layer can later replace the background. You can do the same thing with your camcorder—although it takes practice and careful planning. Keep in kind that the blue screen does not have to be a backdrop. In this task, I intentionally have my subject hold a blue-screen matte so that you can see the effect of adding a layer of video at some random location in the scene.

Your First Blue Screen

Special effects such as blue screens are the most fun and rewarding parts of experimenting with a camcorder. But good blue-screen mattes are hard to get. To get your feet wet, try filming one person in front of a solid wall. You might also try putting a piece of brightly colored poster paper on the wall to get an evening news "weather map" effect. If you have success with these videos, step up to making moving action against a colored backdrop.

Keep the color tolerance low enough so that you don't spill video into the rest of your scene.

Keep the blue screen lit evenly for best results.

Background video.

Use a unique color for your "blue screen."

Foreground video.

1 Find a Backdrop

Your backdrop doesn't have to be blue, but it should be a very different color than anything else in the scene. You needn't fill the whole background with the backdrop; a small square can serve as a weather map or window.

2 Test It First

Before you bank on the backdrop working, test it first. Film the backdrop with your camcorder and then import the clip into VideoWave or Premiere to see whether you can make your particular blue screen work.

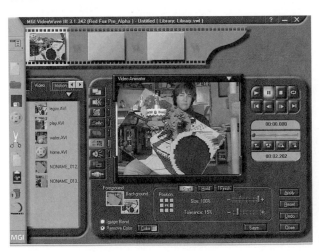

3 Light It Carefully

The backdrop should be lit evenly, with no obvious shadows or highlights. It might take more than one backlight or reflector to illuminate the backdrop properly. Make sure that any people in front of the backdrop don't cast shadows on the material.

4 Edit

After you have your video on tape, you'll need to use the Chroma key transparency filter in either VideoWave or Premiere to let another layer of video "see through" the backdrop.

How to Add In-the-Lens Transitions

Transitions are graphical segues that signal the end of one scene and the start of the next. A transition can be as simple as a fade-out or as complex as seeing one clip fly off-screen as another clip enters the picture. Your camcorder probably has the capability to perform some simple transitions, eliminating the need to create them on the PC. In these steps, you learn how to create a transition directly in the camcorder, without using the PC.

How-to Hint

The PC Does It Better

If you don't want to edit your movie on a PC, adding transitions between scenes in the camera may be okay. But you can get snazzier results with editing software such as VideoWave or Premiere. If you do want to edit your video on a PC, don't use in-camera fades and wipes. If you use fades and wipes, you make it harder to separate scenes for editing because they're "glued together" on tape with a transition.

Camera stores the wipe on tape.

Leading edge of wipe.

Second scene.

First scene.

① Enable Fades or Wipes

Refer to your camcorder's manual and find the menu setting for the automatic transitions, usually called a *fade*, *wipe*, or *dissolve*. You should see a short menu of possible options to choose from.

```
FOCUS         AUTO
EXPOSURE      AUTO
W. BALANCE    AUTO
FADER        [ON]


■ END
```

② Select the Transition

Pick the transition you'd like to use. A *fade* "fades" from black or white; a *wipe* or a *slide* physically moves the new video into the frame while displacing the old video. A *dissolve* fades from one video to the next. For more complex transitions, you'll have to move your video to the PC.

```
FADER
        WIPE-SLIDE
        DISSOLVE
        RANDOM
SEL ▶   OFF
        FADER-WHITE
        FADER-BLACK
```

③ Record Your Scene

The transition effect happens automatically when you press the Record button to start and stop recording. When you are done with the effect, remember to turn off the transition feature in the camera's menu.

④ Don't Turn Off the Camera

If you turn off your camcorder after filming a scene, the ending position will be lost and the camera can't use a transition to ease into the next scene you film.

Task

26

Editing Your Movie

We've finally reached the fun part of the process. With the video *clips*—the scenes of your movie—stored on your PC's hard drive, it's time to mold them into a film. The tasks in this part of the book cover all the basics—generating the overall structure of your film, adding transitions, editing the scenes, and even creating special effects.

Later in the book, you'll learn how to incorporate titles and sound into the movie as well. When all the basics are in place, you'll finish the process by *producing* your movie. That final step takes all the separate video clips and renders them into a single, high-quality movie that can be played back on videotape, the Web, or CD-ROM. As you work your way through the tasks in this part, keep in mind that your movie, at this stage, is still "unassembled"—you can get only a rough idea of the final product when you preview it.

From this point on in the book, we use MGI VideoWave and Adobe Premiere (both are found on the CD-ROM at the back of the book) to create your movies. If you're new to video editing, try VideoWave. It has a lot of features, yet it's extremely easy to use. When you want to try more advanced tricks and discover that VideoWave can't quite get you there, try Premiere. I hand-picked both of these programs for the book because I believe they represent the best video editors on the market. You can't go wrong with either of them.

For now, let's get started laying out your movie.

How to Prepare the Editor

When you first start your video editor, it is not necessarily ready to start creating your masterpiece. In the case of VideoWave, for instance, the video clip library might be filled with sample clips and the Storyline might have unwanted bits of an old video in it. This task explains how you can start the creation of any new video project with a clean slate.

Menu button.

Blank Storyline.

Viewscreen.

New production.

VCR controls.

Library of video clips.

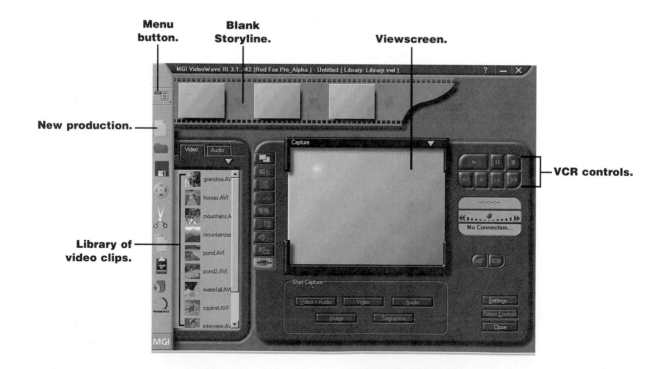

❶ Clear the Storyline

In VideoWave parlance, the *storyline* is the set of panels that run across the top of the screen. Each panel holds one scene in your video. To clear the Storyline and make it ready for a new project, click the **New Production** icon in the toolbar.

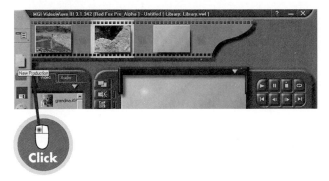

❷ Clear the Library

If the Library is full of clips that aren't a part of your video, you can clear them all out at once by clicking the list menu arrowhead and selecting **New**. To delete individual clips, click the clip you want to delete and press the **Delete** key; when prompted, decide whether you want to remove the clip from the hard disk entirely or just from the Library list.

❸ Load Clips into the Library

Load all the video clips you want to use into the Library. To do that, click the list menu arrowhead and select **Add Files**. In the Open dialog box that appears, locate the video files you captured on your hard drive and click **Open** to make those files available in the Library.

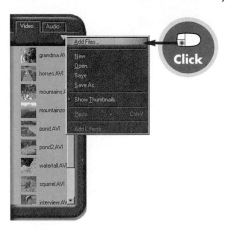

❹ Configure Your Project

Some video editors, such as Premiere, can create a broad variety of video projects. They work best when you configure the software for the kind of video you want to make right at the beginning. Start Premiere and click the **Load** button. Select a preset, or template, that reflects the kind of video you want to make, such as DV. The presets you see in your own copy of Premiere might differ from those you see here, depending on the kind of capture card you have and the kinds of files it supplies to Premiere.

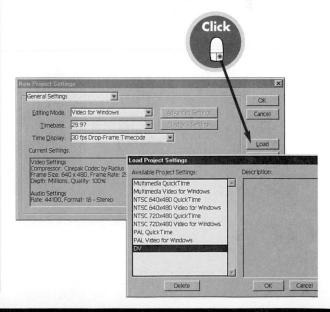

How to Populate the Storyline

The first step in any video project is to lay out the clips you plan to use in the video editor's timeline or storyboard. VideoWave uses a storyboard concept—the panels at the top of the screen represent sequential scenes in your video, which MGI calls a *storyline*. Premiere is more traditional; it uses the concept of a timeline. In Premiere, you drag clips to the Timeline, where they appear stacked like a bar graph.

Storyline.

Drag and drop clips from the Library to positions on the Storyline to rough in the flow of the video.

① Preview Your Clips

Before you drag clips to the Storyline, you can preview them to make sure that you have the right clip in hand. Double-click a clip in the Library. The clip will appear in the Viewscreen. Click the VCR controls to play the clip and make sure that it's the one you want to use.

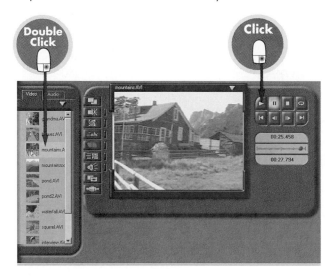

② Drag and Drop

Now drag the clip from the Library and drop it on the Storyline. It'll appear in the first panel. To finish creating the rough draft of your video, continue dragging clips to the Storyline, dropping each to the right of the previous clip.

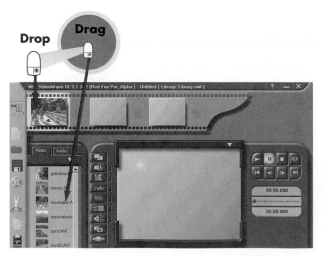

③ Preview from the Storyline

If you need to refresh your memory about what's in a Storyline clip, you can preview it from there as well. Just double-click any panel in the Storyline; the clip appears in the Viewscreen, where you can play it with the VCR controls.

④ Drag and Drop

In Adobe Premiere, the idea is the same—double-click any clip in the Project window to preview it; drag it to the Timeline to add it to the video you are creating. Drag the clip to the Video 1A line; add subsequent clips to the Video 1A track by dropping them to the right of preceding clips.

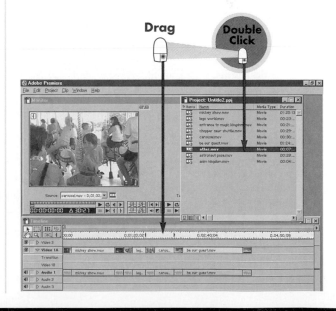

How to Rearrange Scenes

Even with a well-organized storyboard and the best of intentions, you're going to want to rearrange your video after the clips have been added to the Storyline. That's okay; it's easy to do. In fact, that's the magic of nonlinear editing: You can add, remove, and rearrange clips at will.

Remembering the Right Mouse Button

As with most Windows applications, VideoWave uses the right mouse button to simplify your work. Right-click any clip—either in the Library or the Storyline—and get a list of options such as copying, pasting, and deleting the video. Often, this is the most convenient way to work with a clip.

Rearranging Scenes in Premiere

If you're working in Premiere, editing clips is a snap. If you've added a few scenes to the Timeline, you can rearrange them just by dragging and dropping them from one position to another. Likewise, to delete a scene, just right-click the scene and press the **Delete** key.

Right-click the clip for more options.

Select a panel and press Delete to remove the clip from the Storyline (but not from the Library).

Drag from the Library to a Storyline panel to add a clip.

Drag a clip to a new place on the Storyline to rearrange clips.

Drag from the Library between Storyline panels to insert a clip between existing clips.

① Move Clips in the Storyline

If you decide that you want to move a clip to a different part of the movie, you can drag and drop it to the desired location. To move the clip in the Storyline, first click the clip to select it; click again, the second time holding down the mouse button. Then move the mouse, dragging the clip to the new location in the Storyline.

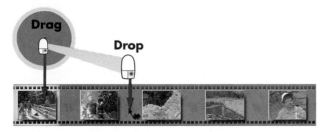

② Delete a Scene

If you want to eliminate a clip from the Storyline, just click the clip to select it and press the **Delete** key on the keyboard. The clip is removed from the video but remains in the Library for you to use again. Alternatively, right-click the clip you want to delete and select **Remove** from the shortcut menu.

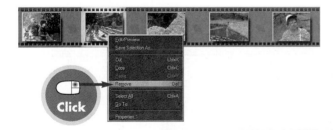

③ Insert a Scene

You already know how to add clips to the end of the Storyline. To add a clip to a location in the middle of the Storyline, just drag it from the Library to a position between two existing clips. When you release the mouse button, the clip will be inserted at that position.

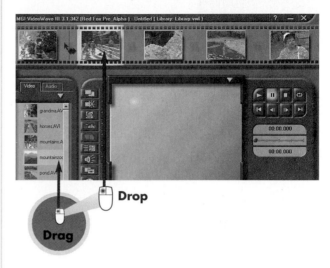

④ Duplicate a Scene

You might want to include the same scene in two parts of your video, especially if you edit them differently (as explained in Task 5, "How to Trim the Length of a Clip"). To copy a clip, right-click the original clip in the Storyline and select **Copy** from the shortcut menu. Then right-click a blank panel in the Storyline and select **Paste** from the shortcut menu.

How to Save and Open Your Project

Because you probably can't create your entire video production and save it to tape or CD-ROM in a single sitting, at some point you'll have to save your work so that you can pick it up again later where you left off.

Getting Help from Preferences

Select **Preferences** from VideoWave's menu button to access a few options that can make your life easier. In general, you should probably select **Save Library with Production** because that way you don't have to reload all your potential video clips every time you start the program. You might also want to select Open Last Production on Start Up because that option saves you the trouble of loading the in-progress production every time you start the program. One last tip: Don't select Show Splash Screen on Startup because it gets annoying after a while.

Select Storyline, Save from the menu button.

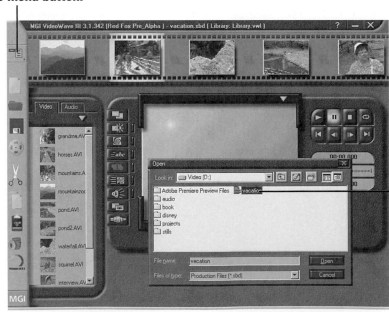

Save your work often so that the most current version of your production is available.

① Save Your Work

Get in the habit of saving your work frequently because VideoWave won't do it for you. Select **Storyline**, **Save As** from the menu button to give your production a name and save it. After the first time you save, you can select Storyline, Save to quickly save your work. By default, your production file is given the extension **.sbd**.

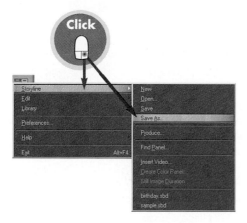

② Open Your Production

When you start VideoWave and want to return to a saved production, select **Storyline**, **Open** from the menu icon. The Open dialog box appears, from which you can select the project you want to work on.

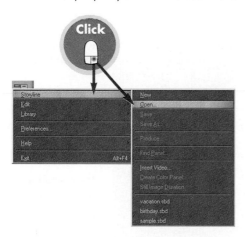

③ Save Your Project

In Premiere, the process of saving your work is very similar to that in VideoWave—but you can also set the program to automatically save your work at set intervals. To do that, select **File**, **Preferences**, **AutoSave/Undo**. In the Preferences dialog box that opens, configure the program to save your work at any interval you desire.

⑤ Open an AutoSaved Project

If you want to open a project that has been automatically saved, you can't just select File, Open. Instead, select **File**, **Open** and look for the Project-Archive folder in the Premiere program folder. (A likely path is something like `C:\Program Files\Adobe\Premiere 5.1\ Project-Archive`.)

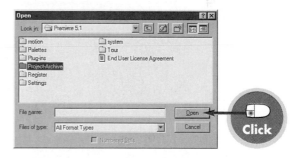

How to Trim the Length of a Clip

Just because a scene you shot on the camcorder is several minutes long doesn't mean it has to stay that way in the final production. In fact, video editors enable you to trim clips down to eliminate unwanted details, or to split a single clip into several scenes (as explained in the next task). In fact, clip editing is a powerful tool that lets you make just the movie you want, regardless of how much extra detail you recorded on tape.

No Fear

Don't worry about experimenting with the trim or split tools. No matter what you do to the clips in your production, the original video you captured and stored on your hard disk (and that appears in the Library list) will never be affected. Only the "copies" of the original that you drag onto the Storyline and use in the video reflect your editing changes.

Imperfect Previews

As you experiment with VideoWave by trimming clips, adding effects, and layering extra audio tracks, you'll discover that the program cannot render all the edits you made to your clips unless you actually produce the movie. If you add an extra audio track, for instance, you won't be able to hear it unless you're in the Audio Studio. To see and hear all your edits, you have to fully render the movie using the Produce tool first—as explained in Chapter 30, "Producing Videotape."

This scene plays with modified start and end times.

Drag the slider to advance through the clip quickly, useful for setting marks.

Here's the current position of the clip.

Mark-in time: when the clip starts.

Mark-out time: when the clip stops.

The original clip is not changed, despite edits.

① Put the Clip in the Viewscreen

To edit a clip, you must first place the scene you want to edit in the Viewscreen. Drag the desired clip from either the Library or the Storyline into the Viewscreen.

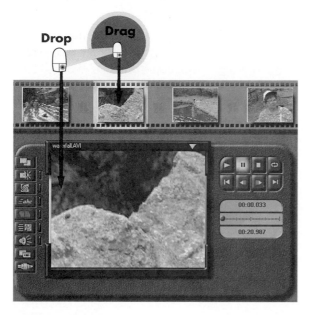

② Go to the Cutting Room

Click the **Cutting Room** button. You should see a console of controls appear under the Viewscreen for editing the clip. (If you click this button—or any of the mode selector buttons—by accident, click it again to return to the basic Viewscreen.)

③ Set the Mark-In Point

Use the VCR controls or the brown slider button to set the point where you want the clip to begin. The slider is handy for fine-tuning the exact point at which you want to start. Notice, though, that you can't hear any audio associated with the clip, so you'll have to use visual cues in the clip to know when you're at the right point.

④ Click the Mark-In Button

After you find the frame at which you want your clip to start, click the **Mark-In** button. This trims video off the front of the clip so that it starts at the point you indicated. Notice that the shortened video clip is also registered in the Duration box.

How to Trim the Length of a Clip, *Continues...*

5 Set the Mark-Out Point

Use the VCR buttons or the slider to find the point in the clip at which you want the video to stop playing (the point known as the *mark-out point*) .

6 Click the Mark-Out Button

Click the **Mark-Out** button to lock in this end point for your video. Again, notice that the shortened clip is registered in the Duration box.

7 Apply the Edit

After marking both the start and end points of your scene, click the **Apply** button. If the clip was already in the Storyline, it is updated with the change. If you dragged the clip to the Viewscreen from the Library, the edited clip is added to the Storyline; the Library clip remains unchanged.

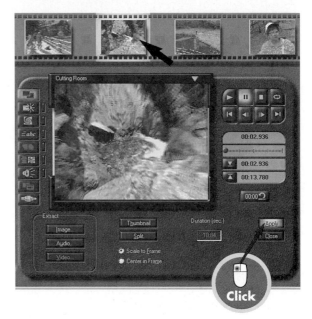

8 Display Clip in the Monitor

Just as you do in VideoWave, you must first add the clip you want to edit to Premiere's Monitor window. To do that, double-click a clip in the Timeline.

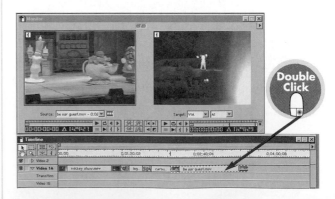

⑨ Set the Mark-In Point

In the Source Monitor, drag the slider around until you reach the frame at which you want the clip to start. Then click the **Mark-In** button to trim the clip to that point.

⑪ Apply the Changes

Click the **Apply** button at the top of the Source Monitor. This causes the changes you made to appear to the clip in the Timeline. Remember that the clip in the Project window remains unchanged.

⑩ Set the Mark-Out Point

Now drag the slider to find the point at which you want the clip to stop. Then click the **Mark-Out** button to trim the end of the clip.

⑫ Review Your Edits

To view the edited clip, double-click it in either the Storyline or the Timeline to play the clip. You should see the trimmed version of the original clip.

How to Split a Clip into Two Scenes

There might be situations in which you want to take a scene you filmed and cut it in half (or into thirds, and so on). By cutting up a scene, you can move different parts of a scene to other places in your movie, or you can perform various tricks or effects on the parts. Splitting a scene is easy and does no permanent damage to the original clip.

Using the Thumbnail Tool

When a clip appears in the Storyline, its first frame is used as a thumbnail to show you the contents of the scene. But if the first frame doesn't really represent most of the action in the clip, you can specify a new thumbnail. Load the clip into the Cutting Room and use the slider to display the frame you want to use as a thumbnail. Then click the **Thumbnail** button in the console below the Viewscreen.

Here's the first clip.

Here's the second clip.

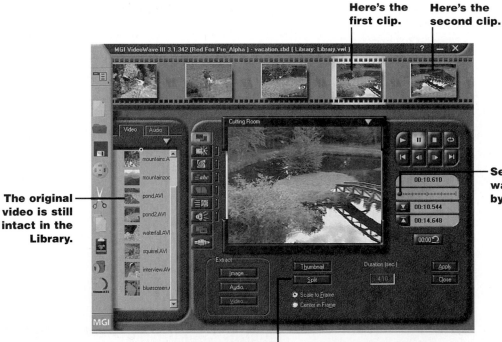

The original video is still intact in the Library.

Select where you want to split the clip by dragging the slider.

Click here to split the clip at the selected frame.

① Go to the Cutting Room

Start by loading your scene (either from the Storyline or the Library) in the Viewscreen and clicking the **Cutting Room** button.

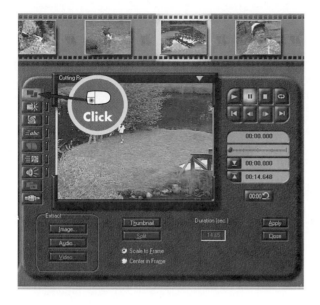

② Find the Split Point

Drag the slider to find the exact point at which you want to split the scene in two.

Drag the slider to the point you want to split the clip into two scenes.

③ Cut the Scene in Two

Click the **Split** button in the console under the Viewscreen. Note that you can't use the button at the very start or very end of the scene, and there's no need to apply the split—as soon as you click, the two halves appear in the Storyline.

④ Use the Premiere Razor

In Premiere, you can split a scene using the Razor tool. Drag the slider until you reach the point in the clip where you want to split it. Then, click the **Razor** tool and click the clip to perform the cut. The clip instantly becomes two clips, cut at the point you clicked.

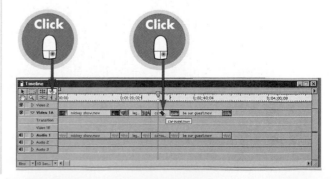

How to Add a Transition Between Scenes

Your scenes don't always have to cut suddenly from one to the next. Instead, you can use a variety of *transition effects* to smoothly go from one scene to another over a short period of time. Transitions such as fades and dissolves are very common techniques in the professional world of video production, and you have the same tools at your disposal on the PC.

Don't Overuse Them

If you're new to video production, you might feel like a kid in a candy store. All those transitions! Boxes, triangles, circles, barn doors…. The list seems endless. But like someone who sees all the fonts in a page layout program for the first time, you're likely to overdo it and create a video that looks like a kindergartner's art project. Stick to just a few transitions and don't use them between every single scene; plain cuts are okay too.

Borrowing from the Video

When you add a transition effect to segue between two clips, remember that the clips themselves are playing at the same time as the transition. In other words, a movie composed of two 1-minute clips is still 2 minutes long, even with a 4-second transition. The transition plays during—and partially obscures—the end of the first clip and the start of the second. Keep that in mind when you preview your film.

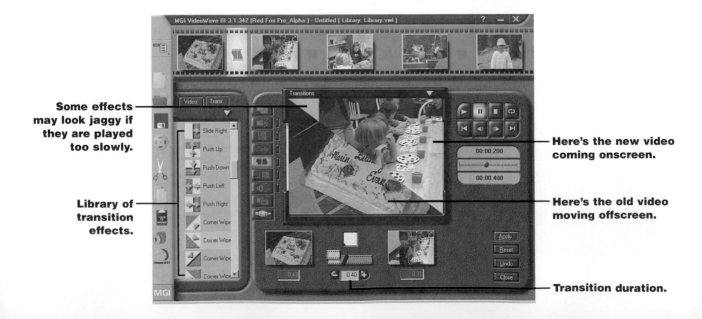

Some effects may look jaggy if they are played too slowly.

Library of transition effects.

Here's the new video coming onscreen.

Here's the old video moving offscreen.

Transition duration.

① Go to Transitions

To add a transition in VideoWave, you must enter the Transitions mode. Double-click the **transition placeholder** between two scenes in the Storyline. You should see the Viewscreen change to the Transitions mode.

② Select a Transition

The Library should now display all the transition effects available to you. Double-click a transition (or drag it to the transition box below the Viewscreen). Click the VCR **Play** button to preview the effect. If you're happy with the result, click the **Apply** button to keep the transition in the video. You can later edit the transition (as explained in the next task).

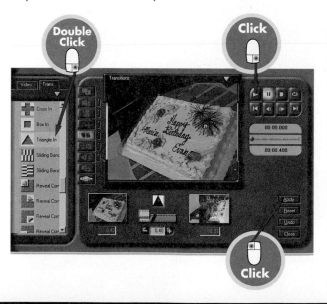

③ Alternate Tracks

Premiere uses a very different way of working with transitions. The two clips must be in alternating video tracks in the Timeline, such as Video 1A and Video 1B. Drag a clip from the Project window to the Video 1A track, and then drag a second clip to Video 1B. Drag the second clip to the right so that it starts just a few seconds before the first clip ends.

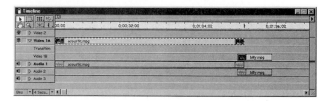

④ Add the Transition

Drag a transition effect from the Transitions window and drop it on the Transition track in the Timeline. The transition will automatically "snap" to the start of the second clip and the end of the first clip. To preview the effect you just added, drag the work bar so that it is over the transition and then select **Project**, **Preview** from the menu.

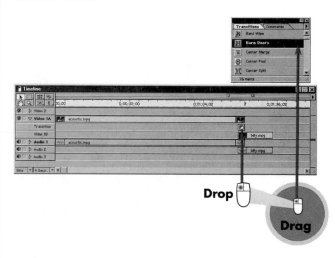

How to Modify Transition Settings

The default settings for video transitions are generally quite good, but they might not be exactly what you're looking for. Thankfully, most video editors—including VideoWave and Premiere—offer ways to edit the basic transitions so that you can apply exactly the effect you need for your scenes.

How-to Hint

Keeping Them Brief

In VideoWave, the only control you have over transitions is their duration. And some videos I've seen capitalize on that, dramatically changing the duration of the transition from one that's so fast you didn't know it happened to one that's several agonizing seconds in length. The reality is that transitions look best when they're rather short, usually just a few seconds or less. You have to try them out for yourself and decide what looks good. Remember, though, that if your transition is too slow, you'll be able to clearly see lots of jagged edges in your video that give away the fact that it was done on a desktop computer and not in a professional broadcasting studio.

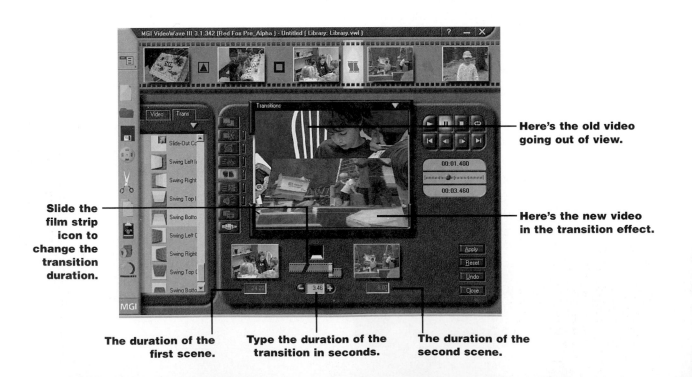

Here's the old video going out of view.

Here's the new video in the transition effect.

Slide the film strip icon to change the transition duration.

The duration of the first scene.

Type the duration of the transition in seconds.

The duration of the second scene.

① Display the Transition

In VideoWave, the only transition option you can change is the duration of the transition. To do that, start by going to Transitions mode—double-click a transition between two scenes in the Storyline.

② Modify the Duration

You can change the duration of the transition by dragging the film strip icons to the left or right, by clicking the plus and minus buttons, or by typing a duration directly into the box. Of course, you cannot specify a transition duration that's longer than the shortest clip.

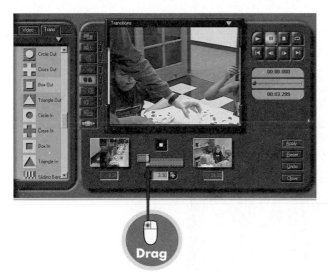

③ Preview the Effect

You can get a sense of what the transition will look like by using the VCR controls. Unfortunately, this preview of the transition happens more slowly than it will when it plays back in the final production.

④ Tweak the Settings

In Premiere, many transitions have supplemental controls that change the look of the effect. The most common is the Border control. Change the transition options by double-clicking its bar in the Timeline. The Settings dialog box opens. If you select a transition such as the Band Slide, you'll see a Border slider, which adds a line around the transition effect. Make your changes and click **OK** to apply them to the video.

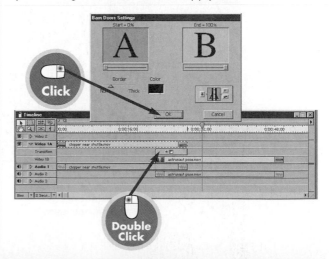

How to Create a Color Panel

*C*olor panels are plain, single-color backgrounds you can use to start and end your video, display titles against, and do other special effects. VideoWave makes it easy to create such panels for your videos.

Making a Color Panel in Premiere

It's easy to make a color panel in Premiere as well. To do that, select **Project**, **Create**, **Color Matte** from the menu. Then choose the color you want and click **OK**. The color panel—or *matte*, in Premiere parlance—appears in the Project window. It has a preset duration of one second, but you can drag its duration to any length you desire after it's in the Timeline.

Color panels can be added anywhere in the video.

You can add titles to color panels.

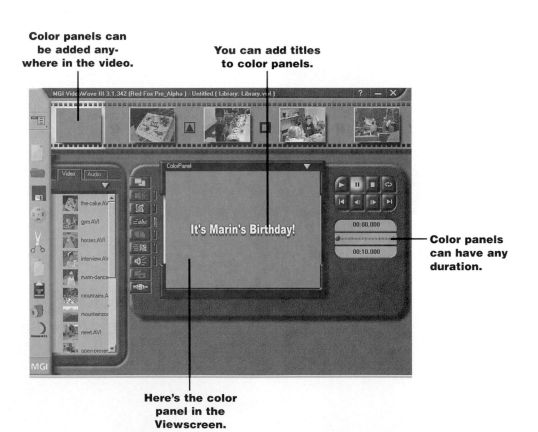

Color panels can have any duration.

Here's the color panel in the Viewscreen.

❶ Select a Blank Panel

The first step to creating a color panel is to click a blank panel in the Storyline, such as the one at the very end of the video. This panel becomes the color panel, although you can later move it anywhere in the production.

❷ Go to the Cutting Room

Click the **Cutting Room** button to get access to editing tools. Although the Viewscreen remains black, be confident that you are working with the panel you selected in the Storyline.

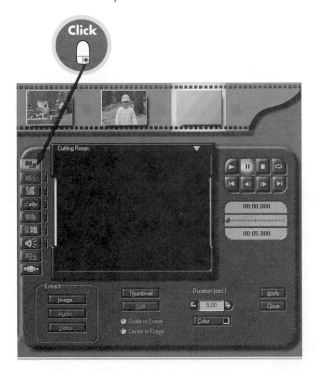

❸ Set the Properties

Set the duration of the color panel by typing the time in seconds or by clicking the plus and minus buttons. To choose a color for the panel, click the **Color** button and select from the millions of shades available. When you have picked the color, click **OK**.

❹ Save the Panel

If you want to add the color panel to the Library (so that you can use it again without re-creating it), click the **Image** button in the Extract region of the screen. Then, click the **Apply** button to add the color panel to the Storyline.

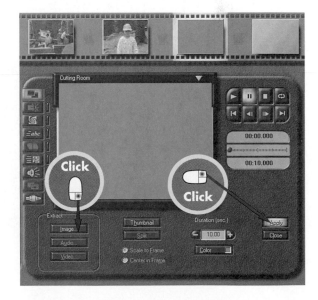

How to Superimpose Video

Superimposed video is cool. If not overdone, it's a great way to combine two video clips into one for an MTV-style effect. In VideoWave, not only is it easy to superimpose video, but the program gives you a fair degree of control over the final look of your scene.

Superimpose Tips

When you superimpose video, it's a good idea to look for clips that complement each other. If both have a lot of action taking place, they can interfere with each other. You might consider muting the color in one clip and perhaps even slowing it down with techniques discussed later in this part of the book. Also, remember that you don't have to superimpose two video clips; you can always lay video over a still image, as I do in this task.

Superimposing in Premiere

You can superimpose video in Premiere as well. To do that, just follow the steps in Task 15, "How to Create Special Effects with a Blue Screen." However, when you open the Transparency Settings dialog box, select **Screen** instead of Chroma for your Key Type. That's all there is to it!

Two clips superimposed.

Video Animator mode.

These controls determine when the Start, Hold, and Finish settings occur to the video.

The video's size, position, and transparency can change through the scene. Use the Start, Hold, and Finish settings to modify these options.

Use the Image Blend option.

These are the settings for the Foreground video.

➊ Put the Clip in the Viewscreen

To superimpose two video clips, start by adding the first image—the background image—to the Viewscreen. Drag it there from either the Library or the Storyline.

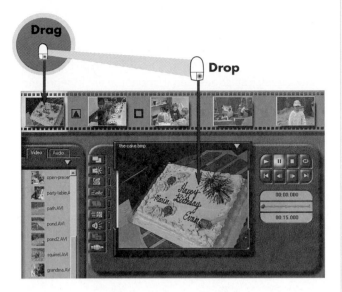

➋ Size Them Up

In most cases, you'll want both clips to be the same length. To do that, start by checking the length of the background clip. Make a note of its duration.

Clip duration

➌ Trim the Foreground

Drag the foreground clip into the Viewscreen and click the **Cutting Room** button. If you're happy with the length of the two clips, go straight to step 5. If not, trim the foreground clip (refer to Task 5, "How to Trim the Length of a Clip") so that it is the same length as the background clip you just measured. Click **Apply** to save your changes to the Storyline.

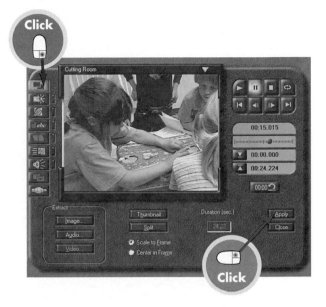

➍ Copy to the Library

Although the edited foreground clip is now stored in the Storyline, it doesn't do us a lot of good there. Drag the clip to the Library to store a copy of it there. (You'll have to name the file before it will be copied.)

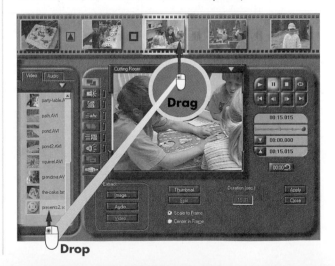

⑤ Load the Background Clip

Now go back to the beginning—load the background clip into the Viewscreen. With all that trimming nonsense out of the way, you're finally ready to super-impose.

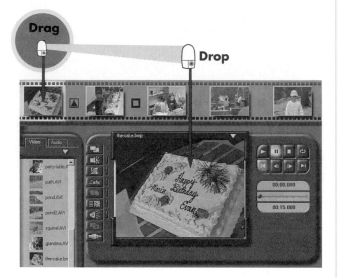

⑥ Go to the Video Animator

Click the **Video Animator** button. In the console area, notice that the loaded clip automatically appears in the Background layer.

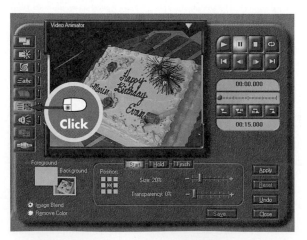

⑦ Add the Foreground

Drag the clip you edited for use as the foreground clip from the Library (where you stored it in step 4) into the Viewscreen. You should see it appear in the Foreground layer.

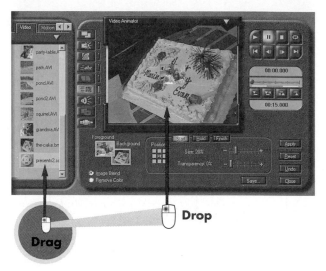

⑧ Select Image Blend

You can do two kinds of video animations: Image Blend and Remove Color. The Image Blend option enables you to mix two layers of video; the Remove Color option plays a second video layer on top of any solid color (it is, in effect, a blue screen effect). In this example, make sure that the Image Blend option is selected.

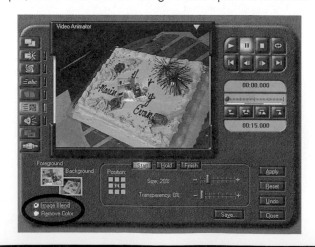

9 Adjust Motion and Transparency

You can make the foreground clip enter the screen from any direction or already be in the middle of the frame at the Start of the scene. You can also set the transparency and size of the foreground clip relative to the background clip. Click the **Start**, **Hold**, and **Finish** buttons to change the motion, size, and transparency of the foreground image for the start, middle, and end of the scene. Alternatively, you can use the presets in the Library's Motion tab to specify a prebuilt motion for the clip.

10 Edit the Timing

The timing controls under the VCR buttons enable you to specify when the Start, Hold, and Finish effects take place. If you want the entire scene to use the Hold position settings, for instance, drag the slider to the extreme left of the clip and click the **Set Beginning of Effect Hold** button. Then drag the slider to the end of the clip and click the corresponding **Set End of Effect Hold** button.

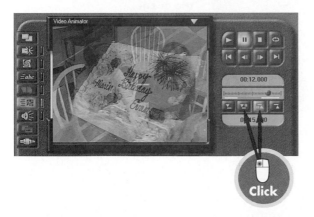

11 Preview Your Scene

At any point, you can get a feel for the effect you've created by playing with the VCR controls and the slider. Move the slider back and forth to see the way the video animation will look.

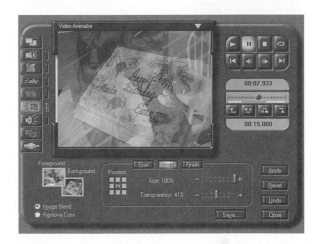

12 Save Your Changes

When you have set up the scene just the way you want it, click the **Apply** button. Your changes will be saved to the Storyline.

How to Add a Video Watermark

Now that you know how to superimpose video clips, let's do something useful. If you watch much television, you've no doubt seen *watermarks* (sometimes called *bugs*). Watermarks are semi-transparent graphics that let you know what channel you're watching or who is speaking. You can add your own watermarks to your video productions and look like a real pro.

How-to Hint

Watch Your Colors

Watermarks are a cool effect, but they can be tricky. In VideoWave, you have to remove the color from the graphic you're using as a watermark so that your clip shows through. You have to be sure to use a color for your watermark that is distinct from the colors used in the video. When you use the Tolerance slider, be sure that you don't overdo it, or you might remove parts of the graphic or video that you want to keep in the finished production.

Select a background color for your watermark that's distinct from the rest of the scene.

Save the watermark as a BMP file in any graphics program.

A watermark can be any graphic, text, or photo.

① Create the Watermark

You must first create an image in a graphics program such as Photoshop or Paint Shop Pro. Make the image 720×480 pixels in size, a solid color, with some kind of graphic or text in one corner so that it looks like you're making a watermark for CNN. Save it as a BMP (Windows bitmap) file.

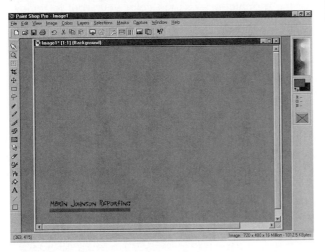

② Load the Watermark

Click the Library's list menu arrowhead and select **Add Files**. Find the watermark graphic you created in step 1 and add it to the Library.

③ Load the Scene

Drag the scene you want to watermark to the Viewscreen from either the Storyline or the Library, and then click the **Video Animator** button.

④ Load the Foreground Image

Drag the watermark graphic from the Library into the Video Animator screen, where it will become the Foreground layer. Also, you probably want to change the watermark's size to 100%.

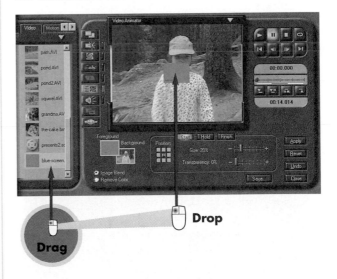

⑤ Remove Color from Graphic

For the watermark to work, you have to "remove" the solid color of the graphic so that the video in the Background layer shows through, leaving only the special graphic or text you added. Click the **Remove Color** option.

⑥ Display the Color Dialog Box

Now that the Video Animator is set to remove color, you have to tell it which color to remove. Start by clicking the **Color** button in the console at the bottom of the screen. The Color dialog box opens.

⑦ Pick a Color

Click the **Pick a Color** button; the pointer turns into an eyedropper. Move the eyedropper over the graphic in the Viewscreen and click anywhere in the solid region of the graphic to select the color you want to remove from the graphic. Click **OK** to accept the selection.

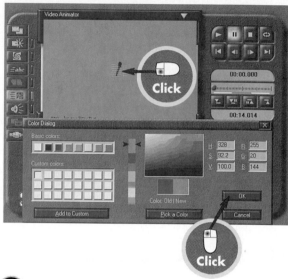

⑧ Set the Tolerance

Drag the **Tolerance** slider to the right. You should only have to move it one increment—about 5%—to see the solid color disappear and reveal the video underneath. The graphic bug is all you should now see of the Foreground layer. Click **Apply** to save these changes to your video.

10 Create the Watermark

If you're watermarking in Premiere, you start the same way you did in VideoWave: Create the graphic in a program such as Photoshop or Paint Shop Pro. Be sure to make the graphic's basic color solid white, however, not some arbitrary color.

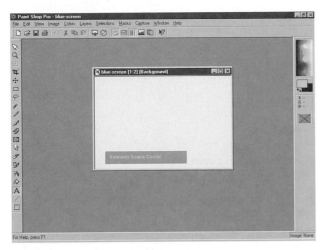

11 Add a New Video Track

For the watermark to work in Premiere, the Timeline must have a track called Video 3. If that track doesn't already exist in the Timeline, click the Timeline list menu arrow and select **Track Options** to open the Track Options dialog box. Click **Add**. In the Add Tracks dialog box, make sure that you're adding one track; then, click **OK** twice to close both dialog boxes.

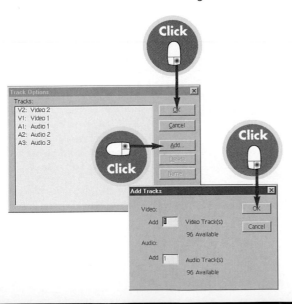

12 Populate the Timeline

From the Project window, drag the video clip to the Video 2 track and the watermark graphic to the Video 3 track in the Timeline.

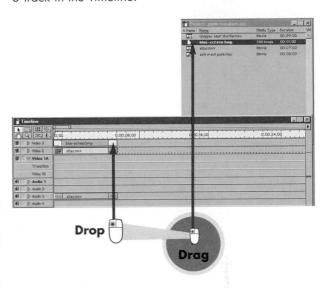

Drop

Drag

13 Use the Track Matte

Right-click the **Video 2** clip and select **Video, Transparency** to open the Transparency Settings dialog box. From the **Key Type** drop-down list, select **Track Matte**. The graphic bug should appear on the video.

Bug.

How to Use Special Effects Filters

Special effects can enhance your movie by distorting video scenes in ways that the viewer won't expect. There are all kinds of filters available, such as swirls, ripples, mosaics, and snow. Using filters, you can make your video look like it's part of a dream sequence, pulled from an old-time TV broadcast, or any of dozens of other effects. It pays to experiment because the possibilities are extensive. Special effects is one area in which Premiere has a leg up on VideoWave—Premiere has more effects, and thanks to an "open architecture," you can buy additional effects as well. Premiere is also more powerful than VideoWave because you can add many layers of video to your movie and perform special effects on each layer. VideoWave restricts you to one layer of effects.

How-to Hint

Customizing Your Effects

By using VideoWave's Effect Level slider with the Start, Hold, and Finish buttons, you can create unique effects for your videos. Instead of creating a favorite effect from scratch every time, however, you can click the **Save** button in the Special Effects console to store customized effects in the Custom tab of the Library.

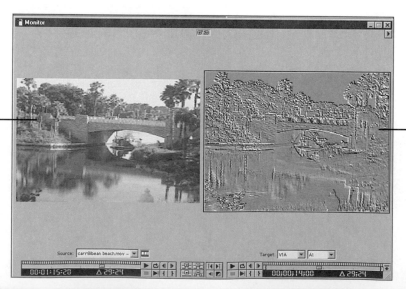

Here's the original video.

Here's the same video with a special "embossed" effect.

❶ Open the Special Effects

Drag the clip you want to embellish from the Storyline or the Library into the Viewscreen and click the **Special Effects** button. The Special Effects console appears under the Viewscreen and the Effects tab pops up in the Library.

❷ Drag an Effect

Find an effect in the Library you want to apply to your video and drag it to the Viewscreen. Experiment with the **Effect Level** slider to vary the intensity of the selected effect.

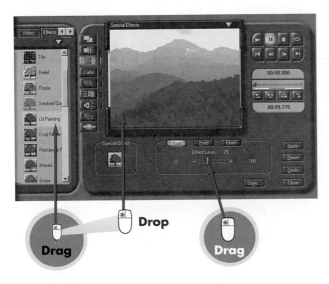

❸ Set Start, Hold, and Finish

The effect can change intensity at the start, middle, and end of the scene. Click the **Start** button and set the Effect Level; repeat for the Hold and Finish options. When you're done, click the **Apply** button to save the scene to the Storyline.

❹ Stack Effects

VideoWave doesn't let you apply more than one special effect to a specific clip. If you want, for instance, to render a clip in digital snow and add a wave effect at the same time, you need Premiere. Right-click a clip in the Timeline and select **Filters** from the shortcut menu. You can add as many filters as you like to the clip— although the processing time becomes enormous if you work with too many effects at once.

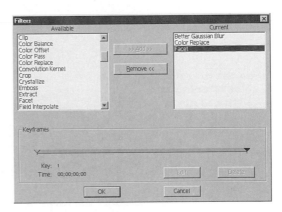

How to Color Correct a Scene

In addition to special effects that change your video in very obvious ways, you can use VideoWave's Darkroom mode to tweak the color balance. You can be subtle—to adjust for too much red in your video, for instance—or you can go over the top and burn in a unique color effect (such as the way in which most of the movie *The Matrix* was a lifeless blue) .

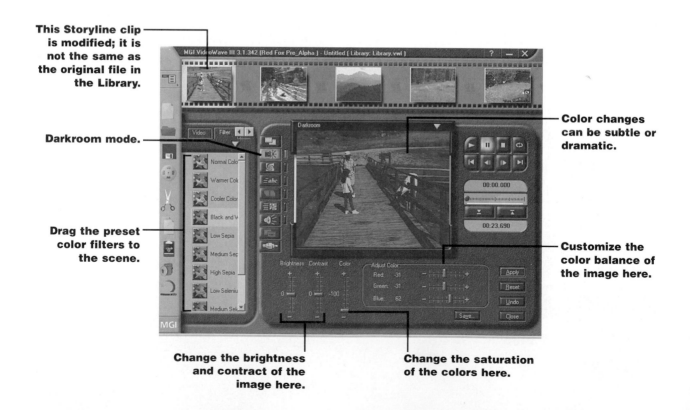

This Storyline clip is modified; it is not the same as the original file in the Library.

Darkroom mode.

Drag the preset color filters to the scene.

Color changes can be subtle or dramatic.

Customize the color balance of the image here.

Change the brightness and contract of the image here.

Change the saturation of the colors here.

➊ Go to the Darkroom

Drag the clip you want to color correct into the Viewscreen and click the **Darkroom** button. A wide variety of color controls and presets appears on the Filter tab in the Library.

➋ Drag an Effect

You can tweak the color of the clip manually or automatically. If you see a preset that corresponds roughly to the effect you want, drag it from the Filter tab of the Library to the Viewscreen. If the color effect is not exactly what you want, you can continue editing the effect in the next step.

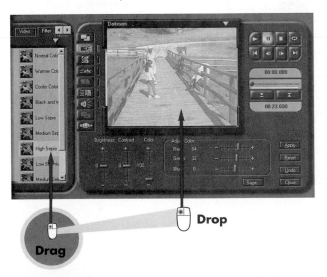

➌ Fine-Tune the Colors

The Darkroom gives you a wide variety of controls for editing color balance. If you want to manually adjust the color levels in the scene, use the **Red**, **Green**, and **Blue** sliders in the Adjust Color area. A rule of thumb for increasing the level of one color is to reduce the level of the other two sliders by half as much at the same time.

➍ Tweak Color Settings

You can modify the brightness and contrast of the image. In general, you will get the best results by changing both the Brightness and Contrast controls at the same time because they have an interrelated effect in the picture. The Color slider is actually the color saturation—you can enhance colors or bleach them out of the picture using this slider.

How to Create Slow-Motion Video

What's more emotional than watching a sports playback in slow motion? Or the explosive payoff at the end of an action flick in slo-mo? Slow motion is a powerful tool for drawing attention to a key scene. In this task, you learn how to apply this effect to your own video production by using Premiere; VideoWave does not have a slow-motion option.

How-to Hint

Clever Video Tricks with Premiere

If you want to get fancy with video effects, you're probably ready to make the move from VideoWave to Premiere. Premiere has many more effects than VideoWave does, and they are especially useful if you're trying to be artistic with your video project. For example, one of the Premiere filters enables you to play a video clip (and its sound file) backwards, something that's impossible to do in VideoWave.

Slow down the video until it becomes too choppy; usually about 25% of normal speed.

Delete the audio track from the video clip.

The effect of slow motion is easily achieved with Premiere.

1 Fast Shutter Speed

It helps to plan ahead for a slow-motion shot by filming the scene with the fastest shutter speed available on your camcorder—try a setting of 1/500 second. That will give you the best source material.

2 Add a Clip to Timeline

Drag the clip you want to produce in slow motion from the Project window to the Timeline.

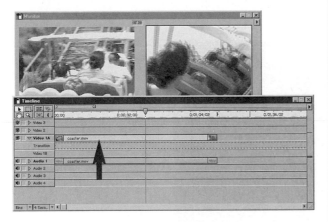

3 Set the Playback Speed

Right-click the clip in the Timeline and select **Speed** from the shortcut menu. In the Clip Speed dialog box, set the **New Rate** to a low value such as **25%** or **30%** and click **OK**. Preview the video; if it's too choppy, increase the **New Rate** value using the trial-and-error approach.

4 Delete the Audio

Most of the time, you won't want the audio to play back in slow motion. Click the **Audio** track in the Timeline and press the **Delete** key.

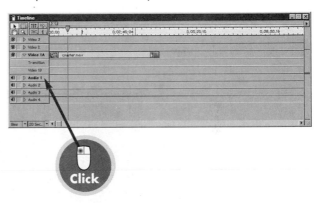

How to Create Special Effects with a Blue Screen

In Chapter 25, "Working with Your Camcorder," we talked about how to film video with a blue screen background so that you could later overlay a second video source. Now it's time to load that video into your editor and actually replace the blue screen with a second video layer. It's easy to do, and the results can be impressive.

How-to Hint

Watch Your Colors

A blue screen doesn't really have to be blue, as we discussed in Chapter 25. In fact, using chroma key color removal, you can use a backdrop of any color. Make sure that it's a color unique to the rest of the video background, though, or you might accidentally paint video over parts of the scene where you don't want video—such as the actor's face.

Here, the edge of blue screen is visible; you can adjust the tolerance levels to eliminate it.

A zoom in on the blue screen can make a clever transition to the next scene.

The blue screen does not have to be blue.

Here's the background video containing the blue screen.

The actor is holding a blue screen.

This is the superimposed video on the blue screen.

❶ Display the Overlay Video

Find the video that you want to show through the blue screen and add it to the Viewscreen. If you were blue-screening the starfield on a *Star Trek* bridge, for instance, this would be the star pattern or a Klingon warship.

❷ Go to the Video Animator

Click the **Video Animator** button to begin editing the video layers. Notice that the video you have loaded is automatically assigned to the Background layer in the console.

❸ Add the Blue Screen Clip

Now drag the clip that actually contains the blue screen into the Video Animator screen. This video clip becomes the Foreground layer in the console. You should see that the clip doesn't actually fill the screen; that's because the size of the clip defaults to 20% in the Start and Finish steps of the scene. Drag the **Size** slider all the way to **100%** and then click the **Finish** button and drag the **Size** slider to **100%** again. Click the **Start** button so that you're working at the beginning of the clip again.

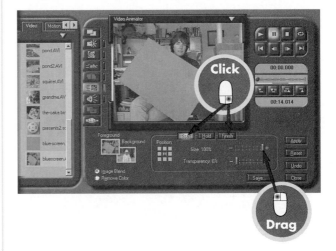

❹ Switch to Remove Color Mode

By default, the VideoWave Video Animator is set to Image Blend mode. Click the **Remove Color** option to enable the chroma key effect that we need for this shot.

5 Pick the Blue Screen Color

Now we need to remove the blue screen from the scene so that we can see through to the other video layer. Click the **Color** button and then click the **Pick a Color** button. Click anywhere in the blue screen to select the color you're removing and then click **OK**.

6 Increase the Tolerance

Drag the **Tolerance** slider to the right until the blue screen disappears and is replaced by the Background layer video (the overlay video), but stop dragging the slider before the overlay video spills into the rest of the scene.

7 Apply Your Changes

To finish the blue screen effect, click the **Apply** button. The scene is updated in the Storyline.

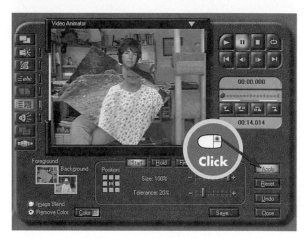

8 Add the Overlay

The process of creating a blue screen overlay in Premiere is a little different. Start by dragging the overlay video—the clip that you want to appear in the blue screen—from the Project window to the Video 1A track in the Timeline.

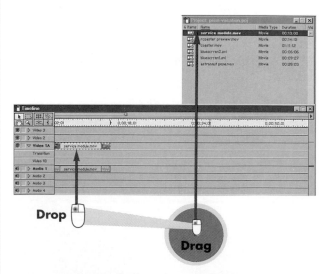

9   Add the Blue Screen

Drag the background video clip (the clip that contains the blue screen) from the Project window to the Video 2 track in the Timeline.

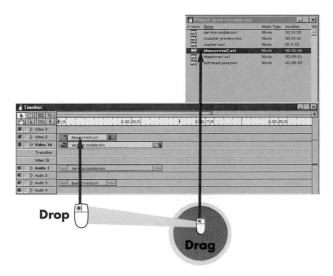

10   Open the Transparency Box

Right-click the blue screen clip in the Video 2 track and select **Video**, **Transparency**. The Transparency Settings dialog box opens.

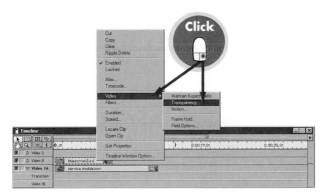

11   Switch to Chroma Key

From the **Key Type** drop-down list, select **Chroma**. Then click the blue screen in the Color pane to select the color you are going to replace with the overlay video.

12   Increase the Similarity

The Similarity slider in Premiere is equivalent to the Tolerance slider in VideoWave. Drag the **Similarity** slider to the right until the blue screen in the Sample pane is filled with the overlay video, but stop before that video spills into the rest of the background scene. Click the **OK** button when you're done.

How to Preview Your Movie on the Computer

Now that you know the basics for editing a movie, you can actually put together a simple film. We haven't discussed titling or audio tricks yet (you'll learn about those aspects of video editing in later parts in the book), but you might be ready to combine some clips and see what they look like. You don't even have to dump the scenes to tape to see them play; in this task, you'll learn how to preview your movie on the computer screen.

How-to Hint

Save Early, Save Often

You should save your work often—and especially before previewing your movie. Although you shouldn't necessarily expect your PC to crash, an editing program such as VideoWave or Premiere can really tax your computer. Generating a preview file could cause your computer to experience a software error—which would be bad if you haven't saved any of your work.

Shift-select the panels you want to preview.

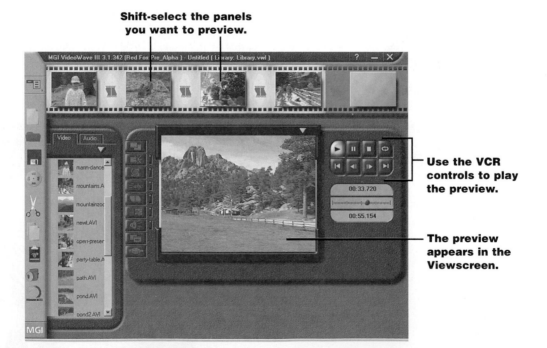

Use the VCR controls to play the preview.

The preview appears in the Viewscreen.

❶ Shift-Select

To preview your VideoWave production on the PC, start by clicking the first panel in the Storyline that you want to see. Then, holding down the **Shift** key on the keyboard, click the final panel you want to include in the preview. All the intermediate panels should be highlighted.

❷ Play the Movie

Right-click the selected panels and select **Preview** from the shortcut menu. The preview might drop some frames—especially if you are using transitions or filters—but they'll all play properly later, when you record the movie to tape. Alternatively, use the VCR controls to play the video.

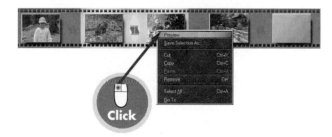

❸ Select a Region

In Premiere, the work area bar is located at the top of the Timeline. Drag the bar to the left or right until it encompasses all the video you want to watch.

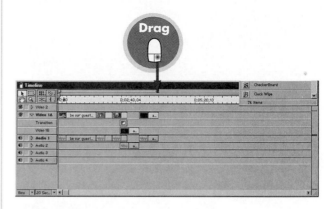

❹ Preview the Movie

Select **Project**, **Preview** from the menu bar. If you haven't yet saved this project, Premiere prompts you to do that. Then Premiere writes the movie to your hard drive and plays it. It can take several minutes or even several hours to generate the preview, so be patient.

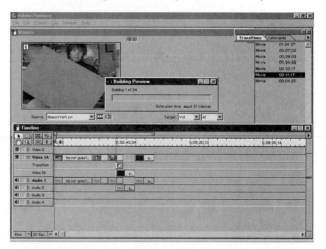

Working with Titles

No video is complete without some titles—text that can leap or fade or dance or spin its way onto the screen to identify your movie or specific scenes. Titles help your viewer immediately understand the context of your movie, and they add a professional touch to your production as well.

Actually, don't think that the only text in your video must be a traditional title scene at the beginning of the film; you can also create captions, credits, and even subtitles! Most people save the credit roll for the end of the movie. *Credits* can mention who filmed, produced, and otherwise slaved over your film. Credits also identify who appeared in the film and what music you used. Just watch a Hollywood movie all the way to the end for some ideas about who to include in your credits. Captions and subtitles are also handy text tools to use in your production. *Captions* can label a scene or identify a location or person onscreen. *Subtitles*, of course, translate foreign-language dialogue or transcribe hard-to-understand speech.

Video editors such as VideoWave and Premiere enable you to use text as a different kind of special effect, complete with colors, transparency, and motion. In this part of the book, I show you how to master text and title tools in both of these programs.

How to Add Titles to a Video

The most basic text effect you can add to a video is the traditional title shot. Titles can cut on and off the screen; you can also use an animation technique to make the title appear and disappear. In this task, we'll start simple and just get the titles into your video.

How-to Hint

A Tale of Two Titles

As you might expect, Premiere enables you to make significantly more sophisticated titles than VideoWave—but at a cost. It takes more effort and expertise to make your video in Premiere. On the bright side, 90% of all the titling effects you can do in Premiere are also available in VideoWave, so feel free to stick with the simpler program for most, if not all, your video projects. If you run into a text effect that there's simply no way to do in VideoWave (such as text that flies in four directions at once), remember that you can always turn to Premiere.

Title.

Make titles large, don't use thin fonts.

Titles are usually a contrasting color.

Titles can appear on video or color panels.

① Display the Video

The title has to be displayed on top of something such as a video clip or a color panel. Select a background for your title and add it to the Viewscreen. In this example, I selected a video clip of a birthday cake from the list of clips and dragged it to the Viewscreen.

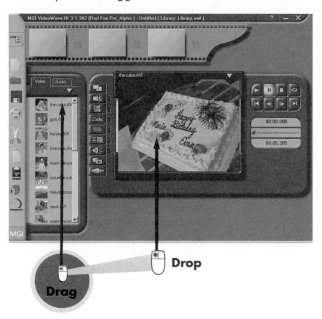

② Open the Text Animator

VideoWave uses a module called the Text Animator to add titles to your productions. Click the **Text Animator** button.

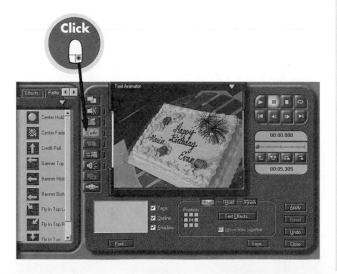

③ Type the Title

In the text box, type the title you want to give your video. Press the **Enter** key to arrange the title on to multiple lines. Keep in mind that the text box doesn't show the text's true appearance. You have to look on the Viewscreen to see what your finished titles really look like.

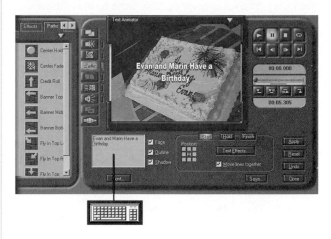

④ Apply the Changes

When your title is complete, click the **Apply** button to add the titles to the clip and update the changes to the Storyline.

5 Create a Blank Title

In Premiere, titles are clips that can be displayed on their own or over any other clip. Start by selecting **File**, **New**, **Title** from the menu. The title window opens.

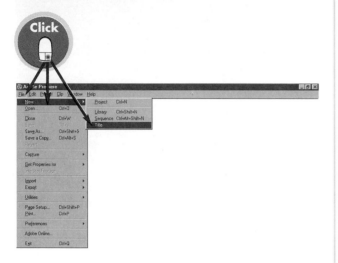

6 Choose a Sample Clip

It can help if you use some video in the background of the title. The video won't be a part of the title, but it will help you position and format the title. Double-click a clip to add it to the Source Monitor window.

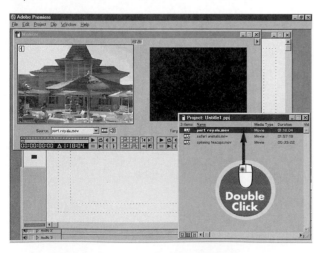

7 Choose a Frame

If you want the first frame of the clip to be your background, drag it from the Monitor window to the title window. If not, use the slider to find the frame you want to use and then select **Clip**, **Set Marker**, **0** from the menu. Then drag the desired clip from the Monitor window to the title window. This process can help you see what the titles will look like over the final video, but remember that the video you add here isn't really a part of the title file.

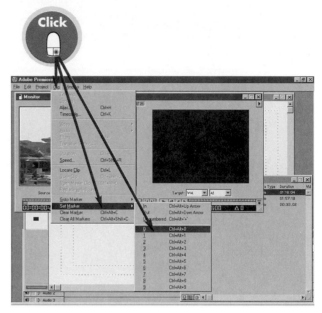

8 Type the Title

Click the **Text** tool in the title window palette and click in the title window to position the insertion point. Type the text that will be your title. You can modify the look of the titles using options in the Title menu, as described in the following task.

9 Save the Title Clip

Now save the title clip by selecting **File, Save As** from the menu. Give the title clip a name and click **Save**. Note that the default extension for a Premiere title file is PTL.

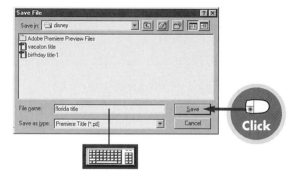

10 Close the Title Window

Click the **Close** box in the title window's toolbar to get rid of the Title window.

11 Load the Title Clip

Now it's time to add the title to the project. Right-click the **Project** window and select **Import**, **File**. The File Open dialog box appears; find the title file and click to select it.

12 Add the Title to the Timeline

Now drag the title file from the Project window to the Timeline. If you want to continue editing the title, double-click the filename in the Project window to reopen the title window.

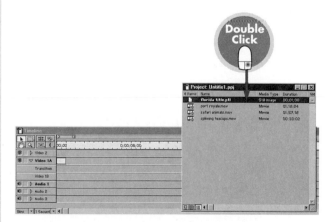

How to Color and Size Your Titles

In the last task, you learned how to make a very basic title—it appears onscreen in a rather ordinary-looking font and it stays there until the scene is over. Let's start making our titles a little fancier—the first step is with color and styles. In this task, I'll show you how to change the appearance of your titles in both VideoWave and Premiere.

Readability Is Paramount

The most important thing about your titles is that the audience should be able to read them. Consider these tips when making titles:

- **They should be big**—Don't use tiny characters, or people will have to put their noses up to the screen to see them.
- **Don't use thin fonts**—Thicker is better—thin fonts tend to be hard to read on television screens.
- **Use high-contrast colors**—Select your colors based on the video behind the text. The color of the text should stand out for added visibility.
- **Leave the titles onscreen longer**—Longer than what? Longer than you think they need to be onscreen. Recognize the fact that many people read slower than you do.

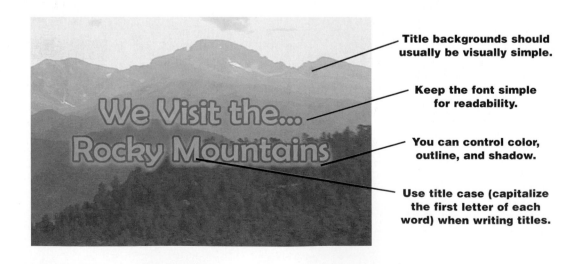

Title backgrounds should usually be visually simple.

Keep the font simple for readability.

You can control color, outline, and shadow.

Use title case (capitalize the first letter of each word) when writing titles.

❶ Open the Text Animator

To edit the text characteristics of your title, start by opening the title scene in the Text Animator. To do that, drag the title scene video clip to the Viewscreen and click the **Text Animator** button.

❷ Create Text

Type the text of your title in the text box.

❸ Select a Font

Click the **Font** button under the text box to display the Font dialog box. Select a font, style, and size. Click **OK** to see what the title looks like with this font selection; return to the Font dialog box if you want to make any changes. Notice that you can also align the text to the left or right margin or center it in the screen.

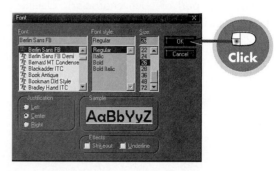

❹ Change Text Color

To change the color of the title, click the **Effects** tab in the Library and double-click a color style that appeals to you.

⑤ Edit the Text Effect

To the right of the text box are check boxes for Face (the main, thick part of each character), Outline (the line that wraps around each character), and Shadow (the backdrop that makes each character stand out from the video). You can turn these elements of the title on or off by clicking the check boxes.

⑥ Customize the Text Effect

If you prefer, you can tweak the text effects by clicking the **Text Effects** button in the Text Animator console. The Text Effects dialog box enables you to change the color and intensity of the face, outline, and shadow of the text. Note that you can make this effect change over time by setting different values for Start, Hold, and Finish (click each of these buttons, located above the Text Effects button, and specify settings). When you're done, click the **Apply** button to save these changes to your video.

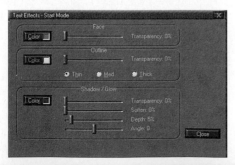

⑦ Enter Text

Premiere gives you much more control over the text, but the program is not as convenient to use as VideoWave. Start by entering some title text in the Premiere screen as explained in the last task.

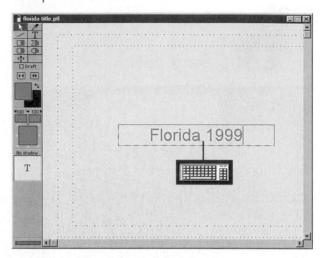

⑧ Select the Text

Perhaps the biggest difference between VideoWave and Premiere is that Premiere enables you to change title attributes on a character-by-character basis; with VideoWave, you change all the text at once. Double-click in the text box and then select the text you want to change.

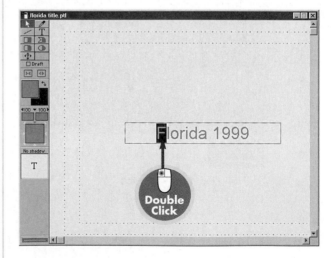

⑨ Choose a Font

With the appropriate text selected, select **Title**, **Font** from the menu. In the Font dialog box that opens, select the font, style, and size that you like. Click **OK** to close the dialog box and apply your font choices.

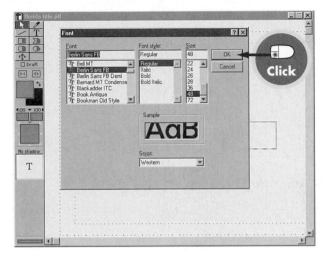

⑩ Size Quick Pick

You don't have to open the Font dialog box to pick a font size; you can also select the text to edit and then select **Title**, **Size**, and the desired font size from the menu.

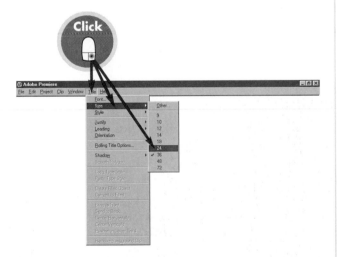

⑪ Select a Color

If you want, each character in your title can be a different color. Select the desired text and then click the color box at the left side of the window. A Color Picker dialog box appears, from which you can choose a color for the selected text.

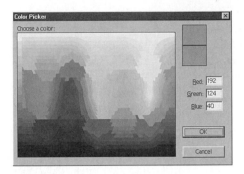

⑫ Choose a Color from a Clip

If you prefer, you can pick a color for the text directly from the sample clip behind the text. To do that, click the **Eyedropper** tool in the palette and then click a spot in the video clip.

How to Make Titles Roll

It's almost a clichè, it's so common: Titles tend to move around on the screen. Sometimes they *roll*—go from the top to the bottom of the screen—and sometimes they crawl. But no matter what you want to do to your video text, the technique is easy to accomplish with VideoWave.

Controlling the Flow

Depending on how you use the Mark-In and Mark-Out points for text animation, you can get radically different effects. Consider some of these tips:

- If you want the text to hover onscreen, set the **Hold Mark-In** and **Hold Mark-Out** points a few seconds apart.

- If you want the titles to roll smoothly without stopping, make the Hold Mark-In and Hold Mark-Out points identical.

- If you want the titles to speed onto the screen but scroll off slowly, make the Hold point closer to the start of the clip. Likewise, put the Hold point closer to the end of the clip to make the titles move in slowly but leave quickly.

Preset paths for your title.

Title enters from lower-right corner.

Title is static in Hold position here.

Title starts to move to Finish position here.

① Choose a Preset Path

The easiest way to make text roll is to use a preset path. Load the scene you want to appear behind the titles. Click the **Text Animator** button if necessary and then click the **Paths** tab in the Library. Double-click the **Credit Roll** option. Click the **Play** button in the VCR controls to preview the effect. If you like it, just click **Apply**.

② Set a Start Position

If you want to create a custom path (for example, a motion that goes from the bottom-right corner to the upper-left corner), use the **Start**, **Hold**, and **Finish** buttons to make these selections. Click **Start** and then click the bottom-right position in the nine-block grid. This setting makes the text start offscreen at the bottom-right corner when the scene begins.

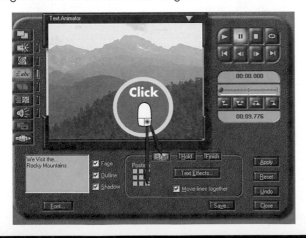

③ Set the Hold Position

Where do you want the text to be halfway through the scene? In the middle of the screen, in this case. Click the **Hold** button and then click the center position in the grid.

④ Set the Finish

At the end of the scene, the text should scroll off the top left of the screen. Click the **Finish** button and then click the upper-left corner of the Position grid.

5 Edit the Path Duration

We've set the motion of the text, but not the timing. Use the Mark-In and Mark-Out buttons to specify when the three motion phases occur. These buttons appear under the VCR controls and enable you to set when the effect should begin, when the effect should hold in the middle of the scene, and when the effect should end.

6 Apply the Changes

With the path of the text set, click the **Apply** button. Click the **First Frame** button and then the **Play** button in the VCR controls to see what your rolling title looks like now.

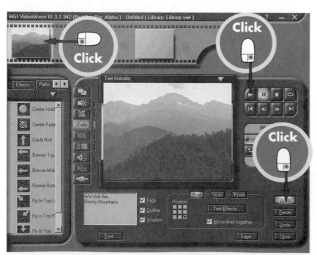

7 Select Rolling Titles

Premiere doesn't have drag-and-drop preset paths for titles to follow, but it's easy to create moving titles nonetheless. Click the **Rolling Title** tool in the tool palette. This tool enables you to create a text region within which the text rolls.

8 Create a Text Box

In the title window, click and drag the **Rolling Title** tool to create a region in which the title rolls.

⑨ Enter Text

Click in the text region and type a title. If you want, you can adjust the font size and type from the Title menu.

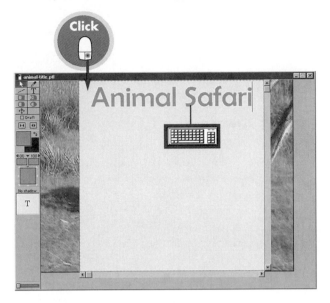

⑩ Add Dead Space

Now add hard returns (press **Enter**) before and after the title so that the text scrolls properly. It might take some experimentation to get the number of hard returns right.

Press Enter before and after title.

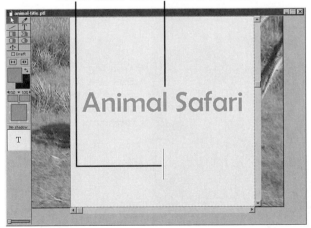

⑪ Select a Path

Right-click the text box and select **Rolling Text Options** from the shortcut menu. In the dialog box that appears, select **Move Down** as the movement you want the text to take and click **OK**.

⑫ Test Your Title Roll

Click and drag the slider in the lower-left corner of the title window. Using this slider, you can test the motion of your titles and add more space before or after the text as needed to get the effect you want.

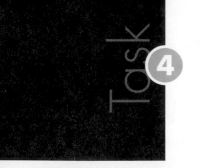

How to Make Titles Crawl

In video lingo, a *crawl* is text moving across the screen—from side to side—as opposed to a *roll*—which is text moving from top to bottom. In the last task, you learned how to make titles move, so the crawl is a piece of cake.

Don't Always Use CG

Your titles don't have to be character-generated text—that is, done on the PC. You can use props and scenery for more natural-looking or clever titles. Consider filming street signs, for instance, and using them when appropriate for titles. You can even film a traffic sign and digitally alter the text on the sign in a program such as Paint Shop Pro or Photoshop—the resulting graphic can be a great title.

Did you ever see the video for Bob Dylan's classic song *Subterranean Homesick Blues*? Just holding up a cardboard sign with words on it has its charms.

Title moves to the left.

This bar indicates that the title will "hold" in the center of the screen for a few seconds.

Banner paths make text crawl.

Title starts off-screen on right.

① Choose the Path

With a clip loaded in the Text Animator, double-click one of the banner paths from the Library. All the banner paths move text across the screen; the speed of the crawl depends on the length of the clip and how much text you need to move.

② Set the Timing

Use the timing controls under the VCR buttons to modify the flow of the text. By default, banner crawls move smoothly from one side to the other, but you can make them hover in the middle of the screen by using the Hold Mark-In and Hold Mark-Out buttons. You can also change the text attributes at various locations along the crawl path by clicking the **Start**, **Hold**, and **Finish** buttons and the **Text Effects** button.

③ Create Rolling Text

Click Premiere's **Rolling Text** tool and drag a horizontal text box on top of the video clip you want to use for the background of your title. Right-click in the text box and select **Rolling Title Options** from the shortcut menu. In the dialog box that appears, select the **Move Left** or **Move Right** option to direct the motion of the text and click **OK**.

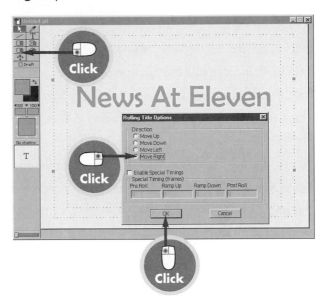

④ Massage the White Space

Type the text for your title and adjust the font, size, and color of the text. Press the **spacebar** enough times so that you add a screen's worth of space on both sides of the text. Test the crawl using the slider at the bottom of the Title window.

Press the spacebar to add spaces before and after the title.

How to Make Credits Roll

A credit roll is actually pretty similar to a title roll; both involve text moving across the screen. A credit roll, however, moves a lot more text than does a title roll. Typically, you want to include a credit roll at the end of a movie to give credit where credit is due—to yourself, the people who appear in the film, the music, and so on. Watch the end of a Hollywood movie for a peek at what professional credits look like. This task explains how to create a credit roll for yourself.

How-to Hint

Moving the Lines Together

You have probably seen the option in the Text Animator console called Move Lines Together. When it's enabled, it keeps all the text moving as a group, regardless of how many separate lines (and hard returns) are in the text. When it's disabled, each line of text moves onscreen independently, one after the other. Although you generally wouldn't want to direct the movements of each line separately in a credit roll, disabling the Move Lines Together option can be effective if you're displaying titles at the beginning of a film—experiment for yourself. Unfortunately, you have no control over how those lines move—it's all preset. To exact precise control over title movement, see the How-To Hints in Task 7, "How to Move Text in Two Directions at Once," later in this part, which use Premiere to do some fancy titling.

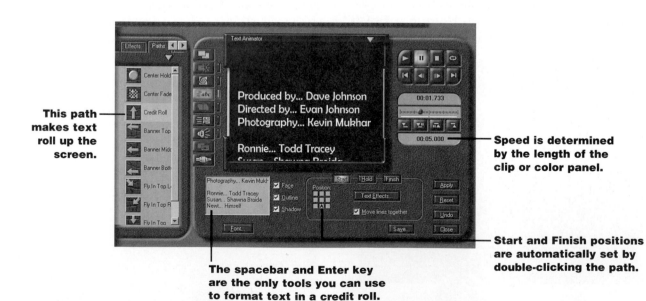

This path makes text roll up the screen.

Speed is determined by the length of the clip or color panel.

The spacebar and Enter key are the only tools you can use to format text in a credit roll.

Start and Finish positions are automatically set by double-clicking the path.

① Create a Color Panel

Most credit sequences occur on a blank background, typically black. Although you can roll credits over video if you want to, for this example, create a color panel and load it into the Viewscreen: Right-click the last blank clip in the Storyline and select **Create Color Panel**. From the console at the bottom of the screen, pick a color for the panel. Keep in mind that the credits will roll as quickly or as slowly as necessary to display completely within the duration of the color panel, so adjust the **Duration** setting accordingly.

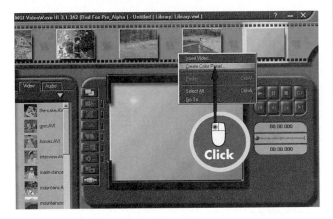

② Open the Text Animator

Click the **Text Animator** button.

③ Type the Credits

Type the text for your credits. Most credits are left justified (click the **Font** button and make sure that the **Left** option is selected). Unfortunately, VideoWave doesn't allow you to line up text using tabs, so you might have to be creative to get an effect you like.

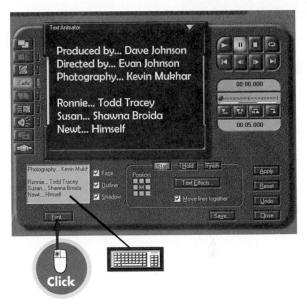

④ Choose the Credit Roll Path

In the Library, double-click the **Credit Roll** path. Preview the credits by using the VCR buttons in the Preview Control Panel and click **Apply** when you're done. Remember that you might need to adjust the duration of the color panel based on how quickly you want the credits to roll across the screen.

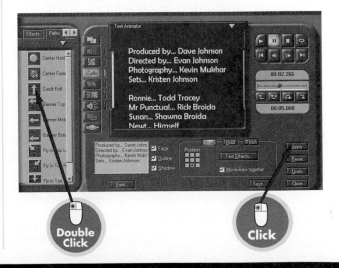

How to Add Captions and Subtitles to a Scene

Captions and subtitles are more kinds of titling that you can easily do with your video editor. Both of these text formats are a little different from titles and credits in that they traditionally don't move; they appear in place on the screen, linger for a few moments, and then leave. This task shows how to create captions and subtitles in VideoWave.

Why Use Captions?

Captions can come in handy. Here are a few reasons why you might want to use them:

- To label people who have just entered a scene
- To describe the location
- To explain what is going on in a scene, such as "This is the final race for the Pinewood Derby championship"

Caption.

Captions needn't be onscreen for the entire scene.

Left-justify captions; center subtitles.

Start, Hold, and Finish positions are the same for a caption.

Use a text effect to make the caption fade in and out.

Keep the font size small for captions.

① Load the Scene

Start by dragging the scene to which you want to add captions into the view screen.

② Go to the Text Animator

Click the **Text Animator** button to switch to the text mode.

③ Add the Caption

In the text box, type the caption or subtitle you plan to use for this clip. What the text looks like is up to you, but I recommend sticking with a simple, easy-to-read font. Avoid special effects—they're distracting in captions. Captions should be functional, not decorative.

④ Set the Start Position

Most often, you'll find captions in the lower-left corner of the screen. (Subtitles, on the other hand, are usually centered at the bottom of the screen.) Click the **Start** button and click the lower-left box in the Position grid to identify this as the location where you want the caption to first appear.

5 Set the Hold Position

Because we don't want the caption to move, click the **Hold** button and click the lower-left box in the Position grid to ensure that the title stays in that position through the middle of the video clip. Remember that the length of the Hold portion of the video is determined by the middle two buttons under the VCR controls.

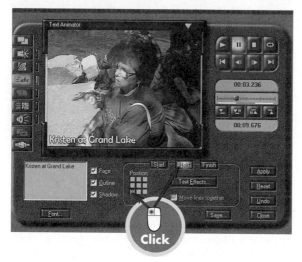

6 Get the Finish Position

Click the **Finish** button and again click the lower-left box in the Position grid. Now the caption won't move through the entire course of the scene.

7 Set the Timing

Now you need to decide when the caption appears and leaves the scene. Drag the brown button on the slider on the right side of the screen until you see the frame where you want to start the caption in the view screen. Click the **Hold Mark-In** button. Drag the brown button until you see the frame where you want the text to disappear and click the **Hold Mark-Out** button. The red Hold line shows you how long the caption will remain onscreen.

8 Start the Fade In

The text of the caption should fade in from the Start mark to the Hold mark. To set VideoWave to do this, click the **Start** button and then click the **Text Effects** button. Drag all three **Transparency** sliders to 100% and click **Close**. (Text that is 100% transparent at the start of the clip won't be seen; it will fade into sight by the time the clip hits the Hold mark.)

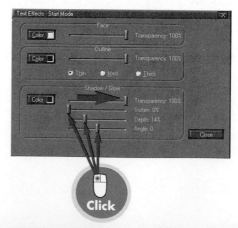

⑨ Verify the Hold Effect

Click the **Hold** button and click the **Text Effects** button. Make sure that the **Transparency** sliders are set to 0%, 0%, and 50%. Click **Close**. (Text that is 0% transparent is solid; a 50% transparent Shadow/Glow effect highlights the text nicely. The solid text appears onscreen when the clip hits the first Hold mark and remains onscreen for the duration of the Hold.)

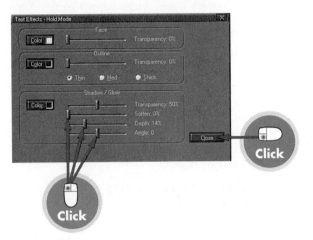

⑩ Finish the Fade Out

The text should fade out from the end of the Hold to the Finish mark. Click the **Finish** button and then click the **Text Effects** button. Drag all three **Transparency** sliders to 100%, just as you did for the Start of the clip, and click **Close**.

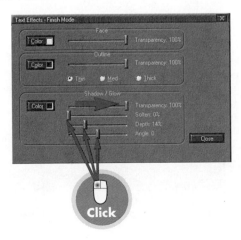

⑪ Preview the Caption

Use the VCR buttons to preview the effect of the caption. Make sure that the caption appears and disappears when you want it to during the scene.

⑫ Apply Your Changes

That's it! Click the **Apply** button to update the scene in the Storyline with the caption.

How to Move Text in Two Directions at Once

How can you create some really snazzy titles that grab your audience's eyes? How about making text fly into the scene from different directions? VideoWave isn't really designed to do that, but here's a technique for doing it that's simple but effective.

How-to Hint

Getting Lots of Text Animation

VideoWave is a powerful program, but it simply can't do some really advanced stuff—such as making four different titles fly into the scene from different directions at once. To do that, you need Premiere. Follow this outline to make four phrases move in from the four edges of the screen and meet near the middle of the screen:

- **Set each box to exhibit the movement you want the text in that box to make**—This can be up, down, left, or right. Make sure that each box touches the side of the screen from which the text will fly in—that way, the text will appear to enter from offscreen.

- **Use the Enable Special Timings option in the Rolling Title Options dialog box to synchronize the different title movements**—By changing the timing value in this dialog box, you change the rate at which the text moves with respect to other text elements on the screen. In other words, text can enter at different speeds.

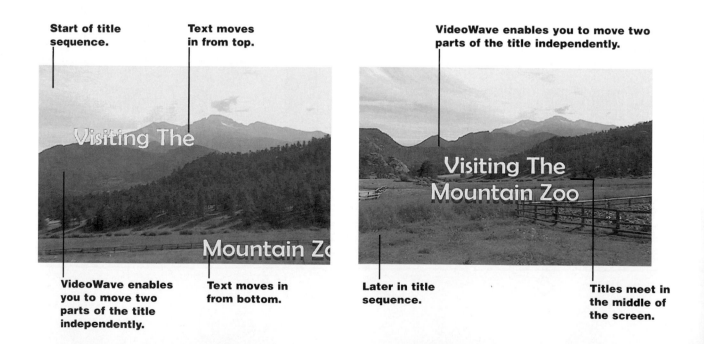

Start of title sequence.

Text moves in from top.

VideoWave enables you to move two parts of the title independently.

VideoWave enables you to move two parts of the title independently.

Text moves in from bottom.

Later in title sequence.

Titles meet in the middle of the screen.

① Create a Color Panel

To have two independent titles moving in one scene, you must have two layers: the video and a transparent color panel. Start by creating a color panel; leave it black.

② Set the Duration

The panel must have a duration that's the same as the video clip that plays behind it. If you don't know the duration of the clip, drag it into the Viewscreen and check the duration under the VCR controls. In the Cutting Room console, set the duration for the color panel based on the clip.

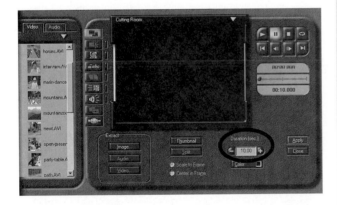

③ Type the Title

Click the **Text Animator** button. In the text box, type the part of the title that will be displayed and animated in this panel. (In this example, I typed the top line of my two-line title; the second line of the title will be created on the video clip itself.)

④ Set the Motion

With an eye on what the finished product will look like, click the **Start**, **Hold**, and **Finish** buttons and use the Position grid to set the motion of the text. You might want one line to roll from the top and stop in the middle, while another line rolls from the bottom and stops in the middle, just under the top word. In a situation like this one, you might have to add a hard return or two above the text that comes up from the bottom so that the two titles don't crowd each other.

5 Apply the Changes

Click the **Apply** button to save this color panel and its text to the Storyline.

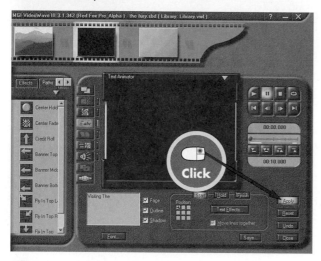

6 Put It in the Library

To use this color panel in the Video Animator, the panel must exist in the Library. Drag it from the Storyline to the Library (click the **Cutting Room** mode selector button if necessary to see the Video tab); when prompted by the Save As dialog box, give the color panel and its title a filename.

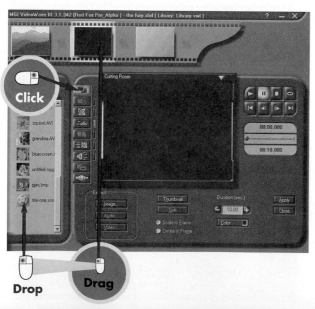

7 Open the Video Clip

Drag the video clip on which you want the titles to actually appear from the Library or the Storyline to the Viewscreen.

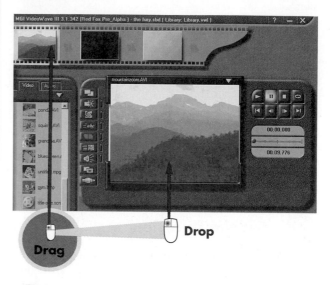

8 Add the Other Title

Click the **Text Animator** button and type the other part of the title that you want to appear in the scene. In this example, I typed the second line of my two-line header; this line will fly in from the bottom of the screen and meet up with the first line in the middle of the screen.

9 Set the Motion

Click the **Start**, **Hold**, and **Finish** buttons and use the Position grid to set the motion for the text you just entered. Make sure that it complements the motion of the text in the color panel—the lines of text shouldn't run over each other, for instance.

10 Switch to the Video Animator

Click the **Video Animator** button to get ready to combine the two layers of this complex title scene.

11 Add the Color Panel

Drag the named color panel with the other half of the title from the Library to the Video Animator screen. (The Foreground square in the console shows the color panel loaded.) Size the color panel to 100% in the Start, Hold, and Finish zones of the scene.

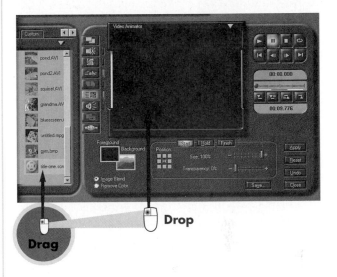

12 Remove the Color

Click the **Remove Color** option and select the black background of the color panel from the **Color** list. You should now be able to preview the titles moving around the scene. If you like the result, click the **Apply** button.

How to Make Titles with Video in the Letters

Imagine a scene in which letters move across a plain-colored background; in the letters themselves, you see moving video. It's as if the letters were cut out of a mask, revealing the scene behind the mask. If that sounds like an effect you'd like to try, you're in luck—this task teaches you how to do it.

Choosing the Right Letters

This technique works well—if you're using the right font. Make sure that the letters are big and fat, not skinny. Use sans-serif fonts (simple letters that don't have tails and fancy legs at their bottoms). And make the letters as large as possible—cover the whole screen and move them across the display slowly so that the viewer can appreciate both what the text says and what the video is behind the letters.

Large crawling title moves to the left.

Make the font big enough so that the viewer can see the video in the letters.

"Transparent" font shows a moving video clip through the letters.

Solid background.

❶ Create a Color Panel

Start by creating a color panel; make it any color you want. (You might want to consider making it a color that will contrast nicely with the dominant colors of the video clip you will be using.)

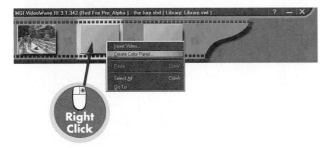

❷ Set the Duration

This panel must play as long as you want the title to appear. Decide on the video clip you want to "poke through" the letters and use the duration of that clip to help you determine the duration of the color panel. Then set the duration for which the color panel will run.

❸ Switch to the Text Animator

Click the **Text Animator** button so that you can type the text that will appear on the color panel.

❹ Add the Titles

In the text box, type the text of the title. Click the **Font** button and choose a big, fat font; to see the video behind the color panel, you'll need a wide, bold font (such as Zurich, Verdana, Kristen, or Litho in bold and large enough to fill the screen, probably over 100 points). Click **OK**.

(5) Apply the Changes

When the title meets your satisfaction, click the **Apply** button to save the color panel and its text to the Storyline.

(6) Add Panel to the Library

To use the color panel and its text in the Video Animator, the panel must first exist in the Library. (Click the **Cutting Room** button if necessary to display the Video tab of the Library.) Drag it from the Storyline to the Library; when prompted by the Save As dialog box, give the panel a filename.

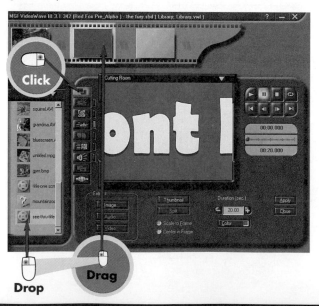

Drop   **Drag**

(7) Add the Video Clip

Find the video clip you want to show through the letters in the title and drag it to the Viewscreen.

(8) Open the Video Animator

Click the **Video Animator** button to begin the process of combining the video clip with the title on the color panel.

Click

⑨ Add the Color Panel

Drag the color panel with the title from the Library to the Video Animator. (The Foreground square shows when the color panel is loaded.) For each of the Start, Hold, and Finish zones, set the size of the panel to **100%**.

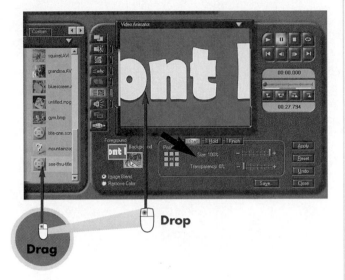

Drag **Drop**

⑩ Remove the Color

Click the **Remove Color** button to set the animator to chroma key mode. In the next step, we actually tell VideoWave which color to remove from the color panel letters so that the video shows through the text.

Click

⑪ Choose the Text Color

Click the **Color** button next to the Remove Color option and click **Pick a Color**. Now position the eyedropper tool, in the Viewscreen itself, over the one of the letters in the title. Click to select the color of the letter (not the background color). Click **OK**.

Click **Click**

⑫ Set the Tolerance

Finally, bump up the **Tolerance** slider until the video shows through the letters for each of the Start, Hold, and Finish positions (you want the letters to stay transparent throughout the video). Preview the effect with the VCR controls and click **Apply** to save your changes.

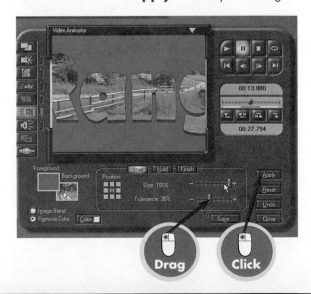

Drag **Click**

28

Working with Audio

In the world of video, the visuals tell only half the story. Less than half the story, if you believe sound engineers. In reality, the *audio*—narration, music, even *Foley effects* (special sound effects for creaking doors, gunshots, and car engines, for instance) if you're really fancy—fills in the gaps and turns your simple video clips into a sophisticated multimedia presentation.

For most of us, 90% of the sound in a home movie comes straight from your camcorder, recorded along with the video at the time you were shooting. Sure, you can add sound effects after the principal photography is over, but I'm guessing you don't have the time or patience for that. Instead, the tasks in this part of the book show you how to add music and other sound effects to the audio you already have, creating a cohesive audio-video product. By using a program such as VideoWave, you can easily capture music from the Internet (in the form of MP3 files) or from audio CDs and apply it to the background of your videos as music soundtracks.

How to Capture a Song from CD

VideoWave makes it easy to capture music from an audio CD and incorporate it into a movie in Windows's common WAV format. In fact, you can use VideoWave to capture CD audio that you want to use in Premiere—the format will be the same.

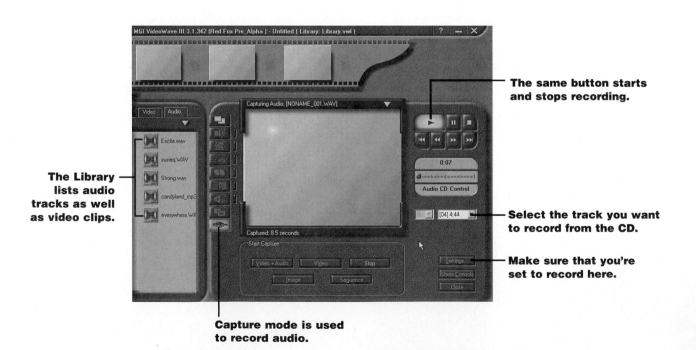

The same button starts and stops recording.

The Library lists audio tracks as well as video clips.

Select the track you want to record from the CD.

Make sure that you're set to record here.

Capture mode is used to record audio.

➊ Go to Capture

Click the **Capture** button to switch to VideoWave's Capture mode. In addition to recording video from your camcorder, this mode enables you to record audio from your PC's CD player.

➋ Verify Your Settings

Click the **Settings** button in the lower-right corner of the console area. The Capture Settings dialog box opens. In the Audio section, make sure that the Capture Device option lists your sound card, not the video capture hardware. Also make sure that you select **Auto-Start CD During Capture**. Then click the **Audio Mixing** button to open the Audio Input Mixing dialog box. Make sure that the Compact Disc Balance option is selected. Click **OK** twice to close both dialog boxes.

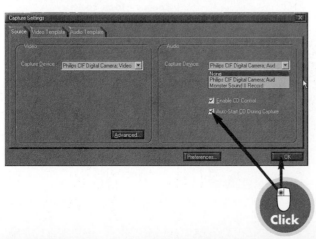

➌ Choose the Track

Make sure that the CD you want to record from is in your PC's CD-ROM drive. From the drop-down list, choose the number of the CD track you want to record. You can also use the VCR controls to select the track you want. When you're ready to record, make sure that the audio is stopped (click the **Stop** button on the VCR controls).

➍ Record the Song

Click the **Audio** button. The selected song will start playing and be recorded to the hard disk. When the song is over, click the **Stop** button. You will find the track with the label NONAME in the Audio tab of the Library; you can rename the file to anything you like.

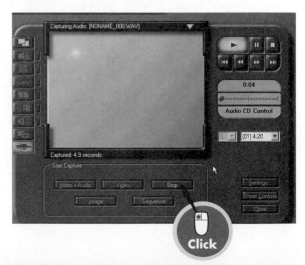

How to Capture Narration

One of the most useful kinds of audio you can add to a video is *narration*. A voiceover can add tremendous value to a video by explaining the situation to viewers. You can do the narration on-scene when you film the video, but you'll generally get better results by recording the voiceover in a quiet studio (such as at your PC) and adding it to the video afterwards.

How-to Hint

Tips for Better Audio

Voiceovers are often an afterthought, but with a little planning, you can get excellent results that really enhance the quality of your video:

- **Use a quality microphone**—The $5 mike that came with your PC simply isn't up to the task of recording quality audio.
- **Get to know the mike**—Speak at the proper distance from the mike so that the sound level is good without "popping" your audio and causing annoying audio glitches.
- **Write a script**—Don't narrate off the cuff. Write down the script and practice it, ideally in front of a running preview of the film.

Use the best mike you can afford.

Speak close to the mike, but avoid "pops" from blowing into mike.

Record narrations and voiceovers "in studio" instead of on location with the camcorder.

❶ Go to Capture

Click the **Capture** button to switch to VideoWave's Capture mode. This is the mode in which you record live audio.

❷ Verify Your Settings

Click the **Settings** button to open the Capture Settings dialog box. In the Audio section, make sure that the Capture Device option lists the device that controls your microphone (probably your sound card). Make sure that the Auto-Start CD During Capture option is not selected. Then click the **Audio Mixing** button to open the Audio Input Mixing dialog box. Make sure that the Microphone Balance option is selected. Click **OK** twice to close both dialog boxes.

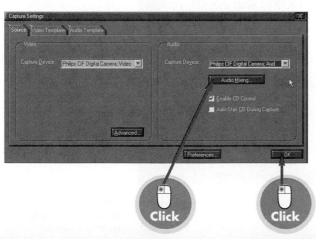

❸ Start Recording

When you're ready to begin, click the **Audio** button and start reading your narration. Make sure that you enunciate clearly, speaking at the proper distance from the microphone to avoid unpleasant "pops" from certain letters you pronounce.

❹ End Recording

When you're done recording the narration, click the **Stop** button to close the audio file and finish the recording. You will find the track with the label NONAME in the Audio tab of the Library; you can rename the file to anything you like.

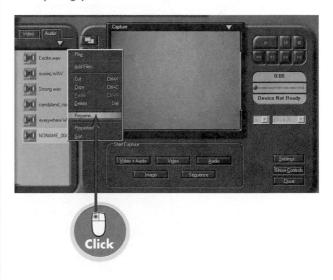

How to Create Background Music

Neither VideoWave nor Premiere has a way to create background music for your video. For that, you must have some musical skill and have access to some instruments—or use a music-authoring program. I like Cambium's Sound Choice, a program with a large selection of soundtrack-quality clips in a variety of styles. Here's how to create some background music in a program such as Sound Choice and then import the sound file into VideoWave.

Why Use Music Software?

Why bother using music-authoring software such as Sound Choice when you can just copy a few tracks from your favorite CD? As mentioned earlier, copyright laws can bite you if you're not careful. Multimedia-authoring software that burns audio tracks for you is designed to be royalty free. That means you can use it in a movie and not worry about having the rights to use it. But watch out for the fine print—some software limits how you can use the music that it generates.

Rolling Your Own

If you want to create your own original music, you can do that, too. It helps to have some good recording equipment, such as some high-quality mikes and perhaps a four-track recording deck to produce your music. You can capture the completed song into VideoWave by connecting the deck with the music to your PC's line-in sound port and use the procedure outlined in Task 1, "How to Capture a Song from CD."

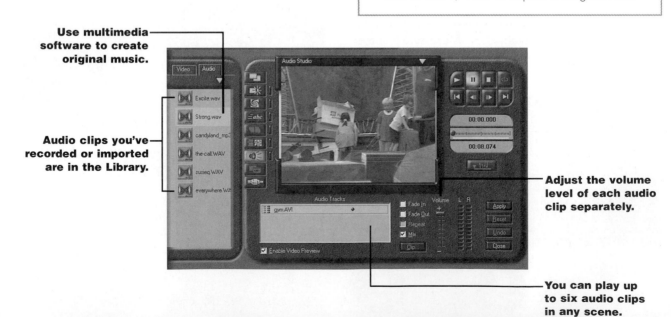

Use multimedia software to create original music.

Audio clips you've recorded or imported are in the Library.

Adjust the volume level of each audio clip separately.

You can play up to six audio clips in any scene.

① Find a Song

Sound Choice, like most multimedia-authoring software, has a library of prerecorded tunes. Surf around the songs and find one that you like. You can also search through the songs by keyword, so you can look for songs that have a specific theme, evoke a particular emotion, or have certain instruments in them.

② Choose a Length

Sound Choice includes several versions of each song in a variety of lengths. Choose the length you need based on how long the scene is that you want to enhance with music. Shorter clips are referred to as "bumps" (hence Bumper), and longer versions are labeled Main. When you select a version, the length appears in the File Information part of the screen.

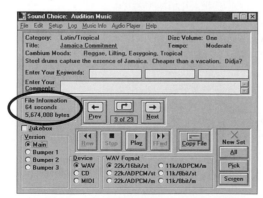

③ Copy the Clip

Click the **Copy File** button. In the Copy Music dialog box that opens, you can shorten the clip by clicking the **Copy Shortened File** button, or you can just click the **Copy Full File** button. If necessary, change the location on the hard disk where the file will be saved and click **Save**.

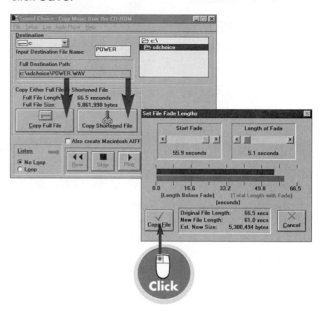

④ Import Audio File into VideoWave

Back in VideoWave, click the list menu arrow in the Library and select **Add Files**. Locate the file you just created and select it. The file should now appear in the Audio tab of the Library, ready for your use in VideoWave.

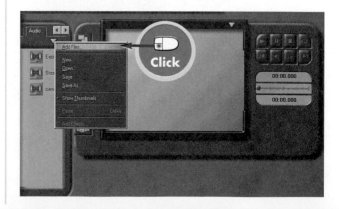

How to Mix Audio Tracks

The preceding few tasks have shown you how to create and import audio tracks into your video editor but haven't really shown you how to use those files. Well, fret no more; this task shows you how to load some audio tracks into VideoWave and Premiere. Although Premiere lets you use up to 99 simultaneous audio and video tracks, VideoWave is a bit more limited—you can add a total of only 6 audio tracks to a single scene. Usually, however, that's plenty.

Audio Formats

Audio on the PC has changed a lot in the past few years. The changes have come about because lots of people are downloading songs from the Internet and listening to music on their computers. Here's what you should know about sound formats:

- **WAV**—The WAV format is quite old. All video editors work with this format, which is *lossless*—that is, there's no compression to degrade sound quality.

- **CD-Audio**—Audio CDs use a high-quality sound format that can be read and converted to other computer formats. VideoWave can read audio CDs, although Premiere cannot.

- **MP3**—The MP3 format compresses sound files to save disk space and download time, but does so without losing the CD quality of the sound. MP3 is extremely popular on the Inter-net. You can also use special software to turn a CD-Audio file into an MP3 file. VideoWave reads MP3 files but Premiere does not.

Audio being previewed in the source Monitor window.

Handles enable you to change sound levels.

You can add multiple audio tracks to any scene.

The audio waveform.

❶ Add the Video

Load a video clip into the Viewscreen. This is the clip to which you will add a second audio track. (The first audio track is the one you recorded when you filmed the video originally.)

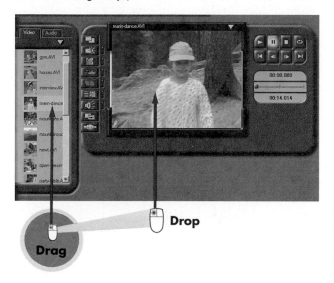

Drag

Drop

❷ Preview Audio Files

If you want to hear a sound clip, click the **Audio** tab in the Library and then right-click a clip in the list that appears. Select **Play** from the menu. Right-click and select **Stop** to end the playback. (Note that you can't preview music if you're already in the Audio Studio; to preview music, click another of the Mode Selector buttons to go to some other part of the program.)

Click

❸ Go to the Audio Studio

Click the **Audio Studio** button to edit the sound in the scene. You should see a suite of audio tools appear in the console.

Click

❹ Add a Sound Clip

From the Audio tab of the Library, drag a sound clip to the Viewscreen. Note that the sound clip's filename appears in the Audio Tracks list under the Viewscreen. It's important to realize that if you add a clip that's longer than the scene, the clip will continue playing into the next scene.

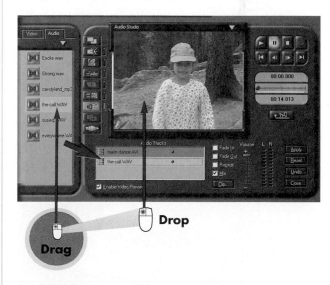

Drag

Drop

5 Select a Level

You can adjust the level of each audio track independently so that one is louder than the other is. From the Audio Track list, select the audio track you just added and adjust the volume level by using the Volume slider. Do the same for the track's primary audio track. Test the results using the VCR controls. VideoWave doesn't let you fade one clip into another; for more precise control over multiple audio tracks, you need to use Premiere.

6 Apply the Audio

You can add as many as five additional audio tracks to the scene if you want. When you're happy with the audio you've added, click the **Apply** button to update the scene in the Storyline.

7 Add Clips to the Project

Before you can begin using audio in Premiere, you must add at least one audio clip to the Project window. Do it the same way you add video: right-click a blank area in the window and select **Import**, **File** from the shortcut menu. Unlike VideoWave, which can read MP3 files, Premiere can understand only the WAV audio format.

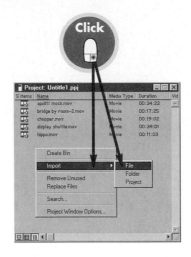

8 Put Audio in Source Monitor

Assuming that you want to preview an audio clip before you insert it in the project, double-click the file-name in the Project window. The file should appear in the Source Monitor window.

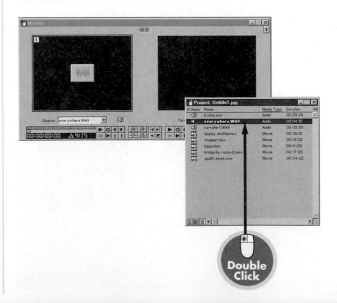

⑨ Preview the Audio

To listen to the clip, click the **Play** button in the Monitor window. Click the **Stop** button to stop the playback of the audio file.

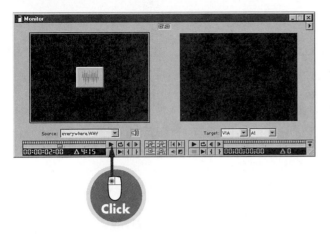

⑩ Add the Audio

Now add the sound clip to the Timeline. Assuming that there's already a video clip in Video 1A (and if there isn't, add one now), you should see its audio component in the Audio 1 track. Drag the audio clip you just auditioned to the Audio 2 track.

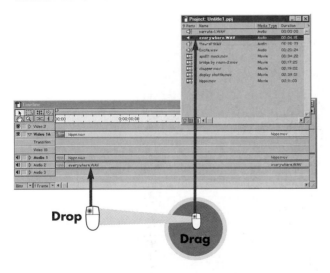

⑪ View the Wave

Now adjust the relative volume of the two audio tracks. Start by clicking the right-facing arrows next to the Audio 1 and Audio 2 tracks in the Timeline window. The tracks should expand to display the waveforms of the two sound files.

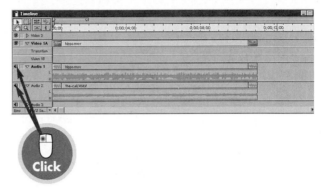

⑫ Change the Level

You should see a red line that runs through the middle of both waveforms. Grab a line by the handle on the left side of the window and drag it down to lower the volume. Drag the right handle down to keep the line horizontal to reduce the volume of the entire clip.

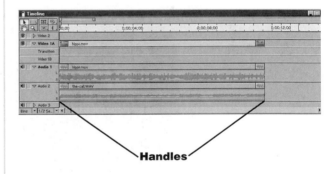

How to Fade Audio

In the last task, you learned how to mix a second (or third) audio track into a scene, as well as to vary the volumes of the sound tracks. Although this is a great technique to implement, even more frequently you'll want to fade the music in at the beginning of the scene or fade it out at the end. As you're about to see, VideoWave makes it easy to do a simple fade; Premiere gives you the power to vary the volume many times throughout the scene.

How-to Hint

When to Fade

Why fade the audio to begin with? There are many reasons to fade, but here are a few to get you started:

- To end music that's longer than the scene
- To introduce music slowly into a scene
- To slowly ramp up the volume of dialogue in a scene while reducing the volume of the background music (or vice versa)

Add handles to vary the volume at any point.

Audio ramps up.

Audio fades down.

① Open the Audio Studio

Load the scene you want to work with in the Viewscreen and then click the **Audio Studio** button. If you don't already have your second audio track loaded, drag it to the Viewscreen now.

② Apply Fade Controls

Click one of the audio tracks in the Audio Tracks list. Then select the **Fade In** and **Fade Out** check boxes to tell VideoWave to fade this sound file in and out of the scene. (You can also select just one or the other of these options.) Click another audio track in the scene and apply the desired fade to that one. Click the **Apply** button to save your changes.

③ Create Handles

Premiere doesn't have a one-click fade control; instead, you can raise and lower the volume of a sound clip many times through the scene. Load the video clip and the additional sound clip files in Premiere as usual. In the Timeline, you should see the waveform for your audio track (if not, click the right arrow next to the desired audio track to expand the display). The waveform already has a volume handle at each end; add two more handles by clicking the red line at two places in the track.

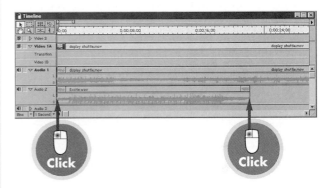

④ Drag the Handles

Drag the handles to create a fade. For example, drag the new handles so that the volume goes up for most of the clip and then goes back down again. You can add more handles and drag them around to create sophisticated audio control of your scene.

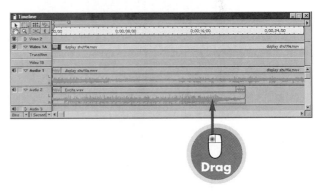

How to Trim Audio

The audio files you create for your movies won't always be exactly the right length. Sometimes, the sound clip is too long, and you'll want to modify the video to fix the problem (as described in the next task); other times, you'll want to trim the length of the audio file itself. Perhaps the sound clip has ugly mike pops at the start or end. This task shows you how to trim VideoWave audio. (In Premiere, you trim audio in the Monitor window, exactly as you trim video.)

Audio That Spans Scenes

A long audio clip can run longer than a single scene in VideoWave. For proof, click the **Clip** button in the Audio Studio console to display the Audio Trimmer dialog box. An audio track that is longer than the video keeps playing into the next scene unless you clip it to stop sooner. When you preview the clip all by itself, the audio stops when the video stops. You have to preview multiple scenes to hear the entire clip. For more precise control over these kinds of audio situations, however, switch to Premiere.

Top blue bar: Scene length.
Bottom white bar: Audio length.

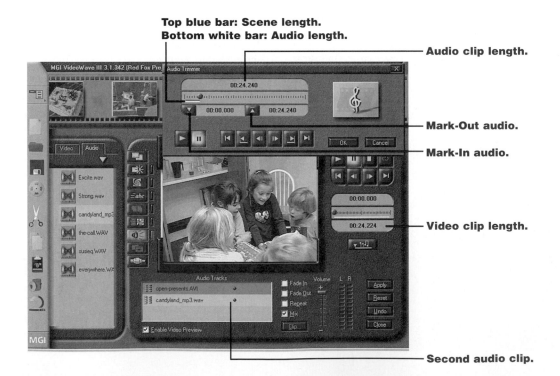

Audio clip length.

Mark-Out audio.

Mark-In audio.

Video clip length.

Second audio clip.

① Go to the Audio Studio

Load a video clip in the Viewscreen and click the **Audio Studio** button.

② Load the Audio Clip

If your video clip doesn't already have a second audio clip associated with it, add a second sound clip to the video by dragging the file from the Audio tab in the Library now.

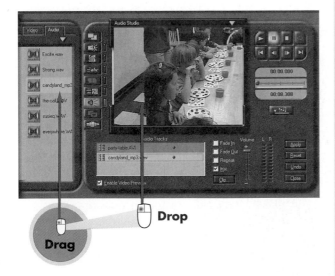

③ Open the Audio Trimmer

Select the new clip in the **Audio Tracks** list and click the **Clip** button. The Audio Trimmer dialog box opens. Note that you can't trim the length of the first audio track (the one that is part of the video).

④ Mark the Start and End

The Audio Trimmer dialog box enables you to play the audio and set the Mark-In and Mark-Out points—in other words, the points in the song where it begins to play and where it stops playing. This is handy if you want only a short section of the middle of a song to play in the scene. Use the **Play** button or the slider to set the location, and then click the **Mark-In Point** when you want the clip to begin playing. Then find the point where you want the song to stop playing and click the **Mark-Out Point**. Click **OK** to complete the process.

White audio file line is much longer than blue video file line.

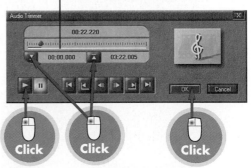

How to Extend Video to Match Audio

Sometimes, your audio track is longer than the video intended to run behind it. You might run into this situation with a background song that runs a little long or a narrator who talks a little too slowly. Whatever the case, you can add more video to fill in the hole, trim the audio short (as explained in the preceding task), or add extra frames to the end of the scene so that a *freeze frame* runs while the audio ends.

How Much Quality Do You Need?

When you record audio, you have a lot of choices for audio quality. VideoWave reduces what could be dozens of options down to just three. Here's when to use each one:

- **AM Radio Quality**—This is 11KHz, 8-bit stereo. It's very low quality and should only be used for recording voice. Even then, I'd avoid using it.

- **FM Radio Quality**—This is 22KHz, 16-bit stereo. It's much better than AM Radio Quality and is good for most home-brewed videos. Use this option for voice and sound effects.

- **CD Quality**—This 44KHz, 16-bit stereo is most appropriate for music. Using this option for voice recordings is probably overkill.

Don't use this technique for more than a few seconds.

The audio file is longer than the video scene.

The last frame of the video "holds" the scene while the audio plays.

Point of transition to freeze frame.

① Go to the Audio Studio

Load the scene that has the too-long audio into the Viewscreen. Then click the **Audio Studio** button.

② Determine the Total Length

If the audio clip isn't already attached to the clip, include it now. Select the too-long audio clip and click the **Clip** button to open the Audio Trimmer dialog box. Note the total audio length and click the **Cancel** button.

③ Apply Your Changes

If you haven't already saved the video clip with the second audio track, click the **Apply** button now.

④ Go to the Cutting Room

Click the **Cutting Room** button so that you can extract the end of the scene as a still frame.

(5) Scroll to the End

In the pane under the VCR controls, drag the brown circle to the very end of the slider to move directly to the end of the video clip.

(6) Extract the Last Frame

With the Viewscreen showing the last frame of the scene, click the **Image** button in the Extract section of the Cutting Room console. The Extract Images dialog box opens.

(7) Add to Storyline

Select the **Add to Storyline** check box and click the **Extract** button to make a copy of this last frame of video and save it as a bitmapped image. Then click the **Close** button to close the dialog box.

(8) Display the Frame

Locate the saved frame at the end of the Storyline. Drag it from there to the Viewscreen so that you can edit it.

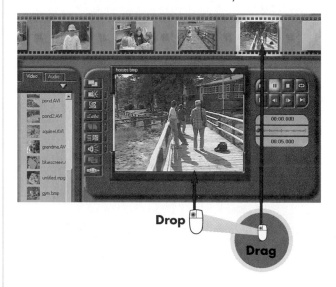

⑨ Go to the Cutting Room

Click the **Cutting Room** button so that you can work on the still image in the Cutting Room. You want to adjust the length of the image so that it perfectly fills in the space between the time that the video would otherwise have ended and when the audio track ends.

⑩ Change the Duration

Set the Duration box for the frame so that the frame remains onscreen long enough to fill in for the over-long audio. You need to subtract the duration of the original video scene from the total length of the audio to determine how long this freeze frame will remain onscreen.

⑪ Apply Your Changes

Click the **Apply** button. The scene now holds on the last frame for as long as the audio continues to play.

⑫ Extract the Last Frame

The procedure to freeze a frame in Premiere is essentially the same as it is in VideoWave, but you have to know how to grab that last frame. Display the scene in the Monitor window and go to the end of the clip. Select **File**, **Export**, **Frame** from the menu and save the frame as a BMP file to your hard disk. You can then load the frame file into the Project window and stretch it appropriately in the Timeline.

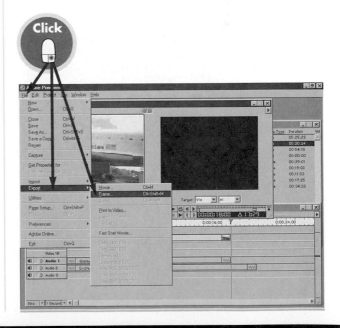

How to Create an Audio Transition

It's a common technique—so common, in fact, that you might not even notice it is happening. Filmmakers like to transition to new scenes aurally, not visually. Often, you can hear the next scene—such as a person's voice, street traffic, or a telephone—a few seconds before you see it happen onscreen. Then the scene changes, and the audio is perfectly in synch with the visuals. You can't do this in VideoWave, but you can in Premiere. Here's how.

Getting the Most Out of Audio Transitions

Audio transitions are more popular than video transitions in most movies. Here are some tips to remember when you create your transitions:

- **Keep them short**—Don't play more than just a few short seconds of audio or the magic of the transition is lost.

- **Don't combine an audio transition with any kind of video transition**—Just use a simple cut instead.

- **Fade the outgoing audio**—However, don't be too obvious about dropping out the audio from the first scene or the effect will be ruined.

- **Use audio transitions on scenes in which you can cut to the next scene at a dramatic moment**—Or use a subtle effect (such as a ringing phone) to signal the scene change.

Second scene.

First scene.

Video 2 "hides" Video 1A.

Videos overlap by few seconds.

The viewer hears the roller coaster screams before the next scene actually starts.

❶ Add the First Scene

For this technique to work, we take advantage of Premiere's video layers: Higher track numbers obscure tracks with lower numbers. Drag the first scene from the Monitor window or the Project window to track Video 2 in the Timeline window.

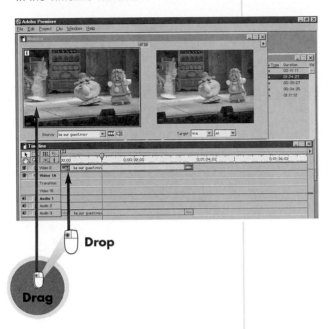

❷ Add the Second Scene

Drag the second video scene from the Monitor window or the Project window to the Video 1A track in the Timeline.

❸ Set the Timing

In the Timeline, drag the clip in Video 1A track back a little so that it starts before the clip in the Video 2 track ends. Back it just up a few seconds at most.

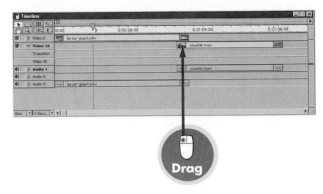

❹ Fade the First Scene

If you want, you can fade the audio at the end of the first scene a little to emphasize the audio that plays from the second scene. When you play these clips, you hear the action in the second scene before you see it. A flair for the dramatic can help you know when to make the cut.

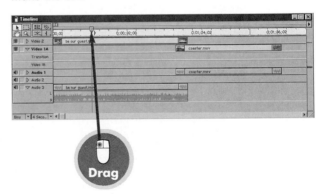

29

Working with Still Images

One of the great things about digital video is that still images and moving video are so closely related. Not only can you extract stills from a video clip, you can also include still images in your movie in a sort of video slideshow. Equipped with just a camcorder, you can make both video and still shots that you can print and email.

Don't be fooled by the marketing hype, either—no matter what kind of digital camcorder you own, you can extract still images from video. Of course, some cameras give you a little more flexibility. Some JVC and Sony cameras, for instance, enable you to take stills and copy the pictures to a removable memory card.

Nonetheless, the ability to pull a still out of video is a great feature. You can shoot continuous video and then grab the one moment that's "perfect" as a still. Or you can grab lots of stills and make a video slideshow out of them, complete with background music.

Interested in the potential of still images? Great. In the tasks in this part, I'll show you how to capture stills from video, edit them in a simple image editor such as Paint Shop Pro, and use them in video.

How to Capture an Image from Video

Unlike analog video you'd get with an ordinary camcorder, digital video can make good still frames that you can extract and print, email, or include in other documents. You can even reuse the still in the video, as you'll see later in the book.

Good Freeze Frames Aren't Easy

Considering the nature of video, every freeze-frame image isn't going to be exactly frozen. Especially with analog video, you can get a lot of noise, blur, and even a mixture of two different images in alternating lines. Jagged edges might also be apparent. If your video capture device has controls for smoothing out extracted images, experiment with them. If not, you can try grabbing the still just a little sooner or a little later on the tape, where the artifacts might be less apparent. By jogging the tape around, you can find the optimum point at which to grab the still.

A still image grabbed from a video clip or imported from a digital camera.

Use the Cutting Room to grab and edit stills.

The Library holds the still images.

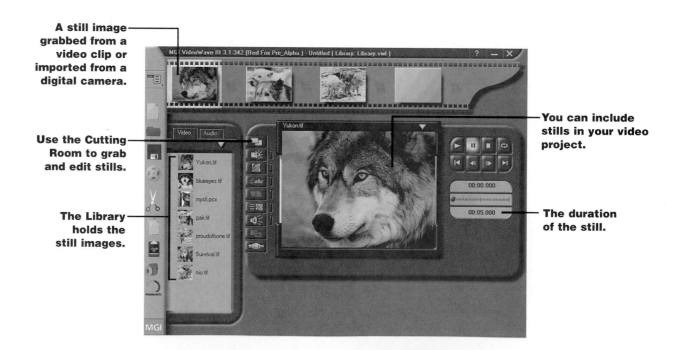

You can include stills in your video project.

The duration of the still.

① Load the Video

Find the clip from which you want to extract a still image and drag it to the Viewscreen.

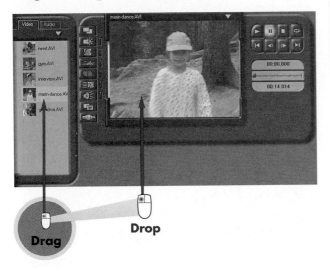

Drag   **Drop**

② Go to the Cutting Room

Click the **Cutting Room** button. The Cutting Room controls appear in the console area.

Click

③ Find the Frame

Using the VCR slider, find the moment in the video clip that you want to capture.

Drag

④ Start the Extraction

In the Extract area of the Cutting Room console, click the **Image** button. The Extract Images dialog box appears.

⑤ Set the Save Location

Where do you want to save this image? Click the **Browse** button and specify a filename and a location on your hard drive where you want to save the image you are going to extract.

⑥ Add to Storyline

If you want this image to appear in the Storyline, select the **Add to Storyline** check box. Otherwise, leave it blank. You can always add the still to the movie later.

⑦ Extract the Image

Click the **Extract** button. After a few seconds, the image is saved to your hard disk. You can work with it just as you would any graphic.

⑧ Close the Dialog Box

The Extract Images dialog box won't close on its own—it stays open in case you want to extract more still images. Click the **Close** button to return to the Cutting Room.

⑨ Load the Video

In Premiere, the process of creating a still image is actually simpler than it is in VideoWave. Start by dragging a clip from the Project window to the Source Monitor window.

⑩ Find the Frame

Use the slider in the Source Monitor window to find the point in the video clip that you want to capture.

⑪ Extract the Image

Select **File**, **Export**, **Frame** from the menu. The Export Still Frame dialog box appears.

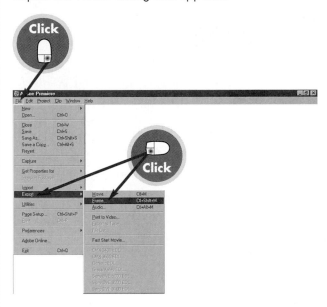

⑫ Save the File

By default, the still image is saved in the BMP file format. If you want to use another format, click the **Settings** button and make the change. Otherwise, simply name the file, select a location on the hard drive where you want to store the file, and click the **Save** button.

How to Change Image Resolution

The *resolution* of an image, measured in *pixels*, represents both the overall file size and the physical size at which the image will print. Images extracted from digital video are usually 720×480 pixels. Although this is a somewhat low resolution for a photograph (a 5"×7" print, for instance, typically is about 1280×960 pixels—8"×10" prints are even bigger), the resolution for the still image might be greater (and the resulting file size bigger) than what you need. If you want to post the image to a Web page, for instance, you might want to shrink the image further. To do that, you should use an image editor. I prefer Jasc's Paint Shop Pro. Any image editor will do—you might already have Adobe PhotoShop or Corel Photo Paint, for instance—but I prefer the simplicity of Paint Shop Pro.

Resolution Explained

It's important to understand the term *resolution* when you work with graphics. Resolution is the density of the pixels in an image. Digital video cameras capture images at a resolution of 720×480, which means 720 pixels in a line by 480 lines. At that resolution, you can't really print the image any bigger than 5"×7", but it's great for Web pages and importing into Word or Publisher documents.

If you want to print images and frame them on your wall, you need a digital camera that can grab images at a much higher resolution. These megapixel cameras take pictures with at least a million pixels in the image, such as 1280×960. Although a few digital camcorders can take high-resolution stills like this, you should look into one of the many megapixel still digital cameras if you want to take pictures for printing and framing.

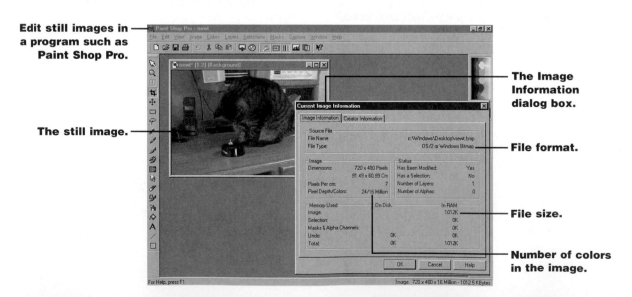

Edit still images in a program such as Paint Shop Pro.

The still image.

The Image Information dialog box.

File format.

File size.

Number of colors in the image.

① Load the Image

In an image editor application such as Paint Shop Pro, open the image file you extracted from a video clip by selecting **File**, **Open**.

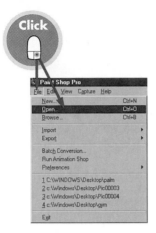

② Crop the Image

If you want to make the image smaller by trimming away unwanted details, click the **Crop** tool in the toolbar. Then click in the image area and drag to frame the portion of the image you want to keep. Click the **Crop Image** button in the Controls window.

③ Set a New Size

You can also shrink the image to a specific pixel size to drop the resolution. If you plan to insert this image in a Web page, for instance, you might want to select a width of 400 pixels—a size at which the image will fit on the screen with enough room to spare in which you can put some text on the side. Select **Image**, **Resize** from the menu. In the Resize dialog box, enter a new width or height in the Pixel Size area and click **OK**. Make sure that the Maintain Aspect Ratio box is selected so that you don't distort the image.

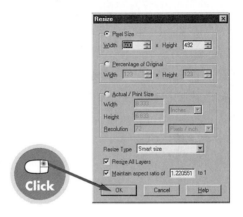

④ Save the Image

When you're done adjusting the image and its resolution, select **File**, **Save As** from the menu to save the image on your hard drive. Note that you might want to give the modified image a different filename than the original image.

How to Change File Format

In a perfect world, there would be one universal file format for everything. Unfortunately, that's not the case. Your video editor might extract an image in BMP format, but you might have to convert it to the JPG or GIF format to make use of it. Converting the format of an image is a snap with an image editor program such as Paint Shop Pro.

Image File Formats

Here is what file formats are most commonly used for:

- **JPG**—The JPG format is great for squeezing huge photographic images down to tiny file sizes while sacrificing only a little image quality. JPG is great for Web pages and email.

- **GIF**—Commonly used in Web pages, GIF files can be made to display first in low resolution and then improve in quality as more data is downloaded.

- **TIF**—This is a great format for preserving all the image quality in a picture, although files can be huge.

- **BMP**—Used by Windows to display "wallpaper" images, it isn't practical for most other applications because of the large file sizes associated with the format.

Shrink the resolution to 640×480 or smaller for Web and email applications.

Use the Image menu to resize the image.

The Crop tool makes the image smaller by discarding extra information.

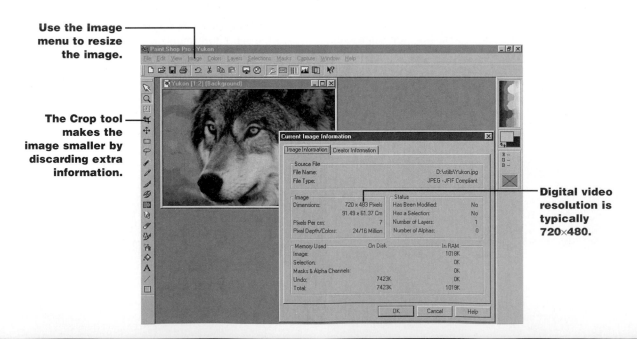

Digital video resolution is typically 720×480.

① Load the Image

In an image editor application such as Paint Shop Pro, open the image file you extracted from a video clip by selecting **File**, **Open**. Recall that images extracted from video clips are typically in the BMP format.

② Open the Save Dialog Box

Select **File**, **Save As** from the menu. From the Save As Type list, select the format you want. The most common formats are JPG, BMP, GIF, PCX, and TIF. Name the file and click the **Save** button.

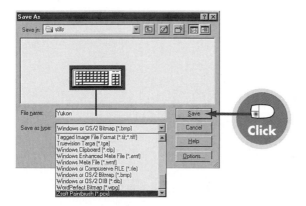

③ Set the Format Options

Sometimes, you might encounter a dialog box that says you're about to save the image in fewer colors—perhaps even as few as two colors. If you see this dialog box, click **No** to close the warning box without saving the file. Back in the Save As dialog box, click the **Options** button.

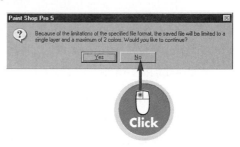

④ Change the Version

In the Save Options dialog box that opens, set the file format to the latest version. The PCX file format, for instance, should be set to Version 5 if you want to save lots of colors.

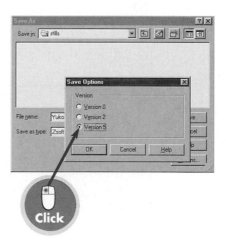

How to Erase Parts of an Image

After you've extracted an image from a video clip, you can edit the image to your heart's content. One common problem with images culled from video is the presence of junk—such as telephone poles or other obstacles—that gets in the way of your main image. You can airbrush such objects out of the image using an image editor program such as Paint Shop Pro.

How-to Hint

Cloning Tips

The Clone Brush in Paint Shop Pro is a great way to wipe out distracting parts of an image. You need to practice, though, to avoid smearing the background. Get in the habit of dabbing the brush on the screen. You can also vary the thickness of the brush tip to get a better erasure effect.

We want to remove this tree from the image.

Editing is obvious if you look carefully.

The tree was painted out by covering it with nearby background colors.

The tree is gone.

① Load the Image

In an image editor application such as Paint Shop Pro, open the image file you extracted from a video clip by selecting **File**, **Open**.

② Select the Clone Brush

Click the **Clone Brush** tool in the toolbar. This tool enables you to paint one part of the image with actual pixels from another part of the picture. We'll use it to eliminate an eyesore from the image.

③ Select the Source Region

Move the Clone Brush over a background part of the scene that's near the element you want to remove. Right-click to select those pixels; they're the pixels the Clone Brush will paint with.

④ Paint

Paint the obstacle out of the image by clicking the left mouse button. It helps to "dab" the brush and work slowly, clicking many times instead of making big, sweeping strokes.

How to Print an Image

After you've extracted and edited an image, you might want to print it to send it to friends or family who do not have access to the Internet or email. Although the images you extract from a video clip are not detailed enough to print and frame, images taken by a two-megapixel digital camera can be impressive enough to hang on the wall.

How-to Hint

File Sizes and Printing

When you print an image, it will come out jagged and "pixely" unless the resolution of the file is sufficient for the size you want to print. Use this chart as a rule of thumb for sizing the images you want to print:

File Resolution	Maximum Print Size
640x480	5"x7"
1 million pixels	8"x10"
2 million pixels	11"x17"

When printing on an inkjet printer, remember that the image quality greatly depends on the kind of paper you use. You get dramatically better results if you use glossy photo paper, available at any computer or office supply store.

You can print an image file from a graphics program such as Paint Shop Pro.

Select File, Print to open the Print dialog box.

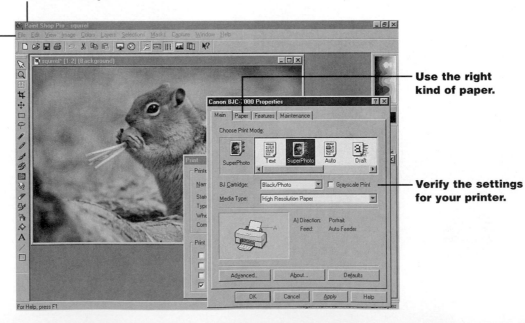

Use the right kind of paper.

Verify the settings for your printer.

① Load the Image

Because there's no printing feature built into VideoWave, you need an image editor program such as Paint Shop Pro to print an image file. Using Paint Shop Pro's **File**, **Open** menu item, load the image.

② Configure the Printer

Select **File**, **Page Setup** to open the Page Setup dialog box; click the **Printer** button. From the Name drop-down list, select the printer you plan to use. If you're using a color inkjet printer, click the **Properties** button and configure the printer to use the appropriate kind of paper.

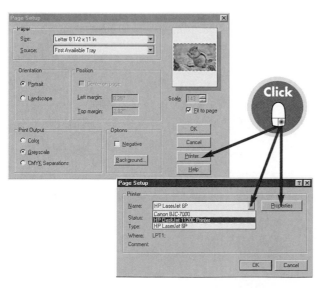

③ Orient the Print

After you close the Printer Properties dialog box, you should be back in the Page Setup dialog box. Select **Portrait** or **Landscape** orientation and then select the scaling you want. (Scaling determines how large the image appears on the printed page.) If you select Fit to Page, the image will print at the full size of the paper. Click **OK** to close the dialog box.

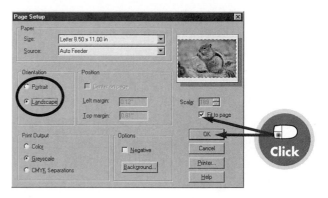

④ Print

Select **File**, **Print** from the menu to print the image. When the Print dialog box opens, check all the settings you have already made and then click the **OK** button.

How to Email an Image

In the previous task, I showed you how to print an image. But emailing images is more efficient, and I always send pictures electronically when I have a choice. The procedure for attaching an image file to an email message is essentially the same regardless of what email program you use; in this task, we'll use Microsoft Outlook.

Quick View might not be installed on your PC; open the Control Panel and select Add/Remove Programs to install it if necessary.

You can email image files using any mail client.

Click to attach the image file to the email message.

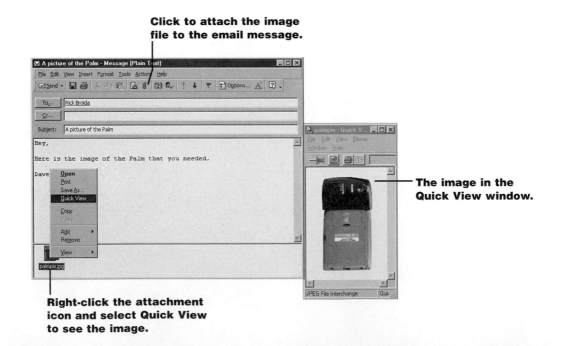

The image in the Quick View window.

Right-click the attachment icon and select Quick View to see the image.

① Create a New Message

With Microsoft Outlook set to the Inbox view, click the **New** button in the Outlook toolbar to open a new, blank email message.

② Fill in the Message

Fill in the header information, such as the recipient's email address and the subject line. Then type the message body.

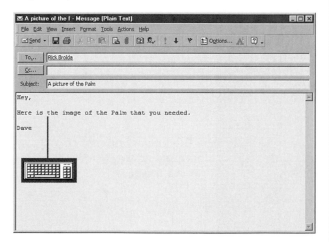

③ Attach the Image

Select **Insert**, **File** from the message's menu and select the image file you want to attach from your hard drive. Click **Insert**. Alternatively, you can drag the image directly from the desktop to the message window. An icon appears at the bottom of the message window, showing that a file has been attached to the email message.

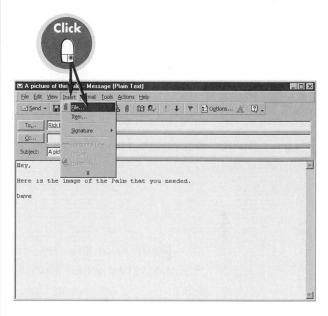

④ Send the Message

When you're ready to send the email message and its attachment, click the **Send** button in the message toolbar.

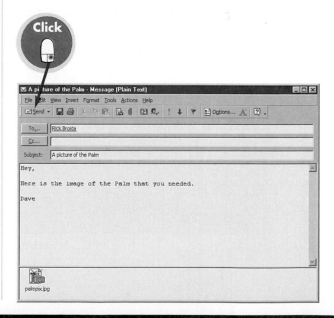

How to Add Still Images to Video

You can mix still images with video in your movies very easily. Still images can be used to fill in gaps between video clips caused by long audio clips. You can also use several still images to create a digital slideshow. The possibilities, in fact, are endless.

Make sure that images are 720×480 or they'll be distorted when they become part of a video clip.

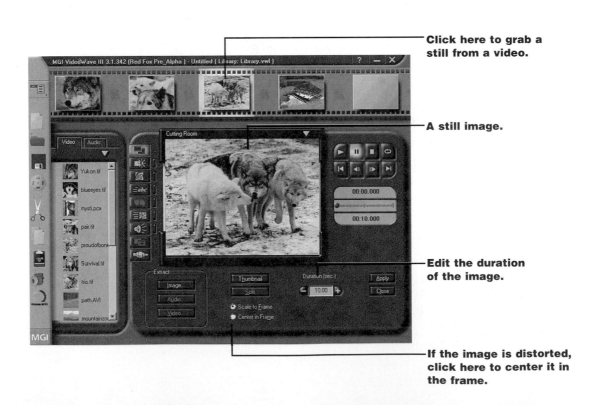

Click here to grab a still from a video.

A still image.

Edit the duration of the image.

If the image is distorted, click here to center it in the frame.

① Drag the Image

In VideoWave, images can be handled the same as video clips. Drag an image from the Library to the Viewscreen.

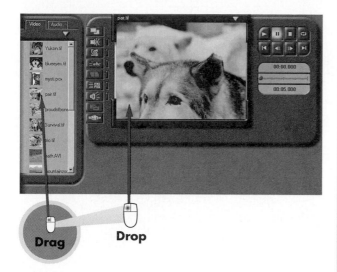

② Change the Duration

By default, images in VideoWave appear for five seconds. To change that, click the **Cutting Room** button and set the Duration to any value. When you're done, click the **Apply** button.

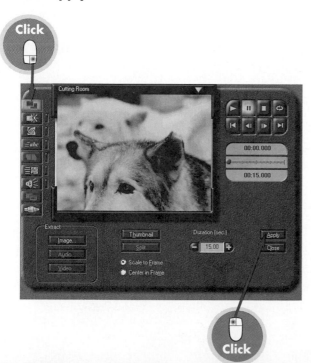

③ Put It in the Timeline

In Premiere, you can add an image to your project by dragging it from the Project window to the Timeline.

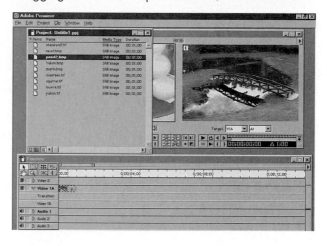

④ Change the Duration

To lengthen or shorten the length of time the image displays, position the pointer at the right edge of the image track and drag it to any length of time you desire. Alternatively, right-click the image in the Timeline and select **Duration** from the shortcut menu. Specify the desired length.

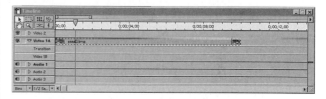

Task

Producing Videotape

After hours of filming, capturing, and editing audio and video, you finally have a finished project on your PC. It doesn't do anyone much good there, though. In fact, so far in the book, I haven't really told you how to produce a watchable movie. Instead, I've had you arrange clips, add titles, use special effects—but the video isn't finished and you can't sit someone down (even in front of the computer) to watch your creation. That's because VideoWave (or Premiere) needs to render your raw files into a finished film.

After the movie has been rendered (another term you might see used for this process is *produced*), you can watch the video as a full-screen film on your PC. That's great, but most likely, you'll want to copy the video onto tape and distribute it to friends, family, or co-workers. In the following tasks, I talk about how to make videotape from a finished production. If you prefer to burn the movie onto CD-ROM or copy it to the Web, hold on to your hat! We'll do that in Chapter 31, "Publishing Video to the Web and CD-ROM."

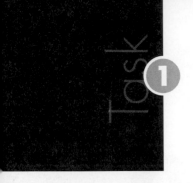

How to Prepare Your Video for Tape

Before you can copy your production to tape, you must *produce* the movie. Producing the movie renders it in its final form and stores it on your hard disk. The produced video becomes the high-quality master from which you can make any number of copies—and those copies will be every bit as good as the first copy. In this task, I explain the process for producing your movie in VideoWave. In Premiere, the process varies depending on the kind of video capture hardware you have in your PC. Check the documentation that came with your FireWire card for details.

How-to Hint

Prepping Premiere

Adobe Premiere uses project settings for your desired output right from the start. Make sure that your project is configured for DV output when you begin the project using the dialog boxes that appear when you start the program.

Producing Part of a Production

Thanks to the magic of digital video editing, you don't have to produce the entire movie. For example, you might want to produce just the first few scenes to make sure that your settings are right. After all, it can take hours to produce the entire movie, and you don't want to find out after an evening of rendering that you chose the wrong format and that your video has been rendered to a small Web-style window instead of in full screen for videotape.

Save your work, and then render the video.

The fully rendered video file ready for transfer to videotape.

The completed production.

A preview of the finished video you can watch on your PC.

① Save Your Work

The first step—before you render the video—is to save the production. From the menu button, select **Storyline**, **Save**. If anything happens during the production, you now have a good backup from which to work.

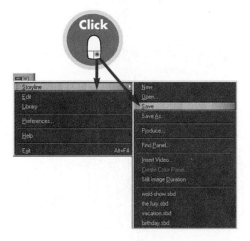

② Select the Panels

You might want to produce only part of the movie. If that's the case, Shift-click to select the panels in the Storyline that you want to appear in the movie. Otherwise, move on to the next step.

③ Start the Production

Click the menu button and select **Storyline**, **Produce**. The Produce Movie Wizard appears.

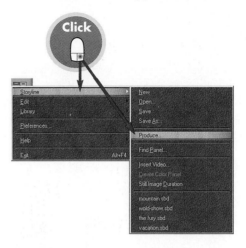

④ Choose the Panels

If you want to produce just the panels you selected in step 2, select the **Highlighted Clips Only** option. Otherwise, select the **Entire Storyline** option.

5 Pick a Template

Now you have to select the correct settings to produce the movie. If you're making a movie in DV format (using a DV camcorder and a FireWire cable), select **DV** from the Select a Produce Template list. If you are using an analog camcorder, select **Full Screen Playback**.

7 Make Changes

In the Settings dialog box, you will find options such as stereo and mono audio or PAL and NTSC playback that you can choose from. Make any changes you want and click the **Finish** button to return to the Produce Movie dialog box.

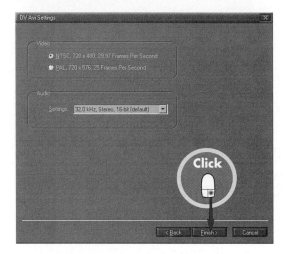

6 Enter Edit Mode

Most of the time, you don't need to tweak the Edit settings. But if you have special needs (for example, if you want to change the size of the rendered movie), click the **Edit** button to open the Settings dialog box.

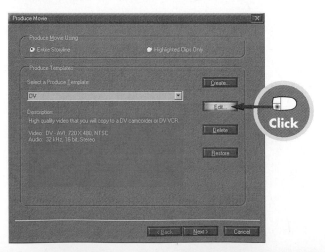

8 Go to the Summary

Now that you've selected a template, click the **Next** button to go to the Summary Page, where you can name the file and prepare to render the movie.

⑨ Name the File

In the Summary Page, give the video file a name. If necessary, click the **Browse** button to locate where you want to save the video. This step takes all the pieces of the video you have made earlier in the book—the clips, transitions, titles, and music—and renders them into a single video file that conforms to the template settings you just made. In this case, we're using a template to make a videotape, but we could just as easily render the production files into a format for the Web or a CD-ROM.

⑩ Produce It!

It's the moment of truth: Click the **Produce** button. The video will be rendered to your hard drive. Don't be surprised if it takes a while—maybe even hours. You can track the video's progress onscreen.

⑪ Watch the Preview

When the production process is complete, the video appears in the Library and in the Viewscreen. Click the **Play** button to watch the completed movie in the Viewscreen.

⑫ See It Full Size

Alternatively, you can use Windows Explorer to find the movie file on your hard drive (the file has the extension **AVI**) and double-click it. The movie should open in a Media Player window and play at its full size.

How to Copy the Finished Video to Tape

Now that the video has been created, edited, and produced, all that remains is to copy it to videotape. After making a copy on DV tape, you can use that copy to make an infinite number of copies on VHS tape, as you'll see in the next task.

How-to Hint

NTSC Versus PAL

If you've never worked with video before, terms such as NTSC and PAL might seem really confusing. Why would you use one format instead of the other? The answer is actually pretty easy. The two formats are similar, but the resolution and display frequency are slightly different. NTSC is the standard for transmitting and displaying video in the United States. If you're in Europe, you use PAL or SECAM. In general, you can't take a video in one of these formats and play it in a VCR made for a different format.

Record to a digital videotape if possible for the highest quality video.

Here's the finished video playing on a DV camcorder.

Use the video-out port on your camcorder to make copies on your TV's analog VCR.

① Load the Video

If the finished video isn't already loaded in the Viewscreen, drag it from the Library to the Viewscreen now. If you just finished producing the video, it should be in the Viewscreen already.

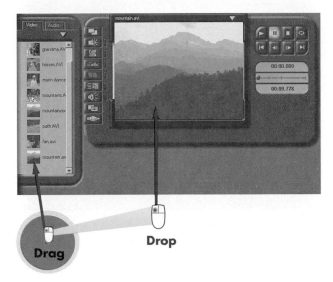

Drag **Drop**

② Connect the Camera

Attach your camcorder to the FireWire or video connector on your PC. Refer to the documentation for your particular camcorder for specific details.

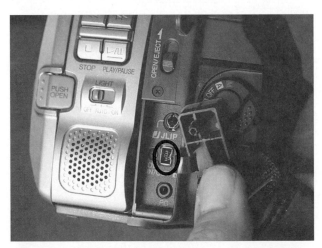

③ Turn On the Camera

Turn on your camera and set it to Play, not to Record. The software on your PC controls the camera and can write to tape only if the camera is turned to the Play setting.

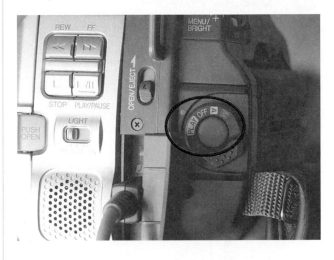

④ Insert a Tape

Make sure that you have a fresh, blank tape installed in your camera. If you accidentally overwrite existing video footage, there's no undo button—you can't get it back.

⑤ Use AC Power

Connect your camcorder to its AC adapter and plug it in to a wall outlet. You don't want to rely on battery power when making the video master because a low battery can ruin your tape.

⑥ Choose Output to Video

In VideoWave, click the **Output to Video** button to switch to Output mode.

⑦ Set the Correct Output

From the Output list, select **DV Output** if you're writing the video to a DV camcorder. If you're recording to analog video, select **Full Screen**.

⑧ Find the Right Spot on the Tape

Use the VCR controls in VideoWave or on the camcorder itself to set the tape to the point at which you want to start recording. Most of the time, you'll probably just want to rewind to the beginning of the physical tape.

⑨ Start Recording: Digital Video

If you are using a DV camcorder, click the **Begin** button when you're ready to start recording the PC file to the DV tape in the camcorder. VideoWave automatically starts the camcorder, and the video will record on the tape.

⑩ Start Recording: Analog Video

If you're using an analog camcorder, you must start recording on the camera manually and then click the **Begin** button in VideoWave. You can also click the check box for **Pause on First Frame**. If you do that, the very first frame of the video holds until you press the spacebar. You might want to hold the first frame because it can take several seconds for the tape on your camcorder to spool up, get past the leader, and begin recording. If your first frame is a black panel or the title, you can write that to the tape for several seconds so that you don't accidentally lose any of the video that follows.

⑪ Check Your Video

When the recording is complete, press the **Stop** button on the camcorder, rewind the tape, and press **Play** on the camcorder. You should see the finished product in the camera's viewfinder.

⑫ Close the Output to Video Screen

When you're done, click the **Close** button to close the Output to Video screen and return to the standard Viewscreen. Congratulations, you've made a video! At this point, you can safely delete the video files from your PC's hard disk and make subsequent copies from the digital tape. If you don't have a digital camcorder and are instead making copies directly to VHS tape, you might want to keep the files on your PC to make additional copies. Remember that, unlike copies from digital tape, copies from VHS are *lossy* and lose resolution and image quality with each copy you make.

How to Work with a Videotape Master

The first physical videotape you record from your PC video file is known as a *master*. The master tape is a high-quality source to which you should return whenever you want to make more copies. Of course, you could use the file on your hard drive as a master, but you won't want to keep that file forever because it takes up so much storage space. Just two or three videos, and your whole hard drive would be filled with old master videos! Instead, connect your camcorder to the VCR and dub copies.

Quality and Generations

Every time you make a copy of a copy of a VHS tape, the quality degrades substantially. Consider this: A standard VHS videotape has only half the resolution of a regular television broadcast, and you lose another 15% of the image quality every time you make a copy. That's why you should start with a high-quality master tape (such as a DV tape) and only make copies from that. If you are working with analog video, the master is actually the production file on the computer; the final videotape you make is already second generation. If you dub a copy from that, you're now looking at a third-generation tape, which most people consider to be at the very fringe of acceptability.

The DV tape is digital and makes the highest quality master.

The DV master tape is identical to the video file on your PC.

Copies made from VHS tapes degrade from copy to copy.

① Wire the VCR

To record from your camcorder to your VCR, you'll need to get analog video and audio cables. Most likely, a set came with your camera or VCR. If not, buy a set from a local stereo store. Connect the Video-Out and Audio-Out jacks on the camcorder to the Audio-In and Video-In jacks on the VCR.

② Insert Tapes

Put the master tape in your camcorder and a blank videotape in your VCR. Rewind both tapes to the appropriate points to start recording.

③ Set the VCR

Now you must configure your VCR to "see" the camcorder. You need to set the VCR's channel to an External Input, usually indicated by the characters Ext or AU. Refer to your VCR's documentation and experiment until you can see output from the camcorder on the TV.

④ Start Recording

Start recording on the VCR and wait a few seconds until you're past the non-recordable leader at the beginning of the tape. Then press **Play** on the camcorder. The video should be copied from the camcorder to the videotape in the VCR.

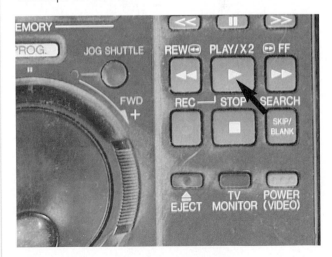

31

Publishing Video to the Web and CD-ROM

In the digital age, video is a very versatile product. Sure, you can copy it to videotape (as we did in the previous part of the book), but you can also include it on Web pages, distribute it to friends or co-workers on CD-ROM, or even include it in a PowerPoint presentation. Web pages are a great convenient mechanism for letting people see your video because all you need to do is tell them where to surf. The downside? Imagine quality is lower, and playback might be jerky if your visitor has a slow modem. In the tasks in this part of the book, I'll show you how to incorporate video in Web pages and CD-ROMs.

How to Prepare Your Video for the Web

Before you can put your video production on the Web, you need to first produce the movie—just as you did for videotape in the previous part of the book. Producing the video renders your movie in its final form and stores it on your hard disk. After rendering the movie, you can then move it to the Internet. In this task, I explain the process for producing your movie in VideoWave. In Premiere, the process varies depending on the kind of video capture hardware in your PC. Check the documentation that came with your FireWire card for details.

Bandwidth Concerns

Planning to publish your movie on the Internet? Keep in mind that although you might have a fast cable modem or DSL connection (I don't know that you really do...I'm just guessing) to view Web pages at high speed, many other folks are still plugging along with 28.8Kbps and 56Kbps modems. Make sure that you keep your movie short—well under a megabyte—so that it doesn't take all day to download. Also consider making the movie *stream* (see Task 4).

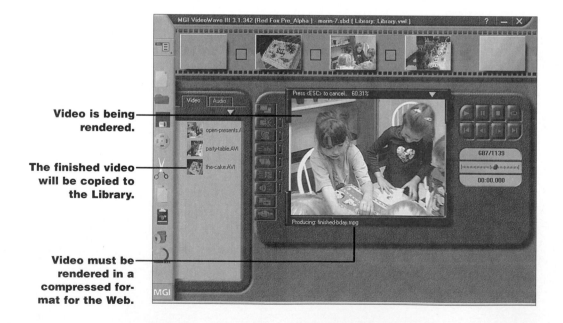

Video is being rendered.

The finished video will be copied to the Library.

Video must be rendered in a compressed format for the Web.

① Save Your Work

Before you render the video, you should save the production. From the menu button, select **Storyline**, **Save**. Now, if anything happens during the production, you now have a good backup to work from.

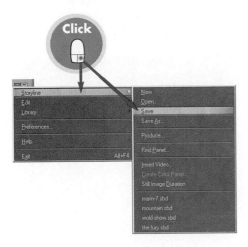

② Select the Panels

You might want to produce only part of the movie. If that's the case, hold down the **Shift** key and click to select the panels in the Storyline that you want to appear in the movie. Otherwise, just move on to the next step.

③ Start the Production

From the menu button, select **Storyline**, **Produce**. The Produce Movie Wizard appears.

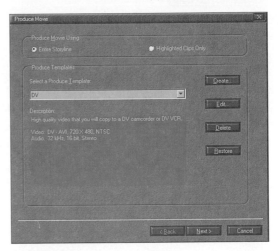

④ Choose the Panels

If you want to produce just the panels you selected in step 2, select the **Highlighted Clips Only** option. Otherwise, select the **Entire Storyline** option.

⑤ Pick a Template

Now select the settings to produce the movie. The Select a Produce Template list provides a trio of preset Web video formats. Depending on how fast you think your audience's Internet connection is, select the **Web Video - Best Quality**, **Web Video - Good Quality**, or **Web Video - Minimum Size** option.

⑥ Enter Edit Mode

You can change the specific attributes of the Web Video template you selected by clicking the **Edit** button. You'll have to edit the settings to ensure that you'll be rendering the video into a size that's appropriate for the Web. Click **Edit**, and the Settings dialog box opens.

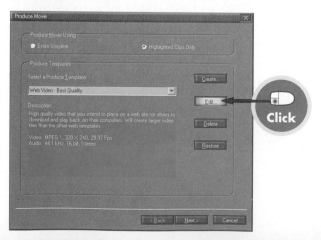

⑦ Make Changes

In the Settings dialog box, click **Next**. On this page, the most important settings are Bit Rate and Audio Channels. Throttle the Bit Rate up or down to affect the quality of the video and the rate at which it plays. The Audio Channel option also affects the quality-to-download rate ratio. Make any changes you want and click the **Finish** button to return to the Produce Movie Wizard.

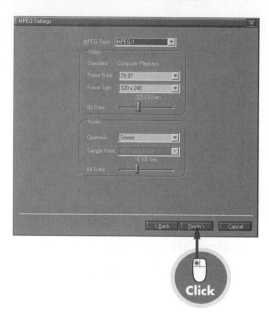

⑧ Go to the Summary

Now that you have made any necessary changes to the video format, click the **Next** button. The Summary Page appears.

⑨ Name the File

On the Summary Page dialog box, name the file. If necessary, click the **Browse** button to find the location on the drive where you want to save the video file. Remember, the file you are about to produce combines the various production components you saved in step 1 into a single, playable video file.

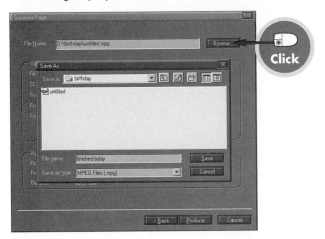

⑩ Produce It!

It's the moment of truth: Click the **Produce** button. The video will be rendered to your hard drive. Don't be surprised if this step takes a while—perhaps even hours. This is the number-crunching part of the process, in which all the bits are combined into a single file. You can track the video's progress onscreen.

⑪ Watch the Preview

When the production process is complete, the video appears in the Library and in the Viewscreen. Click the **Play** button to watch the completed movie in the Viewscreen.

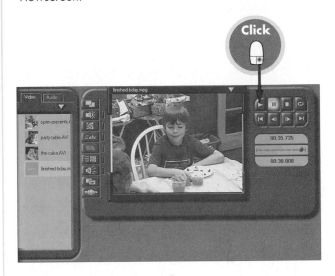

⑫ See It Full Size

Alternatively, you can use My Computer to find the file on your hard drive and double-click it (the file has the extension .mpg). The movie should open in a Media Player window and play at its full size.

How to Insert a Movie into a Web Page

After you produce a movie that you want to display in a Web page, you're only halfway there. You still have to create the Web page itself and get the video file onto the Internet. In this task, you get your Web page ready and drop in the video you've prepared. Because Microsoft FrontPage is so popular, I've chosen to explain the process using that program; if you have another program, the procedure will be quite similar. By referring to this task and your Web editor's user manual, you should be able to figure out the process without too much trouble.

How-to Hint

Optimizing Video for the Web

Posting a movie on the Internet probably means that it's been highly compressed to save space and bandwidth—when you produce your movie in VideoWave, for instance, you select a Web-friendly template so that the video is adequately compressed for playback on the Internet. To make your movie look its best on the Net, try some of these tips:

- **Minimize movement**—The less movement in the video, the more smoothly it plays back in compressed form.
- **Extend transitions**—Make those transitions longer. That way, they won't be destroyed by compression.
- **Make text really big**—If you use titles, make the text even bigger than usual so that the text is legible after the video is compressed.

Videos play in Internet Explorer and Netscape Navigator.

You can optionally create a Web page so that it launches an external video viewer.

Here's the movie embedded in a browser window.

Video player controls.

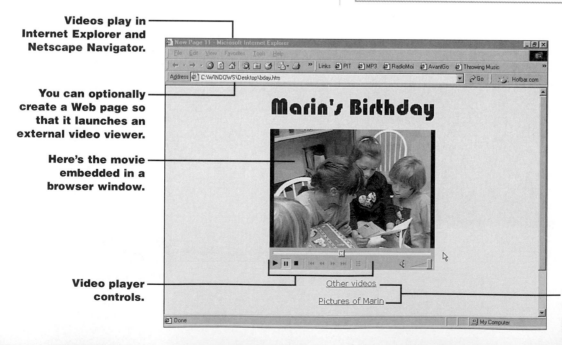

You can add other links, text, and images to the Web page.

① Use FrontPage

The easiest way to get a video clip into a Web page is to use a Web design program such as Microsoft FrontPage. Most programs—including FrontPage—have built-in tools for generating a Web page with video clips.

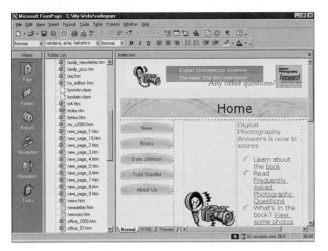

② Insert the Plug-In

If you're using FrontPage, open the Web page you want to insert the clip into and select **Insert**, **Advanced**, **Plug-In** from the menu. FrontPage uses the term *plug-in* to refer to any component (such as video) that needs a special viewer. The Plug-In Properties dialog box opens. Click the **Browse** button and select the video file you've already produced in VideoWave. Click **OK** to add this element to the page. Note that the video clip appears on the Web page as a plug icon.

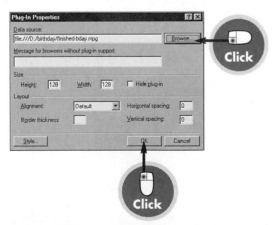

③ Size the Plug-In

Click to select the Plug-In icon on the Web page and drag its sizing handles to adjust the pane in which the video clip will play. Size the pane however you like, and be sure to select the **Preview** tab to see what the finished video will look like in the Web page.

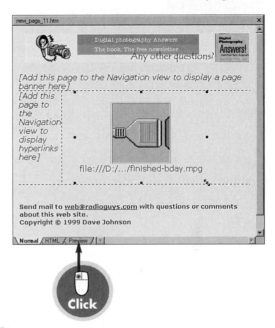

④ Do It Manually

If you are familiar with creating Web pages using HTML, you can include your video clip in a Web page by adding the following line of HTML code in your Web page:

`<embed width="400" height="400" src="movie.mpg">`

Remember to change the `width` and `height` values to match the size of your movie, and set the `SRC` variable to the name of your video file.

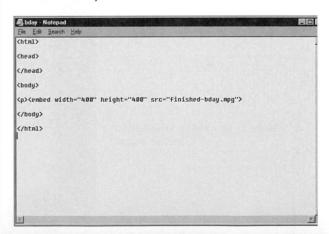

How to Upload the Movie to the Web

After you've created your Web page on your PC and included a video clip or two in the page, you might want to actually publish the Web page on the Internet. Only after this last, crucial step can you actually invite others to your Web site and let them view your video creation.

The program can automatically upload Web pages to the Internet.

This view shows what the page will look like in a real browser.

Beware of FrontPage

If you use FrontPage to upload your Web pages, don't make "manual" changes to your site with an FTP program because you might confuse FrontPage and damage its knowledge about what's stored on your Web server. FrontPage likes to keep track of all the files on your Web site. This actually lets you easily update your Web site because you can make changes to your site on your computer's hard drive and then tell FrontPage to make the appropriate changes to your Web site by publishing changed files. If you change files manually using an FTP program, FrontPage can't tell what has changed and what hasn't. Consequently, it can do real damage to your published site if you later command it to publish changed files to the Web.

FrontPage or another visual Web design program makes creating Web pages easy.

Here is the video embedded in the page.

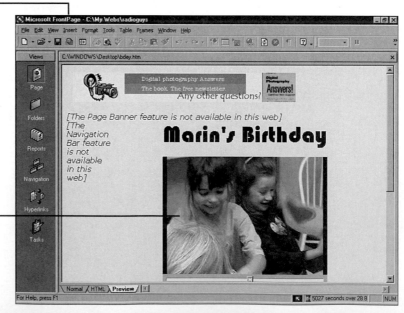

① Do It the Automatic Way

If you are using a Web page authoring program such as FrontPage, the process of uploading the page to the Internet is pretty simple. The program tracks the location of all the files in your Web page, including your video files. Select **File**, **Publish Web** from the menu to open the Publish Web dialog box.

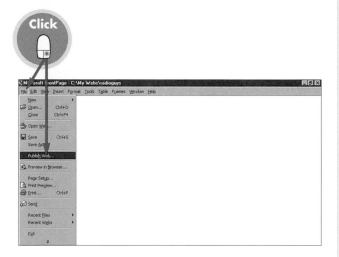

② Specify a Location

Enter the location to which you plan to publish the site—for example, you might enter your domain name. Then click the **Publish** button and let FrontPage do all the work.

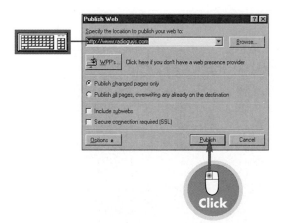

③ Move It with FTP

If you're uploading the page to the Internet more manually than with a program like FrontPage, you need an FTP client. (I like a program called FTP Voyager.) Enter the FTP site name (the location where your Web site will be stored) along with your user ID and password. Then connect to your site.

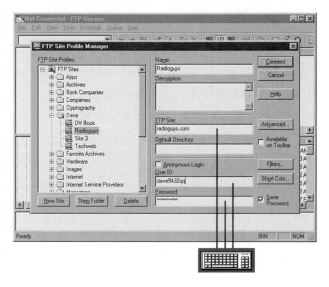

④ Copy the Video File

Use the FTP program to copy the video file to an appropriate folder at your Web site's domain. Be sure that the folder name and filename exactly match the names you used in your Web site's HTML code (as shown in step 4 of the previous task).

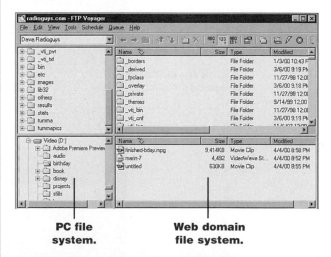

PC file system.   **Web domain file system.**

How to Prepare a Streaming Movie

The video you made and uploaded in Tasks 1, 2, and 3 must be downloaded from the Internet in its entirety before someone can watch it in a Web browser. If your audience has a slow Internet connection, the time spent downloading the video file is often more than the video clip is worth. As an alternative, you might want to use *streaming video* so that visitors to your Web site can watch the movie as it downloads. To stream video, you need to produce it in a special way in VideoWave, and then feed it into another (free) program called RealProducer, which I'll talk about in the next task.

How-to Hint

Finding Streaming Video

If you surf the Web very often, you no doubt know that streaming media is the preferred method for watching video and listening to music—it's more instantaneous than waiting for a file to download completely to your PC. If you want to look for streaming video on your own, the best starting place is **www.real.com**. This site has the necessary viewer software as well as untold riches of movie files to watch.

A Web page created with RealProducer has been enhanced in FrontPage.

Notice that the image quality is markedly lower than in the original video.

Internet Explorer is the browser.

Here is the embedded video.

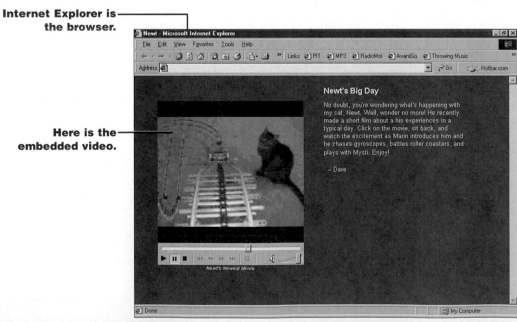

① Create a New Template

With your movie loaded in the VideoWave Storyline, select **Storyline**, **Produce** from the menu button to open the Produce Movie wizard. By default, VideoWave creates movies only in MPEG format, but RealProducer requires an AVI movie. The first time you create a streaming movie, click the **Create** button to make a new template.

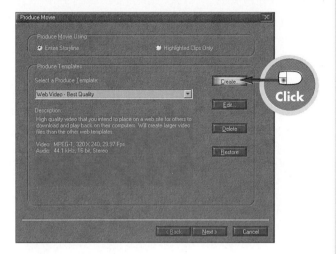

② Name the Template

In the **Template Name** field of the Create Produce Template dialog box, give the template you are about to create a name—something like `Streaming Video`—so that you can find this template again in the future. From the File Type list, select **AVI Compressed**. Click **Next**.

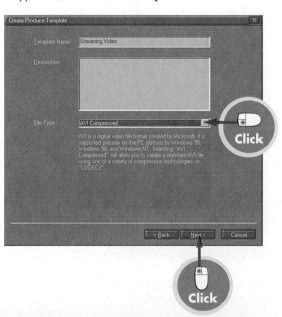

③ Set Video Options

The next dialog box is the AVI Settings dialog box. It looks intimidating, but you can accept the defaults. Make sure that you are using indeo video compression, that the frame size is 320×240, and that the Quality slider is set to High (100%). Click the **Finish** button to return to the Produce Movie Wizard.

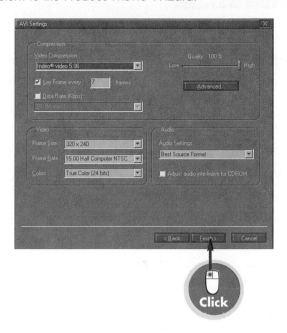

④ Produce Your Movie

Click the **Next** button to go to the Summary Page. Type a name for your movie and click the **Produce** button to create your movie file. Note that the movie isn't in streaming format yet; you have to import it into the next task and finish the job.

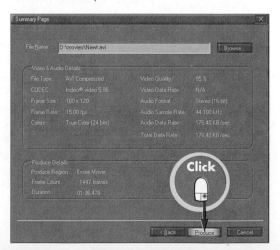

How to Create a Streaming Movie

Streaming video is a popular way to deliver audio and video on the Internet because you don't have to download huge data files to experience the multimedia effects. To create streaming media of your own, you'll need RealProducer, a free program found at www.real.com. The basic version of this program enables you to take a completed video, convert it to streaming format, and post it to a Web site. To actually watch the streaming video after it has been published to the Web, your audience needs a copy of RealPlayer (also a free download). Thankfully, RealPlayer comes preinstalled on most PCs, so they're ready to go right from the start.

How-to Hint

Sprucing Up Your Movie Page

RealProducer has a Web page publisher built in, which makes creating a complete Web page with the streaming video file already embedded easy to upload to the Web. But you don't have to settle for RealProducer's plain, vanilla page. You can take the Web page that RealProducer creates for you and import it into FrontPage or another Web design program to add links, background graphics, additional text, and any other features you expect to find on a page at your Web site. You can then upload the completed page to the Web using your Web editor (such as FrontPage) or an FTP program.

You can download RealPlayer for free from www.real.com.

Player controls.

Here you can watch the streaming video.

Click here to change the size of the video.

① Start RealProducer

After you have created a complete movie in AVI format in VideoWave, start your copy of RealProducer. In the New Session dialog box that appears when you launch the program, select **Record from File** and click **OK**.

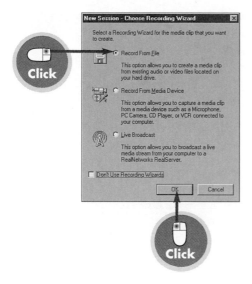

② Find the Video

On the first page of the Recording Wizard, click the **Browse** button and select the filename of the streaming video file you created in the last task. Click **Next**.

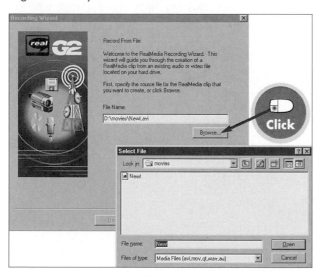

③ Name the File

Now enter the details about your video that will appear on the Web page. Give the file a title, name the author, type a brief description of the video file, and enter some appropriate keywords. The keywords help Web surfers more easily find your video in search engines. Click **Next**.

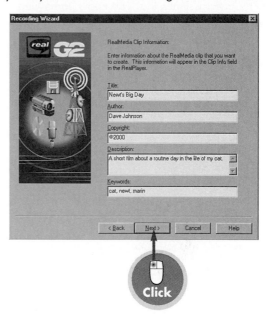

④ Choose a Server Type

Because you're probably posting this video to your own Web server and are not expecting thousands of people to flock to it, select the **Single-Rate for Web Servers** option and click **Next**. (If you had a high demand for your movies, you would want to use a special server that could deliver the movie to many people simultaneously.)

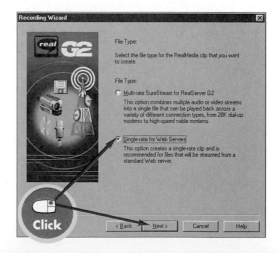

5 Choose a Target Audience

RealProducer assumes that you know something about the kind of people who will view your movie. Select the type of Internet connection you expect most of your viewers to have. If you don't know the modem speeds of your audience, select **56K Modem**. Click **Next**.

6 Choose Audio Quality

Select the option that best represents the kind of audio in your movie. The Stereo Music option takes up more of the available bandwidth than Voice Only, leaving less bandwidth available for the video stream. For most videos, Voice with Background Music is your best bet because it balances the sound quality with video quality pretty well. Click **Next**.

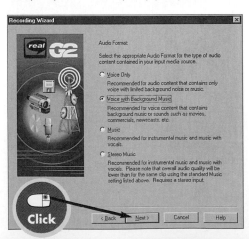

7 Choose Video Quality

Select the option that best represents the kind of video in your movie. Normal Motion Video is usually a good compromise. Don't select Slide Show if you want the video to appear as a motion picture. Click **Next**.

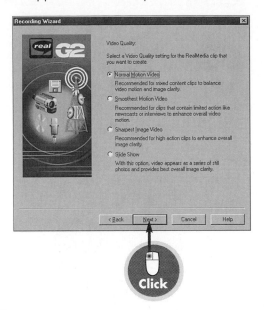

8 Name Your Video

Select a filename and location for your movie. This file, bearing the `.rm` file extension, is the hyper-compressed streaming video file that was rendered based on the VideoWave produced file. It is the file that will be uploaded to your Web site. Click **Next**.

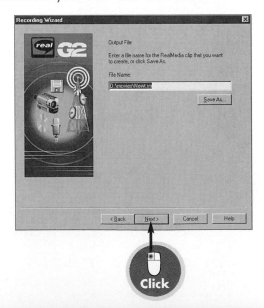

⑨ Verify Your Settings

The next dialog box displays all the data about your movie. Check it over to ensure that it is all correct; click the **Back** button to make changes to these options. When you're satisfied with your movie settings, click the **Finish** button.

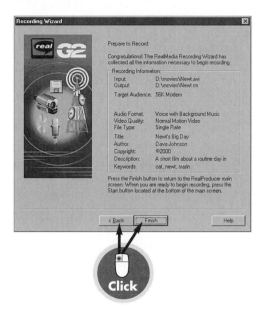

⑩ Ready to Produce

After the Recording Wizard goes away, you finally see the main RealProducer window. This view gives you one last chance to make any changes to your video before you produce it.

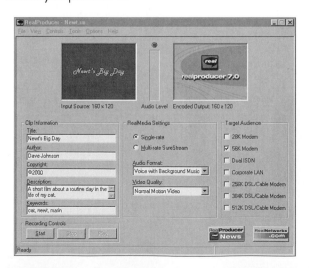

⑪ Start the Encoding

Click the **Start** button. The video will play and encode itself into a streaming video file.

⑫ Post It to the Web

After the file is complete, you can upload it to your Web site. RealProducer includes a wizard for creating and publishing the streaming video file in the Tools menu.

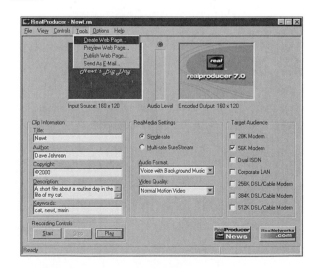

How to Put Your Video on CD-ROM

Creating a video for CD-ROM is very similar to working with video files for the Web. Both are sensitive to data rate—if you try to play a very large, high-resolution video from the Web or from CD-ROM, you will experience choppiness, stutters, and frustrating results. Most people have fairly fast CD-ROM drives these days, however, so it's not too hard to play back good-looking video directly from CD-ROM. Here's how to create that video.

How-to Hint

Using a Front End on the CD-ROM

If you plan to distribute your movie on CD-ROMs, you don't have to just copy the video file to the disc and let users search for the movie file using Windows Explorer. Instead, build your movie files into Web pages using the Web page feature in RealProducer and copy the complete "Web site" you've made to CD-ROM. When the users of your CD start your on-disc Web page, they can click their way around as if they were navigating a real Web site. It's an elegant way to complete a CD-ROM.

The Right Hardware

If you plan to burn CD-ROMs and distribute the discs to friends and family, you'll need a CD-RW drive. Different from a standard CD-ROM drive, CD-RW drives can actually create CDs from blank discs. Although CD-RW drives can write to both CD-R (recordable once) and CR-RW (rewritable, erasable) discs, only CD-R discs are readable in everyone else's drives. The lesson here is to make copies of your videos on CD-R.

The 650MB of space on a standard CD can store a lot of video.

Special, inexpensive label makers can make your CD look professionally published.

Record on CD-R discs; CD-RW discs might not play in everyone's CD-ROM drive.

① Start the Production

From the VideoWave menu button, select **Storyline**, **Produce**. The Produce Movie Wizard appears.

② Pick a Template

Experiment with templates to find what works for you, but a good place to start is by selecting the **Video on a CD-ROM** option. If you don't like the default settings, click the **Edit** button and make the video bigger (that is, change its physical size on the screen during playback) or increase the bit rate, which determines the overall image quality.

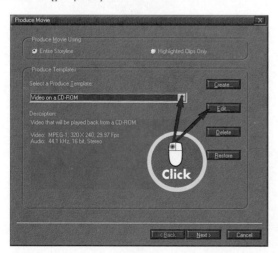

③ Produce the Video

Click the **Next** button to move to the Summary Page. Click the **Produce** button, and the video will be rendered to your hard disk. Don't be surprised if this step takes a while—perhaps even hours. You can track the video's progress onscreen.

④ Burn a CD-ROM

When the video is complete, use the software that came with your CD-RW drive to copy it to a blank CD-R disc. A program such as Adaptec's Easy CD Creator is an excellent choice for copying files to CD-R discs.

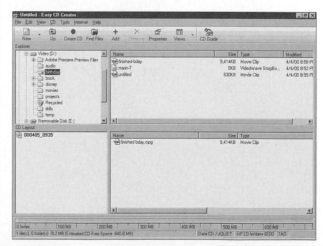

V

Music

32

Listening to Music on Your PC

Several levels of expertise are involved in listening to music on your PC. The simplest level, of course, is simply putting an audio CD into your system and letting it play. However, you might want to extract audio from your audio CDs, using a CD recorder (or *burner*) to store the songs on your hard drive. (See Chapter 37, "Making Your Own CDs.")

But you can also download music. These files will also reside on your hard drive, and you will need a player to listen to them. These music players typically have a browser capability to select sites for music. Players also let you organize your music into *playlists*, so that you can turn your PC into a virtual jukebox. The default player in Windows is Windows Media Player, which we will cover shortly.

Music aficionados often download their own players: WinAmp, RealPlayer, MusicMatch, and others. So, let's download and start one of these players first.

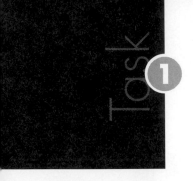

How to Download a Player

You've downloaded other files in parts of this book. The hardest part of some sites, such as Real Networks, is finding the free version of the player you want. Let's use WinAmp as an example of how to download your own player.

1 Locate the Download Link

For WinAmp, you just follow the arrow to the download link and locate the download page. Sometimes you will see a secondary link to click if the download is delayed or doesn't begin.

2 Save the Download File

Click **Save** to save the file to your hard drive. That way, you can always reinstall the file or back up the file to reuse it.

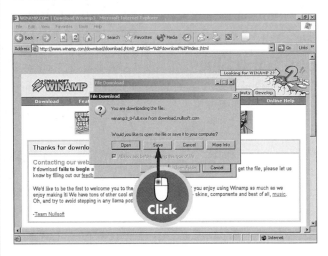

3 Open the File

When download is complete (the file is saved), you can click **Open** to begin the installation.

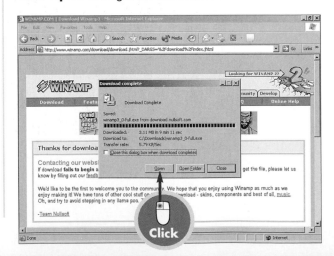

④ Follow the Wizard

The default options for installation will probably work. Click **Next** to proceed.

⑤ Uncheck File Associations

Unless you love WinAmp, you should probably uncheck the files for which you want it to serve as the default player (file associations). Leave the Preserve File Associations and Create Desktop Icon options checked. Click **Next** to finish the wizard.

⑥ Complete the Installation

When the installation is finished, WinAmp launches in a window at the center of your desktop. Notice that, with a Web connection, a browser fills up on the right with links to download and streaming music sites.

How-to Hint

Downloading Tips

Generally, you should set a folder aside for downloads (`C:\Downloads`) and then keep your downloaded files there (or in subfolders) for backup.

Downloading a song is similar to downloading a program, only you must use a player to open the song from the folder to which you downloaded it.

Privacy

If you value your privacy, you can tell WinAmp to leave you alone and not send you any more stuff during installation.

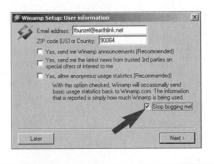

How to Tour Windows Media Player

Unless you truly have a problem with Microsoft, you will keep Windows Media Player as your default music player. The version of Media Player included in Windows XP is similar to what you used to have to download. It has all the bells and whistles.

Let's take a look at some basics for playing music in Windows Media Player. You'll learn how to organize music into playlists in Media Player later.

❶ Open Media Player

Select **Start**, **All Programs**, **Accessories**, **Entertainment**, **Windows Media Player**. Or, you can double-click the **Media Player** icon on your desktop.

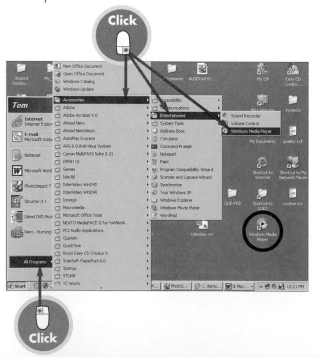

❷ View Media Selections

If you open Media Player while connected to the Internet, your browser goes to MediaPlayer.com and gives you immediate access to online music. You are in the Media Guide.

❸ Listen to a CD

Insert an audio CD into your CD-ROM or CD recordable drive. Then, click **Now Playing**; you will see a *skin* (a virtual animation linked to the audio) and a listing of the tracks of the album. Drag the slider to lower or raise the volume.

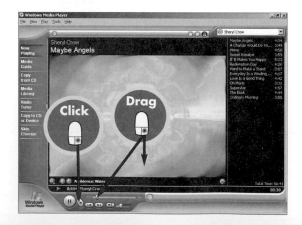

④ Change the Skin

Click the **Skin Chooser**, and try another skin to accompany your music.

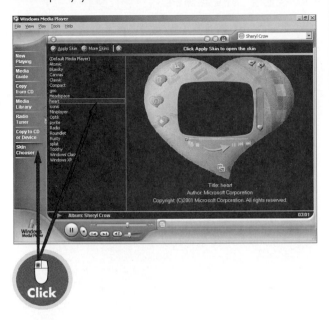

⑤ Look at the Media Library

Click the **Media Library**, and you should see the Sample Playlist. This is where you can organize any content—audio or video—that is on your computer.

⑥ Look at Copy Music

With your CD in a CD recorder, click **Copy from CD**. You will see how Media Player lets you select songs to copy (extract) to your hard drive.

How to Quickly Find and Stream Music

Just as you can download music online, you can also *stream* the file, which means that even though you don't possess it, you can listen to it directly over the Internet through your player. With streaming, you just click the link, the file *buffers* (meaning it gets set to play), and then the music plays according to the speed of your connection.

1 Find Streaming Music

Open Media Player to the Media Guide, and click **Listen to Music**.

2 Pick a Station

Click a link to a type of music you want to stream; the music plays automatically.

3 The Music Streams!

The page for the station loads in Internet Explorer, and you can listen to the music in real-time without downloading.

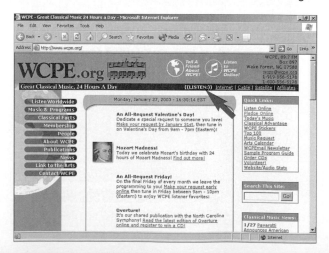

④ Change the Station

Click **Media Player** on the taskbar to return to the Media Guide. Then, search for an artist by typing it the name and clicking **Go**.

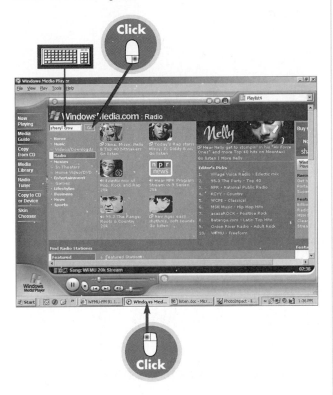

⑥ Site Opens and Plays

The site with the content opens, and the video plays.

<table>
</table>

Accessing Streaming Content

Internet radio is the fastest and easiest way to access streaming content online. Other streaming sites also use the Windows Media Player to stream their content over servers or provide content by download. They might also use playlists from other player programs, such as WinAmp, which was showcased earlier.

How-to Hint

⑤ Select the Song or Video

Select the song or video you want; then, you can check the bandwidth, which is modem, cable, or DSL.

How to Access Other Audio Sites

Microsoft Media Player is by no means the only way to access Internet radio or other streaming audio sites. You earlier saw that WinAmp has a browser attached to it. Real Networks, Apple QuickTime, and other software and content providers have their own solutions to streaming media and Web sites that make media available in their streaming formats. Let's see some of these solutions.

1 Open the WinAmp Browser

Open WinAmp and make sure the browser is open.

2 Open the Radio Section

Click the **Radio** tab to begin to locate music according to your taste.

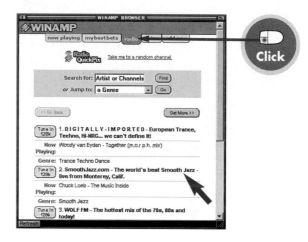

3 Go to WinAmp's Site

In some cases, Internet Explorer opens to WinAmp's site. Now you can find more content or try the other major music sites.

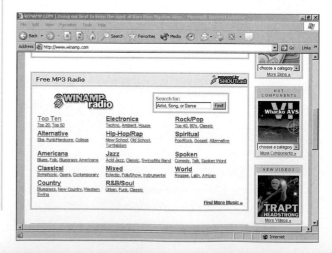

4 Go to RealPlayer

Go to **www.real.com**, and see whether you can find the link to the free player on this page.

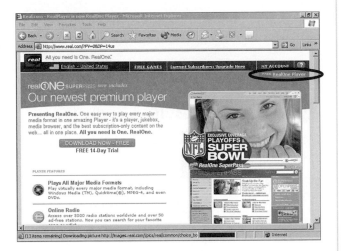

5 Download the Free Player

Click the download link to get the free version. This gives you access to more radio sites and lets you play all types of media files.

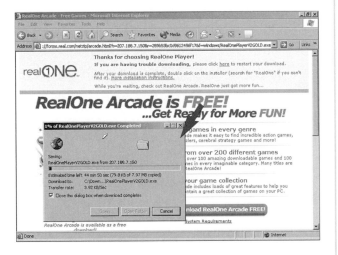

6 Get QuickTime

Even with a Windows XP PC, taking advantage of QuickTime content is cool. You can download the latest player at **http://www.apple.com/quicktime/products/qt/**. This lets you view streaming MPEG4 QuickTime movies and even navigate through QuickTime VR panoramas.

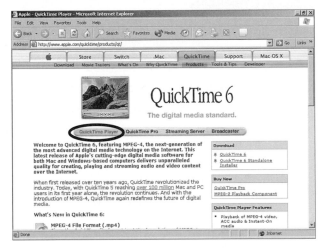

How-to Hint

Watch for New Versions

Each of these players requires frequent upgrades to view content. With QuickTime, even if you get a version with other software, you will probably need to download some or all of the components from Apple to view Web content. Real Networks releases a new version often enough to annoy you, and sometimes you can't listen to content until you upgrade.

Watch Your Format

Each of these content solutions has its own format, so the last one you install can become the default player for all your media files unless you pay attention during installation and don't let it change your file associations.

Don't Enable Cookies

Enabling cookies in your Web browser allows most of these sites to remember your favorite selections and find your music more efficiently, but there are also privacy issues you should consider. Also, the more sites you access and join, the more junk email you'll receive.

How to Find Other Streaming Sites

After you have a player, especially one with a browser included, finding audio in your format is generally just a matter of pointing and clicking. But let's look at some other places to go.

❶ Use Yahoo! or Google

Doing an advanced search in Yahoo! or Google should provide some cool sites to search. Enter keywords to search for, and click **Search**.

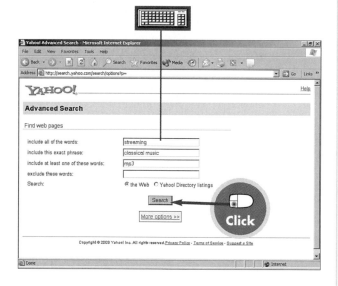

❷ See the Results

Now you can select from more than 10,000 links to streaming MP3 digital classical music.

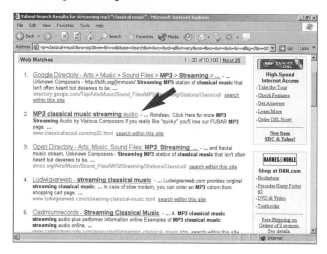

❸ Go to Yahoo!'s Launch Site

Click **Radio** or **MP3** on Yahoo!'s main page to go to Launch.com, a huge music site.

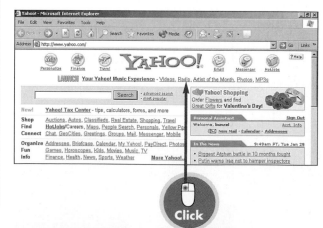

④ Pick Your Style

Now you can select either free or subscription-based music in streaming or download MP3 format.

⑤ Try WinAmp's SHOUTcast

SHOUTcast.com is WinAmp's music distribution site. Click the drop-down arrow on the **Genre** selector to quickly find radio sites with your favorite type of music.

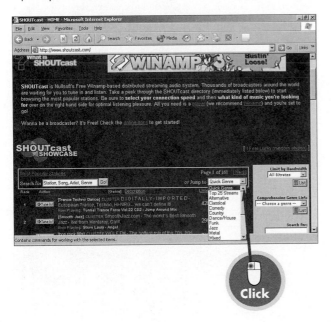

⑥ Try Free Sites

Free streaming sites are available all over the Web—there's even one called **www.thefreesite.com**. This one features the RealPlayer format, so you need to download that player to take full advantage of the site.

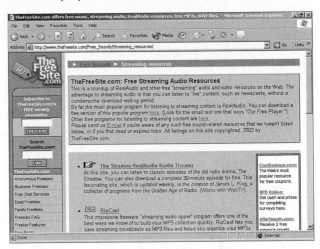

Task

How to Use MP3s

So far we've looked at ways to use a player program and your Web browser to listen to MP3s online. With Media Player, we also quickly noted how to use it with an audio CD and pointed out its media library.

Now, we'll cover the best ways to get, save, and keep your own music—in a special format called an *MP3*.

How to Understand MP3

You've downloaded other files in parts of this book. You probably noticed that in all cases, they reside in a folder on your hard drive as specific files. MP3 is just a digital file format, like a Word document or an Excel spreadsheet, but it is compressed digital audio.

❶ Examine an Audio CD

Open **My Computer**, right-click, and select **Explore** for an audio CD in Windows.

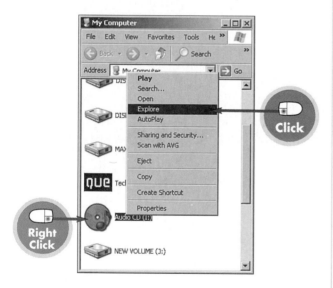

❷ Look at the Results

If you look at the details of these files, you will see that they're 1KB in size! Can this be right? No, it can't because they aren't the digital audio files themselves; they're *references* to the CD tracks. That's because CD audio is not truly a computer file—it's just digital stuff that plays in an audio CD player.

3 Check Digital Audio's Size

When you convert or extract digital audio into a normal computer audio file, which in Windows is called a wave or .WAV file, 3 minutes of music can easily be 30MB in size because of its excellent digital quality! This would make a 12-song album more than one third of a gigabyte.

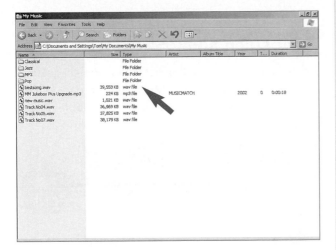

4 What Is MP3?

As we said, MP3 (which stands for MPEG 1 Audio Layer 3) is just another computer file format that can play the same piece of audio but compressed by a factor of 12! That means you can store 12 times more music on your computer in this format than you can in the Windows WAV file format.

5 What Can You Do with MP3?

MP3s can be music or any type of audio file, including books. As you've seen, by compressing files to small sizes, they can be streamed in real-time over Internet radio and other servers. And after they're converted from an audio CD or downloaded, MP3 files can be saved on a hard drive and organized into collections to turn your PC into a virtual jukebox.

6 Look at an Example

You will learn how to create folders of types of music and populate them with audio files in MP3 format that are much smaller than their WAV counterparts and yet have very acceptable audio quality.

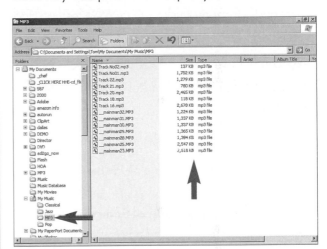

How to Extract Audio in Easy CD Creator

Many of you have CD recorders, and they usually come with burning software. One of the most popular types is Easy CD Creator from Roxio, which can be used to extract audio from an audio CD in WAV, Windows Media (WMA), or MP3 format. In this task, you'll use Roxio Easy CD Creator to get audio from an audio CD in WAV format, add effects, and finally convert it to MP3.

(We could have used Nero just as well for this process, but the MP3 converter in Nero is free for only 30 days.)

① Open the Project Selector

Click the **Start** button, and select **All Programs**, **Roxio CD Creator 5**, **Project Selector**.

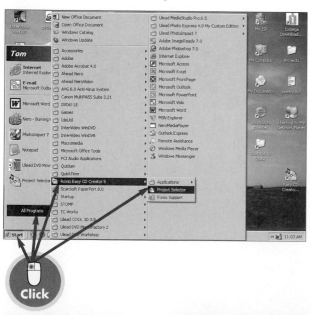

② Open SoundStream

Hover your mouse over the first icon in Project Selector and click **SoundStream**. Make sure an audio CD is in a fast CD-ROM, CD-RW, or DVD recordable drive.

Hover

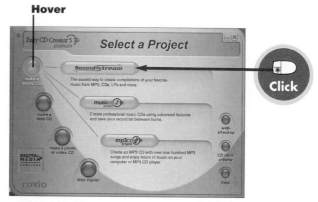

③ Open the File Folder Destination Panel

Click the **File Folder** icon in the Destination panel. Then, click (highlight) a folder that you will remember as the location for your music files. Notice that the default file format is *.**WAV**. Leave it as is, although you can click the drop-down arrow to see the other choices: MP3 and WMA. For now, use the WAV file format unless you have very little hard drive space. Finally, click **Select Folder**.

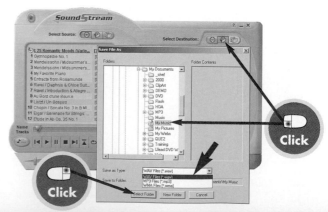

4 Select and Add Your Tracks

Now your new destination folder appears in the destination area. Notice that it also has a Windows audio file extension, **.WAV**. Depending on whether you have added other tracks to the library previously, the destination panel might have entries. But notice that the new folder location and file type (WAV) are now at the top. Click to select all or some of the tracks you want in the library album. Click the arrow with two music symbols to add them all. To add individual tracks, hold down the **Ctrl** key as you click to select. To add consecutive tracks, hold down the **Shift** key as you click to select. Then, click the **Add Selected** button (for specific tracks).

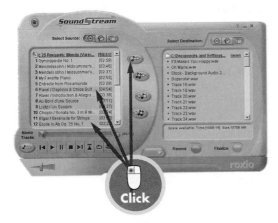

5 Record the New Selections

Now when you click the red Record button, the same record panel opens that you saw for burning a CD, but you're now recording to a destination folder on your hard drive. Click **Record** in the panel, and watch as your CD audio files are saved to your hard drive. When you're done, you can play your library files without the disc being present in the computer!

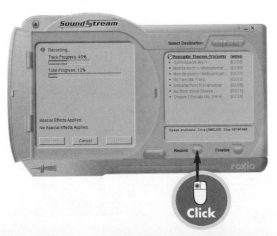

6 Locate the Files

If you followed the previous directions, your new WAV files are in the My Music folder of My Documents. Open it and see the files. Note the size of the various tracks you extracted; they're big—more than 30MB. Click the drop-down view selector arrow and select **Details** to see the file sizes instead of the file icons.

Creating a Destination Strategy

In SoundStream's destination panel, you can record a music library of WMA files or save files to a Windows folder in the WMA, MP3, or WAV file format. Which should you use? Any Windows program that works with audio will accept WAV files for playback and some for editing. Many will also accept MP3, which are compressed audio files with excellent quality. WMA is less popular and much smaller. Your decision will depend on your hard drive capacity and what you intend to do. If you want the maximum functionality from the audio files, save them as WAV audio files in a folder and remember their location.

How to Add Effects in Easy CD Creator

Now that you've seen SoundStream, let's explore some extras, including the ability to change the sound of your audio tracks.

① Open SoundStream

Hover your mouse over the first icon in Project Selector and click **SoundStream**. Make sure an audio CD is in a fast CD-ROM, CD-RW, or DVD recordable drive.

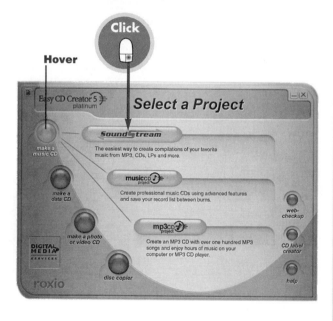

② Open a Destination

Click the **Select Destination** button to select a music library or folder destination. Then, click the **Show Options Drawer** icon.

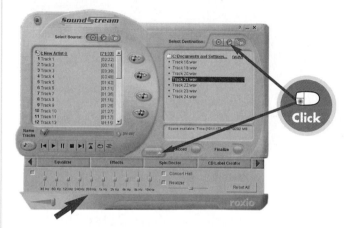

③ Activate the Equalizer

Use trial-and-error and drag the sliders until you are pleased with the results. Click **Play** to hear the results.

Click to select a destination track, and click **Play** to hear the changes. Then, either click **Concert Hall** or click to activate the track and drag the **Realizer** for other effects.

④ Try the Effects Panel

Select the **Effects** panel. As you play your audio, see whether you enhance its sound by adding and adjusting the Sound Cleaning or Pop Removal level. Dragging the Normalizer can also enhance the audio's sound.

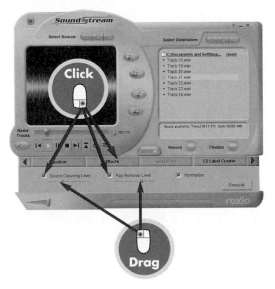

⑤ Open the Spin Doctor

So far, you have worked only with files you extracted from a CD-RW. What about using analog audio files? Open the Spin Doctor in the Effects panel to record analog audio through the line-in jack of your sound card. Your sound card (if properly configured) is visible under Select Source. The level indicator will blink to show audio coming in. Click the **Record** button to capture the audio track, and use the LP, CD, and audio cassette presets to enhance the recording.

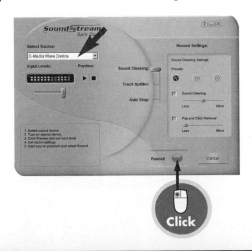

⑥ Create a Filename and Record

You will be prompted to select a folder as you did with the destination folder. Remember the location, and then enter a filename (note it's a WAV file) and click **Start Recording**. When your segment ends, click **Stop Recording**. Your newly recorded WAV file is in the folder you designated.

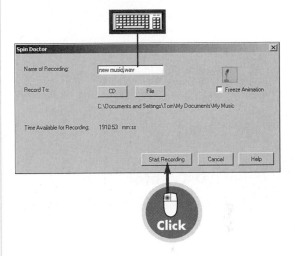

How-to Hint

Recording a CD from Your Folder

Click **Folder** in your Source panel, and select your **My Music** (destination) folder, and click **CD** in the Destination window.

You will see the new audio file you just recorded, along with your other extracted WAV files, in the Source panel ready to be burned to a new audio CD!

When you create an audio file in Windows, your most useful choice of file format is the WAV file if you have plenty of space. If you want to store music in quantity, you should convert your files to MP3, which we will show you how to do next.

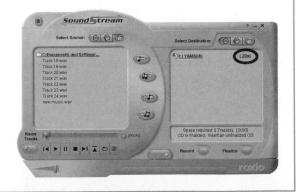

How to Convert Music to MP3 in Easy CD Creator

Easy CD Creator can be used in different ways as an MP3 converter. This task shows you how to extract your music from an audio CD directly into MP3 format.

1 Open CD Creator

Hover your mouse over the **Make a Music CD** icon in Project Selector and click **Music CD Project**. Before you make an MP3 disc, you need to *rip* (another word for extract) the music.

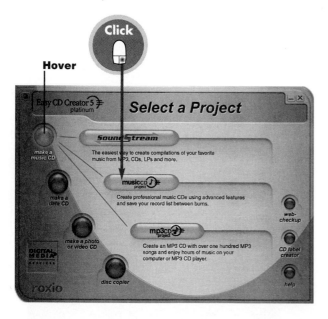

2 Select Tracks to Rip

Click the tracks you want to select them for your MP3 disc. Hold down the **Ctrl** key as you select to choose individual tracks; hold down the **Shift** key as you select to choose consecutive tracks. Then, click **Convert**.

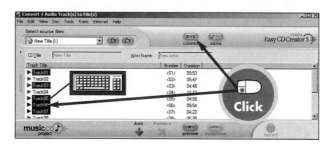

3 Enter the MP3 Format and a Name

Navigate to the folder where you want the files stored. (You can click to create a new subfolder called MP3 in My Music and then double-click it to put the songs there.) Select **MP3** from the drop-down list for CD quality, and if you have saved other files in that folder, you will see them there. Enter a name (of the artist) for your sequential files. Then, click **Open**.

④ Extract the Files

The files are ripped and named sequentially with the name entered. When ripping is complete, you can close CD Creator. (Select **File**, **Save As** to save the project first, if you like.)

⑤ Open a MP3 CD Project

Click the **Project Selector** (which has now appeared) to open an MP3 CD project.

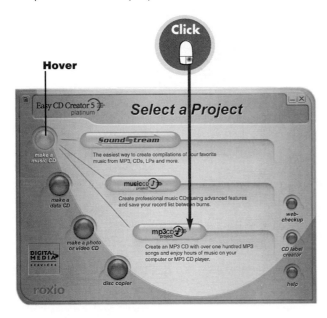

⑥ Add and Record Your MP3 Files

Now you can drag and drop your stored MP3 files and burn them directly from your hard drive. The source folder is in the top panel, and the disc space is on the status bar. However, you do not have transition options (as you do with a normal audio CD). Click the **Record** button to start the burn process.

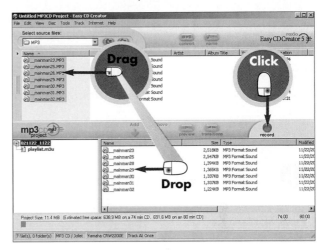

Setting Your Play Order

How-to Hint

Your play order depends on the order in which you dragged your MP3 files. If you want to reorder them, you can double-click the MP3 playlist to open the MP3 Playlist Editor. You can click to select a file(s) to move up and down and then click the up and down arrows to make the change.

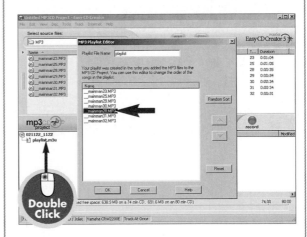

How to Convert WAV to MP3 in MusicMatch

MusicMatch is a free program you can download from the Web that lets you rip CDs to MP3, burn CDs, and convert to and from MP3 and WAV formats.

1 Download MusicMatch

Go to **www.musicmatch.com** and download the latest version of the product.

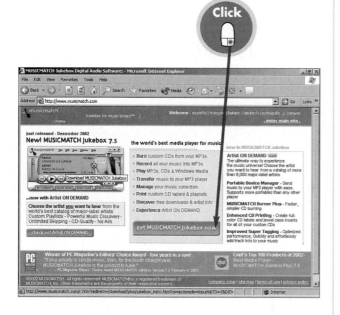

2 Install MusicMatch

Remember where the file went, double-click it to install.

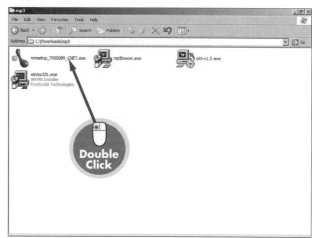

3 Open MusicMatch

Click **Start** or a double-click a desktop shortcut to open MusicMatch.

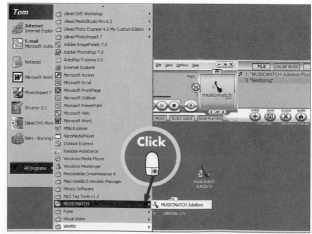

4 Open the Converter

Select **File, Convert Files in MusicMatch**.

5 Set Your Folder Options

Click to open a folder with WAV files; then click to open a folder with the MP3 files to which they will be converted and sent. Set your file format choices from the drop-down menu.

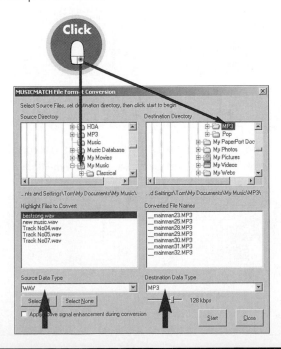

6 Select Your Files and Convert

From the Source Folder list box, select one or more files. Then, click **Start**. (For now, leave the bit rate set at the default of 128 and make sure the Apply Active Signal Enhancement check box is enabled.) Click **Start** to begin the conversion.

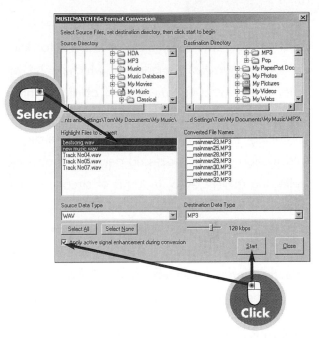

How-to Hint

Finding Your MP3 Files

When conversion is complete, your new MP3 files (with the same name but now with the **.mp3** file extension) are in your destination folder.

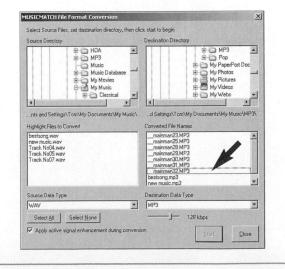

How to Set Bit Rate Options in MusicMatch

Just as a file has a definite size in bytes (or kilobytes or megabytes), a media file, which plays over time, processes a certain amount of digital information per second. This is called a *bit rate*, and essentially, the higher the bit rate, the more digital information can be processed per second and the better the quality. Also, in terms of streaming, the higher the bit rate, the higher the bandwidth necessary to accommodate streaming. And more important, in terms of downloading, the higher the bit rate, the bigger the underlying file—meaning it will take longer to download (but it might be worth it).

1 Open the Music Match Converter

In MusicMatch, select **File**, **Convert Files**.

2 Set Your Folder Options

Open a folder with WAV files, and then open a folder with the MP3 files to which they will be converted and sent. Set your file format choices from the drop-down menu.

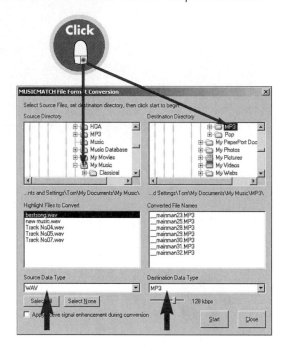

3 Select Your Files and Convert

From the Source Folder list box, select one or more files to convert (you can use Ctrl+click to select multiple files).

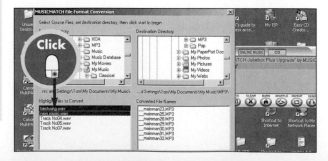

➍ Reduce the Bit Rate

For the selected songs, drag the slider to reduce the bit rate to 64Kbps. Click **Start**.

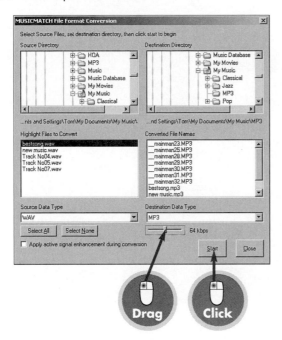

➎ Increase the Bit Rate

For another song, increase the bit rate to 320Kbps; then, click **Start**.

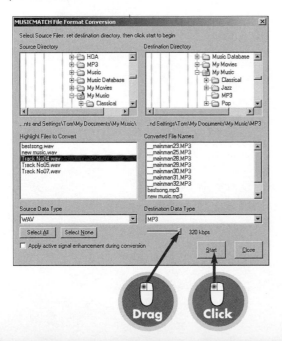

➏ Compare the Results

You will have to listen to the songs to compare which audio is acceptable. But note the huge difference in file sizes: The 320Kbps version is enormous, whereas the 64Kbps version is tiny but doesn't sound nearly as good.

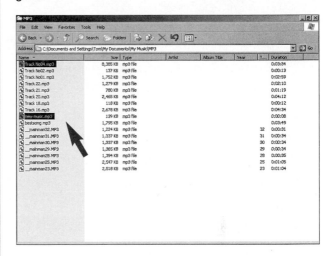

How-to Hint

Keeping Different Versions

You might have tried to convert the same song to the same folder as an MP3 with the same name but different bit rate. If you did, you overwrote and lost the original song. You can keep different versions of the same song in different folders and use the high bit rate version to listen to and the low bit rate version to share or email to others.

Task

34

Finding and Sharing MP3s Online

Now that you understand what an MP3 is and have worked with a few conversion and ripping tools, let's go back online and find some other ways to find and even share MP3 files.

Besides music, you'll look around for audio books in the compressed audio format MP3. You'll explore some other download sites and then take a look at an expanding concept—the peer-to-peer file sharing approach pioneered by Napster and now used by other companies such as WinMX and KaZaA.

How to Find Audio Books

Although music comprises the bulk of audio downloaded from the Web, it shouldn't surprise you to know that audio books are a fast growing area of interest. You can listen to the books on your PC or laptop, but you can also download them into an assortment of MP3 players, some of which you can get free from audio book clubs.

① Books That Find You

If you've bought real books on Amazon.com, it's not unusual to get an email ad for audio books. You can just click the link to go to the Web site.

② Look at the Site

audible.com is just like a regular book of the month-type club. Instead of ordering through the mail, however, you download an MP3 version of the book. As an inducement to join, you can get a portable MP3 player.

③ Search for Audio Books

A quick Yahoo! search reveals more than three million sites that offer some type of audio book link. Some of these offer audio CDs, audio cassettes, and MP3 CDs.

❹ Search for Download Books

An advanced search on Google.com lets you enter the concept of download and MP3 to the search criteria.

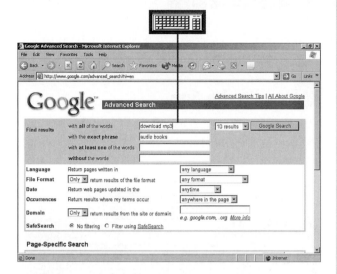

❺ Check the Results

Now the choices are narrowed to 11,000 pages, including Apple's I-Tunes solution and Christian selections.

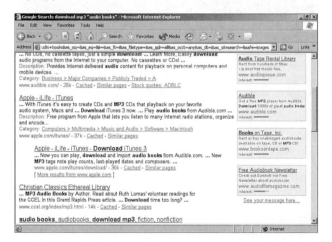

❻ Free Audio Books

There's even a site with downloadable audio books for free. Go to **http://www.audiobooksforfree.com**.

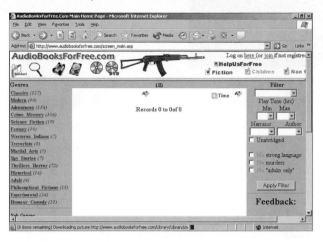

How to Use AudioGalaxy and MP3.com

We've looked at how to search for files on Yahoo! and Google, but let's just explore a couple of more super sites that feature both streaming and downloadable MP3 audio.

❶ Open AudioGalaxy

audiogalaxy.com has both a free site and a subscription site called Rhapsody. You can also enter search parameters and find more specific audio files.

❷ Join the Site

You can log in with a username and password and read unflattering messages about those who enjoy classical music.

❸ Search by Labels

audiogalaxy also lets you find links directly to specific music labels to see whether they have legal downloads of samples or complete songs.

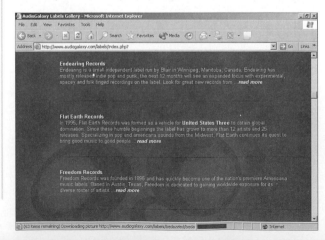

④ Visit MP3.com

MP3.com is one of the oldest streaming and download music sites on the Internet. It is a community of visitors who want to enjoy music and participate in forums.

⑥ Locate the Files

The downloaded MP3 version of "Hotel California" joins some extracted WAV audio files in a general music folder on my PC.

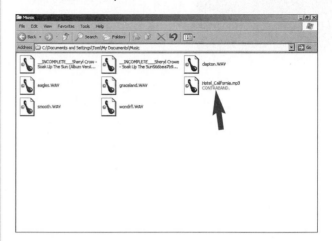

⑤ Download Top Selections

At MP3.com, you can download entire songs in the MP3 format directly to a local folder, just as you ripped them from CD-ROM in the previous chapter.

How-to Hint

Creating a Download Strategy

Now that you've seen two CD burning programs and how they extract audio, and even seen some download sites, you can begin to organize your My Documents subfolders (My Music) into categories for MP3, WAV, or music according to your taste. To create a subfolder in any folder, just right-click and select New Folder from the pop-up menu.

How to Start WinMX File Sharing

Ever since Napster, there's been a lot of buzz about file sharing, or so-called peer-to-peer networks. Over most of the Web, servers distribute content and your browser is the client to these servers. This lets you use a common browser and implement standards of security.

When you join a peer-to-peer network, the concept is that everyone is equal—there is no server with security features, and it's every machine for itself. Theoretically, you set aside one or more folders on your computer to share. In effect, you might be opening up your entire machine or network and even giving away some of the CPU processing power. But let's explore one of these services, WinMX.

1 Locate WinMX

The first thing you need to do is download the WinMX application to your local machine from www.winmx.com.

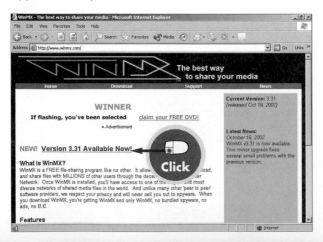

2 Download WinMX

The download is fast because the file is only 752KB. Click **Open** when the download is complete to begin the installation.

3 Begin the Wizard

Like many installation programs, WinMX uses a wizard. Click **Next** to proceed through a series of screens.

④ Select a Local Folder

You should select a local folder that you know has files you are willing to share or has no files in it that will conflict with your downloaded files (same names or different formats). Then, click **Next**.

⑤ Choose a Username

You'll need a name to identify you on the network and to associate with your shared files. Enter it and click **Next**.

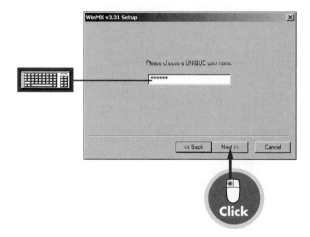

⑥ Choose Which Files to Share

You will be prompted to select the file types (extensions) that you will let other network users download from your machine. Select them and click **Next**. You're almost ready to log on.

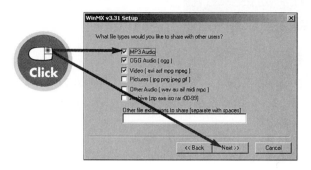

Setting a File Share Folder

How-to Hint

One of the last steps in setting up WinMX is giving permission to others to download files from one (or more) of your folders and subfolders. Choose carefully, and then finish the Installation Wizard.

How to Use WinMX File Sharing

Now that you've downloaded and installed WinMX, you run it like any other Windows program. But remember, it's not exactly a Web browser—it's a way to receive files, but it's also a way to grant permission to others to download your audio files. WinMX is a program that invites itself onto your system tray. It needs to be on most of the time to complete your downloads and uploads.

① Open WinMX

Right-click WinMX in your system tray, and select **Show**.

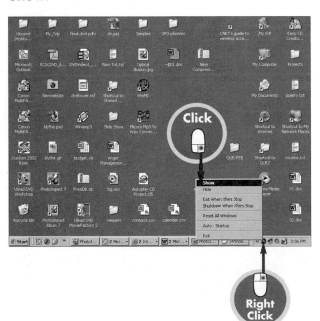

② Begin the Search

With the full screen open, you are ready to search and download music and other files. Click **Search**.

③ Search the Files

Enter the name of an artist and click **Search**. Almost immediately files and users fitting your parameters appear onscreen.

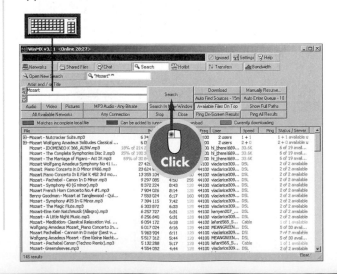

④ Download the File

Right-click a file you like and select **Download**. Note the bit rate and file size.

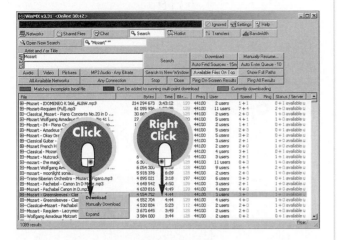

⑥ Search by Bit Rate

You can also narrow your search by bit rate and other parameters to find files that might download more quickly.

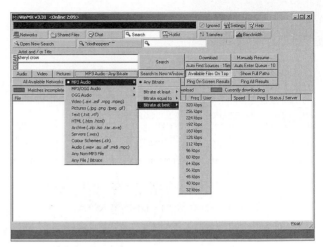

⑤ Watch the Progress

You can see the potential length of time for a download—the network can be slow at times.

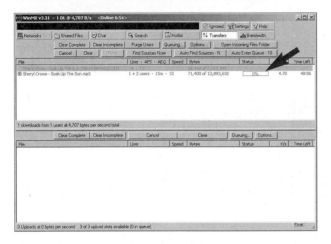

How to Set Security for WinMX

As you can see, setting up WinMX can also set up your computer to be accessed by anyone else on the peer-to-peer network. Because you're not using your normal Web browser or email program, you should keep your antivirus program up-to-date and take some precautions.

① Shut Down When Transfers Stop

One precaution you can take is to shut down WinMX when transfers are complete. Set this option by right-clicking the icon in the system tray and selecting **Shutdown When Xfers Stop**.

② Open WinMX

To open WinMX, right-click the system tray icon and select **Show**.

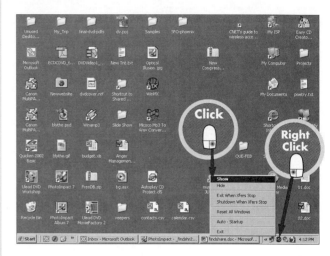

③ Open Settings

Click **Settings** to access the WinMX setup options.

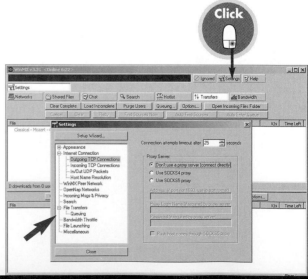

④ Limit Message Access

Click **Incoming Msgs & Privacy**, and reduce the range of users who can contact you through WinMX by unchecking the boxes.

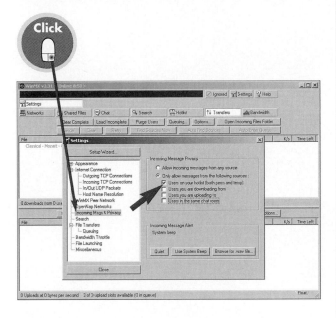

⑤ Set TCP/IP Connection Options

Note that WinMX is set up to operate without a firewall. So, to use a firewall, you need to adjust these settings. Click **Incoming TCP Connections**, and select the corresponding radio button.

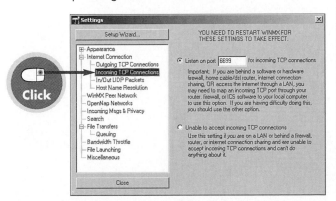

⑥ Download a Software Security Program

If you remain uncertain about the settings in WinMX or letting others access your folders, go to www.download.com and select a software security program specifically designed for peer-to-peer networks.

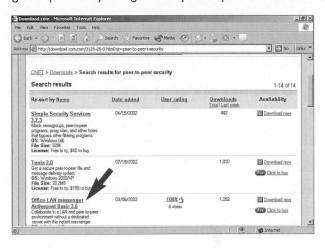

Protecting Your System

How-to Hint

WinMX has a dangerous file type warning in place; do not suppress it unless you know what you're doing.

Consider downloading a software firewall such as BlackICE Defender and adjusting its settings to allow some peer-to-peer activity.

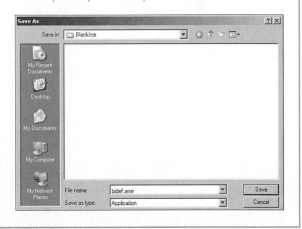

35

Tagging and Organizing MP3s

One of the neat things about storing your audio as files on your hard drive is that you can organize them in folders and easily access them within the players as playlists. You can add information to each file, such as the artist name, genre, and title, which makes organization easy. This is called *tagging*.

This hour examines some of these scenarios using MusicMatch and Windows Media Player. First, you'll add files to the MusicMatch Library, and when you use MP3 files, you'll tag them so they will be easier to locate later. You can also export them to a portable MP3 player.

How to Add to the MusicMatch Music Library

You already saw how you can use the downloaded MusicMatch player program to convert your WAV music files into MP3s. Now that some have been converted, let's add them to the MusicMatch Library.

1 Open the Add Tracks Panel

In Music Match, select **File**, **Add Track(s) to Music Library**.

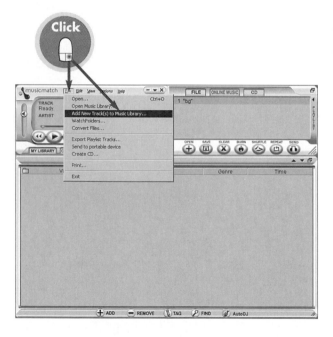

2 Find Your MP3 Folder

You should locate the folder that has your MP3 audio files—perhaps in My Documents\My Music.

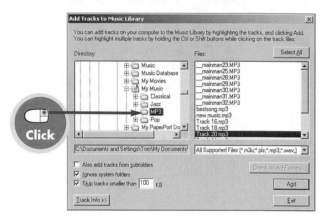

3 Select the Files to Add

Click to select one or more MP3 files to add to the current Library. Use Ctrl+click to select individual files, or use Shift+click to select a range of consecutive files. Then, click **Add** and click **Exit** to close the Add Files panel.

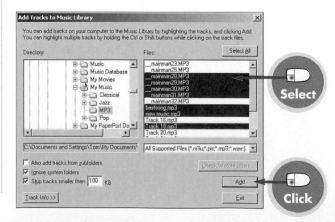

④ Check the Library List

The songs you selected are added to the MusicMatch Library.

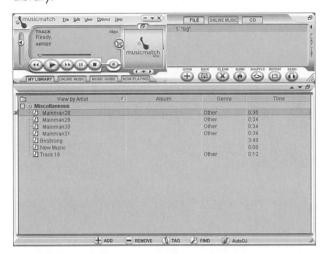

⑤ Add to the Playlist

Now that the library files are available, you can drag one or more of them to the playlist.

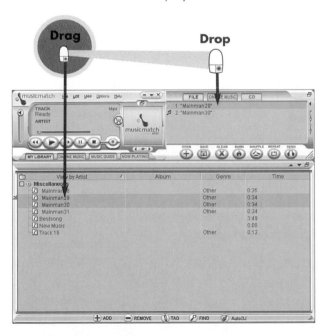

⑥ Save the List

You can save this compilation of songs in the playlist as a new playlist file. Click **Save Playlist**, type in a name, click **Save**, and click **Exit**.

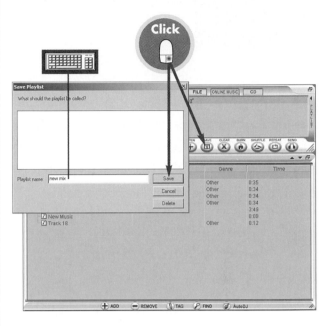

Where's My Folder?

Remember that in Windows XP, if a file browser doesn't locate your My Documents folder, you can find it under your username in the Documents and Settings folder under the main **c:** drive. On my machine that would be **C:\Documents and Settings\Tom\My Documents\My Music\MP3**.

How to Tag Your MP3 Files

When you've accumulated many MP3 files and perhaps moved them around on your PC or uploaded them to a portable player, you might want to add tags to the songs to keep track of them by track name, artist, and even genre.

① Select a Library Song

Click a song in the Library that you want to tag.

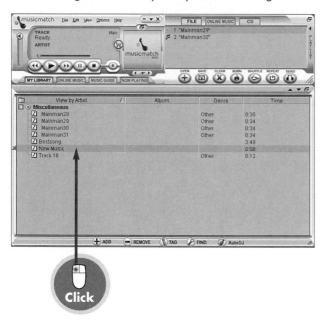

② Edit Its Tag

Right-click the song you selected, and select **Edit Track Tag(s)**.

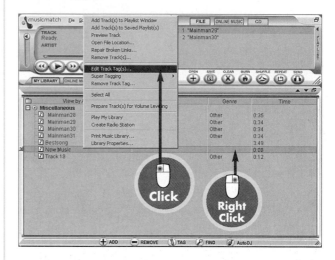

③ Enter Your Information

Enter your information in the Artist, Album, and Genre text boxes. Then, click **Apply** and click **OK**.

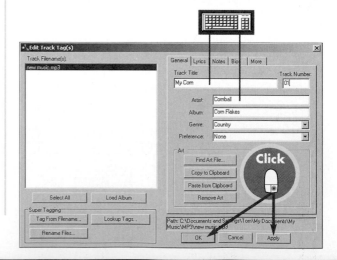

4 Review the Tag

Now the album is listed in the Library. Click the **+** symbol to expand it, and the cut you renamed is properly tagged by genre, album, and artist.

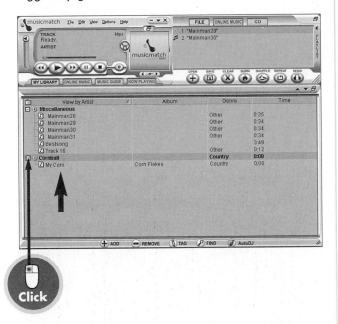

5 Add to Playlist

Now, drag and drop the tagged file into the playlist, where it plays automatically.

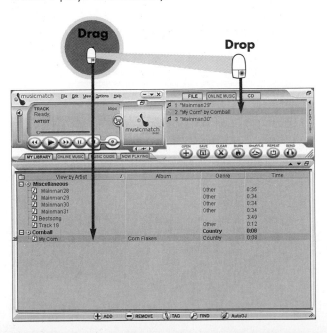

6 Music Library Options

You can rearrange the Music Library in various ways, including clearing its contents. Click **Music Library** to see its drop-down menu.

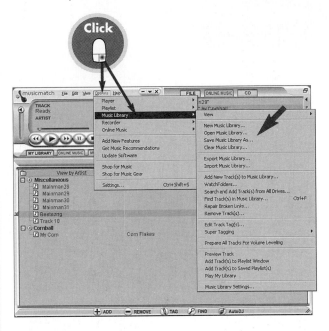

How-to Hint

Playlist Options

MusicMatch actually uses Media Player to play the audio files. It can also import playlist files created in Media Player (see the next task).

How to Organize Audio Files in Media Player

Another way to use the files you've stored on your hard drive is to play different lists in Windows Media Player.

① Open Windows Media Player

Select **Start**, **All Programs**, **Accessories**, **Entertainment**, **Windows Media Player** to open Windows Media Player. You can also just double-click the Windows Media Player shortcut on your desktop.

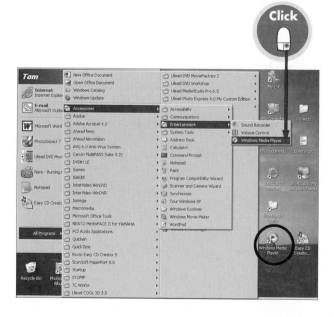

② Open the Playlist Panel

To create a playlist, click **Media Library** and then click **New Playlist**.

③ Name the Playlist

Type in a name and click **OK**.

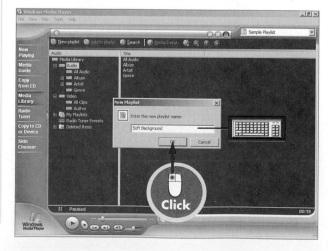

④ Access Your Music Files

Click to select the new playlist in Media Player; then, open the My Music folder to the location of the files you want to add.

⑤ Add Selected Files

From the main My Music folder or a subfolder (such as Classical), select and drag and drop your files into the new playlist.

⑥ Enjoy Your Playlist

Select the top (or any song), and click the **Play** button to hear the cuts from that point on. Click **Now Playing** to view the skins.

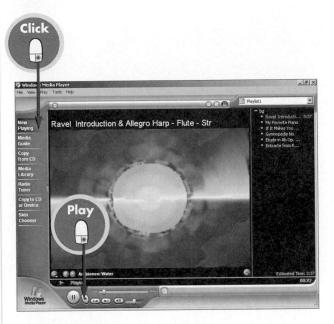

⑦ Save Your Playlist

Select **File**, **Export Playlist to File** to create a text file with your selections, which you can reuse or import. (Name and save the file as a text file.)

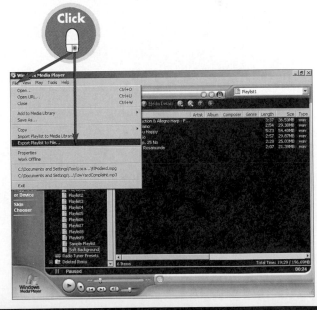

Task

Recording and Customizing Your Songs

You've already seen how you can extract music from audio CDs and add some basic effects using Easy CD Creator. Now you'll see how to record music from an analog source and do some quick and dirty edits of your songs.

The important thing to remember is that all sound cards have two parts—playback and record. Both are accessed either through the Control Panel or by right-clicking the speaker icon on your system tray. You need to have some knowledge of your audio system, and particularly the line-in and microphone settings, to take full advantage of the tips in this section, but we will give you some hints along the way.

How to Record Analog Music

Analog music, or music that is not on an audio CD, generally comes into your system through the line-in connector of your sound card. This can be connected to an output from your stereo amplifier, tape player, or even an external audio CD player (although that would be used only if you didn't have digital audio extraction available).

You'll use Easy CD Creator again in this task, along with a neat feature of Windows XP called the Sound Recorder.

❶ Open the Project Selector

Select **Start**, **All Programs**, **Roxio Easy CD Creator 5**, **Project Selector**. Or, you can just double-click the shortcut on your desktop.

❷ Open SoundStream

Hover your mouse over Make a Music CD and click **SoundStream**.

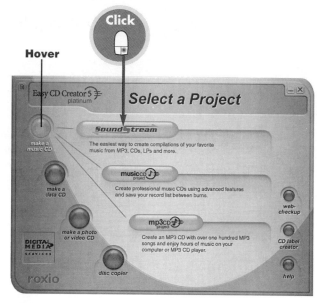

❸ Open the Effects Drawer

With SoundStream open, click the arrow to open the Effects Drawer; then click **Spin Doctor**.

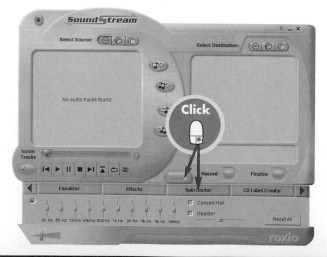

④ Check the Level

Start playing your audio source. The level indicator will blink to show audio coming in. Click the **Record** button to capture the audio track, and use the LP, CD, and audio cassette presets to enhance the recording.

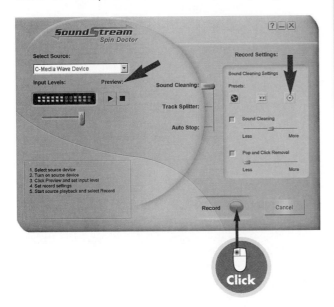

How-to Hint

Checking Your Sound Card Software

Your sound card also might come with its own recording software, including an audio mixer and a graphic equalizer that lets you combine tracks from CD and analog audio.

⑤ Create a Filename and Record

You will be prompted to select a folder as you did with the destination folder (not shown). Remember it, and then enter a filename (note it's a WAV file) and click **Start Recording**. When your segment ends, click **Stop Recording**. Your newly recorded WAV file is in the folder you designated.

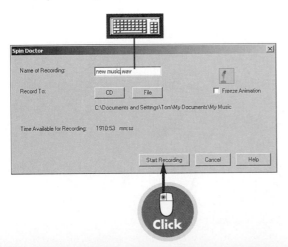

How to Troubleshoot Audio

If you don't hear your audio, you need to check your sound settings. As noted, a typical sound card has a line input (for connection to an external source), a microphone input (for voice) and a speaker output. Some cards have multiple inputs and outputs, as well as internal connectors to your CD player(s). If you aren't hearing sound, check your cable connections and then the Windows audio controls.

① Open Volume Control

Right-click the **Speaker** icon on your system tray, and click **Open Volume Control**.

② Open the Properties

Click **Options**, and then select **Properties**.

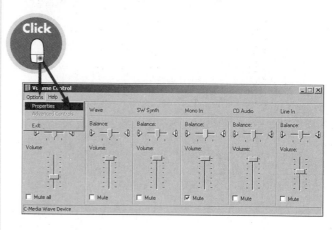

③ Choose Recording

Click **Recording**, and click **OK**.

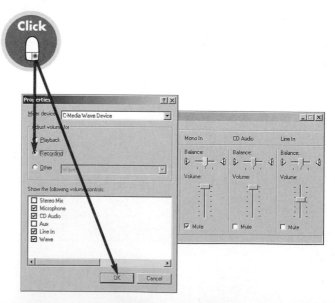

④ Check Your Settings

Your sound card will probably allow only one input source at a time. Frequently, it is set to microphone, which is fine for narration. To allow the system to accept input through the external jack from another source, click the check box labeled **Select** under Line-in.

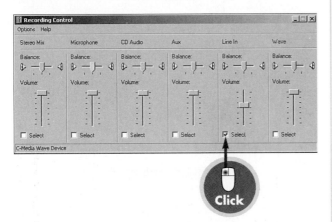

⑤ Adjust the Volume Level

As long as your application (SoundStream) has its own volume or level control, you can set your line-in up high by dragging the slider.

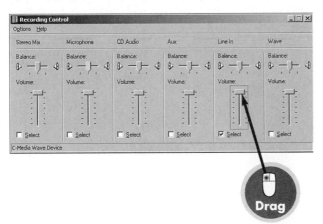

⑥ Check Your Application

Exit out of the controls and recheck the audio coming into your application. If you minimized it and kept the analog source playing, it should now be audible.

Video Capture Issues

How-to Hint

If you are using an analog video capture card, it might be connected to the line-in of your sound card, especially if it has an external box. (See Chapter 24, "Getting Started with Digital Video.") Some hardware DVD graphics accelerators also use this jack. You might want to use a simple switch box to alternate external audio sources, or even an inexpensive analog mixer if you want to get fancy.

How to Trim Your Audio Files

What happens if you extract an audio CD cut from an album and you only want a certain portion of it? To solve this problem, you'll use one of the unsung heroes of Windows (pun intended): the Sound Recorder. Although this tool is typically used with the microphone input of your sound card to record narration, it can open any audio file on your PC, edit it, and change its properties.

➊ Open the Sound Recorder

Select **Start**, **All Programs**, **Accessories**, **Entertainment**, **Sound Recorder**.

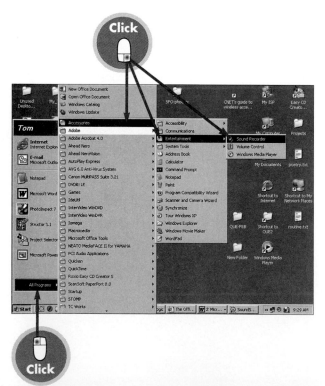

➋ Open Your File

Select **File**, **Open**.

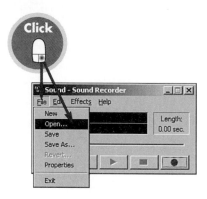

➌ Select Your Song

Locate and select the song you want to trim; then, click **OK**.

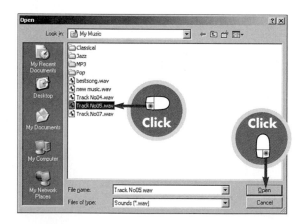

④ Find Your In Point

Click to play your song to the point where you want it to begin; then, click **Stop**. Note the change in the position bar and the second counter.

⑤ Edit the Song

Select **Edit**, **Delete Before Current Position**. (If you want the beginning of the song until that point, select **Delete After Current Position**.)

⑥ Save the New Version

Select **File**, **Save As** and give the new version a different name (unless you intend to replace your original tune). Note that the sound setting is still full digital quality audio, if that's what you're working with.

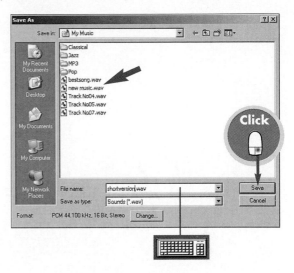

What About MP3?

Sound Recorder accepts only WAV files, so you need a converter to work with MP3 songs (see Chapter 33, "How to Use MP3s," for details on using MusicMatch as an audio file converter).

Sound Recorder has some capability of saving files in MP3 format. You do so by clicking Change in the File Save dialog box and selecting MPEG1 Layer 3 from the drop-down menu. You then select All Files from the Files of Type selector and manually give it an MP3 extension.

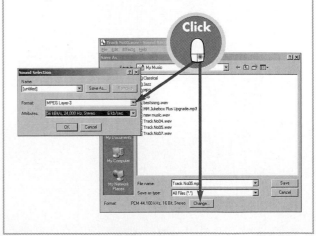

Task

37

Making Your Own CDs

The two major programs for making your own CDs are Easy CD Creator from Roxio and Nero. Some of the download programs also will find your CD recorder and create music CDs, and Windows Media Player can do it, too.

Let's take a quick look at all three.

How to Create an Audio CD in CD Creator

You've already had a quick look at SoundStream, a part of CD Creator that makes it user friendly. But now let's use the full power of CD Creator to make professional-style audio CDs and a new greatest hits album.

❶ Open the Project Selector

Select **Start**, **All Programs**, **Roxio Easy CD Creator 5**, **Project Selector**. Or, you can double-click the shortcut on your desktop.

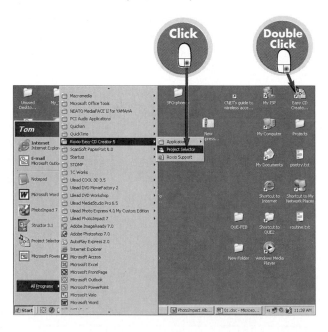

❷ Open CD Creator

Hover your mouse over the first icon in Project Selector (Make a Music CD) and click **Music CD Project**. Make sure an audio CD is in a fast CD-ROM, CD-RW, or DVD recordable drive.

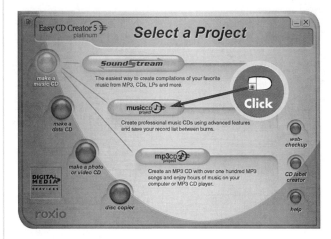

❸ Name Your Album and Tracks

Now you're in the main interface of CD Creator, and your source audio tracks are in the top panel. Directly below it, type in a name for your new album and the artist. You can manually rename the tracks by right-clicking or (if you have a Web connection) clicking Name Tracks to access the Roxio online database.

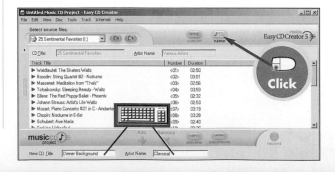

4 ⬤ Select Your Tracks

Click the tracks you want to select for your new greatest hits album. Hold down the **Ctrl** key as you select to choose individual tracks, or hold down the **Shift** key as you select to choose consecutive tracks. If you forget which tracks you want, you can click to preview one or more tracks.

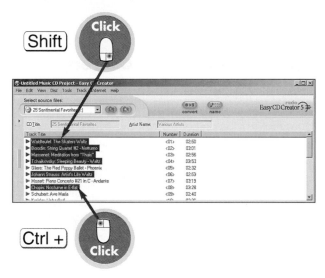

5 ⬤ Add Your Tracks

With the tracks you want from the source CD selected, either drag and drop them into the lower panel or click **Add**. Note the length of time and amount of disc space used, the number of tracks, and the amount of disc space remaining on the status bar.

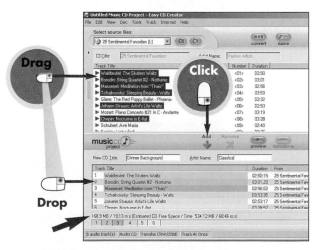

6 ⬤ Include Another Album

Eject the audio CD from the CD-RW or DVD recorder, and replace it with another if you want. Another set of source tracks will appear in the top panel. Click **Add** or drag and drop to add them to your new album.

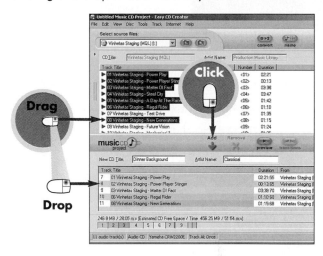

7 ⬤ Record Your New Album

Click the **Start Recording** button to begin the recording process. Because you are using more than one CD for your source, and perhaps only one drive, you need to be ready to insert your source discs as prompted. You will see the Record CD Progress dialog box. When you're prompted, insert a blank CD into your CD-RW drive.

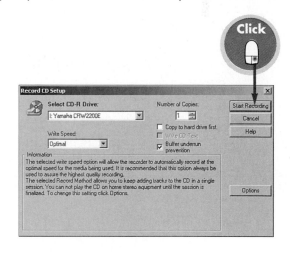

How to Use Your Own Audio Files in CD Creator

If you've been following along, you have probably grasped the difference between CD audio content (digital goo) and actual WAV files that you've previously stored in your My Music folder. If not, don't worry—you're going to convert more files now.

① Open CD Creator

Hover your mouse over the first icon in Project Selector (Make a Music CD) and click **Music CD Project**. Make sure an audio CD is in a fast CD-ROM, CD-RW, or DVD recordable drive. (To open the Project Selector, double-click the **CD Creator** icon on your desktop or select **Start**, **Program Files**, **Roxio**).

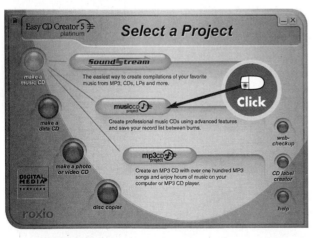

② Select Tracks to Convert

Click the tracks you want to select for your personal collection. Hold down the **Ctrl** key as you select to choose individual tracks, or hold down the **Shift** key as you select to choose consecutive tracks. Then click **Convert**.

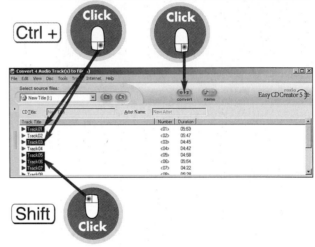

③ Enter a Name and Format

Navigate to the folder in which you want the files stored. Select **WAV** from the **Save As Type** drop-down list and, if you have saved other files in that folder, you will see them there. Enter a name (for the artist) for your sequential files; then click **Save**.

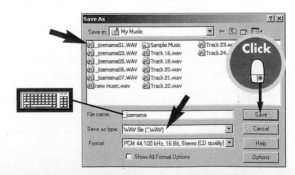

④ Extract the Files

The files are extracted and named sequentially with the name you gave them. (The extraction speed is also shown.)

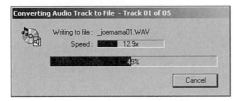

⑤ Locate Your File Collection

Click the drop-down arrow to navigate to the folder with your extracted files on your hard drive. Then, click to open it.

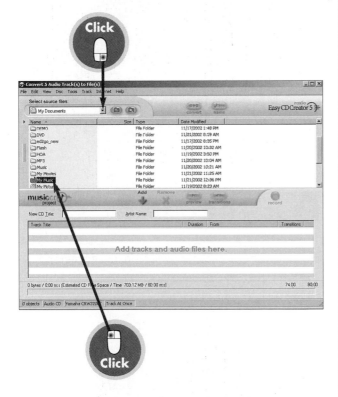

⑥ Record Your File Collection

Now you can drag and drop your stored files and burn them directly from your hard drive. Just click the **Record** button to start the burn process.

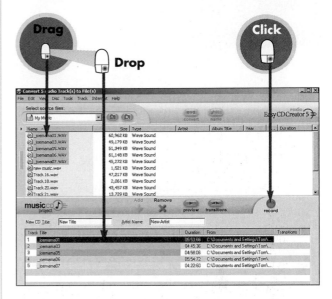

Saving Your Project Files

To save your projects for later revisions, select **File**, **Save As** on the main menu, name the project, click **Save**, and remember where you saved it. You can then double-click the project file anytime to open CD Creator with the same combination of source and destination files.

But don't confuse your project files with your new WAV audio files—one is a record of the choices you made, whereas the others are the actual audio files in digital format on your hard drive.

Other Naming Options

Remember that the Name Files button can access the online database to name your files before extraction.

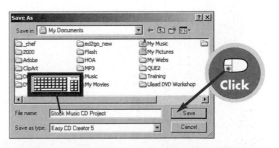

How to Apply Transitions in CD Creator

A nice touch you can add to audio CDs is simple fade-in and fade-out effects between tracks. You do this just before you burn the CD, and when you save the project (see the previous task's how-to hint), these choices are saved along with it.

① Select a Track for a Transition

In the lower (to be burned) panel of CD Creator, select an audio track to which you want to apply a transition. Then, click the **Transitions** button.

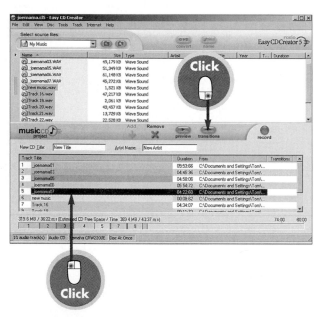

② Adjust Your Fades

Set a duration for the fade in and fade out to and from the selected track.

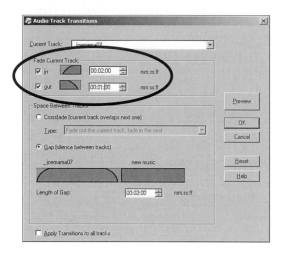

③ Create a Crossfade

Or, select the **Crossfade** radio button and set a duration for the time the current track will fade into the next one.

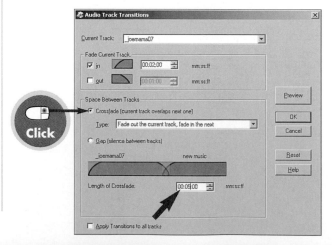

④ Preview Your Transitions

Click Preview to open a player that plays your tracks with the transitions you selected.

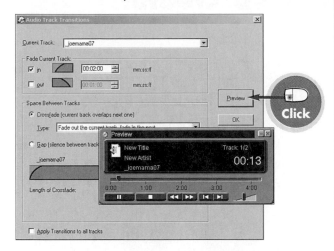

⑤ Change the Gap Length

Instead of a transition, you can change the length of the interval between tracks from the default of 2 seconds. If you do, your record option will be labeled Close the Disc (Finalize).

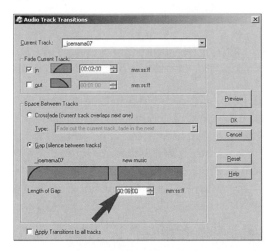

⑥ Apply the Transition

Click **OK** to apply your choices to the track(s) you selected. A transition icon appears next to the track(s) to indicate that a transition has been applied. (You can double-click it to open the transition and change it before burning.)

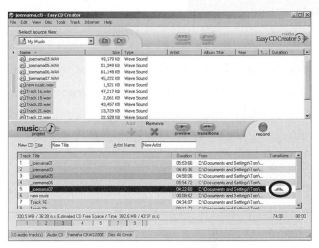

How-to Hint

Applying a Universal Transition

To quickly apply a transition setting to all tracks simultaneously, select the **Apply Transitions to All Tracks** check box.

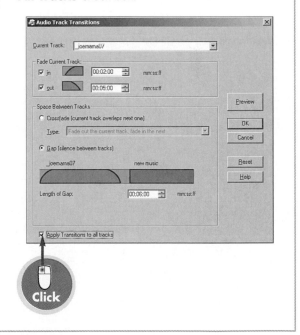

How to Create a CD with MP3 Audio in CD Creator

So far, you've burned CDs with true digital audio and saved (extracted) digital audio as WAV files. You also learned that the SoundStream music library files are, in fact, highly compressed Windows Media (WMA) files.

You've probably heard of MP3, which is a compressed audio format popular on the Internet and in portable devices. So, let's make an MP3 disc.

❶ Open CD Creator

Hover your mouse over the first icon in Project Selector (Make a Music CD) and click **Music CD Project**. You do this because, before you make an MP3 disc, you need to extract, or *rip*, the music.

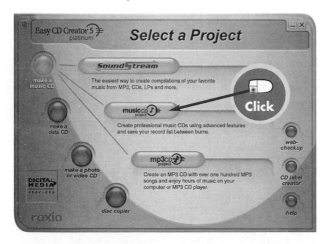

❷ Select Tracks to Rip

Click the tracks you want to select them for your MP3 disc. Hold down the **Ctrl** key as you select to choose individual tracks, or hold down the **Shift** key as you select to choose consecutive tracks. Then, click **Convert**.

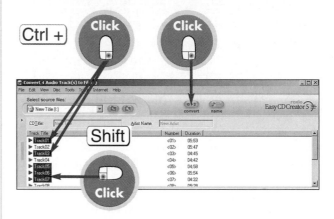

❸ Enter the MP3 Format and a Name

Navigate to the folder in which you want the files stored. (You can click to create a new subfolder called MP3 in My Music and then double-click it to put the songs there.) Select **MP3** from the drop-down list for CD quality and, if you have saved other files in that folder, you will see them there. Enter a name (for the artist) for your sequential files. Then, click **Open**.

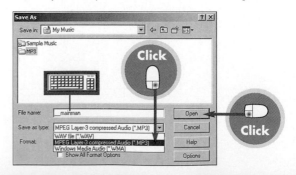

4 Extract the Files

The files are ripped and named sequentially with the name you entered. When the ripping is complete, you can close CD Creator. (Select **File**, **Save As** to save the project first, if you want.)

5 Open a MP3 CD Project

The Project Selector now appears. Click **MP3CD Project** to open a project.

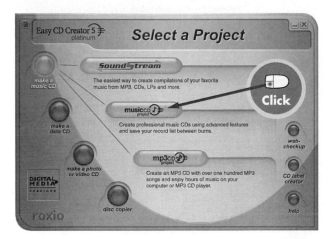

6 Add and Record Your MP3 Files

You can drag and drop your stored MP3 files and burn them directly from your hard drive. The source folder is in the top panel and the disc space is on the status bar, but you do not have transition options. Click the **Record** button to start the burn process.

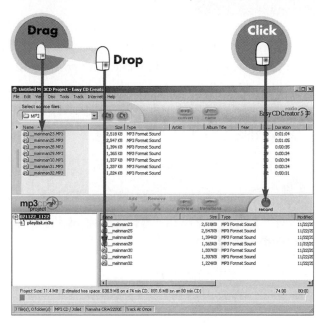

Setting Your Play Order

Your play order depends on the order in which you dragged your MP3 files. If you want to reorder them, open the MP3 Playlist Editor. Click to select a file(s) to move up and down, and then click the up and down arrows to make the change.

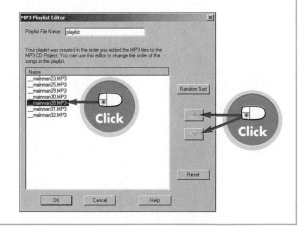

How to Begin an Audio CD with Nero

I'm sure you're anxious to make your own greatest hits audio CD. You'll need the music you want to compile (source discs) and a blank CD-R or CD-RW disc.

1 Open Nero - Burning ROM

Select **Start**, **Programs**, **Ahead Nero**, **Nero-Burning Rom**.

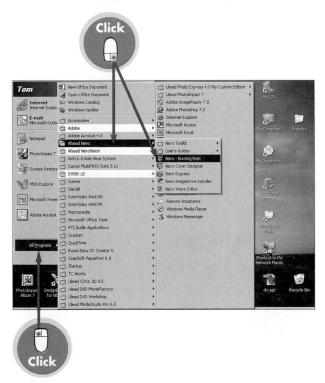

2 Advance Through the Wizard

You'll probably tire of the wizard soon enough (see the following how-to hint). But for now, click **Next** until you get to the step where you select the CD type. Select the **Audio CD** radio button, and then click **Next**. (One more wizard window (not shown) appears; just click **Finish**.)

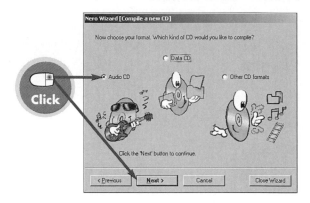

3 View Your Tracks

You might not see your CD audio tracks right away—just the drives and folders appear in the right panel. Drag the slider down to locate your audio CD, and click its icon.

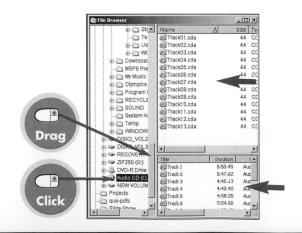

4 Select Your Tracks

Click the tracks you want to select for your greatest hits album. Hold down the **Ctrl** key as you select to choose individual tracks, or hold down the **Shift** key as you select to choose consecutive tracks.

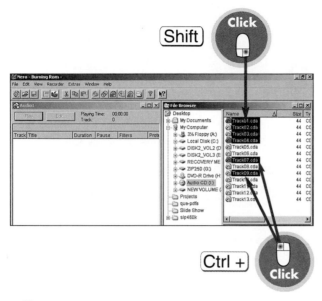

5 Add Your Tracks

With your tracks selected, drag and drop them into the compilation area (the left panel). In a moment, the extraction process begins and moves the audio files to your hard drive.

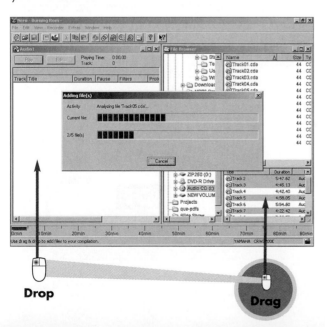

6 Name Your Compilation

A database window opens; click **Cancel**. Next, a window pops up in which you can name your audio CD. Type in a name, and click **OK**.

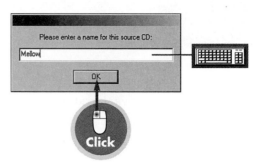

How-to Hint

Windows XP Interference

Windows XP sometimes pops up and prompts you for an action when you insert a new CD of any kind. You should select the **Take No Action** option in the middle of a project.

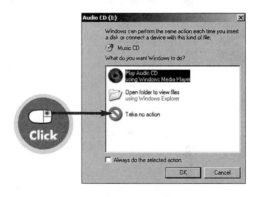

Killing the Wizard

You can always stop the wizard from appearing by clicking **Help** and unchecking **Use the Wizard**.

How to Complete Your Greatest Hits Compilation

Some of the more adventurous of you might have clicked the Burn button and already begun the process of creating an audio CD of your own.

Others might have continued to add more tracks from more audio CDs to the mix.

Now, you're almost ready to do finish with Nero.

① Preview Your Tracks

Click the **Play** button to ensure that the correct track is listed. Drag and drop a track to a new location to change the play order.

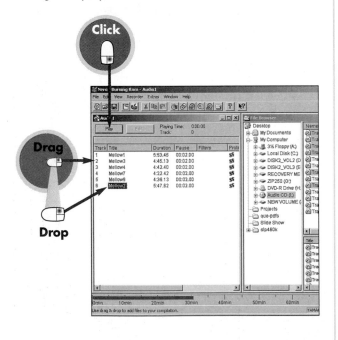

② Add Another CD

Insert another audio CD into your drive, and drag more tracks into your compilation. When the dialog box appears, type in another name and click **OK**.

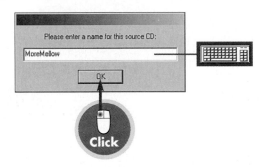

③ Save Your Compilation

Click **Save**, give your compilation a name, and click **Save** again. Note where you saved it for future use. (Remember, this is only the compilation, not the audio files themselves.)

4 Begin the Burn

Insert a blank CD and click the **Burn** button. In the Write CD dialog box, select the best speed for your burner and your blank media. If you have disc space and think you might want to add more tracks later, uncheck **Close Disc**. Then, click **Write**.

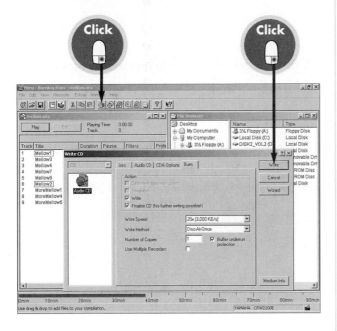

5 Monitor the Burn

I believe it's bad luck to watch your disc burning slider—it leads to errors. But if you like, you can see it happen.

6 Use the Burn Wizard

If you're a glutton for punishment, click the **Wizard** button in the Write CD dialog box. This lets you create an image file for reuse or adjust your burn speed.

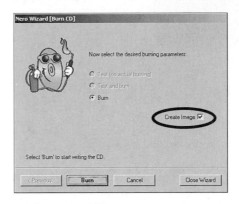

How-to Hint

These Audio Tracks Are "Just Visiting"

The audio tracks in your compilation are temporary files. To continue with the project file and reuse these tracks, you still need the original audio CD(s) when the program prompts you for it.

How to Create a Music Collection in Nero

In the last task, you moved tracks from an audio CD into Nero and burned them to your own greatest hits compilation disc.

But what if you want to keep these tracks available to play or to burn again in different combinations? You need to save the audio tracks as computer files on your hard drive.

Let's take a look at creating a personal collection.

1 Open an Audio CD Project

Open Nero - Burning ROM from the Start menu. If you have killed the wizard, you will see the new Project Options panel. Click **Audio CD**, and then click **New**. (Okay, okay, go ahead and click **Wizard** if you must.)

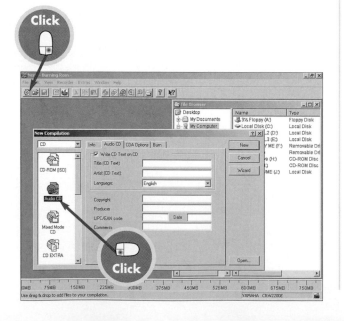

2 Begin the Extraction Process

On the main menu, select **Recorder**, **Save Track**.

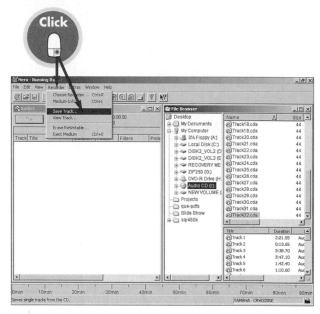

3 Choose Your Source Drive

Click the drive that holds your audio CDs. (This might not be necessary if you have only one CD or DVD drive in your system.) Then, click **OK**.

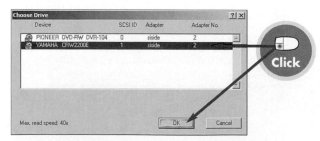

4 Close the Database

A database menu opens; click **Cancel** to close it for now. Then, close the dialog box that explains that the Nero MP3 converter can be used only 30 times without a program upgrade. *(This box is not shown.)* Check the box not to show this again.

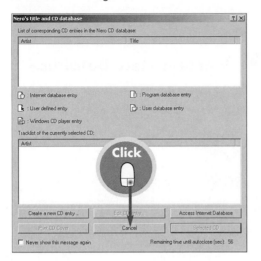

5 Save Your Selections

By default, all the audio tracks on your CD are selected. To deselect them, click a single track to select it and then hold down the **Ctrl** key as you select to choose other individual tracks. Or, hold down the **Shift** key as you select to choose consecutive tracks. Click the drop-down arrow to change the file type from MP3 to PCM Wave audio. Notice that the default destination puts the files directly into your My Documents folder. Click **Browse** to select a new folder (such as My Music), and click **OK**. Then, click **Go**. You can watch the digital audio literally being sucked from the disc and renamed as Windows-friendly WAV audio files.

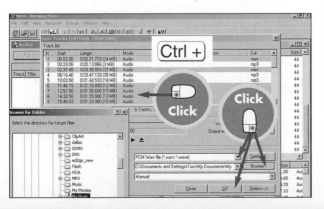

6 Reuse Your WAV Audio Files

Use the file browser in Nero to access the location of your files. Click **My Documents**, click **My Music**, and drag the slider to scroll down to your extracted tracks. Then reselect them, and drag and drop them back into a new compilation. Finally, click **Play** to play the tracks from the compilation panel.

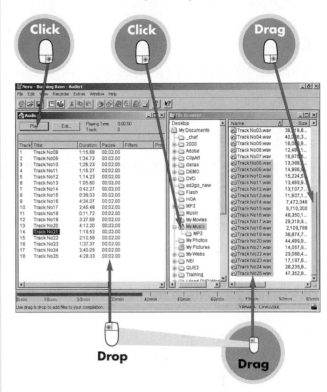

How-to Hint

Naming Your Tracks

Before you extract your audio from an audio CD, you can change the filename creation method from manual to user defined. Click the drop-down arrow and then name the sequential tracks with your own name.

Renaming Your Tracks

If you're very careful, you can use Windows Explorer to rename your tracks. Open My Music, right-click the file, click **Rename**, and type in the name of the song. *Do not alter the file extension—only the name itself—and do this very slowly and carefully.*

How to Create a Music Database in Nero

So far, you have seen and cancelled out of the Database Window in Nero as you performed various tasks. Some advanced users will love the database, so I'll summarize it here. The database is similar to a file cabinet that keeps track of your CDs, album titles, artists, and tracks, but it takes effort to create and maintain it.

① Create a Database Folder

The database is a file that needs to be stored in a folder. Right-click your My Documents folder; select **New**, **Folder**; and rename it `Music Database`.

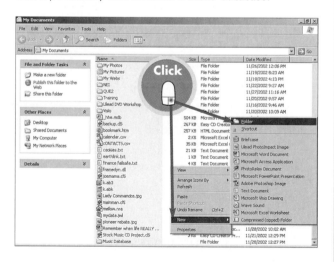

② Create a New Database

Click the **Extras** menu in Nero, and then select **Create a New User Database**.

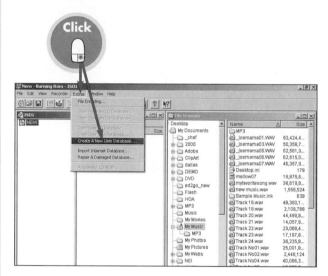

③ Select Your Destination

Click **Browse** and select **Music Database** under My Documents. Then click **OK**. Nero tells you that is creating the file. When it asks you to accept it, click **Yes**.

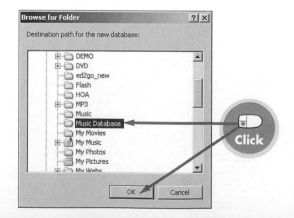

4   Open the Database

On the main menu, select **Extras**, **Open User CD Database**.

5   Add Your New CD Record

Click **Add New CD**, and make sure your audio CD is in your drive. Click **OK** if Nero asks to access the CD—sometimes it can read the information directly for the disc. If necessary, let Nero know which CD drive contains the disc you will be adding to your database.

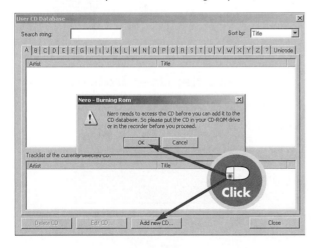

6   Open a New CD Record

Click **Create a New CD Entry**.

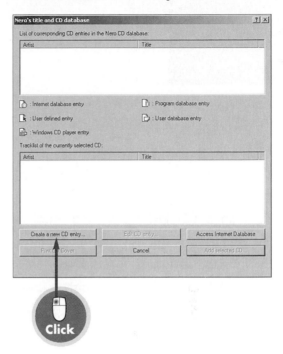

7   Fill In the Title Information

Type in the title and artist information. Next, select the **Title** check box and click **Next**.

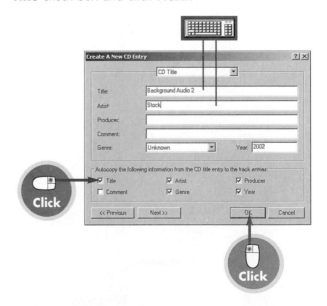

How to Use a Music Database in Nero

If you've come this far, you should know three important things about the database. First, it reads the track and time information of any CD you've entered and finds it automatically. Second, it also works with a CD text feature that most newer drives use to let you access your own burned music discs with the database. And finally, a huge Internet database of titles and artists is available that you can use and connect to through Nero.

1 Fill In the Track Information

Click the **Track** drop-down arrow, scroll down, and highlight the last track before you close it. Then click **OK**.

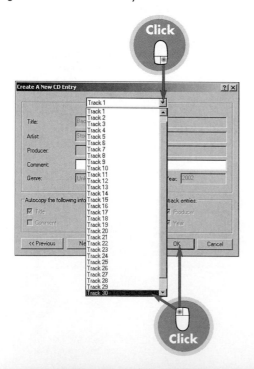

2 Add It to the Database

In the main database window, click **Add Selected CD**.

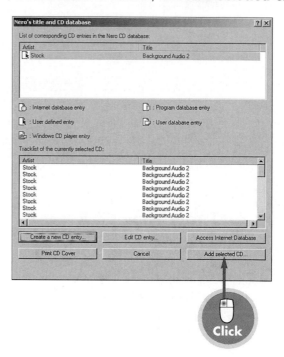

3 Access the User Database

Click **OK** to the prompt that the entry has been successfully added.

④ Find Your New Entry

You should now be able to easily locate your new entry. Click the **Sort By** drop-down arrow and choose whether to sort by title or artist. Then, click the appropriate alphabetical tab and look at the entries.

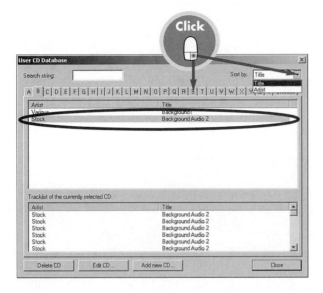

⑤ Start to Extract the CD Tracks

On the main menu, click **Recorder**; then click **Save Track**. Notice that now when the database opens, it has found your CD! Click the **Selected CD** button.

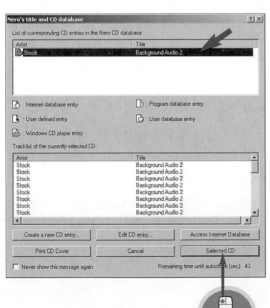

⑥ Select and Save the CD Tracks

Select the tracks to save your hard drive, and choose a file format (WAV) from the drop-down list. Now, however, the name has been filled in from the database. Click **Go**.

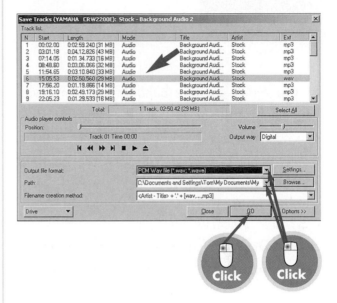

How-to Hint

Creating CD Text

Now that you've seen the database, you can understand how CD text works. When you click to open a new audio CD as a project, just use the CD text window to enter information. But be sure you also click **Write CD Text on CD** when you insert the disc (after it has been burned, you can instantly add your new album to your user database as a new entry).

Importing an Internet Database

If you're a huge music fan, you can explore the Import Internet Database option under Extras on the main menu. This is a somewhat difficult process that connects your user database with volumes of information online that identify albums by their number of tracks and track lengths. For most users, entering their own data is probably much easier.

How to Burn a CD with Media Player

If you didn't get any bundled programs with your CD recorder or don't like the ones you have, you can also use Media Player, along with the Playlist option described in Chapter 35, "Tagging and Organizing Your MP3s."

① Open Windows Media Player

Select **Start**, **All Programs**, **Accessories**, **Entertainment**, **Windows Media Player** (or use a shortcut).

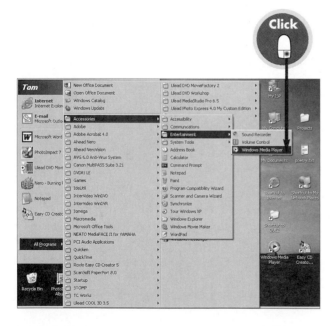

② Open a Playlist

Click **Media Library**, and then click the playlist you want to burn to CD.

③ Open the Burn CD Panel

Click **Copy to CD or Device**, making sure a blank CD is in your burner.

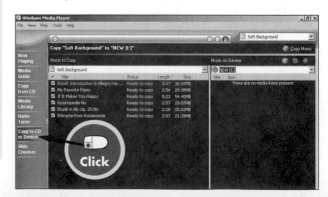

4 Access the CD Recorder

Click the drop-down arrow to make sure that the drive with your blank CD is set as the burner.

6 Burn the Files to Disc

Make sure that the newly imported files are also clicked (checked); then click the **Copy Music** button.

5 Add More Files

From the main My Music folder (or elsewhere), select and drag and drop your files into the playlist.

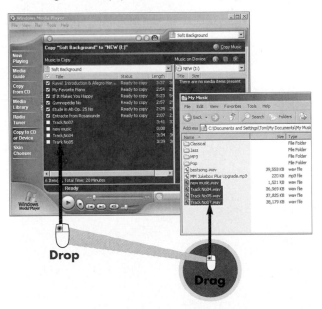

Drop

Drag

Task

Using MP3 Players

You might have been wondering why we went through the tagging process using the MusicMatch software. The reason is that so many people now want to keep dozens or even hundreds of files organized on their hard drives, create different mixes, and then export them to a portable player—to use during exercise or for a serene walk by the ocean.

In general, most players come with some software to simply upload and download MP3 files—generally through a USB or FireWire connector. Some also work as file storage devices or let you record memos through a microphone. But to make the most use of your player, you will want an organizer, which the utility software might or might not provide.

How to Find Software for Your Player

The most obvious place to get software for your player is on its Web site. Like a lot of downloaded software, free introductory versions will be available, as will more full-featured versions that require you to pay a fee.

1 Creative Labs

If you're using the Creative Labs Nomad, it uses software from SoundBlaster that includes a full-feature mixer and organizer, the capability to synchronize, and a file manager.

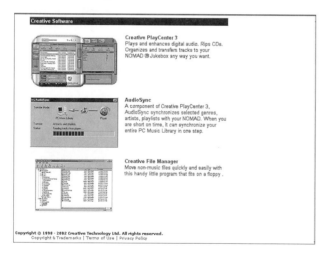

2 Rio's Download Option

Rio's software is available on the SONICblue Web site as a popular program called MoodLogic, which you can download by clicking the **Download Now** button.

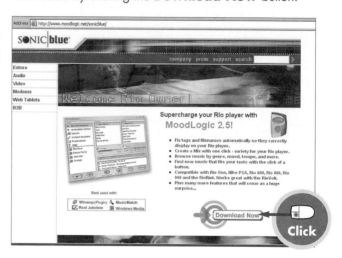

3 Use iRiver

iRiver's device also has a download option for MoodLogic, and it gives you a peek at its organizational capability.

④ Use MusicMatch

MusicMatch features the capability to connect to these players and others through plug-ins. Click **Send to Portable Device** to open another panel, where you can see whether your device is already found (loaded).

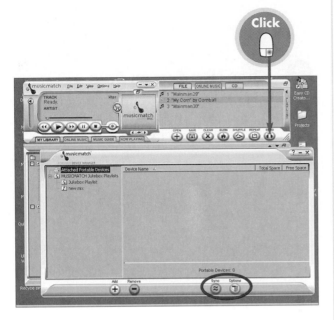

⑤ Load a Plug-in

If your device is not found, click the **+** sign to add your device to MusicMatch. You will need a Web connection, and the plug-in will be downloaded. You should also have your device switched on and connected to your computer.

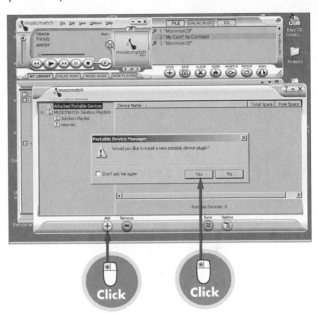

How to Install MoodLogic

Because MoodLogic is downloadable from at least two MP3 player Web sites, let's go through its installation. First, you will download the software.

① Install the Software

Double-click the installer file after you have downloaded it into a folder (such as `C:\Downloads\MP3`). (Notice that this one was for iRiver.)

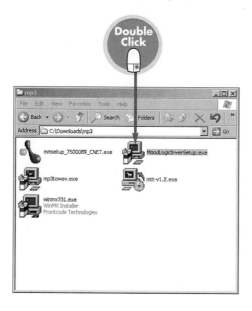

② Choose a Screen Name

First-time users will need a screen name. For users with multiple devices and installations, a common screen name can be entered. Click **I Need a Screen Name**.

③ Enter Your Information

Enter the usual data that lets MoodLogic connect to the Internet for you; then click **OK**.

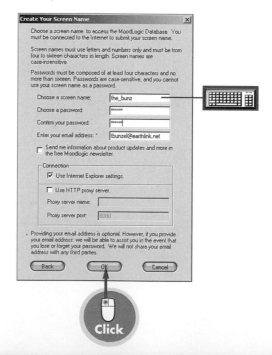

4 Find Your Music

Select the **Scan My Computer for Music Files** option and click **Next** to let MoodLogic scan your system.

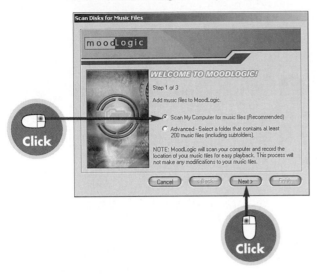

6 Check the Results

Now you can see how the tags you created for MP3 files in MusicMatch can be used.

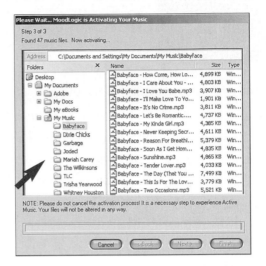

5 Continue Activation

Let MoodLogic find all your music files, including WAV and MP3 files.

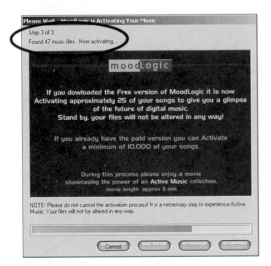

How to Use MoodLogic

After you've activated MoodLogic, it sorts through your artists and albums by genre. If you have tagged your songs, this process will be easier. However, if you have names such as Track 1, Track 2, and so on, you will need to manually add your songs to the mix.

1 Open MoodLogic

Like any other program, you can open MoodLogic from the Start menu—select **Start**, **All Programs**, **MoodLogic**, **MoodLogic**.

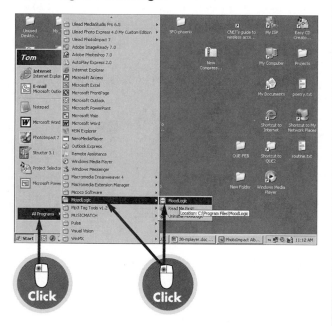

2 Check Your Music Files

Typically, some of your favorite songs will already be found and sorted, but others will need to be tagged or renamed.

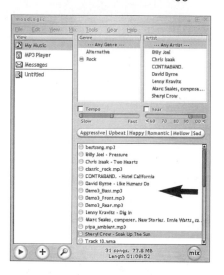

3 Sort Your Music

Clicking a genre, such as Rock, filters the songs that were scanned for selections from that genre.

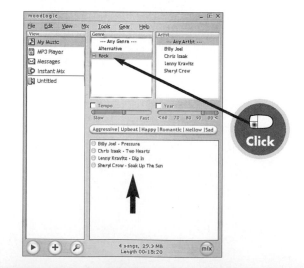

4 Select the Songs

Select the songs you want to add to a mix. (Press **Ctrl+click** for individual songs, or press **Ctrl+A** to select all the songs.)

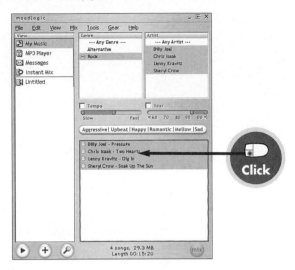

5 Create a New Mix

Click the **Add** icon to create a new mix with these songs.

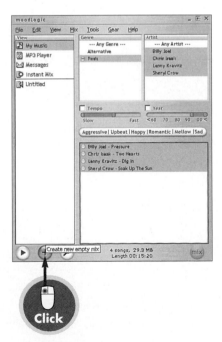

6 Rename the Mix

Right-click the mix and select **Rename** to rename it for future reference.

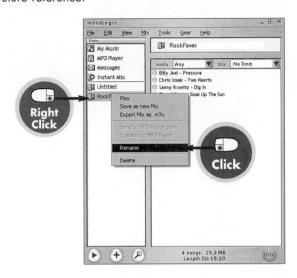

7 Upload the Mix

After it has been configured, you can open the MP3 player to upload the mix. In the status bar, you can see the lengths and file sizes of your songs. You can also click the **Limit** drop-down list to set a maximum capacity for the memory of your device.

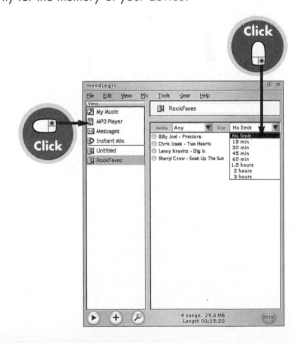

Glossary

A

activate   Windows XP requires that you activate your product within a set number of days; otherwise, you won't be able to continue using it. Activation is a separate process from registration. During activation, a small snapshot of key pieces of hardware on your system is sent to Microsoft. No personal information is required, and none of the hardware information can be used to identify you. In theory, activation prevents people from installing the same copy of Windows on more than one computer—an action that violates the software licensing agreement. *See also* register.

adapter card   *See* expansion card.

add-in card   *See* expansion card.

administrator   A user account created during Windows installation that gives full permission to use the computer and modify settings. Administrator is also a title given to a person who manages a computer network or system.

AGP (Accelerated Graphics Port)   A bus specification that enables 3D graphics to display quickly on a computer. The AGP bus is dedicated solely to graphics and offers more bandwidth than the PCI bus. It is required for graphically demanding applications.

analog video   Video captured by an older camcorder that uses a format such as VHS, S-VHS, 8mm, or Hi-8. These formats are all relatively low in overall video resolution and degrade with each copy that is made from the original source tape.

antivirus software   Software that checks a computer for viruses and eradicates them if it finds them.

aperture setting   The size of the opening that lets light through the lens to hit the film. The bigger the aperture's f/stop—expressed as f/2, f/5.6, or f/22, for instance—the smaller the aperture opening.

applet   A small program. In Windows, the programs you can access from the Control Panel window (Display, System, and Mouse, for example) are often called applets.

application   A program, such as Microsoft Word, that is separate from Windows.

archive   A collection of files copied to a specific location as a backup. When you install a Windows XP service pack, you have the option of archiving Windows files that the service pack will replace so you can uninstall the service pack later.

associate   A document file is associated with the program that created it. Files of a certain type (for example, text files with the file extension `.txt`) are associated with the Windows applet Notepad. If you double-click a file to open it, the program associated with that file type launches and opens the selected file.

ATA   A series of standards for IDE drives and devices. It covers a wide variety of features, including how the controller is integrated onto the drive itself.

ATAPI   An IDE disk interface standard for devices such as CD-ROM or tape drives.

attachment   A file that is inserted into an email message and sent to a recipient.

ATX   A commonly accepted standard for the layout and form factor of the motherboard and power supply for PCs.

audio   The portion of a recorded file that provides the narration, music, or sound effects that accompany the visual portion of the film. Adding audio to your video can fill in the gaps and turn your simple video clips into a sophisticated multimedia presentation. Most video editors enable you to add several layers of video to your scenes in addition to the audio that was recorded on tape when you recorded the original scenes.

audio cable   A cable that runs between a CD-ROM drive and a sound card and enables the sound card to play audio CDs.

audio transition   A technique in which the video transitions to a new scene aurally, not visually. For example, while watching the end of the first scene, you will hear the beginning of the next scene (such as a person's voice, street traffic, or a telephone) a few seconds before the second scene actually appears onscreen. Then the scene changes visually, and the audio is perfectly in sync with the visual.

Automated System Recovery   A feature of the Windows XP Backup utility, Automated System Recovery backs up certain system files and then creates an emergency rescue floppy disk you can use to restore your system following a failure.

automatic updating   You can configure Windows XP to automatically monitor the Windows Update Site for updates and even to download them automatically when it finds them.

B

back up   To copy files from your primary computer to separate media (such as a floppy disk or Zip disk) in case the hard disk on the primary computer fails.

backlight   A light that is reflected off the background to add a sense of depth between the subject and the background.

backplate   A metal plate that helps secure add-in cards to the motherboard.

backward compatibility   The capability of hardware or software to work with older versions of the same hardware or software.

bandwidth   The amount of data that can be processed by a given device. An analog modem has very little bandwidth compared to a high-speed cable modem, for instance, and it cannot download video from the Internet nearly as quickly.

baud   The prevalent measure for data transmission speed until it was replaced by a more accurate term: bits per second (bps).

bidirectional parallel port   A parallel port enabling data to flow in two directions between the PC and printer.

BIOS (basic input/output system)   The system that performs all the basic functions of your computer, such as sending information from your keyboard to your PC. The system BIOS is contained on the BIOS chip.

BIOS chip   A chip that contains a system's BIOS. On many systems, it can be updated with a flash utility.

bit rate   The speed at which a video file can stream from the Internet. When you create your streaming video file, you can control the bit rate at which the file will stream.

blue screen   A specially colored backdrop that is later replaced with another video layer. For example, you can film your subject holding a blue screen (a uniquely colored board) that you will later edit to contain a second video.

BMP   A file format used by Windows to display wallpaper images. The BMP format isn't practical for most applications because of the large file sizes associated with it.

bookmarks   Shortcuts to your favorite Web sites, also called *favorites*. This feature is available in Netscape Navigator, Internet Explorer, Opera, and other Web browsers. You can save bookmarks to sites you visit often, letting you more easily load them in your browser.

boot To start a computer. During the boot process, the many files that make up the Windows operating system are loaded into memory.

boot disk A floppy disk that can be used to boot your computer. Boot disks are often used to recover from a system failure or to install Windows.

bootup screen The first screen you see when you start your computer.

briefcase A special folder designed primarily for users who want to transfer files to another computer. The briefcase contains functions for moving and synchronizing files.

broadband connection A connection to the Internet that's at least 10–20 times faster than you can get using a dial-up modem. Most broadband connections are made using television cable or DSL telephone line technology and cost about $40–$70 per month. Contact your local cable or telephone company to see whether it offers high-speed Internet connections. Broadband connections do not use your computer's modem; they require special hardware that might need to be set up by a professional, such as a cable TV or phone installer.

browser A program, such as Internet Explorer, that can display a Web page. Some browsers can display text, graphics, and frames; other browsers can display only text. Popular browsers other than Internet Explorer include Netscape Navigator and Opera. *See also* Web browser.

bug *See* watermark.

bus A pathway in the PC over which data travels.

C

cable connection *See* broadband connection.

cache memory Random access memory (RAM) that a computer microprocessor can access more quickly than regular RAM.

caption Text that labels a scene or identifies a location or person onscreen.

capture To put a moving image on a tape by using a video camera or camcorder. Also, to transfer a video from a camcorder to the PC through a video card using video editing software.

cascade A way to arrange multiple windows onscreen. The multiple windows are layered, one on top of the other, so that the title bars of all the windows can be seen.

CCD (charge coupled device) A light-sensitive chip that acts like film in a traditional camera. The CCD renders the image projected through the lens, which is then written to videotape. The quality of a CCD is determined largely by its resolution, measured in pixels.

CD-Audio A high-quality sound format used by audio CDs that can be read and converted to other computer formats. VideoWave can read audio CDs, although Premiere cannot.

CD-ROM drive A device that can run CD-ROMs.

CD-RW drive A CD-ROM drive that lets you write data many times per a special CD.

chat The most immediate way to communicate with someone over the Internet. A chat is a live (real-time), back-and-forth discussion that takes place between two or more people over the Internet instead of over voice telephone lines or in person.

chip puller A tool for removing chips from your PC.

clean installation An installation of Windows onto a blank, formatted hard disk. *See also* upgrade.

click To position the mouse pointer over a file or folder and click the left button on the mouse once. Clicking is used to select files in Windows and to follow a link on the Internet.

clip A short piece of video, sometimes called a *scene*. When creating a movie (or film or video project), you string together several clips that will play in sequential order to tell the story of your movie. The transitions between clips can help the progress of the movie, as well.

Close button The button with the – on it, found in the upper-right corner of most windows and dialog boxes. You click the Close button to close a window.

CMOS battery A small battery that provides power to the CMOS chip.

CMOS chip A chip containing a record of the hardware installed on your PC. The CMOS battery supplies it with power, so the data remains stored even when the computer is off. The CMOS stores the information contained in the BIOS settings as well as maintains the clock. Older systems have a separate chip, whereas newer systems have the function integrated onto the motherboard chipset.

CMOS setup screen   A screen that enables you to change your CMOS settings.

cold boot   Starting a computer from a state in which the power is off.

collection   A group of associated pictures or video clips in Windows Media Player. Collections are used for organizational purposes.

color depth   The number of colors displayed on your screen. Common color depths include 16 colors, 256 colors, 16,000 colors (24-bit), and millions of colors (32-bit). You change the color depth used by Windows using the Display Properties dialog box.

color matte   What Premier calls a *color panel*.

color panel   A plain, single-color background you can use to start and end your video (or appear at any point within the video), display titles against, and do other special effects.

COM port   *See* serial port.

compression   A way to store data so that it takes up less disk space than normal. Windows XP offers built-in compression that does not require a separate application.

computer name   A name of up to 15 characters given to a computer. On a network, this name helps distinguish the computer from other computers.

Control Panel   A special folder that contains applets used to configure various Windows settings, such as display, mouse use, and sound.

Controller   A device found on an add-in card or on the motherboard that connects the motherboard to a hard drive.

Controller card   An add-in card that has a controller on it. *See also* Controller.

CPU (central processing unit)   The main processor on a PC, such as a Pentium or Athlon chip.

cradle   A device into which a PDA is inserted that enables it to synchronize its data with a PC's.

crawl   When title text goes from left to right across the screen (or vice versa).

credit   Text that tells who filmed, produced, and otherwise slaved over a film. Credits also identify who appeared in the film and what music you used. Watch a Hollywood movie all the way to the end for some ideas about who to include in your credits.

crop   To make an image physically smaller by trimming away unwanted details. Cropping also reduces the size of the computer file.

cut   To appear suddenly onscreen without any other type of transition effect. The cut is the most basic type of transition for changing scenes and dropping titles onto the screen.

D

daisy-chain   A configuration in which devices are connected one to another in a chain-like fashion, one attached to the next. USB devices can be connected in a daisy-chain.

decryption   To remove the encryption from a file or folder. *See also* encryption.

default   A setting automatically selected by Windows or another program if you do not specify another setting.

defragment   *See* fragmented.

Defragmenter   Software that allows a hard disk to run more quickly by defragmenting it—placing all related pieces of files next to one another so they can be called into memory more quickly.

depth of field   The amount of the scene in front and in back of the focused subject that remains in focus. You can control the depth of field by adjusting the amount of zoom, the shutter speed, or the aperture setting of the camera. Use depth of field to isolate the subject from the foreground and background or to keep the entire scene in focus.

desktop   The metaphor used by Windows to display your file system. The desktop is the main screen in Windows on which various icons are displayed.

desktop theme   A coordinated collection of background colors, wallpaper, mouse pointers, and sounds used to provide a unique feel to your desktop.

device driver   A file that controls and is required for running a particular type of device attached to your computer. Device drivers exist for printers, displays, CD-ROM readers, disk drives, and so on.

Device Manager   An application used to control the settings for hardware on your computer. The Device Manager is used to enable and disable hardware devices, as well as to control driver versions and other settings.

DHCP (Dynamic Host Configuration Protocol)   A computer protocol that assigns a different IP address to a computer each time it connects to the Internet. When you set up a home network to share a high-speed Internet connection, such as a cable modem, you often must also set up DHCP.

dialog box   A small window that opens on your computer as a program is running, often to ask a single question that can be answered by clicking a button containing a label such as Yes, No, or Cancel.

digital camera   A camera that records and stores photographic images in digital format, which can be read by a computer.

digital image stabilization   A camcorder's digital attempt to reduce the apparent jitter or shakiness in a scene, especially when you're using the zoom.

digital video   Video that conforms to the new standards of DV, miniDV, or Digital8. These formats record video and audio as computer data is recorded and are thus not subject to generational loss, like analog video is.

digital zoom   A way of enlarging the image you see through the viewfinder (and record on film) using electronic trickery. Specifically, a digital zoom uses only the pixels in the middle of the CCD and enlarges them, often producing a noisy, grainy, and relatively ugly image. Avoid using the digital zoom too often—try to stay within the limits of the camera's optical zoom. *See also* optical zoom.

DIMM (dual inline memory module)   A type of RAM used in newer PCs, it attaches to the motherboard via a series of pins.

DIN connector   A connector between the keyboard and the computer.

DIP (dual inline package)   A type of RAM used in older computers.

DIP switch   A switch on an add-in card or on the motherboard used to configure a computer or peripherals.

disable   In a list of check box options (as in a dialog box), this removes a check mark from the check box for a particular option. In contrast, you enable an option by clicking an empty check box to place a check mark in the box.

display adapter   *See* graphics card.

dissolve   A video transition in which one video clip fades into the next.

DMA (Direct Memory Access)   A way in which data moves between a device and system memory without the use of the CPU.

docking station   A piece of hardware attached to a laptop that enables the laptop to use expansion cards and devices such as external monitors and keyboards. It is sometimes called a *port replicator*.

domain   A way of grouping computers and users in a fairly complicated network. Domains are often used at large companies, where powerful computers called *servers* provide security, Internet access, file storage, and much more to less powerful computers called *workstations*. If your computer is on a Windows network, it is either part of a domain or part of a workgroup. *See also* workgroup.

double-click   To position the mouse pointer over a file or folder and click the left mouse button twice in rapid succession. Double-clicking opens, or *launches*, a file or folder.

download   To copy a file from another computer to your system, using a network such as the Internet or another means of connecting computers. You can download data files, programs, and many other types of files from sites all over the Internet to your local server or hard drive. A word of caution: Downloaded files are a major source of computer viruses, so you should have up-to-date antivirus software on any computer to which you are actively downloading files. You also should download files only from sources you know and trust.

DPI (dots per inch) A measurement of the quality of the output of a scanner, printer, or computer monitor. The more dots per inch, the higher the quality.

draft mode To print a document in a special mode offered by many programs that reduces the amount of ink used during printing and the quality of the printed document.

drive bay A bay inside a PC into which you install devices such as hard disks, floppy disks, and CD-ROM drives.

driver A piece of software used to enable a peripheral, such as a printer or video card, to work with your PC.

DSL connection *See* broadband connection.

DSL modem A device that enables your computer to access the Internet at a high speed via special DSL lines. Although it's called a modem, it uses technology different from modems, which use traditional telephone lines.

dual-boot A computer on which two operating systems have been installed. When a computer is configured to dual-boot, you are presented with a menu when the computer first starts that prompts you to choose the operating system you want to use.

dub To make a copy from one tape (usually the master tape) to another tape.

DVD decoder card An add-in card that helps play DVDs.

DVD drive A drive that can run DVD discs or play DVD movies.

DVD-RW drive A DVD-ROM drive that lets you write data to special DVDs.

E

EDO RAM (extended data output RAM) A type of random access memory.

email Electronic mail messages sent between different users on a network, such as the Internet. Some email systems are configured only on a local network, and email messages can only be sent between other users on the network.

enable In a list of check box options (as in a dialog box), it places a check mark in the check box for a particular option. In contrast, you disable an option by clicking a check mark to make the check box empty.

encryption To translate data into a secret code that only certain users can access. Windows XP provides built-in encryption. After a user encrypts a file, only that user can decrypt the file. It's also a way to encode data so that it remains confidential. Some Web servers can encrypt Web pages and other data so that you can enter confidential information on a site, such as when you are buying a product online and want to transmit your credit card information.

enhanced parallel port A parallel port that offers transfer rates of up to 2MBps. It can be used for printers and other devices.

enhanced parallel port cable A cable you must use to take advantage of the enhanced parallel port. The numbers and IEEE 1284 are printed on the side of an enhanced parallel port cable.

EPP/ECP (Enhanced Parallel Port/Enhanced Capability Port) A type of parallel port offering transfer rates of up to 2MBps for use with peripherals other than the printer. It enables higher data transfer rates than the original parallel port. EPP is for non-printer peripherals; ECP is for printers and scanners. *See also* enhanced parallel port and enhanced parallel port cable.

Ethernet A standard for tying together computers in a local area network.

Ethernet card A network card that adheres to the Ethernet standard. Virtually all network cards sold for PCs are Ethernet cards.

event An occurrence in Windows, such as when you delete a file or empty the Recycle Bin. An event can also be an occurrence you don't cause, such as when Windows displays an error message. Most such occurrences can be associated with sounds.

Everyone group A special security group that includes all users of the network. By default, the Everyone group is given read access to all files and folder on your computer that you share with the network. You should remove this group and narrow the focus of users to whom you allow access to a resource.

expansion card Also called *adapters* or *add-in cards*, these plug in to the motherboard on expansion slots and expand how your PC can be used. Video cards, disk controllers, and graphics cards are just a few of the expansion cards you can add to a PC.

expansion slot A slot on the motherboard into which expansion cards can be plugged.

Explorer *See* Windows Explorer.

extension The three-letter suffix following the dot in a filename. The extension usually identifies the type of file (for example, a `.doc` extension identifies the file as a Microsoft Word document, and a `.jpg` extension identifies the file as a JPEG image file).

extranet A company network built using Internet technologies that is available to business partners of a company as well as to the company itself.

F

f/stop The aperture setting—that is, the size of the camera opening that lets light through to the film. The wider open the aperture, the smaller the f/stop setting value. For example, the most-open aperture for your camera might be f/2; when the aperture is shut down to its smallest diameter, the f/stop setting might be f/22.

face The main, thick part of a text character.

fade A video transition in which the scene fades from black or white into another scene.

FAT (file allocation table) Maintained on a hard disk by an operating system, it's a table that provides a map of the clusters (the basic unit of logical storage on a hard disk), detailing where files have been stored.

FAT32 A version of the file allocation table (FAT) disk format used mainly in Windows 98 and Windows Me. Windows XP can also use the FAT32 file system. When using FAT32, Windows XP cannot use several advanced features, such as encryption and compression. For that reason, you should use the NTFS file system with Windows XP whenever possible.

favorites A special folder that contains links to favorite Web pages in Internet Explorer. *See also* bookmarks.

feedback rating A numeric ranking listed with every eBay buyer or seller, so that you can evaluate whether you want to do business with that person.

file A collection of data that is stored as a single unit on a disk drive and given a name. Almost all information stored on a computer, including Windows itself, is stored as files.

file sharing The practice of downloading files from other people and making your own files available to others, which is most popular among people who are exchanging MP3 files. Millions of people use file-sharing programs such as WinMX or services such as AudioGalaxy and Gnutella, a source of ongoing controversy because these services do nothing to stop people from exchanging copyrighted music by popular musicians.

fill light A light that is reflected off another surface onto the subject. The reflector softens the effect of light on the subject.

firewall A system designed to prevent unauthorized access to a computer or an entire network. Firewalls can be hardware based or software based. Windows XP comes with a software firewall. Using a personal firewall is a good idea when setting up a home network connected to the Internet because it can prevent attacks. *See also* proxy server.

FireWire A standard that enables devices to be easily connected to a PC without having to open the case and allows devices to communicate at high speeds. It is also called *IEEE 1394*.

Flash memory A type of memory easily updated by running a patch or piece of software. BIOS chips often contain flash memory, so they easily can be updated by running software. Flash memory is also called *flash ROM*.

floppy disk A removable disk that can hold up to 1.44MB of data. Floppy disks are commonly used to transfer information between computers and to back up small amounts of data.

floppy drive A drive that stores information on removable disks that hold 1.44MB of data.

focal length The distance from the lens to the point behind the lens at which the rays of light focus and create an image. Typically, the longer the focal length of the lens, the higher its magnification. The focal length also affects the overall look of your scene. A telephoto lens, for example, compresses the foreground and background while keeping only the subject in sharp focus. More moderate lens magnifications can keep everything in the scene in focus at the same time. Not all lenses have a fixed focal length; if you have a zoom lens, the focal length can actually change depending on the zoom's setting.

folder A Windows object that can contain files and other folders. Folders are used to organize storage. (On older, nongraphical systems, folders are called *directories*.)

Foley effects Special sound effects you can add to your video to suggest creaking doors, gunshots, and car engines, for instance.

format To prepare a storage medium, such as a hard disk or floppy disk, for writing data. Windows includes utilities for formatting disks.

fragmented When data is deleted from a hard drive, the data is not actually removed. Instead, it is marked so that it can be overwritten. When new data is stored, it is written to any empty spaces on the drive. These spaces are not necessarily contiguous, which leads to a condition known as *fragmentation*. Fragmented drives are usable but can slow down a system. Windows XP includes a defragmenting program that rewrites the data on a drive so that it is contiguous.

frames A way of dividing a single Web page into separate sections, each of which can have its own scrollbar and border. Clicking a hyperlink in one frame often causes a page to be opened in a different frame.

freeze frame A technique in which a particular frame of video is held onscreen. Sometimes the audio portion of the scene continues playing.

G–H

game port A port into which you plug a joystick or other gaming device.

generational loss The drop in video resolution that results when you make a copy of an analog videotape. The original videotape is called first generation; a copy of that is second generation, and so on.

GIF A file format used in Web pages. GIF files can be made to display first in low resolution and then improve in quality as more data is downloaded.

grain Texture on the film that occurs when there isn't enough light to make a good shot or when the camera uses its digital zoom. Grain usually refers to chemically processed film, but the digital equivalent of grain appears in video as well.

graphics accelerator A graphics card, chip, or chipset that speeds up the display of graphics on a PC.

graphics card An add-in card that gives your computer the capability to display graphics and video on your monitor.

handle A screen name that identifies you to the Internet-using public. Comparable to a CB radio handle, an Internet handle can say something about your personality (`Grumpy1`), your career (`BeanCount`), or your hobbies (`QuiltingB`). Of course, it can also be an easy-to-remember moniker such as `FirstName.LastName`.

hard drive Where data and programs are stored, even when you turn off your computer.

hardware driver *See* driver.

heatsink A device attached to a CPU that cools down the CPU so that it doesn't overheat.

host In the context of the World Wide Web, to make pages and other documents (a Web site) available to users of the Internet. Many Internet service providers offer a limited amount of free space on their servers for you to publish your Web pages; companies are also available that host sites for free. The provider's server then becomes the host for your site.

hover To position the mouse pointer over an area without clicking the mouse button. Hovering the mouse pointer over a hyperlink on a Web page displays the filename or the URL of the page that will load if you click that hyperlink. Hovering over an area in a program window frequently displays a ScreenTip or ToolTip.

I

icon   A small picture on the desktop or in a folder that represents a file or folder. The icon usually helps indicate what type of file or folder an object is.

IDE (Integrated Drive Electronics)   A standard that details the way in which a computer's motherboard communicates with storage devices, such as hard disks.

IDE/EIDE hard drive   A hard drive that connects to the motherboard via an IDE/EIDE controller card.

IEEE-1394   *See* FireWire.

inbox   The folder in an email program to which new messages are delivered.

indicator light   The light or lights on the front of the PC that show the computer is turned on or that the hard disk or CD-ROM drive is being used.

infrared recording   A feature that permits the camera to record images in absolute darkness using an infrared emitter. Sony Handycams have this feature and call it NightShot. Infrared recording creates a greenish monochrome image similar to what you would see through night-vision goggles.

ink cartridge   A cartridge for inkjet printers.

install   To load software (such as Windows or Microsoft Office) onto your computer. Most programs are installed using a setup program that guides you through the installation step-by-step. The term *install* is also used to refer to the process of setting up other devices and software configurations on a computer. For example, configuring a printer to work on your computer is often referred to as *installing the printer*, and hooking up a new hard drive inside your computer is referred to as *installing the hard drive*.

instant messaging   A style of chat in which you keep track of people you know who are using the same software. A server tells you when selected people are online and provides the same information about you to others. You can send private messages that are received instantly on another user's computer.

IP address   A set of numbers, such as 150.2.123.134, that identifies each computer connected to the Internet. To use many Internet services, each computer must have a unique IP address.

IRQ (interrupt request)   A connection between a device and a controller. Only one device at a time can use a particular IRQ.

ISP (Internet service provider)   A company that provides access to the Internet for a monthly fee.

J–K

joystick   A device for playing games that plugs in to the game port.

JPG   A file format that can compress huge photographic images into tiny file sizes while sacrificing only a little image quality. It's great for Web pages and email.

jumper   A small set of pins set in a particular way on the motherboard or add-in card to configure devices to work with a PC.

key light   The main light in the room; it provides the principal light on the subject.

keyboard port   A port into which the keyboard is plugged. Most often, it is a PS/2 port.

keywords   Descriptive words that help identify files on the Internet. Keywords can let Web surfers more easily find your video files in search engines.

L

LAN (local area network)   *See* local area network.

lasso   The dotted rectangle that follows the mouse pointer when you drag around a group of objects. The lasso encircles the objects and selects all the objects at once.

LCD (liquid crystal display)   The type of display used in laptop computers.

leader   The beginning of the physical tape on a videocassette. It is a strip of nonrecording tape that connects the actual recording tape to the spindle on the cassette. Most cassette tapes have about five seconds of leader before the actual recording media portion of the tape begins.

link   On a Web page, a selection of text or a graphic that, when clicked, causes the Web browser to load another Web page.

local area network (LAN) A network of computers connected together so they can share files and printers and also share a high-speed Internet connection, such as a cable modem. This enables them all to access the Internet from one connection. This type of computer network spans a relatively small area, such as a single building. LANs can be connected to one another to form a wide area network (WAN).

local printer A printer that is connected directly to a computer. This differs from a network printer that might be connected to a different computer on a network or directly to the network itself.

logon Because it is a secure system, Windows XP requires that you enter a username and password so that it can register you with the network and determine the permissions you have been given on a computer.

lossless compression The condition in which no elements of a picture are lost during compression, resulting in higher picture quality and often larger sizes of picture files.

lossy compression The condition in which certain elements of a picture are lost during compression, resulting in lower sizes of picture files but also reduced quality of pictures.

LPT1 The name given to the primary parallel port on a computer. The first printer attached to a computer usually uses the LPT1 port.

lux value A camera rating that indicates how low the light can be before the camera can no longer record an image. Lux values are subjective and are not standard, but typically a 2-lux camera can record an image in candlelight.

M

MAC address A number that identifies a network card. Each network card has a unique MAC address so that it's the only one in the world with that address. When you install a cable modem, you must give your cable provider your network card's MAC address; otherwise, you cannot connect to the Internet.

mailing list A group discussion that takes place entirely with email. People who are interested in a list's topic send email messages to a specific address to subscribe. If the list allows public participation (as many do), you can use a special email address to send a message to all the list subscribers. Any message sent by another member to the list of subscribers appears in your Inbox.

Makebt32 The program used to create the set of floppy disks used for Windows XP installation. Makebt32 can be found in the BOOTDISK folder on the Windows XP installation CD.

manual override To force the camera into settings different from those it would choose automatically. For example, you can manually override the exposure settings of most cameras, and you can trick the camera into focusing on something other than your subject. You override the camera's settings to achieve special effects.

map To create a shortcut to a shared resource on the network by telling your computer to treat the resource as a separate drive on your computer. Because not all programs know how to work with Network Place shortcuts, you can fool these programs into working with shared resources by making them think that the resources are on a different drive on your computer.

Mark-In point The point in a longer video or audio clip at which you decide to start the clip. You can shorten a lengthy clip or crop out unwanted leading frames or noise by setting the Mark-In point. Keep in mind that when setting a Mark-In point, the beginning of the clip isn't physically deleted. Instead, the video editing software is smart enough to start playing the clip at the Mark-In point, which can be changed or deleted at any time during the movie production.

Mark-Out point The point in a longer video or audio clip at which you decide to stop the clip. You can shorten a lengthy clip or crop out unwanted trailing frames or noise by setting the Mark-Out point. Keep in mind that when setting a Mark-Out point, the end of the clip isn't physically deleted. Instead, the video editing software is smart enough to stop playing the clip at the Mark-Out point, which can be changed or deleted at any time during the movie production.

master The first tape you create from your PC video file, also known as the *first-generation tape*. The master tape is a high-quality source to which you should return whenever you want to make more copies. Although you could use the file on your hard drive as a master, you probably won't want to keep that file forever because it takes up so much storage space. If you're using analog video, however, the PC file is your master source and first generation; the first physical tape you record is considered to be a second-generation tape.

maximize   To cause a window on your desktop to grow to maximum size, filling your screen.

memory bank   A series of slots or sockets on the motherboard that holds RAM.

memory socket   A socket on the motherboard into which RAM is installed.

menu   A collection of related commands in a program that is accessed by clicking once on the menu's title.

microprocessor   *See* CPU.

Microsoft Network (MSN)   *See* MSN.

Microsoft Passport   A free account you can use on all Microsoft Web sites and more than 125 other sites, including 1-800-Flowers.com, Buy.com, eBay.com, RadioShack.com, and Starbucks.com. On Windows XP, you can associate a different Passport account with each person who uses your computer. To set up a Passport, you must have an email account.

minimize   To cause a window on your desktop to be removed from view. After it's minimized, you can access the window using its taskbar button.

modem (modulator/demodulator)   A device for connecting a computer to other computers or the Internet. Modems can be located outside the computer (called *external* modems) or inside the computer (called *internal* modems).

motherboard   The main part of the PC—a very large board into which the CPU, add-in cards, chips, RAM, and many other devices are plugged.

motion blur   The effect of tracking a speeding object and thus blurring the background because of the motion.

mounting rails   Rails inside a drive bay to which hard drives and other storage devices are attached.

mounting screws   Screws that secure a drive into a drive bay.

mouse port   A port into which the mouse is plugged.

MP3   A popular format for sound files. MP3 compresses the sound file so that it takes up less room on the hard disk and takes less time to upload or download to and from Web pages. The compression scheme does not affect sound quality noticeably; it's often just about CD quality. VideoWave reads MP3 files, but Premiere does not.

MP3 player   A small, portable device that can play MP3 files.

MSN   Previously known as the Microsoft Network, MSN is a free Web portal that includes news, email, travel and consumer information, instant messaging, and Web hosting. To visit the site, type the URL http://www.msn.com into your browser's address bar and press Enter.

MSN Explorer   A simplified Web browser that provides quick access to many MSN-related services, such as Web-based email, a calendar, and personalized Web services.

My Computer   A special folder located on the Windows desktop that contains all the drives (hard disks, floppy disks, CD-ROM, and network drives) available on a computer.

My Documents   A special folder located on the Windows desktop meant to hold all the documents and personal files you create.

My Network Places   A special folder located on the Windows desktop used to browse other computers available on the network.

My Pictures   A special folder in the My Documents folder that has special features for viewing and working with pictures.

N

nanosecond   The speed at which RAM is rated. The lower the nanosecond rating, the faster the memory. For example, a 7-nanosecond chip is faster than a 12-nanosecond chip.

narration A voice that explains what is happening on the video. A voiceover can add tremendous value to a video by explaining the situation being shown to viewers. You can do the narration onscene when you film the video, but you'll generally get better results by recording the voiceover in a quiet studio (such as at your PC) and adding it to the video afterward.

NetCam *See* WebCam.

netiquette Commonly accepted standards for behavior on the Internet.

network Several computers (and sometimes other devices) that are connected together so they can share software, data files, and resources. *See also* local area network and wide area network.

network card (NIC) An add-in card that enables a computer to be connected to a network or to a cable system or DSL line to get a high-speed Internet connection.

network drive A shared resource, such as a folder, treated as a drive on your computer. A network drive gets its own drive letter and shows up in the My Computer window.

network hub A device to which PCs are connected that enables them to communicate with one another as part of a local area network. Also, each PC can access the Internet through the hub.

Network Place A shortcut to a resource (a file, folder, or device) on the network. The shortcut you set up to that location works only on your computer; other computers on the network might or might not have the same Network Places you do.

network printer A printer connected to another computer on the network or to the network itself and for which an icon is created in the Printers and Faxes folder on your computer.

news In the context of Usenet, public messages contributed to the newsgroup.

news server An Internet site that can send and receive Usenet newsgroup messages.

newsgroup An Internet-based forum in which you can participate in threaded discussions. *See also* Usenet.

NIC (network interface card) *See* network card.

noise The random errors generated by your camcorder when filming in low-light situations. A camcorder's CCDs are designed to work with a certain minimum level of light; videotaping with less light results in the CCDs creating phantom pixels in the video that appear as noise.

nonparity RAM chips RAM chips that do not perform error checking to see whether any other memory chips are not functioning properly. Most RAM sold today is nonparity.

NTFS The native file system format used by Windows XP. *See also* FAT32.

O

object An item on your screen (usually an icon) that represents a program, file, or folder.

OEM (original equipment manufacturer) A company that buys computers in bulk, customizes them, and then sells them under its own name.

offline folders Folders that have been marked to be accessible when your computer is not connected to the network. Files in offline folders are periodically synchronized with the actual files on the network.

offline viewing Looking at a Web document while not actually connected to the Internet. If your telephone and your computer share the same line, you can look at pages offline as you're talking on the phone—which you can't do if you're viewing them online.

operating system A program or group of programs that controls the file system, drive access, and input for a computer. Windows XP is an example of an operating system.

optical zoom A way of enlarging the image you see through the viewfinder (and record on film) using the camera's optics. *See also* digital zoom.

outline The line that wraps around a text character—especially obvious with large, thick fonts.

overlay video When creating special effects with a blue screen, the clip that appears in the blue screen. The scene that surrounds the overlay (for example, the actor holding the blue screen on which the overlay video plays) is called the *background video*.

P

Palm   A small, handheld computer commonly used for keeping track of contacts, appointments, to-do lists, and similar items. It uses the Palm operating system.

Palmtop   A generic name for a PDA. *See also* PDA.

parallel port   A port into which the printer is plugged. It also can be used for scanners and other external devices. *See also* LPT1.

parent folder   In a hierarchical list of folders on your computer, the parent folder is the folder above (and thus the folder that contains) the folder you are currently in.

parity RAM chips   RAM chips that perform error checking to see whether any other memory chips are not functioning properly. This is generally an older type of memory. Usually, 486 PCs and Pentiums use memory that is nonparity. Parity RAM chips have nine chips on them, instead of the eight found on nonparity memory.

partition   A separate portion of a hard drive. It can also be used as a verb: You divide a hard drive into sections by partitioning it.

Passport   *See* Microsoft Passport.

password   A word; phrase; or combination of letters, numbers, and punctuation that you must use to gain access to a Web site, online store, Internet service provider, or another service on the Internet. You should make your passwords impossible for others to guess; one way to do this is to make a password two unrelated words separated by a punctuation mark (such as `eve*school` or `ace!radar`). *See also* username.

path   The description of the location of a file or folder on your computer or a network. A typical path might include the drive letter, folders, and name of the file (for example, `C:\My Documents\invoice.doc`).

pause printing   To stop a document in the print queue from printing. The document remains in the print queue but does not print until you choose to resume printing. Other documents waiting in the queue continue to print. *See also* restart printing.

PC Card   A credit-card-size add-in card that plugs in to a laptop computer and gives it extra functionality. Modems and network cards are common PC cards.

PC Slot   A slot into which a PC card is plugged.

PCI (Peripheral Component Interconnect)   A bus standard developed by Intel that enables fast bus speeds.

PCMCIA card   An older term for PC card.

PCMCIA slot   An older term for PC slot.

PDA   A generic name for a small, handheld computer designed to keep track of contacts, appointments, to-do lists, and similar items.

peer   On networks with no main server, all computers are part of a workgroup and are considered peers that can share their own resources and access other resources on the network.

peripheral   A general term that refers to any device, such as a printer, modem, scanner, or others, that isn't required for the basic functioning of a computer but that can be used to enhance the way it works or give it extra functionality.

permission   On a secure system such as Windows XP, users are given specific rights (such as the ability to read or change a file) on objects.

phishing   An attempt to steal a user's password or credit card information. On America Online and other places where instant messages and chat are popular, a person might masquerade as a system administrator who needs your password or credit card number because of a problem of some kind. This is always a hoax: No legitimate employee of an Internet provider asks for this information in email, via instant messages, or in a chat room.

phone jack   A connector into which you plug a telephone wire to connect your modem to the telephone system.

pickup tool   A tool for picking up small objects that have fallen into your computer.

pixel   A dot on the computer screen, usually used to describe image resolution. Every computer image is created from an array of pixels, usually 640×480, 800×600, or 1024×768 pixels.

plug-in   A generic term for a special element you insert into a Web page. FrontPage uses the term to refer to any component (such as video) that needs a special viewer. When you want to include a video clip on your Web page, for example, the clip is called a plug-in to the Web page.

pointer   A small graphic (an arrow, by default) indicating the placement of the mouse on your screen.

pop   The annoying sound on a voice recording that accompanies an inexperienced narrator's pronunciation of certain letters. For example, many people blow out the letter *p*, which results in a pop when they speak into a microphone. You can minimize popping by varying your distance from the mike, changing the angle at which you speak into the mike, and using a foam cover on the mike.

POP3 (Post Office Protocol version 3)   A protocol used by servers that deliver email. When you set up an account with an Internet service provider, your provider often gives you the name of a POP3 server to use when receiving mail. Save this information; you need it to set up an email program, such as Outlook Express.

pop-under window   An extra browser window that opens as you are visiting a Web page but is immediately minimized and out of view. The window shows up on your taskbar with other browser windows that have been opened but are not currently visible. Similar to pop-up windows, these are used most often for advertising purposes.

pop-up window   An extra browser window that opens as you are visiting a Web page, usually to display advertising. The name comes from the way they pop up on the screen in front of the page you're trying to view.

port   A connection on your computer into which you plug a cable, connector, or device.

port replicator   *See* docking station.

portal   A commercial Web site that functions as a gateway to the Internet. If you designate a portal as your browser's home page, you can start every online session on that page, giving some structure to your Internet experience.

power cable   A cable that connects the power supply and provides power to devices in the PC, such as hard drives and floppy drives.

power supply   A device inside your PC that provides power by converting the current from your wall outlet to the type of power that can be used by your PC and all its components.

presets   Shortcuts to your favorite Web radio stations in Windows Media Player 7. You click a preset to begin listening to a particular station.

print device   In Microsoft lingo, the actual printer hardware connected to a computer is referred to as the *print device* and the icon in the Printers and Faxes folder that represents the device is referred to as a *printer*.

print queue   A list of documents waiting for their turn to be printed by a specific printer.

printer   *See* print device.

priority   The status a document has in a print queue. A document's priority governs when it prints related to other documents in the print queue. By default, all documents being printed are given a priority of 1, the lowest priority available. The highest priority is 99. Increasing a document's priority causes it to print before other waiting documents.

produce   To render a video production on your PC in its final form, storing it on your hard drive. The produced video becomes the high-quality master from which you can make any number of copies—and those copies will be every bit as good as the first copy.

product activation   New versions of Windows require that you register and activate the operating system over the Internet or by phone so you can continue to use it beyond a short trial period.

product identification key   The serial number found on the back of the Windows CD-ROM case and entered during the installation process, it helps identify you as the proper owner of the software.

Program Access and Defaults   A feature included with Windows XP Service Pack 1 that lets you control the default applications associated with certain files (such as Web pages) and activities (such as email). This feature also lets you specify whether icons for Microsoft versions of certain built-in programs are shown on your desktop and Start menu.

Properties   A dialog box available for most files and folders that contains various settings relating to the object. You can access this dialog box for most objects by right-clicking the object and selecting the Properties command from the shortcut menu.

proxy server   A server set up between your computer and the Internet (generally in an office or academic environment). To get to the Internet, you must go through the proxy server, which performs security checks to ensure that outsiders cannot access your company's network illegally. Also called a *firewall*.

publish   To upload files to a Web server to make those files available to users of the Internet. One way to design Web pages is to create them on your computer and then publish the pages to a Web server that has direct access to the Internet.

Q–R

queue   A list of the documents waiting their turn to be printed.

RAM (random access memory)   Memory where programs are run and data is stored while the data is being manipulated. When you turn off your computer, any information in RAM is lost.

RAM cache   Memory that sits between your CPU and your main RAM. Information is shuttled here from the main RAM to be available more quickly to the CPU. Cache is faster than normal RAM and includes intelligence. It is not part of the main memory in a PC and on most cases is not found directly on the motherboard.

RAMBUS   A type of high-speed RAM.

RealPlayer   The standard playback software, distributed by Real Networks, for enjoying streaming media (such as audio and video) on the Internet.

RealProducer   A free program that can be used to convert video into a Web-friendly streaming format. RealProducer is distributed by Real Networks to enable users to easily and quickly upload streaming video to the Internet.

Recent Documents   A special folder available on the Start menu that contains shortcuts to the documents you have most recently opened.

Recycle Bin   A special folder on your desktop that temporarily holds files you delete from your computer.

When the Recycle Bin becomes full, the oldest files are permanently deleted to make room for new files to be added. You can also empty the Recycle Bin manually, permanently deleting all the files inside.

reflector   A card, fabric, or other reflective surface you can use while shooting a scene to direct ambient light onto the subject. Reflectors are available at most photo and video stores, and they can dramatically enhance the quality of your film.

register   During registration of Windows, you provide certain personal information (name, address, phone number, and so on) to Microsoft so that the company can record you as the owner of a Windows license. Registering is optional. When you register, you are eligible for technical support, warranty, and software bulletins; you also can receive special promotions from Microsoft on other products. *See also* activate.

removable drive   A device that stores data permanently like a hard drive or a floppy drive does, but on removable disks. These disks commonly hold several hundred megabytes or more of data.

Reset button   A button that turns off your computer and then automatically turns it back on.

resolution   The number of pixels used to display an image. Digital cameras capture images at a resolution of 720×480 (720 pixels in a line by 480 lines). When printed, this resolution maintains the image's integrity only up to about 5''×7'' (good enough for Web pages and importing into Word or Publisher documents). For images with higher resolutions, you need a megapixel digital camera.

restart printing   To begin printing a paused document again from the beginning. Restarting a print job can be useful if, for example, you start to print a document and then realize the wrong paper is loaded in the printer. You can pause the document, change the paper, and then restart the document. *See also* pause printing.

restore point   A special backup of system files and settings used by the System Restore application to return your computer to a particular state.

ribbon cable   A wide ribbon-like cable that connects a drive to a disk controller.

right-click To hold the mouse pointer over a certain object and press the right mouse button once. Right-clicking an object usually opens a shortcut menu that contains commands relating to the object.

RIMM (RDRAM inline memory module) A form of high-speed memory used by the newest, most powerful computers.

roll When title or credit text goes from the top to the bottom of the screen (or vice versa).

ROM (read-only memory) Memory that is not volatile, meaning it can be read but not changed or can be changed only under specific conditions.

ROM BIOS chip A chip that holds the code necessary for starting your computer and for the basic functions of receiving and sending data to and from hardware devices, such as the keyboard and disk drives.

router A device that can connect networks and that routes information to and from the Internet. Routers are commonly combined with hubs in home networking devices to enable PCs to be networked and share an Internet connection.

S

scale When printing an image, scaling reduces or enlarges by a specified percentage.

scene In VideoWave parlance, a clip that is already in the Storyline. The term *scene* is really just another way of describing a clip, and the two terms are frequently used interchangeably. *See also* clip.

scheduled task A job (such as launching a program or backing up files) defined in the Task Scheduler application to run at a certain time.

screen name *See* username.

screen resolution *See* resolution.

screensaver A small program that displays graphics on your screen when the computer has been idle for a certain amount of time. Although designed to prevent images displayed too long from permanently burning themselves into your monitor (a phenomenon that does not often occur on newer monitors), screensavers are used mainly for entertainment and security in conjunction with a screensaver password.

ScreenTip A small pop-up box containing text that defines or describes a particular area of the screen. You can display a ScreenTip by hovering the mouse cursor over the area of the screen in question. Some applications call the ScreenTips that appear for toolbar buttons *ToolTips*.

script Text that identifies what everyone in the scene you are filming is going to say. The script can help you identify any weaknesses in the storyboard and flesh out the video you are about to film.

scroll To move the display in a window horizontally or vertically to view information that cannot fit on a single screen.

SCSI (small computer systems interface) A hardware interface for connecting hard disks, scanners, CD-ROM drives, and other devices to a PC.

SDRAM (synchronous dynamic random access memory) A generic name for various types of DRAM synchronized with the clock speed for which the microprocessor is optimized.

search engines World Wide Web sites that use computers to catalog millions of Web pages, which you can use to search for specific text. Some of the most popular search engines are AltaVista (`http://www.altavista.com`), Google (`http://www.google.com`), and HotBot (`http://hotbot.lycos.com`).

secure system A computer that can be assigned a password so unauthorized users are denied access.

secure Web server Most often used for online shopping. A secure server encrypts information (such as a credit card number) that is sent to the server and received from it so confidential information is hidden from anyone who might try to view it. These servers use Secure Sockets Layer (SSL), a protocol that protects private information over the Internet.

security certificate A special browser window that vouches for the authenticity of a program's author. After you see the security certificate, you can decide whether you want to let the program run on your machine. A security certificate is required only when you're working with ActiveX technology; Java doesn't require this type of direct action by the user.

select To click once and bring the focus to an object. For example, in a list of files displayed in an open folder window, you can click a file to select that file. Information about the selected object is frequently displayed.

Send to A submenu available on the shortcut menu for most files and folders that contains commands for quickly sending files to certain locations, such as the floppy drive, desktop, and My Documents folder.

serial port A port into which modems and other devices are plugged.

server A computer that sends information to other computers, either in response to a request or through an automated schedule. A popular type of server on the Internet is a Web server.

service pack A collection of updates and features issued by Microsoft since the original release of a Windows operating system. Service packs are numbered (Service Pack 1, Service Pack 2, and so on) and are cumulative. For example, Service Pack 3 would contain all the updates found in Service Packs 1 and 2. At the time of this writing, Service Pack 1 is the only service pack issued for Windows XP, although more recent individual updates might be found on the Windows Update site.

shadow The optional backdrop that can make a text character stand out from the video background.

share To allow network access to a file or folder on your computer. After you share an object, you can define which users can access the object and exactly what they can do with it.

shortcut A small file that targets another file on your computer. Double-clicking the shortcut launches the target file.

shortcut menu The menu available by right-clicking most files and folders. The shortcut menu contains various commands associated with the particular object.

shutter speed The amount of time each frame of film is exposed to light.

signature file Text that is automatically appended to email, Usenet postings, and similar documents. These files often contain your name, email address, favorite quote, and other personal information.

SIMMs (single inline memory modules) A type of RAM, SIMMs attach to the motherboard via a series of pins.

slide *See* wipe.

SMTP (Simple Mail Transfer Protocol) Similar to POP3, it's a protocol used by email servers. When you sign up with an Internet service provider, your provider often gives you the name of an SMTP server to use when sending mail. You need this information to set up an email program, such as Outlook Express.

socket The way certain Intel Pentium microprocessors plug in to a computer motherboard so they make contact with the motherboard's built-in wires or data bus. The many socket standards include Sockets 7, 8, 370, 423, and A.

sound card An add-in card that enables your computer to play music and sounds.

spam A type of unsolicited Internet marketing in which thousands of email messages are sent out to anyone with an email account. An electronic version of junk mail, spam often promotes unsavory businesses and is forged so that the sender's identity is hidden. Spam is a widely loathed practice that is illegal to send in a few jurisdictions. The name was inspired by a *Monty Python* comedy sketch and is unrelated to the Hormel spiced meat product of the same name.

SSL *See* secure Web server.

standby When your computer enters a mode in which the power to the monitor, hard drive, CD-ROM drive, and most other elements is turned off or reduced. Just enough power is fed to the computer's memory so that Windows remembers which programs were running and which windows were open. When your computer leaves standby, it should return to the same state it was in before it went to standby.

Start menu The menu that opens when you click the Start button in the lower-left corner of your screen. The Start menu provides access to all your programs, special folders, and Windows settings.

status area *See* system tray.

still frame *See* freeze frame.

storyboard A series of cartoon-like panels you draw that describes, scene by scene, what happens in your movie. The storyboard can be either crudely drawn in pencil or elaborately produced on a computer. Regardless of how it is created, you'll find the storyboard handy for staying on track and on schedule.

storyboard template In VideoWave, it's a dummy video you can use to help structure your own video. If you need help organizing your film, open an appropriate storyboard from the `VideoWave\Media\Storyboard` folder. Each panel in the storyboard includes text that suggests a specific flow for your movie.

Storyline In VideoWave parlance, it's the set of panels that runs across the top of the screen. These panels contain individual video clips that, in the sequence presented, become the video movie you are creating. You can think of the VideoWave Storyline as your movie's storyboard.

streaming audio Sound on the Internet that begins playing as soon as the file is selected rather than at the end of a complete download of the sound file. This format is especially well suited for concerts and live radio.

streaming video Video that plays onscreen even as it is being downloaded from the Internet to the viewer's PC. If the video file contains audio sounds, the audio portion of the clip streams right along with the video.

subtitle Onscreen text that translates foreign-language dialogue or transcribes hard-to-understand speech.

synchronization In Outlook Express, the process of receiving new messages in Usenet newsgroups to which you have subscribed.

synchronize To cause offline files or folders to be in unison with the actual files and folders they represent. Files in either location with newer modification dates replace files with older modification dates.

System Restore A Windows application that creates restore points (backups of certain system settings) and that can restore Windows to any particular restore point. *See also* restore point.

system tray The part of your Windows taskbar that's next to the current time (usually in the lower-right corner of the display screen). This is also called the *status area*, and it can contain icons representing your Internet connection, speaker volume, antivirus software, and other programs running on your computer.

T

talking head A film segment that shows just the head and shoulders of a person who is talking. This tight focus is often used in interview situations in which the background is not as important as the talking subject is. It is also convenient in a movie destined for the Web because the small amount of movement in a talking-head shot compresses well for the Internet.

tape drive A drive enabling data to be copied to a tape. The tape can hold hundreds of megabytes of data and is commonly used to back up data and hard disks.

taskbar The strip along the bottom or side of your Windows display screen in which the Start button, the buttons for all active programs, the current system time, and the system tray appear.

TCP/IP (Transmission Control Protocol/Internet Protocol) The basic communication language or protocol of the Internet. It also can be used as a communications protocol in the private networks called intranets and in extranets.

terminator Attaches to a device on the end of a SCSI daisy-chain and lets the chain know the device is the first or last device in the chain.

thread A group of replies to a single message in a newsreader program, such as Outlook Express. When you reply to a message, your reply becomes part of the thread.

ticker symbol A short, unique code assigned to a company by the stock exchange on which that company trades.

TIF A file format that preserves all the image quality in a picture, although files can be huge.

title Text that can leap, fade, dance, or spin its way onto the screen to identify your movie or specific scenes. Titles help your viewers immediately understand the context of your movie, and they add a professional touch to your production.

title case   A capitalization convention in which the first, last, and all important words in the headline are given an initial capital letter. Most newspapers and magazines capitalize their headlines using title case; when you add titles to your videos, you should typically use this capitalization convention, too.

toner cartridge   An ink cartridge for laser printers.

ToolTip   *See* ScreenTip.

track   To follow a moving subject with the camera lens.

transition   A graphical segue that signals the end of one scene and the start of the next. The most basic transition is a cut: The first clip stops suddenly, and the second clip begins without preamble. More artistic transition effects include fades, dissolves, and wipes in which the first clip somehow blends into the second clip.

troubleshooter   A special file in the Windows Help program that walks you through steps to take in determining the cause of a problem with Windows. The troubleshooter frequently suggests resolutions to these problems or points you toward more information about the problem.

U–V

UART (universal asynchronous receiver/ transmitter)   The chip that controls a computer's serial port and the interface to serial devices such as modems.

uniform resource locator (URL)   A unique address that identifies a document on the World Wide Web. The URL for a Web page generally includes the type of file (such as `http`), the computer on which the file is located (such as `www.microsoft.com`), the folder on that computer where the file is located (such as `/Windows/`), and the name of the actual file (such as `default.htm`). You can direct your browser to a particular Web page by typing the page's URL into an address field and pressing Enter. A site's address can take many forms, but most of the largest Web sites have similar-looking and simple URLs, such as `http://www.yahoo.com`, `http://www.quepublishing.com`, and `http://www.metafilter.com`.

Universal Serial Bus (USB)   A standard that enables devices to be easily connected to a PC without having to open the case.

upgrade   To install Windows XP over an existing installation of a previous version of Windows (such as Windows 98/Me/2000/NT).

uplink port   A port on a network hub that connects the hub to a cable modem or other external device for accessing the Internet.

URL (uniform resource locator)   *See* uniform resource locator.

USB hub   A device that enables many USB devices to connect to a computer at the same time.

USB port   A port that uses the USB standard and enables USB devices to easily connect to a PC.

Usenet   A collection of public discussion groups covering a diverse range of topics. Usenet groups, which also are called *newsgroups*, are distributed by thousands of Internet sites around the world.

username   A short version of your name, nickname, or handle that identifies you on a Web site or another service offered on the Internet. On America Online, a username is called a *screen name*. A username is usually paired with a password, and many Web sites, such as Yahoo!, require both of these when you log in to access the personalized features of the site.

V.90   A standard that enables 56Kbps modems to communicate.

V.92   A standard that builds on the V.90 standard and adds features such as those that make connections more quickly.

video port   A port on the back of a graphics card to which the monitor is connected.

virus   A program that creates copies of itself—usually without permission—and can cause damage to files on your computer or reveal personal data to others. Viruses can be spread on floppy disks and by email, so you should protect yourself by installing an antivirus program on your computer. You also should not open any attached file you receive in email unless you know the sender (especially if the file is a program).

visualization In a sound player such as the Windows Media Player or WinAMP, an animated program that reacts to sound as it is being played.

voiceover *See* narration.

volume label The name of a disk. When formatting a floppy disk, you can provide a volume label for the disk if you want; alternatively, you can leave the disk unnamed, as most people do.

W–X

wallpaper A picture displayed on the Windows desktop behind any icons.

warm boot Restarting a computer by using software rather than either turning the power off and back on or pressing a reset button.

watermark A small, semitransparent graphic that identifies a scene or speaker. Many TV broadcasts use a watermark to let you know which channel you're watching.

WAV An older, but still popular, format for sound files. All video editors work with this lossless format. By default, VideoWave captures sound in the WAV format.

Web browser The tool that lets you view pages on the World Wide Web. After you connect to the Internet, you load a browser; then you can see and interact with pages on the Web. Some of the most popular browsers are Microsoft Internet Explorer, Netscape Navigator, and Opera. Internet Explorer 6 is used in many of the tasks in this book. *See also* browser.

Web directory World Wide Web sites that use human editors to categorize thousands of Web sites according to their content and make recommendations about the best sites. The main way to use these directories is to navigate to the categories you are interested in. Web directories include Yahoo! (`http://www.yahoo.com`), Lycos (`http://www.lycos.com`), and the Open Directory Project (`http://www.dmoz.org`).

Web page A document that is usually one of many related documents that make up a Web site and that is available for anyone to view with a Web browser, such as Internet Explorer.

Web server A server on the Internet that sends Web pages and other documents in response to requests by Web browsers. Everything you view on the World Wide Web is delivered by a Web server to your browser. *See also* server.

Web site A group of related Web pages. When you are creating related Web pages in a program such as FrontPage Express, you should make an effort to link all the pages together as a site.

WebCam A small, inexpensive video camera that attaches to your computer and lets other people see videos of you live over the Internet.

weblog A Web site published as a series of diary-style entries, usually with the most recent entry listed first. Weblogs often are used to link to interesting Web sites and share personal details of the publisher's life. Two good examples are CamWorld (`http://www.camworld.com`) and MetaFilter (`http://www.metafilter.com`).

white-balance To adjust the camcorder so that it properly reproduces all the colors in your scene based on the available light. Because different light sources—such as daylight, florescent light, and candlelight—all generate different colors, they cause all the colors in your scene to shift unless you compensate. White-balancing is a simple process in which you show your camcorder true white. When the camera knows what color white is, all the other colors come out accurately as well. Your camera usually adjusts for color balance automatically, but you can get better results by manually white-balancing your camcorder—especially indoors, in low-light situations, when using a camera light, or with unusually tinted overhead lights.

wide area network (WAN) Two or more LANs connected together over a distance. *See also* local area network.

Windows Explorer A tree-based application used to browse the file system on your computer.

Windows Media Player A program installed with Windows XP that is used to display picture files, music files, and movie files of various formats.

Windows Messenger Instant messaging software from Microsoft that has an estimated 25 million users. You can send and receive instant messages, keep a list of contacts you communicate with regularly, and send email when one of the contacts is not connected to Messenger.

Windows Movie Maker A program installed with Windows XP that is used to create movie files out of still pictures and recorded video and audio.

wipe A video transition in which the new video physically moves into the frame while displacing the old video.

wireless base station A hub/router the connects PCs wirelessly to one another and lets them communicate and share resources and an Internet connection, using the 802.11 wireless communications protocol (also called *Wi-Fi*). A small radio transceiver in the base station sends and receives data via RF frequencies in the 2.4GHz range.

wireless network A network that enables PCs to communicate with one another without wires. Most wireless networks are based on the 802.11 wireless communications protocol, also called *Wi-Fi*.

wizard A Windows program that walks you through the steps involved in the installation or configuration of a Windows component or program. Most software developed by Microsoft includes an installation wizard that simplifies the process of setting up the program on your computer.

workgroup A group of computers operating as peers on a network. *See also* domain and peer.

Y–Z

Y2K bug The incapability of certain computers or computer functions to work when the year 2000 occurred.

ZIF (zero insertion force) socket A socket that lets you insert or remove a chip without using a special device.

Index

Symbols

B

D